Taming Ares

Legal History Library

VOLUME 26

Studies in the History of International Law

Series Editor

Randall Lesaffer
Tilburg University, Catholic University of Leuven

VOLUME 10

The titles published in this series are listed at *brill.com/shil*

Taming Ares

War, Interstate Law, and Humanitarian Discourse in Classical Greece

By

Emiliano J. Buis

BRILL

LEIDEN | BOSTON

Cover illustration: Achilles tending Patroclus wounded by an arrow, identified by inscriptions on the upper part of the vase. Tondo of an Attic red-figure kylix, ca. 500 BC. From Vulci. Antikensammlung Berlin F2278. Public domain, via Wikimedia Commons.

Library of Congress Cataloging-in-Publication Data

Names: Buis, Emiliano Jerónimo, author.
Title: Taming Ares : war, interstate law, and humanitarian discourse in classical Greece / By Emiliano J. Buis.
Description: Leiden : Brill, 2018. | Series: Studies in the history of international law ; 26 | Includes bibliographical references and index.
Identifiers: LCCN 2017061442 (print) | LCCN 2018004830 (ebook) | ISBN 9789004363823 (E-book) | ISBN 9789004359734 (hardback : alk. paper)
Subjects: LCSH: War (Greek law)–History. | War (International law) | Humanitarian law. | Peace treaties. | Athens (Greece)–History. | Greece–Politics and government–To 146 B.C.
Classification: LCC KL4384.2 (ebook) | LCC KL4384.2 .B85 2018 (print) | DDC 341.60938–dc23
LC record available at https://lccn.loc.gov/2017061442

Typeface for the Latin, Greek, and Cyrillic scripts: "Brill". See and download: brill.com/brill-typeface.

ISSN 1874-1793
ISBN 978-90-04-35973-4 (hardback)
ISBN 978-90-04-36382-3 (e-book)

This book is printed on acid-free paper and produced in a sustainable manner.

δεῖ δὴ τὸν κατ' εἰρήνην βίον ἕκαστον πλεῖστόν τε καὶ ἄριστον διεξελθεῖν.

It is the life of peace that everyone should live as much and as well as he can.

PLATO, *Laws* 803d (tr. BURY)

•••

τέλος γάρ, ὥσπερ εἴρηται πολλάκις, εἰρήνη μὲν πολέμου σχολὴ δ' ἀσχολίας.

Since, as we have said repeatedly, peace is the end of war, leisure of business.

ARISTOTLE, *Politics* 7.13.16–17, 1334a (tr. RACKHAM)

•••

ἀλλὰ μέντοι ὅτι μὲν πόλεμοι ἀεί ποτε γίγνονται καὶ ὅτι καταλύονται πάντες ἐπιστάμεθα, καὶ ὅτι ἡμεῖς, ἂν μὴ νῦν, ἀλλ' αὖθίς ποτε εἰρήνης ἐπιθυμήσομεν.

Moreover, we all know that wars are forever breaking out and being concluded, and that we—if not now, still at some future time—shall desire peace again.

XENOPHON, *Hellenica* 6.3.15 (tr. BROWNSON)

Contents

Foreword

Randall Lesaffer

The subject of *Taming Ares*, the regulation of war among Greek city-states in the classical age, has suffered from long neglect in the historiography of international law. This stems from two truisms which for a century have overshadowed and determined the views which prevailed in the field about the contribution of Greek and Roman Antiquity to the long-term development of international law.

Firstly, the State-centeredness of mainstream international legal history, which endured from the inception of the historiography of international law in Europe and the Americas in the late 19th century to the late 20th century, led to a reduction of the field's purview to the historical pedigree of the modern, sovereign state. This ostracized the centuries of Roman supremacy from historical narratives of international law as Roman imperialism arguably destroyed the conditions for an inter-state law premised on the co-existence of formally equal polities. In this respect, the classical Greek world (6th–4th centuries BCE) with its plurality of city-states fared better. Nevertheless, the prevailing narrow and formalistic interpretation of law as a secular, autonomous body of rules which derived from clear, constitutional actions by state-like bodies and their institutions led to the disqualification of the norms which regulated classical Greece's inter-polity relations.

Secondly, the subject of the legal regulation of war has suffered from the tenacious view that war in classical Greece was not only omnipresent, but also barbarous and unmitigated by humanitarian concerns. This prejudice roots in the earliest works of the history of international law from the 18th and 19th centuries, which in turn were construed on the notion that humanitarian concerns sprang from Christian morality.

In this book, the Argentinian scholar Emiliano Buis challenges both views one at a time. In the first part of the book, Buis argues that the regulation of Greek inter-polity relations deserves the sobriquet 'legal'—without insisting on the term. It entailed a discourse and practice of inter-polity relations that was vested on acknowledging, disputing and settling claims to binding rights and obligations. For this, while expressly referring to modern debates on the theory of international law or on legal personality in international law, the author chooses to leave this discourse behind and offers an insight into Greek inter-polity law in terms of the Greeks' own understanding of the normative and of its place in the wider social and political setting of that day and age.

His investigation begins with an analysis of the understanding of law within the Athenian city-state in the second half of the 5th century BCE, on the scene of Athenian democracy, before he turns to a reconstruction of inter-polity law. Making ample use of epigraphic as well as literary, rhetorical, and historiographical sources, Buis persuasively shows that there is a strong parallel between the functions and understanding of normativity at the inter-polity level and the level of domestic Athenian law. This, in part, comes from the permeability of the intra-polity and inter-polity spheres in terms of actors and relations. In brief, the search for 'international law' should not be limited to a perusal of the actions of 'states', but extend to those of individuals. This allows one to cast a web which captures much more 'custom' than the study of treaties and other forms of 'state' behavior can.

In the second part of the book, Buis forays into the regulation of war and force between Greek city-states, focusing on the era of the Peloponnesian War. He structures his work along the modern division of *jus ad bellum* and *jus in bello*. His readings of Herodotus and Thucydides allow him to conclude that the classical Greeks did think of self-defense as a legal right and that it held a central place in their discourses of persuasion and justification. With this, Buis falls in line with some of the trailblazers of the modern historiography of ancient international law such as Wolfgang Preiser and Karl-Heinz Ziegler, who defended the view that 'just war' is among the institutions which can trace their history all the way back to Antiquity. Buis' exploration of the practices of warfare itself forms the most substantial part of the book. The context of a warfare which was centered around fixed battles between citizen armies of hoplites and phalanxes offered fruitful ground for a formalistic, ritualized organization of armed conflicts that steered, regulated, and restrained political decision-makers, armies and individual soldiers from top to bottom.

Taming Ares paints a rich canvass of how the resort to war and the waging of war were regulated through binding, legal norms which were part and parcel of a wider set of religious, moral, social, and cultural conceptions that created the scene of contest on which Greek city-states, their agents, and members acted. These norms derived largely from customary, often standardized and ritualized practice and discourse and were part of common legal consciousness that bound the classical Greek world together. Through their impact on the Hellenistic and Roman eras that followed, and the central referential role of Rome, Roman politics and law for the formation of Christian Europe, they deserve a place in the grand narrative of the European, and ultimately, global history of international law.

Preliminary Considerations

1 Editions of Reference Works

The aim of this work is to analyze the documentary sources in their original language; therefore, all Greek texts—and those in Latin—reproduced in this research follow a critical edition specified in a note and/or included in the corresponding bibliography section at the end of this book. I have selected canonical editions from ancient authors that are accompanied by a critical apparatus (for the purposes of specifying the different readings offered by the manuscripts through which the text was transmitted) and, in most cases, an introduction and commentaries to the work.

2 Translations

Given that this book proposes an interdisciplinary study of ancient sources and is mainly intended for legal historians interested in the origins of international law in antiquity, I decided to include the corresponding translation into English to accompany all texts in Greek. Note that, except in those cases indicated (where I provide short translations elaborated by myself), all translations into English of ancient authors included in this book correspond to the relevant editions listed in the final bibliography.

3 Transliterations

All transliterations of Greek words follow phonetic criteria, indicating aspirations through the letter "*h*" and the guttural dull sound, identified in Greek with the "χ" grapheme, as "*kh*". Thus, in all cases "φ" has been transcribed as "*ph*" and not as the fricative sound "*f*". For the purposes of this work, I did not find it convenient to mark vowel length; therefore, both "ε" and "η" have been equally transliterated as "*e*", while "ο" and "ω" both appear as "o". The letter "υ" has been transcribed as "*y*", while I decided to keep the Greek diphthong "ου" as "*ou*". In all cases, no stress is included in the transliteration. In the case of proper names commonly used in English that can be easily identified by the reader, I have chosen to depart from the strict phonetic transcription criteria in order to include the versions (generally Latinized) most widely used in our field: thus—for instance—I preferred "Pericles" instead of *Perikles*, "Socrates" instead of *Sokrates*, or "Athens" instead of *Athenai*.

4 Chronological References

Since this research is focused on the study of sources that are mostly dated before the Common Era, for the purposes of identifying historical periods related to ancient documents (generally corresponding to the fifth and fourth centuries before the Common Era), I decided to eliminate any reference to "BCE" as I deemed it unnecessary.

Acknowledgments

A research work, even one that is presumably the result of intense individual effort of thinking and drafting, can only be completed thanks to a pooling of spiritual and material strengths that merge into a true collective effort. This book, an updated version of a postdoctoral work carried out at the University of Buenos Aires (2012–2014)—which readdresses and completes some of the ideas proposed in various personal contributions specified in the bibliography at the end of this book—is certainly not the exception, and many people have directly or indirectly, knowingly or unknowingly, made a major contribution to the words contained here. Without them my first ideas would never have experienced the light of another day.

Firstly, I would like to thank the School of Law of the University of Buenos Aires (UBA)—especially its former Dean, Mónica Pinto—where I hold teaching and institutional positions, for having offered me an outstanding working environment in both roles, marked by professionalism, positive energy and friendship among colleagues, renowned professors and enthusiastic apprentices who share their queries under an *animus academicus* and a *furor sapientiae*. Hortensia D.T. Gutiérrez Posse, who did me the honor of leading me onto this academic path, has been my guide, an essential anchor that drove me to take postdoctoral studies and to move forward. She offered me her vast knowledge to pave the way of a topic that could sometimes be slippery. I am enormously grateful for her trust, and I hope this modest contribution will be an adequate compensation.

I would also like to thank the National Scientific and Technical Research Council (CONICET) for having offered me through my research career, for several years now, the institutional support necessary for long-term projects. I am also thankful to Harvard University's Center for Hellenic Studies, the Alexander S. Onassis Public Benefit Foundation, and the Center for Epigraphical and Palaeographical Studies (Ohio State University) which have honored me throughout this work with generous research scholarships and have allowed me to share some of the ideas explained in this book with colleagues from around the world—in Washington, Athens and Columbus, respectively. The Max-Planck-Institut für europäische Rechtsgeschichte, the Oñati International Institute for the Sociology of Law, the Uppsala University Hugo-Valentin Centrum, the Centre de recherche sur les droits de l'homme et le droit humanitaire (Université Paris-II Panthéon-Assas) and the Centre de recherches Anthropologie et Histoire des Mondes Antiques (Bibliothèque Gernet-Glotz) have also provided me with material and sources that would have otherwise been unavailable.

I would like to express my endless gratitude to my friends from the School of Philosophy and Literature (who, against all odds, stood by me through my doctoral journey and are still there), especially the members of *UBACyT* research projects I co-direct with Elsa Rodríguez Cidre, Hellenists of heart and soul, who share their inspiring passion for Greek literature. Thanks to Laura Giosa and all the wonderful people in the course we share at the School of Law of the National University of the Center of the Buenos Aires Province (*UNICEN*), whose enthusiasm made my ongoing trips to Azul a great pleasure.

I do not want to forget to mention my undergraduate and graduate students at UBA and UNICEN, and my research assistants—especially Zacarías Reidel, Lourdes Paz, Juan Francisco Padín, Daniela López, José Ryb, Ramiro Escudero Giménez and Martín Barros—, who have partially read this work and have always enlightened me with their comments and questions, helping me delve into many questions raised in these pages. I have also contracted huge debts of gratitude towards friends and colleagues, especially Sophia Adam, Victor Alonso Troncoso, Ilias Arnaoutouglou, Morten Bergsmo, Inés Calero Secall, Charles Delattre, Viviana Gastaldi, Pedro López Barja, Daniella Marouda, Kaius Tuori, Muriel Ubéda-Saillard and Gabriel Valladares, who among others helped me improve many of my arguments during the correction process.

I owe special thanks to Randall Lesaffer, who encouraged the inclusion of an updated English-speaking version of this study in the Series "History of International Law", as well as Jennifer Obdam, Wendy Scholma and Gera van Bedaf from Brill Publishers, for their constant support. Also to María Marta Montesano and Christopher Welser for the inspired translation of several of these chapters. They have all been the best possible.

Last, but not least, I am deeply thankful to my family, who honored me with undeserved pride and have always been interested in my enquiries, never hesitating to support my exotic enterprises in this postmodern world. I reserve my last acknowledgment to my wife Natalia, whose smile and patience, accurate comments and wise opinions have made possible the happiness of my *kosmos*.

Columbus (Ohio), January 2018

List of Figures and Maps

Figures

Maps

MAP 1 *Greece in classical times*

Introduction

Πόλεμος πάντων μὲν πατήρ ἐστι, πάντων δὲ βασιλεύς,
καὶ τοὺς μὲν θεοὺς ἔδειξε τοὺς δὲ ἀνθρώπους,
τοὺς μὲν δούλους ἐποίησε τοὺς δὲ ἐλευθέρους.

War is the father of all and the king of all, and has revealed
that the ones are gods and the others humans,
and has made the ones slaves and the other free.

HERACLITUS, fr. 22 B53 (DIELS-KRANZ), D64 (tr. LAKS and MOST)

∴

1 Between Ares and Athena

An apple. Ever since Adam and Eve's original sin, the apple of temptation has probably been the first and best known example of human responsibility and penalty. The Greek world was not oblivious to the metaphor and that fruit aroused new appetite on the occasion of a second union. After the wedding of divine Tethys and mortal Peleus—future parents of Achilles, the warrior *par excellence*—, young Paris—son of the king of Troy—was summoned by Olympus to resolve a controversy: he was chosen by Zeus to give a golden apple to the most beautiful goddess.[1] Athena, Aphrodite and Hera competed for the triumph and, unable to reach an agreement, Zeus (father of two of them, and husband of the third) asked the messenger, Hermes, to lead the three goddesses to Mount Ida in order for Paris to resolve the dispute. The first debate; the first trial.

Each of those goddesses sustained her position with arguments, and the arbitrator was offered gifts aimed at buying his will. The first bribes: Athena promised prudence and victory in all battles; Hera offered absolute power over Asia; Aphrodite, on the other hand, limited her commitment to trying to get the beautiful Helen of Sparta. Not seeking military or political power, the boy was carried away by love: the final decision of Paris in that first trial was in favor of Aphrodite.[2] As a result of the award, the abduction of the wife of Menelaus, the most beautiful of all women, was imminent.

---

1 As regards the origin of the apple in the mythical tradition of Troy, see Severyns (1950–1951).

2 The history of the Judgment of Paris was not discussed in many canonical literary sources (in

 | DOI: 10.1163/9789004363823_002

While the Trojan War began with an apple, that origin should not however be put down to nature or chance. The story behind the myth is that the fruit was given to the divinities to promote fighting and confrontation by a goddess who had not been invited to a nuptial celebration due to her special character: the apple was thrown by Eris, *Strife* or *Discord*, a character as enigmatic and mysterious as the Greeks' ties with conflict.[3]

Many sources account for Eris' ambivalence as a divinity. Thus, in the *Iliad*—the first attested literary work of the Western world—Homer said that Eris glorifies herself by causing an armed struggle (4.440–445):

... καὶ Ἔρις ἄμοτον μεμαυῖα, Ἄρεος ἀνδροφόνοιο κασιγνήτη ἑτάρη τε, ἥ τ' ὀλίγη μὲν πρῶτα κορύσσεται, αὐτὰρ ἔπειτα οὐρανῷ ἐστήριξε κάρη καὶ ἐπὶ χθονὶ βαίνει· ἥ σφιν καὶ τότε νεῖκος ὁμοίϊον ἔμβαλε μέσσῳ ἐρχομένη καθ' ὅμιλον ὀφέλλουσα στόνον ἀνδρῶν.[4]	... And Discord [Eris] that rageth incessantly, sister and comrade of manslaying Ares; she at the first rears her crest but little, yet thereafter planteth her head in heaven, while her feet tread on earth. She it was that now cast evil strife into their midst as she fared through the throng, making the groanings of men to wax.

Epic allusions seem to indicate that, when it comes to *Eris* (as a divinity, or *eris* simply as "discord"), there always appears an illegitimate disruption of the established order.[5] However, that rupture alternates in the text of the *Iliad* with much more positive notions about dispute, as in the case of the desirable struggle for status as a warrior (ἀλκή, *alke,* military force or strength) that liberates warlike emotions and is praised for guaranteeing safety.[6] Hence, negative violence alternates with the rage of the fighter. Similarly, in the *Theogony,*

fact, the *Iliad* only contains a brief reference in 24.28–30) but in other ancient fragmentary texts, mainly in a fragment of the *Cypria,* a lost poem of the Trojan cycle composed after the *Iliad*; cf. Bernabé Pajares (1979: 93–104).

3 For more on Eris, see Grimal (1986: 168), who collects old sources referring to her. In fact, the sources—among them the aforementioned *Cypria*—indicate that it was Zeus who actually had the idea of starting war among mortals (perhaps to fight against overpopulation) and used Eris and the golden apple as instruments for his great plan; cf. Reeves (1966).

4 The version of the Greek text here, as well as its translation, is Murray's (1924). A frequent scene: for example, at the beginning of book 11, Eris is sent by Zeus to incite the Greeks (11.1).

5 Hogan (1981) has argued that "oddly" enough, Eris is almost always seen as a negative character in Homer.

6 As to the relation between these concepts, see Nagler (1988), who focused on their antagonism rather than their overlapping within Homeric passages.

Hesiod—one of the few complete sources we possess from the archaic world—identifies the despicable Eris as the daughter of Night and progenitor of a bizarre lineage of dark characters (vv. 226–232):

αὐτὰρ Ἔρις στυγερὴ τέκε μὲν Πόνον ἀλγινόεντα
ἤθην τε Λιμόν τε καὶ Ἄλγεα δακρυόεντα
Ὑσμίνας τε Μάχας τε Φόνους τ' Ἀνδροκτασίας τε
Νείκεά τε ψευδέας τε Λόγους Ἀμφιλογίας τε
Δυσνομίην τ' Ἄτην τε, συνήθεας ἀλλήλῃσιν,
Ὅρκον θ', ὃς δὴ πλεῖστον ἐπιχθονίους ἀνθρώπους
πημαίνει, ὅτε κέν τις ἑκὼν ἐπίορκον ὀμόσσῃ.[7]

And loathsome Strife [Eris] bore painful Toil and Forgetfulness and Hunger and tearful Pains, and Combats and Battles and Murders and Slaughters, and Strifes and Lies and Tales and Disputes, and Lawlessness and Recklessness, much like one another, and Oath, who indeed brings most woe upon human beings on the earth, whenever someone willfully swears a false oath.[8]

The lineage of Eris includes the most violent confrontations—such as battle (μάχη, *makhe*) or murder (φόνος, *phonos*)—but also false and ambiguous words (ἀμφιλογίαι, *amphilogiai*),[9] precisely because they embrace certain inconsistencies inherent to the Hellenic approach to confrontation. The passage also highlights voluntary involvement in taking false oaths, reflecting the treacherous nature of the one who promotes strife.

The remarkably poor treatment of Eris in some sources is undoubtedly confusing and productive of uncertainty, and the content of some passages is surprising. We should not disregard the fact that Hesiod, in *Works and Days* (5. 11–26), distinguishes two different "Erises" (*Erides*) from the same lineage: a very cruel Eris, who favors evil war and confrontation (ἣ μὲν γὰρ πόλεμόν τε κακὸν καὶ δῆριν ὀφέλλει, 14); and another one, who is "much better for mankind" (ἀνδράσι πολλὸν ἀμείνω, 19) because she encourages work by promoting rivalry.[10] The former is honored by men only because their gods force them to do so, and this seems to be the epic Eris who threw the apple and gave rise to confrontation in Troy. Zeus identifies the latter with the "roots of the earth"

7 The Greek text of Hesiodic works corresponds to Evelyn-White's edition (1914).
8 Translation by Most (2006).
9 Note the interesting alliteration in the repetition of the same morpheme: λόγος (*logos*) means "word" or "discourse", while *amphilogy* presents the same word with a pre-verb (*amphi-*) that usually indicates alternation or contrast. Thus, it indicates an expression whose meaning is subject to variation, and that has a double scope; cf. Bailly (2000: 110, s.v.).
10 du Bouchet (2012: 61–63).

(19–20) and, therefore, reveals a profile that is much more humane. As stated in the *Theogony*, the goddess who marches on the earth triumphs gloriously.

Hence, there is a dual treatment of Strife and Discord (its positive and negative features) in Greek thinking, which is subject to gray areas and inaccuracies. As the frequent target of praise and of reprimand on other occasions, the "hateful Eris" (ἔριδι στυγερᾷ, a dative frequently used by Euripides)[11] appears as a two-sided, duplicated entity, as a strategically ambiguous divinity: she entails destructive conflict though at the same time constructive competition.[12] Thus, for instance, going back to Heraclitus' archaic thinking in contrast with Homer's, Aristotle believes that some defend Eris insofar as perfect harmony can only result from antinomy and antagonism (*Eudemian Ethics*, 1235a25–30):

οἳ δὲ τὰ ἐναντία φίλα, καὶ Ἡράκλειτος ἐπιτιμᾷ τῷ ποιήσαντι "ὡς ἔρις ἔκ τε θεῶν καὶ ἀνθρώπων ἀπόλοιτο" οὐ γὰρ ἂν εἶναι ἁρμονίαν μὴ ὄντος ὀξέος καὶ βαρέος, οὐδὲ τὰ ζῷα ἄνευ θήλεως καὶ ἄρρενος ἐναντίων ὄντων.[13]	The other party says that opposites are friends, and Heraclitus rebukes the poet who wrote—*Would strife* [*Eris*] *might perish out of heaven and earth*,[14] for, he says, there would be no harmony without high and low notes, and no animals without male and female, which are opposites.[15]

Iconography contributes to such a confusing portrait of that divinity. Indeed, having been described in texts as bloodthirsty and "horrible to see" (αἰσχίστη τὸ

11 This expression appears around the year 426 in the tragedy *Andromache*, for example, in vv. 122 and 279. In the play, the Trojan War is actually caused by a "female Discord" (γυναικείαν ἔριν, 362). In *Helen* (412), the Judgment episode is mentioned when referring to "the Eris of the three goddesses" (708) and Discord is described as "miserable" (ἔριν ἔριν τάλαιναν, 248). For more on the function of references to Eris throughout Euripides' production, and the apparent shortage of mentions in other classic Greek authors, cf. Wilson (1979). The mention of Eris and the story of the Judgment of Paris in Euripides should not be surprising given the important influence that the topics discussed in the *Cypria* had for this author, as remarkably shown by Jouan (1966).

12 Thalmann (2004: 364–365), sees Hesiodic originality in this "duplicity" of the divinity—given the nearly absolute lack of other records mentioning "two-sided" gods—and chooses to identify each of the two Erises not in ethical terms (good/bad), but rather through a positive/negative or constructive/destructive polarity. We adhere to that criterion here.

13 The edition used here is Susemihl's (1884).

14 See Achilles' words in Homer, *Iliad* 18.107.

15 Translation by Rackham (1961) with minor corrections.

FIGURE 1 *Eris. Tondo of an Attic black-figure kylix, ca. 575–525 BC*

εἶδος ἐοικυῖα),[16] it is surprising to find that in a cup from the sixth century—now in Berlin—,[17] the name of Eris is clearly spelled out next to the image of a graceful winged woman, without any weapons that could connect her to the extreme violence of her actions.[18]

All in all, there are reasons to recognize a liminal condition in Eris, which fosters cleavage, but at the same time social cohesion through an agonistic structure where the spoken and physical counterpoints become an underlying unity.[19] Divinity and humanity, horror and beauty; her complex status also

16 Pausanias, 5.19.2.

17 Antikensammlung Berlin, F 1775 (*LIMC* III: 847, s.v. "Eris", No. 1, pl. 608). See Figure 1.

18 Isler (1969: 34) attempted to justify that peculiarity by stating that the image in that cup corresponds to the positive Eris described by Hesiod; Hurst (1971: 126, n. 22) is opposed to that idea—he rejected the ethical interpretation of the painter's aesthetic options—but nonetheless does notice the unique nature of that piece of art.

19 That is precisely Thalmann's (2004) thesis: according to him, Eris can symbolize in her

applies to the other gods associated with physical violence, who arouse similar contexts of attraction and rejection. In Olympus, indeed, there exists no pacifism[20] and tensions—which even affect mortals, promoting armed conflict—are evident among the gods themselves. Hence, the works of the murderous evil Ares, the god of war and Eris' mournful brother (as shown above), are described as destructive by the elegiac poet Tyrtaeus (Ἄρεος πολυδακρύου ἔργ ἀΐδηλα, 11.7).[21] The chorus of the *Phoenician Women* by Euripides (year 410 or 409), who referred to Eris as "terrible" (ἦ δεινά τις Ἔρις θεός, 798), will address Ares, the one of many sufferings, to enquire as to the reasons for his being possessed with blood and death (ὦ πολύμοχθος Ἄρης, τί ποθ αἵματι / καὶ θανάτῳ κατέχῃ, 784–785).[22]

The dissolute passion of Ares, who in the epic poem rallied Achaeans and Trojans to bloody battle,[23] also finds in the *Iliad* a specific constraint in the words and actions of the goddess Athena, who is more inclined to play a conciliatory role.[24] The latter divinity, born of Zeus' head with her weapons ready, is the personification of Athenian military virtue; it should be recalled that her gold and ivory-made sculpture, with a spear and a shield, was magnificently located at the center of the Parthenon, in the heart of the city.[25] Yet, she is

---

"two-sided" nature the need for cooperation that the city-state requires. This work will address the "agonistic" nature of Greek society in chapter 1.

20 Crowley (2012: 96–97).

21 West (1992).

22 Similarly, in Aeschylus' *Suppliants*, Ares is defined as a destroyer of choirs and citharas and a generator of tears (ἄχορον ἀκίθαριν δακρυογόνον Ἄρη, 681).

23 Ares is described in the *Iliad* 5.761 as a madman who ignores justice. For more on these aberrant aspects of violence and the reaction of pacifism, cf. Raaflaub (2006: 15).

24 Burkert (1985: 169), Darmon (1991: 114–115), Ager (2005: 414–415), Neff (2005: 16).

25 The oldest description of the magnificent chryselephantine statute of Athena Parthenos, built by Phidias and erected in the Parthenon, is found in the geographer Pausanias (1.24.5–7): "The statue itself is made of ivory and gold. On the middle of her helmet is placed a likeness of the Sphinx (…) and on either side of the helmet are griffins in relief (…) The statue of Athena is upright, with a tunic reaching to her feet, and on her breast the head of Medusa is worked in ivory. She holds a statue of Victory about four cubits high, and in the other hand a spear; at her feet lies a shield and near the spear is a serpent" (αὐτὸ δὲ ἔκ τε ἐλέφαντος τὸ ἄγαλμα καὶ χρησμοῦ πεποίηται. μέσῳ μὲν οὖν ἐπίκειταί οἱ τῷ κράνει Σφιγγὸς εἰκών (…), καθ' ἑκάτερον δὲ τοῦ κράνους γρῦπές εἰσιν ἐπειργασμένοι. (…) τὸ δὲ ἄγαλμα τῆς Ἀθηνᾶς ὀρθόν ἐστιν ἐν χιτῶνι ποδήρει καί οἱ κατὰ τὸ στέρνον ἡ κεφαλὴ Μεδούσης ἐλέφαντός ἐστιν ἐμπεποιημένη· καὶ Νίκην τε ὅσον τεσσάρων πηχῶν, ἐν δὲ τῇ χειρί δόρυ ἔχει, καί οἱ πρὸς τοῖς

described in Homeric verses as a promoter of wariness and prudence that ultimately prevailed on several occasions, as opposed to the debauchery of Ares' conduct.[26]

However, said simplified contrast is not that simple and must be reviewed:[27] the character of Ares is deeply ambivalent.[28] Pausanias points out that, after learning that Poseidon's son had outraged one of his daughters, Ares murdered him and "was the first to be convicted upon trial for that murder" (δίκην ἐπὶ τούτῳ τῷ φόνῳ γενέσθαι πρῶτον, 1.21.4).[29] But the convict also serves as a judge. Thus, mournful Ares—perhaps the most violent divinity in the pantheon—will also contribute with his ambiguity to the development of civilizing justice: he is designated by Aeschylus as "he who solves conflict" (λυτὴρ νεικέων, *Seven against Thebes* 941) protecting the *polis*. The great killer and attacker is, in turn, the guardian of Athens.

The Greek world is marked by the anthropomorphism of violence; even Polemos (πόλεμος, war) is personified in the sources,[30] described by Heracli-

---

ποσὶν ἀσπίς τε κεῖται καὶ πλησίον τοῦ δόρατος δράκων ἐστίν). The text corresponds to Jones and Ormerod (1918) and the translation is by Jones (1978).

26 Burkert (1985: 141–169). Indeed, Athena expels Ares from combat (5.29–36) and frequently controls him throughout the poem (5.855–867, 15.123–142, 21.392–414). For more on the conventions of war in Homeric epic, see Karavites (1992: 157).

27 Deacy (2000: 285–298) has detected interesting parallelisms between both divinities: since war is in essence contradictory (between defensive controlled violence and aggressive wildness), Ares and Athena share in the same contradictions. In that regard, see also Vian (1968: 53–68), Ager (2005: 421) and Contensou (2014: 238–241).

28 According to Graf (1996: 152), Ares is an "embodiment of the ambivalent (destructive but often useful) forces of war".

29 This case is the basis for the court of the *Areo-pagus* ("the hill of Ares"), which will represent the most important judicial institution of political life in the city until the democratic reforms of Ephialtes in the mid-fifth century; cf. Iriarte and González (2008: 38).

30 That is undoubtedly the most frequent term to refer to the concept of "war" in ancient Greek. Note also that the word στάσις (*stasis*), frequently used in literature of the time to account for political unrest and rebellions inside the *polis*, usually refers to what is now identified as *internal conflict* or *sedition*. I will go back to this distinction later in this work. As regards the complex notion of *stasis* in classical Athens, cf. Loraux (1997), Rebuffat (2000: 38–41), Price (2001: 67), Wolpert (2002), Hanson (2005: 10) and, in particular, Gehrke (1985). Some recent works have examined the cases of low-intensity conflicts that do not reach the threshold of *polemos* and that involve unorganized groups of outlaws, guerrillas and citizens who take up arms; cf. Loreto (2006: 133–141) and Börm (2016: 18).

FIGURE 2 *Athena and Ares separated by Zeus. Attic black-figure volute-krater, ca. 540–510 BC*

tus as father and sovereign in the quotation included at the beginning of this chapter.[31] His masculinized representation usually opposes the feminine image of Peace (εἰρήνη, *eirene*).[32] In the comedy called *Peace* by Aristophanes, performed in 421 at the Great Dionysia, Polemos is seen as a character who—having locked Peace in a cave—appears on stage accompanied by *Kydoimos* (the Riot of Combat), with a huge mortar through which he crushes Greek cities (223–288). Thucydides also personifies War, when making it clear in the Corinthians' speech—during the Peloponnesian League congress—that "war [Polemos] least of all conforms to fixed rules" (ἥκιστα γὰρ πόλεμος ἐπὶ ῥητοῖς χωρεῖ, 1.122.1).[33] Moreover, when addressing civil war in Corcyra, the historian will add that "war, upon suppressing daily welfare, turns out to be a master of violence and arranges the anger of the majority according to the circumstances" (ὁ δὲ πόλεμος ὑφελὼν τὴν εὐπορίαν τοῦ καθ' ἡμέραν βίαιος διδάσκαλος καὶ πρὸς τὰ παρόντα τὰς ὀργὰς τῶν πολλῶν ὁμοιοῖ, 3.82.2).[34] War is, according to the Greek structure of mind, disruptive of the ideal of tranquility,[35] but—just like Eris—Polemos is actually capable of educating (he is a *didaskalos*) through hardship. Indeed, both these characters entail an alteration of human order:

31 In fr. 53 (Diels); cf. Jacquemin (2005: 121).

32 Interestingly, if war is intended for men, the chastity of Athena as the city guardian was a metaphor for the city's masculine impregnability (Nevin, 2017: 21).

33 Translation by Smith (1894).

34 Vial (1999: 139).

35 In that regard, cf. Demont (1990).

just as Polemos does not conform to an established order (ἐπὶ ῥητοῖς χωρεῖ),[36] Eris is, according to Hesiod, the mother of *Dysnomy*, lack of justice.[37] However, even though divine laws or oaths do not seem to be binding in times of civil war (Thucydides, 3.82.6–7), the logical conclusion is that they should remain in force in those contexts, since acts of war may ultimately infringe legality (3.82.8).[38]

In the end, the personification of war and conflict in classical Greece accounts for the ambiguities of a critical approach: the discovery of its inhuman nature coexists with the inevitability of its existence. From this conceptual basis, the negative image of discord has its limitations. The role of religion (and divinities), in that regard, provides a framework for understanding ambiguous behavior in relation to armed conflict,[39] but the moral and legal scope of these ambiguities should be taken into consideration as well. The purpose of this work is to explore those intermediate spaces of violence which arise between gods and men, between strife and cooperation, between the two Erises, and between Ares and Athena. The sources I will discuss suggest some limitations of warfare and the need to tame the exacerbated violence of the most aggressive gods.

2 Between Custom and Convenience: Rules and Pragmatics

It could be said that the omnipresence of *polemos*—marked in the sources through characters such as Ares or Eris—has led historians of the ancient world to perceive classical Greece as an anarchic place subject to excessive violence,

36 The lyric poet Pindar in *Pythia* 8 (1–4) invokes "kindly Peace, O maker of greatest cities and daughter of Justice, you who hold the supreme keys of counsels and war" (φιλόφρον Ἡσυχία, Δίκας / ὦ μεγιστόπολι θύγατερ, /βουλᾶν τε καὶ πολέμων /ἔχοισα κλαΐδας ὑπερτάτας). The text is that of Sandys (1937) and its translation is from Race (1997).

37 I will later refer to the Greek concept of *nomos* that serves as the basis for the noun *dysnomia*. In a poem by the famous legislator Solon (fr. 4.31–38), *Dysnomia* is opposed to the correct order established by sound legislation, *Eunomia*, civic virtue that must regulate sound cities. Also personified, in Hesiod (*Theogony* 901–902) *Eunomia* was considered one of the *Horai* along with Justice (*Dike*) and Peace (*Eirene*).

38 Shanske (2011: 207). Paradoxically, the myth suggests that it was *Themis*—the divinity of Justice, as explained below—who advised Zeus to unleash a large-scale war among men by sending Eris. It seems that, in the aim to avoid overpopulation, Eris responded to a "fair" plan.

39 Cf. Jost (1999).

lack of controls and frequent hostilities. The habitualness of the phenomenon of war can be—almost unanimously—explained by an absolute lack of legal rules (δυσνομία, *dysnomia*, lawlessness) to restrict or limit the conduct of armies in struggles with other neighboring communities or even within their own territory. However, note that such an interpretation, common to many authors, is based on a discretionary and partial selection of Greek (literary and epigraphic) testimonies and, consequently, a complete review of the historical sources is desirable. Hence, what I propose here is to rethink the analytical approach through a legal examination of the issue. Therefore, I will suggest that, in fact, the Hellenic cities (πόλεις, *poleis*) of the fifth and fourth centuries—at least based on what can be inferred from classical documentary sources—relied on a discourse stating true rules of law applicable to armed conflict that quite often were inconsistent with some of the prevailing practices.[40]

Based on an interdisciplinary analysis that combines legal thinking with the contributions of philology, history, religion and anthropology, this study will try to prove that the rituals of warfare, the regular need to justify the use of force and the existence of common laws in Greek cities—as revealed in the sources—suggest a discursive precedent for modern State practices, a foundation in archaic custom and ancient roots, which could be the source of some current legal rules of international law regarding *ius ad bellum* and *ius in bello*.

Even though it is not possible to describe a factual situation based on the (scarce) available sources, the aim of this research is to prove the existence in classical Greece of a debate over practices that—to date—are long-established. This debate may shed light on current theoretical discussions on customary rules. Our point of departure is provided by the rule-making sources of international law today: treaties—understood as agreements made through the will of States and other entities with sufficient capacity to commit themselves to creating legal rules through a meeting of the minds—; custom (i.e., the practice of those subjects in the belief that such behavior depends on a legal obligation); and general principles of law, as set forth in Article 38 of the Statute of the International Court of Justice.[41] A historical study such as the one contained in these pages focuses on surveying the existence of similar rules in ancient Greece—through an analysis of the treaties, customs and general principles of law known to us regarding interstate relations in classical times. Hence,

40 On the interaction of practices and narratives, Keil (1916: 5) suggested that peace was only a rare interruption of the normal state of war. For the arguments contesting this view on the basis of the relevant sources, see Alonso Troncoso (2007: 209).

41 Thirlway (2014: 5–8).

the purpose is to show that, in many cases, the content of the rules currently binding upon States regarding the use of force and the regulation of armed conflict have a specific precedent in sources from those times, where νόμος (*nomos*) represents an unwritten law sanctified by tradition.

All of the above is expected to contribute to a greater awareness of the customary basis of current international law and the historical basis of its mandatory character. Thus, we should consider whether the archaic rules surveyed herein could serve today as a basis for proving the binding nature of certain rules which are now applicable in times of armed conflict. In turn, that would lead to the conclusion that, given that those regulations have been essential to the international discourse since ancient times, they bind all States as a whole under a common legal framework.

Therefore, the hypothesis that justifies the present research is composed of different sub-hypotheses, which are closely interrelated. On the one hand, a re-examination of original Greek sources from the fifth century (both epigraphic and literary) allows us to challenge the traditional assertions regarding the lack of regulations on armed conflict in the ancient world. On the contrary, in that context, there existed an awareness of a true *ius commune*—intra-Hellenic or inter-*polis*—, which (both similar to, and different from, modern international law) helped in setting limits at the beginning of armed conflicts and in restricting the excessive use of violence in belligerent situations.

Furthermore, as stated, it is assumed here that the identification in ancient Greece of legal regulations referring to conduct that is considered compulsory at different points in the conduct of hostilities results in interesting considerations relating to the current customary nature of certain rules from international law on the use of force and international humanitarian law.

Lastly—insofar as States tend to project their own interpretations on international law and negotiate with other States based on their best interest—a study of ancient Greece reveals that, when dealing with rules applicable in times of armed conflict, it is often possible to identify a hegemonic intent leading to the application of humanitarian rules that follow circumstantial criteria of appropriateness. Such utilitarianism—still in force as it is inherent to any efficient international law system—in no way hinders the existence of a series of customary regulations on the use of force or the conduct of hostilities (as mentioned in the sub-hypothesis above), though it warns us about the underlying reasons for accepting or invoking such legislation.

3 Toward International Law in the Ancient World: Practices and Contexts

An analysis of a legal system based on historical criteria is especially interesting when we consider that law is a dynamic social construction.[42] The characteristics of human-made legal rules in force in a given period can only be grasped upon an adequate study of their relation with the society in which they operate. For that reason, an evolutionary approach to the legal phenomenon, taking into account the chronological dimension, is essential for an appraisal of its true nature in accordance with socio-political circumstances.

In the case of international law, these somehow disregarded considerations have become particularly interesting in the last few decades, and a series of studies and papers—mostly published by European scholars—have opened the discussion as to the need to consolidate a diachronic thinking adequate to explain the evolution of international law.[43] Given that this area of law is constantly evolving and is nowadays marked by a series of proposals for change, its historical basis should be examined throughout the centuries to detect its preliminary expressions and first signs.

---

42 These considerations are from Kolb (2010: 20–21), who translates and employs the guidelines outlined by Preiser (1976) and holds that the importance of studying the history of international law is threefold. Firstly, it allows detection of the fundamental reasons for the rules by expressly stating their material sources. Secondly, it allows us to think about comparative law techniques and to conclude that the solutions provided by a legal system are not the only possible answers. Lastly, it indicates the contingency and the relativity of the legal regulations of a given time.

43 On the history of international law as the subject-matter of recent studies, including the classical period, see Redslob (1923), de Visscher (1955), Verzijl (1968), Grewe (1984), Truyol and Serra (1998), Hueck (2001: 194–217), Laghmani (2003), Gaurier, (2005 and its enlarged edition of 2014), Renaut (2007), Craven (2007) and Ziegler (2007). Koskenniemi (2001) offers an interesting perspective, stating that the intellectual origin of modern international law should be sought in the *esprit d'internationalité* which, under a liberal movement, inspired the new thinking of experts from 1869 to 1885 (at some point, this argument departs from the lines of thought presented earlier in Koskenniemi, 1989). In that regard, Koskenniemi constitutes a turning point in the historical theorization of International Law, as sustained by Galindo Bandeira (2005: 539–559). Anghie (2005) is another author who has also marked a milestone by proposing that the basis of international law can be traced back to the period of Hispanic colonization of the New World, together with the theoretical discussion arising from the debates of Spanish scholasticism. For a comprehensive and thorough approach to the historiography of international law, see also Lesaffer (2007: 27–41).

International law is understood as a complex system of legal rules aimed at regulating the relations occurring mainly among its subjects (mostly, States as the core of rule enforcement, exclusively entitled to be vested with rights and obligations within their territory). Hence, it seems indisputably false to hold that classical ancient societies were not aware of what it meant to use law to regulate conduct among different communities or—in particular—city-states.[44]

The foregoing observation is not intended to assert the existence in the ancient world of a system of international law similar to that currently in force. However, as shown below, ancient peoples—taking into account their special features—were already aware of the recognized diverse sources of law capable of having legal impact on the relations established beyond the boundaries of their own territory.

During most of the last two centuries, some scholars emphatically denied the existence of international legal rules in the pre-modern world. For instance, we can mention the works of François Laurent—a jurisconsult from Luxembourg (1810–1887)—, who authored three volumes entitled *Histoire du droit des gens et des relations internationales*, later compiled as part of his *Histoire de l'Humanité* (1855–1878). In those three volumes—concerned with the East, Greece and Rome—, Laurent argued for the lack of international regulations in the ancient world. His arguments—which were rapidly embraced by his followers—were aimed at showing that ancient peoples lived in a condition misleadingly called "natural", where everyone was at war against everyone else and where power was in the hands of the strongest: that completely hindered the development of a true law of nations.[45] The lack of a concept of humanity (hence, of universal law)[46] and the non-recognition of equality and fraternity as ideas capable of founding a science of international law[47] were considered by the author sufficient reasons to believe that a regulatory framework to govern the relations among different 'primitive' peoples was impossible.[48]

---

44 I do not intend to expand here on the similarities between States—understood under their modern concept—and Greek city-states, but merely to mention that classical cities in continental and insular Greece possessed territory, population and governing bodies that made them sovereign and independent. As to the legal nature of the various cities and their connection within some sort of international legal system, see Martin (1940), Ehrenberg (1969: 103), Fouchard (2003) and Lonis (2007). Cf. chapter 2.

45 Laurent (1850, i: 15).

46 Laurent (1850, i: 130).

47 Laurent (1850, iii: 328).

48 This skeptical position is still widely accepted among scholars. Eckstein (2006: 37), for

From a theoretical point of view, attempting to recognize sovereign equality among States in a manner similar to that which sustains current international relations entails, however, projecting a modern conceptualization of international law into other historical and cultural contexts based on clearly different patterns.[49] In that regard, we could argue that the fact that there was no universal balance among politically organized communities in the ancient world[50] should not lead us to deny the existence of *inter potestates* relations, interstate connections, or established diplomatic or political ties, mainly aimed at negotiating agreements, for example, on issues related to war or peace.[51] Moreover, we cannot deny a clear awareness in ancient times about the convenience of preserving and promoting such relations, as well as the relevance of guaranteeing preservation of frontiers or opportunities for territorial expansion through embassies and sound foreign policy.[52]

---

example, argues today that ancient Greek city-states existed in a world that basically lacked international law. The result, in his opinion, was a constellation of heavily militarized and diplomatically aggressive societies among which war was a commonplace. Given a world that was mired in anarchy—as formally defined—, it would be impossible to assess legal patterns of conduct.

49 These ideas have recently been put forward by an internationalist critique of 'Eurocentrism', which tries to reframe international standards based on new patterns that take into account different legal traditions. In that regard, see Becker Lorca (2012: 1034–1057).

50 Elsewhere, I have attempted to prove that it is also possible to find in the Greco-Roman world evidence for a balance between the parties to a treaty. However, in those circumstances and even today, the discourse is often typical of international law, which is intentionally based on the principle of "sovereign equality" and thus seeks to conceal a profound subjectivity that protects the great international participants in imposing regulations in their favor or whose interpretation they control. Cf. Buis (2011: 73–117).

51 Hall (2007: 85–88). Giovannini (2007: 14) analyzes these interactions among city-states and argues that, unlike what happens in current society, the Greeks were united by a common language, religion and moral values, so that "inter-national" relations in the classical Greece corresponded, in fact, to ties among states within what could be conceived as a single nation. In that regard, we think of interstate regulations that exist as such irrespective of cultural differences among nations (and, therefore, can occur within a single nation).

52 Some authors claim that the term "international law" should be historically replaced by other concepts more suitable to the pre-modern context: "The very concept of 'international' must be carefully applied to or projected on to the past. The concept of inter-cultural, inter-religious, trans-cultural, trans-religious, or trans-civilizational may be more appropriate to express relations between the politico-religious entities under the rule of politico-military-religious leaders in the pre-modern days" (Onuma, 2010: 277).

Such a conclusion was reached by several authors during the twentieth century, such as Phillipson,[53] Bickerman[54] and—more recently—Bederman.[55] They all recognized in the Greco-Roman world the existence of certain institutions like those in what today is known as "public international law".[56] For those experts, legal writers and historians, observing the different ways in which ancient civilizations interacted—exploring provisions of diplomatic relations, the conduct of hostilities or the treatment of foreigners—allows us to provide a strict analysis of the law, subject to a philosophical and anthropological approach to justice and its specific manifestations in connection with other organized communities.[57] Contrary to the "denial" theory, this line of thought claims that examining the background of a discipline such as international law constitutes an innovative method for the analysis of positive rules in a given historical period. Based on the connections between law and history, the examination of ancient civilizations could help us rethink the subject-matter under study from a diachronic and comparative perspective, arousing a critical spirit about the first expressions of the law of nations and warning about the circumstantial anchorage of a legal development of the relations *inter nationes*.[58]

---

53 Phillipson (1911).

54 Bickerman (1950: 99–127).

55 Bederman (2001). Other scholars will be mentioned in chapter 3 (n. 82).

56 Also in Latin America, special mention should be made of the work of Brazilian legal writer Borba Casella (2012). In Argentina, I should emphasize the original (and little-known) work by Ruiz Moreno (1946), who synthesized previous theoretical contributions, classifying them as affirming, denying or eclectic based on whether they accept the existence of a system of international law before the Common Era. The new joint volume directed by Bouineau (2011) in France does not include specific works on ancient Greece; therefore, this study seeks to carry further some of the thoughts contained there. I will deal with the relevant bibliography in chapter 3, section 5.

57 Kaczorowska (2002: 1) claims that "it is impossible to fix a precise date or a period in history to mark the beginning of international law as it predates recorded history! It began when a politically organized group came into contact with another group and was prepared to treat that group as equal and, at the same time, felt the need to develop a system of rules to regulate their relations. Evidence of rules and procedure regarding international law dates back over 5,000 years".

58 I share here the analysis made by Koskenniemi (2004: 61–66).

4 Inhumane Acts, Human Words: Analyzing the Restrictive Discourse of War

Since the earliest times, the Greek world-view concerning war has been marked by the ubiquity of the *polemos* phenomenon. In the early legendary period delineated by the Trojan epic cycle, Homeric references to barbarism in military confrontation are undoubtedly frequent: bloody episodes occur in the story one after the other, as the Argive army fights King Priam's forces in the ninth year of the siege of the walled city of Troy. However, the fact that the sources mentioning hostile practices are numerous does not mean that we cannot also find other references suggesting a set of specific regulations on humanitarian protection.[59] Nevertheless, despite these various references to certain humanitarian trends, whose origin can be traced back to the oldest Eastern civilizations,[60] the study of the law of armed conflict has very often disregarded any references from the Hellenic world.[61] In Western societies, the first humanitarian considerations in the context of hostilities are usually alleged to date back to the universalization of Christian values during the Middle Ages.[62] Based on these ideas, Jean Pictet—one of the most experienced

59 "Brutal treatment and noble generous conduct are manifested at the same epoch, in the same war, and apparently under similar circumstances" (Phillipson, 1911, ii: 207). Bederman (2001: 245–246) agreed. Rebuffat (2000: 188–189) supports a negative perspective about the legal limits of warfare phenomena, but he nonetheless mentions some sort of easily breachable code of conduct.

60 We think, for example, of the laws of Hammurabi in Babylon, which established a series of criteria designed to prevent the weak from being oppressed by the powerful. Texts such as the *Mahabharata*, the Bible or the Koran all stress the need to respect and treat the opponent with humanity. In China, the *Art of War*, by Sun Tzu (from the sixth century BC) or in India the Sanskrit treatise of *Manu Sriti*, possibly written between 200 and 200 CE, strictly prohibited the killing of prisoners of war and laid down specific guidelines for limiting weapons that could cause excessive damage to the opposing army; cf. Levie (2000: 339–340).

61 In general, the points of contact between old rules and those governing today are random, as stated by von Glahn (1965: 35) "similarities of Greek practices to modern rules of law were just that—accidental similarities and little more. Modern practice cannot be traced, at least on a basis of true international law, to the customs of the Greeks". We will try to offer a different reading on that perspective.

62 Cf. Meron (1998: 1–10). Kwakwa shares that idea (1992: 9): "The current rules on armed conflicts have their roots in the practices of belligerents in the Middle Ages". Note that, in maintaining this idea, the author is thinking about the seminal works by Grotius. However, we should take into account that there is a methodological problem at this point,

commentators on the Geneva Conventions that regulate the fate of victims of armed conflict—[63] stated that, although war is as old as the planet itself, Greek history goes through a series of landmarks that reproduce inhuman and unrestrained acts already detected in the Trojan war.[64]

At least one point raised by these theorists should be recognized: the passion of Greek πόλεις (*poleis*) for war brought about predictable consequences.[65] Since these *poleis* usually confronted each other, there is often a permanent expectation of preserving a substantial military force. Armed conflicts were, therefore, one of the main functions of the city-state,[66] and peace was only a limited reality.[67] Along with other *poleis*, Athens—for example—participated in numerous confrontations and took part in an armed conflict against the Persians that lasted more than forty years (i.e., from 520 to 479). Shortly afterwards, the Athenians fought against the Spartans and other less developed cities in the so-called Peloponnesian War (431–404), which many authors consider one of the first signs of decadence of classical Greek civilization.[68] The ubiquity of the phenomenon of war during the classical period (between the sixth to the fourth centuries) is indisputable, but this fact does not nevertheless entail an absolute lack of regulation; yet there are only a few (non-systematized) isolated works dedicated exclusively to surveying the logic underlying such restrictions on violence. Studies aimed at conceiving these limits in terms of law are even less frequent.

It is precisely on the basis of the theoretical framework described above that this specific research on the discursive treatment of the legal rules governing armed conflict in ancient Greece can be justified.[69] Taking into account the

---

since the scientific development of a discipline (in this case, international humanitarian law) should not be confused with the beginning of a practice itself, which generally precedes theoretical development.

63 I refer to the four Geneva Conventions, adopted on August 12, 1949, which will be referred to later when discussing the scope of their provisions.

64 Pictet (1983: 16). Kolb expresses a similar idea (2003: 19).

65 Pritchett (1974), Garlan (1972).

66 Adcock (1957). Rawlings expresses a similar idea (2007).

67 According to Nail (2014: 30), "les paix n'ont jamais été que des trêves plus ou moins longues".

68 Perrin-Saminadayar (1999: 147) considers that it was the "première des guerres totales, en raison de sa durée, du nombre des belligérants, des destructions qu'elle engendra, ou encore des exactions qui l'ont accompagnée"; cf. Thucydides 1.23.1–3.

69 For a reading of international humanitarian law as a counterpoint between the allegorical values that Ares and Athena represented in the Olympic pantheon, see Durham (2007: 248–258).

recent developments in international humanitarian law and the debates on the limitations of the use of force, a study of the ways in which Greeks reacted against the extreme violence of Ares is both necessary and timely.

In order to examine the original sources in greater depth, I have decided to focus specifically on the sources from the second half of the fifth century—particularly, from the three decades of the Peloponnesian War—, given that the records available from that historical period are larger in number. Taking into account that the sources from that period are still scarce, I will resort not only to epigraphic legal documents (preserved in hard copy such as stone, marble or metal carvings), but—above all—to the numerous extra-legal or literary texts available. Within the latter category, my work will focus more precisely on historiography, in addition to sources from the dramatic genre (tragedy and comedy), oratory and political philosophy.[70] I will privilege the study of Thucydides—recognized as the writer of a *History of the Peloponnesian War*—[71] and Xenophon, author of the *Hellenica*.[72] However, these core readings will be supplemented with prior or subsequent documents, provided they are deemed useful for clarifying on war-related matters and applicable regulatory limits.

Given the exploratory nature of this survey, which is aimed at focusing on the evolution of specific legal conduct and the progressive consolidation of discourse on certain customary rules, I suggest the classical period as a flexible time frame. Even though emphasis will be put on the context of the Peloponnesian War, I will also resort to sources from other historical periods (i.e., the archaic and post-classical periods) in order to provide a broader picture of the phenomenon I intend to describe.[73]

By way of preliminary consideration, it should be noted that the historical horizon to be explored by this research reveals a plurality of city-states

70 In Athens—the city for which we have the most sources—contemporary debate about the Peloponnesian War was reflected in a variety of literary sources. cf. Vial (1999).

71 At this point, I will resort to the statements made by Sheppard (2005), who outlined—though in a brief and incomplete manner—some possible approaches to reading Thucydidean references as regards the regulation of war.

72 The *Hellenica* is a historiographic work that, precisely, chronologically supplements the text by Thucydides, as it covers the last few years of the Peloponnesian War, discussing events from the year 411 until the years that followed the battle of Mantineia (362).

73 In this sense, my aim is not to provide a comprehensive study of all possible sources, but only to show how different literary and non-literary documents provide us with sufficient information to identify in classical Greece a normative discourse on the regulation of warfare in classical Greece.

openly and explicitly interacting through a series of behaviors that were regulated over time. This framework of shared rules allows us to understand such regulatory networks in terms of a system of "international" law, which—as explained in the chapters below—the ancient Greeks conceptualized and defined as "inter-*polis*", "common" or "universal" law.[74]

Based on the considerations above and for the purposes of successfully surveying the narratives of legal regulation of armed conflict in classical Greece, this study will be divided into two main parts. The first one—general—will address key concepts; the second one—more specific—will take up the ideas studied in the first part in order to analyze and interpret the rules of *ius ad bellum* and *ius in bello* mentioned in the sources. In the end, that will lead me to attempt some final conclusions.

More explicitly, in Part 1, I will first examine the historical characteristics of international law and its political-ideological constraints. Based on an analysis of its rules in terms of the will to impose internal systems in the pre-modern world, I propose a review of the concept of local "law" for each *polis* in the Greek world (particularly Athens), beginning with a survey of key notions (*dike, themis, nomos*) and the performative nature of justice (chapter 1). Then, after defining those concepts and the law-making procedure implemented under the Athenian regime (which, of course, offers almost the only evidence we have for that period), this study will address the issue of the "subjectivity" of non-individual persons under Athenian law. These observations will help me examine the nature of relations among Greek *poleis* in order to understand the scope of their international "subjectivity" and the nature of treaties as sources of "common" law in Greek cities (chapter 2).

---

74 One could challenge the identification of the ancient legal system in terms of "international" law. Indeed, throughout this work I will frequently resort to expressions such as "common law of the Greeks", "inter-*polis* law" or "panhellenic law". That being said, I share the understanding of Lafont who discussed in a recent work the existence of international relations in the ancient Near East. He claims, from a theoretical perspective, that the expressions used today could be methodologically inappropriate in that context but are useful, explicit and hard to replace: "Et l'on verra que les notions d'*ambassade*, d'*immunité diplomatique*, d'*usages protocolaires*, de *traité négocié*, de *droit international*, de *souveraineté*, d'*équilibre entre puissances*, etc., ne sont peut-être pas, en réalité, si anachroniques que cela quand on les utilise dans le contexte de l'histoire ancienne du Proche-Orient, même si elles n'ont bien sûr jamais été conceptualisées ni categorisées en tant que telles" (Lafont, 2011: 12–13). It is undoubtedly necessary, in any case, to survey the sources comprehensively to discover the terminology present in ancient documents, as proposed in this research.

After identifying those core elements, which are of the essence for theoretically supporting this research, in Part 2 (chapters 3–4) I will particularly examine the discursive references to the regulation of armed conflict in Greek *poleis*. In chapter 3, I will examine classical sources on rules limiting the use of force, focusing specifically on those that relate to the legality of commencing hostilities. In chapter 4, I consider references to limits on the conduct of armed conflict, and explore evidence for the existence of a principle of distinction and criteria of proportionality which relate to the protection of non-combatants and civilian property, as well as to restrictions on the means and methods of combat.

It is my hope that this study on the 'humanitarian' narrative of Greek sources related to warfare will help to provide a working basis for a historiography of international law and the regulation of war in the pre-modern classical world.

PART 1

The Concepts

CHAPTER 1

Normativity, Hegemony, and Democratic Performance: The Case of Classical Athens

1 International Normativity, Subordination, and Political Imposition in the Ancient World

For purposes of this work, I proceed from the idea of public international law as a system of legal norms that regulate relations between the subjects of the international community.[1] In contrast to national law, which developed with an inward orientation for the purpose of centralized control over individual subjects, "international law" (as it was called for the first time by Jeremy Bentham in the eighteenth century)[2] arose with the aim of giving a normative framework to the connections between States themselves.[3] Despite its fundamental differences from systems of domestic law, we can say that international law fulfills the same social function that characterizes law generally, in that it serves as a means to regulate and control the actions of the relevant subjects, directing their behavior in the service of a supposed common good.[4]

At present, therefore, we can define it in terms of those subjects to which we refer historically as States (the principal subjects) and other actors to which the system itself grants juridical identity.[5] Despite the existence of new actors who play very notable roles in international affairs, we nevertheless usually say that international law remains, even today, a system that is created *primarily* by States.[6] Such, ultimately, is the "international legal order."[7]

---

1 Moncayo, Vinuesa and Gutiérrez Posse (1997: 14), Ruzié (2008: 1).

2 Cf. the edition of Bentham's text by Lafleur (1963).

3 For the relevant terminology, cf. Fisch (2012: 28–30).

4 Allott (1999).

5 Since the end of the nineteenth century, States—as the principal subjects of the world order—have attributed international rights and obligations to organizations, individuals and other actors who thus become secondary subjects with limited legal capacity. The problem of international subject-status, and its usefulness for the ancient Greek world, will be developed in more detail in chapter 2.

6 Malanczuk (1997: 2). Initially, many authors described public international law as that which governs the conduct of "civilized States," as is shown by the various traditional definitions reproduced in Verma (2004: 1).

7 Diez de Velasco Vallejo (1973: 51).

 | DOI: 10.1163/9789004363823_003

I consider that this formulation, obviously positivistic, fails to take account of other features that appear to be essential to the concept of international law, especially with respect to what constitutes its moral foundations.[8] It is not, however, the aim of these paragraphs to survey the many definitions that have been elaborated in legal theory over the centuries in order to make the concept more precise.[9] It is preferable, for purposes of this investigation, to point out that the notion of international law, in its various formulations, always emphasizes the idea of an order that States have created to regulate their own actions.

This has led some authors to argue, from the perspective of domestic legal systems, that international law does not share the essential characteristics of what we call "law."[10] Thus, for example, the philosopher John Austin spoke of a "positive morality" in reference to international law, since it was a legal order in which the rules dictated by a sovereign were not supported by any sanction or punishment.[11] Hans Kelsen, on the other hand, maintained—also from the perspective of domestic law—that we are faced with a "primitive" order in which the degree of centralization needed to impose legal rules by means of coercion has not yet been achieved.[12] Similarly, Hersch Lauterpacht thought that international law was a "primitive law" because it lacked a centralized legislative authority and courts with mandatory jurisdiction.[13]

These skeptical or "negationist" arguments begin from the assumption that national codes of law are the legal "model" that must be followed, and they therefore conceive of international law as a system that lacks the features necessary to allow it to be assimilated to the former.[14] In this book, however,

8 In this connection I should mention John Rawls, who proposes a legal order to regulate the relations beween peoples (rather than States) that are "reasonably liberal" and "decent" (1999: 23–25; 64–67). A study of this text and its vision of international law can be found in Tasioulas (2002).

9 Brownlie (2008)—perhaps the most important textbook in the field—chooses not to define international law except insofar as he concerns himself with analyzing the different ways in which it is created (its sources). Regarding a generic "mistrust" of definitions of international law, cf. Barboza (2008: 11–12).

10 These views are generally inspired by the ideas of Thomas Hobbes (1588–1679); on these positions and the critiques of them, cf. Mégret (2012: 72–81).

11 Hart (1954).

12 Kelsen (1952: 22).

13 Lauterpacht (1933: 405).

14 Cassese (2001: 3–46) has concerned himself with the study of international law and its substantive differences from domestic law. He argues that international law is a type of

it will be maintained that international law *is* law in the proper sense of the word (even if different in its nature from domestic legal systems) insofar as its rules create obligations and rights that are accepted by its subjects for the sake of their coexistence.[15]

Although it should not be confused with international politics or the international economy, the political-economic nature of public international law is evident from the outset. And although we must identify the particular characteristics that define it as a concept—the fact that it constitutes a system of legal rules—it is not appropriate to assume a separation in practice between law and other dimensions of normativity.[16] Only an interdisciplinary perspective, in which the legal, the religious, the moral, and the political are interwoven, can do justice to each field of study through a comprehensive view of the phenomenon in question. This becomes even more evident in the case of the classical world, in which—leaving aside disciplinary differences—it is not possible to identify a domain of "law" set apart from other levels of social regulation.

One often reads that international law in modernity finds its opportunity to develop in the mutual recognition of sovereignty as an essential characteristic of the State.[17] Such interpretations, which place sovereignty at the center of the discussion, conclude that international law has its origin in the establishment of a new political, legal, and religious order in Europe during the sixteenth and seventeenth centuries, with the consolidation of the great powers such as Spain, Portugal, France, the Netherlands, and Sweden.

The so-called Peace of Westphalia of 1648, which ended the Thirty Years' War between Catholics and Protestants, is seen by such authors as a turning point, inasmuch as one can discern in the treaties that constitute it (the so-called Münster and Osnabrück agreements) a regulatory mechanism based on the balance of power.[18] This first attempt to "contractualize" interstate relations in Europe[19] defines the particular features of a new system of European law

---

law that does not take the individual into consideration and that its special features are explained by the unique nature of the global order. Contra, see Cançado Trindade (2010).

15 As Henderson (2009: 5) points out, it is possible to speak of a "voluntary compliance" and thus to conceptualize international law as law in the true sense of the word.

16 Higgins (1995: 2–4) has pointed out that, insofar as social construction cannot be independent of political reality, international law cannot be reduced to mere "rules." Rather, it is a process that is closely related to the exercise of authority.

17 Croxton (1999).

18 Moncayo, Vinuesa and Gutiérrez Posse (1997: 31).

19 Cf. Bull (1977).

shaped by the recognition of an international community characterized by the principle of the sovereign equality of its States. States, according to this principle, are reciprocally recognized as equals in terms of law: each of them is sovereign over its own territory and, consequently, cannot be viewed as being dependent upon the other States, which also exercise their authority, respectively, each in its own zone.[20]

The idea bequeathed by Westphalia is that the limitation of each State's desires for power and expansion somehow ensures that States will respect the integrity of foreign areas of sovereignty. The logic thus established was reiterated in peace treaties at least until the end of the nineteenth century. I perceive here a program for the peaceful coexistence of States which have diverse interests, and do not yet share common aims.[21]

It is usual to fix the origin of public international law in this period because of the belief that the legal equality of States imposes limits on the hegemonic aspirations of the most powerful. It provides a normative framework that can only emerge from agreement among entities that find themselves in a perfect equilibrium.[22] The anointing of the Peace of Westphalia as the original charter of public international law implies a conception of the "new" legal order as a decentralized,[23] horizontal[24] system in which States are subjects that create rules through free and voluntary agreement and in which there is no higher authority that can exercise control.[25] The actual differences among States lie concealed under a pretense of equality that—along with the foundational idea

20 It is for this reason that we speak of an "international" rather than a "supranational" order. At present, there is no supranationality in the field of public international law, at least if we define that field today (as I do in this book) in terms of a system that emerges from a shared desire among sovereign States and one that is characterized primarily by coordination on terms of relative equality. Some authors, such as Gutiérrez Posse (1995: 285–292), tend to speak of a subsystem of quasi-subordination in the specific case of the control exerted over the lawful use of force by the United Nations Security Council. Study of the rules in Greco-Roman treaties, however, reveals the frequent imposition of norms upon one party by another.

21 Oakeshott (1991).

22 In truth, it is possible to regard the Peace of Westphalia as a foundation myth: for this, see Beaulac (2004).

23 Barboza (2008: 15–16).

24 Cheng (1991: 33).

25 Combacau and Sur (1997: 2–3) identify a (decentralized) *interstate* law that occupies an intermediate position between what they call state law (at the domestic level) and *suprastate* law (in which there exists a third party superior to the States).

of sovereignty—allows for a successful fiction that will continue to characterize international law down to our own times.[26]

The Westphalian turning point, however, seems arbitrary from a diachronic perspective. In fact, beneath the supposed equality of sovereign States, there are hidden notorious real inequalities that frequently determine the rules in the international arena. The *pax Westphalica* has created a useful rhetorical mechanism to preserve the *status quo* in international relations.[27]

It is true that since the twentieth century—and especially since the creation of the United Nations in 1945—a sort of "rule of law" has begun to establish itself in the international arena: in many cases a sort of universal legal order does exist and create obligations beyond the will of States as traditional actors.[28] Nevertheless, it would be naive not to think that, even in this new era, the international legal system is (as it has always been) the outcome of a series of interactions between entities that in practice prove notoriously different and that relate to one another on a very unequal basis. Ultimately, this has meant that the States with the greatest capabilities and opportunity to impose their world-view are those that succeed in shaping legal rules (and imposing them on the weakest or poorest States) according to their advantage and interests.[29] As a result, it is indispensible that there should be a counter-voice on the part of developing States in the Third World for the sake of reinterpreting the hegemonic tradition of the law of nations.[30]

This reading, however, belongs to a political view of the phenomenon, which subordinates law to the decisions of States that exercise greater power relative to others. The basis for this outlook is of course historical, because it is believed

26 Some scholarship has been concerned with demonstrating the limits of this theoretical construct: see, for example, Simpson (2004).

27 On a revision of the Westphalian provisions from a historical perspective, cf. Lesaffer (1997, 2004), Eyffinger (1998), Cutler (2001), Osiander (2001), Teschke (2002) and Winkel (2004). According to Beaulac (2004: 90), "… the principal objects and material provisions of the Osnabrück and Münster Treaties do not at all support the traditional position that the *Peace of Westphalia* constitutes a paradigm shift whereby the political entities involved gained exclusive power over their territories. The two main purposes of the agreements related to the practice of religion and the settlement of territories, not to the creation of distinct separate polities independent from any higher authority". Similarly, Hurrell (2009: 54–55).

28 Concerning this feature of contemporary international law, which has permitted the establishment of a kind of legality in the present-day normative order, cf. Pinto (2004: 55).

29 Krisch (2005).

30 See, for instance, the recent contribution by Eslava, Obregón and Urueña (2016: 11–94).

that, since the earliest beginnings of the first politically organized communities, the most influential states tried to dominate the less fortunate through a series of legal rules that benefitted themselves.[31]

Undoubtedly, this imbalance is what most characterizes pre-modern international law. As we shall see, Greek antiquity offers us a number of interesting cases that allow us to think about how international law has served, in such contexts, as an unmistakable tool of domination by the powerful. In these earliest examples, we see a law which is poorly systematized, lacking a theoretical or scientific basis (since, as far as our sources can suggest, no doctrine to describe or explain it existed), and with an essentially particularistic character: the rules in question lacked universal validity but did create rights and obligations between neighboring communities (generally by means of customary norms and bilateral treaties) according to the abilities of the involved parties to persuade, defend their interests, and promote their points of view.[32]

Later in this book, I will examine how, in the case of the classical Greek city-states, an international law was built up from particular agreements imposed by the most powerful *poleis*. Here it is enough to observe that that international law has traditionally arisen from the necessity for States (especially those with the greatest bargaining power) to regulate their mutual behavior and interactions. This necessity was itself a consequence of an urgent need for mutual relations.[33]

Whatever theoretical support may undergird the foundations of international law, one cannot deny that the most powerful States, which could obviously ignore international law given the absence of any means of enforcing it, have instead always tried to justify their behavior by reinterpreting existing law (e.g., through new institutions and doctrines such as preemptive defense, humanitarian intervention, the responsibility to protect others—to mention only some of the most recent) while never acknowledging that they have committed actions that violate its norms.[34] Given this background, we

31 Concerning the existence of both large and small States throughout the nineteenth century, see the fundamental study of Wolfke (1961). As we shall see, the Greco-Roman world had the same political structure, likewise hidden beneath a fiction of legal equality.

32 By contrast, modern international law, which finds it origin myth in the Peace of Westphalia of 1648, presents itself as a universal, decentralized, and horizontal ordering of aims.

33 In fact, the international community—like all social groupings—requires a law that creates rules and imposes them upon its members; cf. Sinagra and Bargiacchi (2009: 1).

34 As Pinto (2004: 163) argues, "debe rescatarse a favor del derecho internacional que aun en el unilateralismo más descarnado, los criterios del derecho siguen guiando las reacciones."

must examine how States with greater political authority seek legitimation for their own behavior with respect to third parties.[35]

The conservative history of international law as a pure product of negotiations *inter pares* has recently produced an opposing revisionist movement which seeks to lay claim to the contested spaces of a peripheral vision of international relations.[36] According to this new interpretation, international law turns out to be an instrument of power and a pragmatic discourse that adapts itself to diverse interests.[37] To speak of an international legal system among civilized and sovereign States therefore implies a Eurocentric construction of the discipline that would exist in different forms according to the need to ratify the values of the "colonialist" States in the dominated non-European world.[38]

From the most critical readings of the phenomenon, we may deduce other advantages of an international law that is common to all: the establishment of a common terminology that creates an adequate sphere of communication

---

The example cited therein of the U.S. President's search for reasons to justify a coalition against Iraq is significant, since, as we shall see, it reveals the existence of a legitimizing discourse in international law.

35 On the crisis of legitimacy in international law—produced in many instances by forced interpretations of the rules or the search for exceptions to explain a lack of compliance—cf. Charlesworth and Coicaud (2010), Buchanan (2010: 79–96), and Tasioulas's response in the same volume (2010: 97–116).

36 See, for example, Rajagopal (2003) and Orford (2011). Among the theorists of the so-called TWAIL ("Third World Approaches to International Law") movement, we may also include Chimni (2012). These "marginal" and novel theories of international law, which challenge previous advances instead of complementing them, have been rejected by authors such as Müllerson (2000: 66–67), on the grounds that they do not contribute to the "mainstream" development of the discipline.

37 Douzinas (2007). The same conclusion is reached from a Marxist perspective by Zolo (2006), for whom international law is an instrument for the exercise of power by the most powerful. Feminist readings of international law tend to see in this normative order the embodiment of a patriarchal regime in which the most powerful States, seen as masculinized, impose themselves upon the weaker—feminized—nations, which are conquered and dominated; cf. Charlesworth and Chinkin (2000). On the United States, its "imperial" ambition, and its manipulation of international law, see Saito (2010). In an age of globalization, the proper response to this conception of international law as a system of unilateral advantages lies perhaps in a greater democratization of international institutions; cf. Condorelli and Cassese (2012: 24–25). For a more revolutionary position reacting to the moral indignation produced by current international law and its manifest inequities, see Allott (2004) and his social idealism.

38 This is the central thesis of Anghie's monograph (2005).

between States.[39] That shared language provides an appropriate means for States to declare their intentions, offers mutual clarity concerning their future policies, establishes with some precision the nature of agreements—including their limits and preconditions—and bestows formality upon agreements in such a way as to create expectations concerning their stability.[40]

In the ancient world, international law presupposes a narrative and a rhetoric that are outstandingly useful for describing and justifying the actions of state actors;[41] hence, it seems not to challenge but to reinforce the imperial hegemony that has historically characterized international relations.[42] Thinking about the regulation of international connections in the ancient world thus implies conceptualizing a logic by means of which the normative patterns of

---

39 Shaw (2008: 7).

40 Bull (1977: 142). It may be said that the success of a uniform vocabulary, however, is paradoxically a result of the fact that many of the key terms in international law are deliberately left undefined by States in the relevant documents (one may think of expressions such as "use of force" or "armed conflict," which, although frequent in treaties, are lacking in specific content). This allows considerable scope for each State to sustain a particular interpretation of rules.

41 Goldsmith and Posner (2005: 167–172).

42 Thus Grewe (1984), identifying historical periods based on different nations' hegemonies: a Spanish era (1494–1648), a French era (1648–1815), and a British era (1815–1919). These three periods represent the greatest degrees of imperialistic expansion by the respective nations. On this topic, see Cohen (2004). Today an interesting reality prevails: this "hegemonic" tendency inherent in international law is counterbalanced by a complementary tendency, an abstraction of "normativity" that causes the rules to bear a certain imprint, converting them into an autonomous system and augmenting its contents without always relating them to the specific reality of States' immediate interests. What we have is a cross between a normative system created to justify the actions of States in a specific historical moment (the sociological-political aspect) and an order based on the doctrinal elaboration of more abstract ideas such as "peace," "international security," and "a clean environment," among others (the philosophical aspect). In truth, we see the simultaneous coexistence of a traditional Grotian model—in which the international community is based on States, which work together but have their own interests in view—and a modern Kantian model—in which transnational solidarity is sought not so much among States as for the sake of humanity, which thus becomes the principal party in the international system. Immanuel Kant, in his 1795 work *On the Perpetual Peace* (*Zum ewigen Frieden, ein philosophischer Entwurf*), expressed the hope that, although there was no possibility of establishing a "world State," civilization should be promoted so that a universal federation of republics might eventually emerge. On this subject, see Koskenniemi (2012: 53). On Kantian influence among later philosophers of international law, such as Rawls or Habermas, see Perreau-Saussine (2010).

the domestic order are projected externally. Therefore, before moving on to the content of international rules in ancient Greece, it is best to begin with a review of the inherent characteristics of the legal order within the city-state. The case of Athens in the classical period (which, although we must handle it with care because of its sometimes unique character, is the only one for which our sources provide anything like complete information) will allow us to determine how we should think about the phenomenon of law in classical times and its practical logic as derived from imperialist aims.[43]

2 Justice, Law, Laws, and Decrees: The Issue of Terminology

In this section, I will offer a vision of law in the Greek world in light of certain theoretical views that envision citizen participation as performance. This regulated implementation of behaviors that materialize in personal interaction will be essential, as an interpretive framework, for understanding the legal limits on the practice of war in our surviving texts. We may begin by asserting that the procedures for elaborating and modifying legal rules in classical Greece constitute one of the most problematic topics in discussions of the history of law in antiquity; yet they are fundamental for an understanding of how public participation in the city's various spaces was understood.

In contrast to what had happened in the archaic period, when the promulgation of statutes by legendary lawgivers—like Zaleucus or Charondas—served to preserve the more conservative contours of political power and promote a shared sense of national identity in the nascent *polis*,[44] the legislative function in classical times (that is, in the fifth and fourth centuries) becomes more closely associated with patterns of social and civic activity that equate the citizen's presence in the Assembly to his participation in the courts, the theater, and—of special interest given the hypotheses already presented—the army.

The absence of documents and records in Athens (the *polis* for which we always have the most data) allows us at least to conclude that before the end

43 In the case of Athens, this imperialist tendency is very apparent during the Peloponnesian War, when frequent attempts were made to impose Athenian national legislation and the Athenian judicial system on "others" at the international level; cf. Balcer (1978: 125). This, as we shall see below, implied a progressive loss of αὐτοδικία (*autodikia*)—the right to one's own jurisdiction—by the weaker cities. Cf. Ténékidès (1954: 9).

44 Gagarin (1986: 140–141).

of the fifth century there were no amendments to, or re-codifications of, the traditional laws set forth by the famous archaic lawgivers like Draco (seventh century) and Solon (ca. 638–559). In concrete terms, we may state that, before the revolution of 404/3, a majority decision within the city's civic institutions was required for the abolition of existing laws or the creation of new ones.

Traditionally, it is the evidence provided by oratory which constitutes our most complete source for attempting to reconstruct the mechanisms of legislative action in Athens in the classical period. Here, however, in contrast to the usual procedure in works devoted to the subject, our aim is to relate different systems of legal rules to the broader background of Athenian democracy. We cannot examine the work of rule-creation in the Athenian context without examining its relationship to other civic and political institutions in which citizens took an active part. An isolated study of legislative activity does not allow us to account for the complexity of the phenomenon in cultural and ideological terms, nor to relate it—as I seek to do in this work—to institutions associated with the conduct of hostilities during armed conflicts.

Thus, after reviewing the literary evidence for the means by which laws and decrees were approved, amended, and abolished, this chapter will deal briefly with the importance of the Athenians' public participation in dramatic spectacles and in the activity of the lawcourts. By comparing the work of the Assembly with what was happening in the theater and the courts, we achieve an overview of the logic of the democracy and of citizen participation in the legal rules that prevailed in the community. In the second part of this investigation, these lines of inquiry will be taken up once again in order to understand discussions of the formal "limits" of military performance that appear in the various literary genres.

To explain how the legislative system worked in Athens, one must begin with a clarification of terminology. The Greeks in the classical period used a number of terms to refer to what we call "law". The concept of *dike* (δίκη), for example, originally referred to justice between families and, in a concrete sense, to ordinary human laws. Related to a verb (δείκνυμι, *deiknymi*) that means "point out" or "indicate," the substantive *dike* suggests a right that is identified as such when it originates from an authority with competence to dictate it.[45] There is debate as to whether in the works of Homer and Hesiod, the earliest literary evidence, the term was already used in a moral sense or whether, on the other hand, it was used exclusively to indicate a settlement of disputes or a sort of

45 On the word's range of meanings and etymological signification, cf. Benveniste (1969: 107–110).

legal procedure.[46] From an abstract idea of correction or rectification, and because technical terms find their basis in everyday vocabulary, *dike* at some point came to signify the legal process as a whole.[47]

With the evolution of the Athenian procedural system, private lawsuits, initiated by an interested party, received this denomination in order to contrast them with actions that any citizen could initiate (called *graphe*, γραφή).[48] The procedural sophistication of Athenian law meant that, in many cases, it was possible for a citizen to select a desired type of action (public or private, i.e. *graphe* or *dike*) based perhaps on evidentiary considerations or on political goals relating to the desired impact of the procedure.[49]

The concept of *themis* (θέμις), meanwhile, is connected with an idea of justice within the family, and its character was originally primitive and divine.[50] The first appearances of the term show that its meaning reflected a justice derived from someone who was legitimized to express the will of the gods. The Greek verb τίθημι (*tithemi*), from which the noun is derived, implies the idea of "placing" or "setting down," so that the concept is associated with the imposition of a superior order that must be respected. Thus, while *themis* represents a household organization set forth and established by the divinities, it has been said that *dike* corresponds rather to the ethical range of a justice meant to limit abusive actions by human beings.[51]

One might claim that in the middle of the fifth century *themis*, as opposed to *dike*, represents the innate sense of fairness in contrast to the external fact of official legality, moral conscience in contrast to positive law, and divine justice

46 The first position is favored by Dickie (1978); he opposes the second position, which is supported by Gagarin (1973), among others.

47 Jones (1956: 26), Hirzel (1907: 56–227).

48 These two essential meanings of *dike* coexist in the Greek world. Thus, Chantraine (1954: 47) distinguishes adjectives derived from *dike* in the sense of "justice" (such as *dikaios*) from others that come from its connotation of "judicial process" (e.g., *dikanikos*).

49 "Since most offences for which the law specified *graphē* could be redefined to fall within the scope of a law specifying procedure by *dikē* it was frequently possible for an Athenian litigant to choose between processes. The man who acted by *dikē* had to act himself but ran no risk; the man who wanted action by *graphē* could prosecute himself or find another who was willing to do so, and whoever undertook the prosecution faced the possibility of a heavy fine if completely unsuccessful. The variety of actions both constrains a man and frees him to fit his actions to his circumstances" (Osborne, 1985: 43). Thus, for example, it was possible to choose between a public and private action in cases of theft: cf. Moneti (1991).

50 Benveniste (1969: 102), Hirzel (1907: 18–56).

51 Méndez de Fraboschi (1985: 13).

in contrast to human justice.[52] It must be said, however, that the sources do not always employ these concepts in such as way as to establish a clear distinction between the positive embodiment of justice in a community and that right decreed by the gods.

Only with the word *nomos* (νόμος)—which itself shows considerable variability in its meaning—does this distinction appear to find textual support: although in many cases it may be appropriate to translate term *nomos* with the English word "law", which is a concept sufficiently broad to embody many of its particular denotations, in other languages *nomos* can from a legal point of view refer either to *ley* or *derecho* (Spanish), *loi* or *droit* (French). From a formal point of view, *ley* and *loi* denote any of the normative instruments that emanate from a duly constituted authority, while *derecho* and *droit* denote a system of legal norms that regulate relations among those whom the same system designates as its subjects. These denotations do not, however, exhaust the range of meanings implied by *nomos*,[53] which extends from "convention" or "custom" to the idea of customary law, whether written or not.[54] In any case, as we shall see below, what is essential to the concept is its normative character and the impossibility of limiting it to what we today conceive of as the "legal" sphere.[55]

Nomos, then, can refer to both law and custom,[56] and at the same time may refer to both written and oral law.[57] The oral transmission of rules, the only method of passing on knowledge in the early period, is steadily set aside by the middle of the fifth century in favor of a growing confidence in the writing down of statutes.[58] Nevertheless, after 403, in the wake of the revision of the law

52 Glotz (1904: 22); cf. Eggers Lan (1997: 33).

53 See Todd and Millett (1990: 11–12).

54 As Ostwald argues (1965: 120), "the term *nomos* has many different connotations in Greek, ranging from 'law' as a written political enactment to a custom or habit which may or may not have absolute validity, and from the rules of a game to that ordered state of society on which civilized existence rests."

55 Hirzel (1907: 359–386).

56 In the absence of law—or together with it—the term may represent a custom that is just as capable of producing recognized legal consequences; this happens, for example, in the commercial sphere: "… in the absence of a juristic framework, the law and the custom of sale (*nomos* in both senses) may be combined" (Millett, 1990: 194).

57 In calling attention to the world's multiple legal denotations, Aristotle provides a classification of various types of *nomos* (Aristotle, *Rhetoric* 1368b5 et seq.). On *nomos* as law (*Gesetz*), see Quass (1971: 19–23) and Triantaphyllopoulos (1985: 9–13).

58 Thus, for example, we find passages in which written law is conceived as a guardian of justice: see, for example, Gorgias fr. 11a § 30; Solon 36w.

code, the term *nomos* refers exclusively to written law.[59] Ever since the reforms of Cleisthenes the idea of written law had been gaining ground; the older laws of Solon, by contrast, received the label of *thesmoi* (θεσμοί).[60]

It is necessary, at this point, to consider what was meant in classical Athens by "unwritten laws" and to discuss, beginning from the opposition between natural right and positive law, the advantages and disadvantages of the transition from oral norms to a written body of law. This discussion is essential in order to address, in the later sections of this work, the nature of an international *nomos* that emerges rarely from written agreements and more commonly from customary norms which are not written down but which have the weight of historical authority.[61] We should recall that the first references to unwritten law only appear in the tragedy *Antigone* (442/1) with explicit mention of the *agrapta nomima* (ἄγραπτα νόμιμα, v. 454)[62] and this undoubtedly has to do with the fact that it is only around this time that one begins to think in terms of the existence of written law. The appearance of written laws offers a new outlook: it typically indicates that at some point the oligarchic segments of the citizen body, which had previously manipulated the unwritten body of law which was not well known and could easily be modified, became constrained in their administration of the laws. The publication of rules in writing, which now is linked to legislation by the people, allowed anyone to have access to what the laws enjoined. *Nomos* therefore has an essentially democratic character.[63]

This thesis is interesting, though in fact it presents only a partial reading of reality. Although it may be useful as a means of examining the first stages in the process of the publication of laws, it is obviously insufficient to explain the situation that develops as we approach the end of the fifth century. In fact, it was the process of the revision of the laws, which took place during the last years of that century (and came to an end in 403/2), that established the absolute primacy of written law and forbade any future appeal to an *agraphos nomos* that had not been explicitly incorporated in the text of the codified laws.[64] This is a

59 Cf. Thomas (1996: 14). Prior to this date, the sources seem to indicate that the word could be used to indicate both written and oral law.

60 Hirzel (1907: 320–358), Ostwald (1969), Quass (1971: 11–14).

61 Phillipson (1911: i, 52–60), Bederman (2001: 38–41), Lanni (2007: 6).

62 The idea also appears in Thucydides 2.37.

63 In his conclusion, Thomas (1996: 30) emphasizes that "written law can be—and often is—fundamental in checking arbitrary judgment: when justice was in the hands of a few elders and governed by unwritten law, it was clearly open to arbitrary judgment and inconsistency."

64 Andoc. 1.85–87, cited by Ostwald (1986: 164).

clear indication that it had previously been possible to challenge a written law with a law that traditionally had been transmitted orally; it demonstrates that any conflict of legal rules posed a problem that urgently required a solution. By the end of the fifth century the argument had not been resolved in a definitive way, and the existence of two sources of legal authority allowed opposing positions to be maintained with equal plausibility in the course of litigation.

As one example, we may recall that in the case against Andocides, accused of involvement in the profanation of the Eleusinian mysteries (in 415), there arose the question of the punishment to be imposed for the placement of a suppliant's branch on the altar in the Eleusinium. Two positions are preserved in a passage from the orator (1.115–116): while Callias held that there existed an ancestral law which prescribed that the one committing this act should be condemned to death without trial, Cephalus (a supporter of the accused) pointed out the existence of a stele that sanctioned the same act with a fine of one thousand drachmas. The contrast between the arguments is clear and attention to their terminology is essential: even for those who would reject the full extent of the lesser penalty preserved in the law written upon the stele, the unwritten law (in the plural, νόμοι ἄγραφοι, *nomoi agraphoi*) is a νόμος πάτριος, *nomos patrios*: a "paternal" law, based on ancestral tradition.[65]

The example just given suggests various interpretations. It may be true that with writing the law becomes objective and its use is initially controlled in practice, but there is no guarantee that a system of rules set forth in writing constitutes a remedy for arbitrariness in the interpretation of the law. Moreover, nothing allows us to connect the existence of *agrapta nomima* with consequences rejected by every legal regime as "arbitrary judgment and inconsistency". In *Antigone* the main character is caught between respect for a customary rule, of divine origin, that requires her to bury her brother, and obedience to a written law imposed by a (human) political power that seeks to prevent her. This has been read—ever since the origin of the idea of unwritten law—as the positing of an opposition of major importance in debates concerning the philosophy of law: natural law vs. positivism.[66]

In general, therefore, the idea of a positive, written law cannot be related directly to the achievement of permanent freedom and equality, values inher-

65 Ostwald (1986: 162–163).

66 This is not the place to cast doubt on this idea; suffice it to say that some recent interpretations have succeeded in asserting, based on a reading of the text itself, that *Antigone* instead represents an opposition between two different ways of manipulating the meaning of the word *nomos*; cf. Harris (2006).

ent in the political logic of unrestricted citizen participation. In speaking of this, Aristotle himself argues that written rules should not remain forever sealed but should be susceptible to change. In changing the laws, however, one should proceed with great caution (*Rhetoric* 1269a12–14). Written law can be equally subject to manipulation if one does not notice its possible opposition to law that is unwritten, customary, natural,[67] derived from morality or religion, i.e. ἄγραφος (*agraphos*) and πάτριος (*patrios*). Written law is a human creation, and such it is subject to improvement: in any open legislative debate, one must take care in creating, modifying, and interpreting it.

Although *nomos* can therefore be interpreted as oral law, it is necessary to emphasize that already in the second half of the fifth century it also refers to a positive, written law that therefore is presented as being in opposition to nature or to that which is natural (φύσις, *physis*).[68] With the rise of sophistic thought in Athens during this period, it began to be argued, on the basis of a distinction between the *natural* and the *conventional*, that laws were based on conventions[69] and that all positive, written law—insofar as it is manipulated by men and sets itself against the conservative ancestral traditions established by time—is open to debate:[70] one may defend one position or another and—to return to the beginning of this topic—the same facts may be attacked or defended in the courts in terms of contradictory but equally valid laws.[71]

---

67 The expression "natural law" emerges only with the establishment of the sophists' opposition between nature and convention, "mais, pour le fond, Aristote ne s'y est pas trompé: la loi non écrite représente bien la loi naturelle" (de Romilly, 1971: 48). However, as we will see, unwritten customary law is part of interstate *nomoi* and, as such, it does not allow itself to be conflated with natural law.

68 "L'opposition de la loi et de la nature, née de la réflexion philosophique et renforcée par l'analyse sophistique, avait, en fait, pénétré de façon rapide le vocabulaire de l'époque; et elle y avait été exploitée par tous ceux qui, dans un domaine ou un autre, tendaient à s'affranchir des lois" (de Romilly, 1971: 97). On this opposition, cf. Heinimann (1945).

69 Varela (1984: 77).

70 The predominance of customary over written law is evident even in Aristotelian philosophy itself (*Politics* 1287b).

71 This is by no means to say that written law does not contribute to the development of democracy, only that in the democracy as it existed at the end of the fifth century we do find individuals abusing the rules. Christ supports this (1998: 223) when, contrasting a literate elite with an illiterate general public, he concludes that "Athenian juries were inclined to view legal sophistication and subtle argumentation based on written authority with considerable suspicion."

Thus, the sophistic approach enshrines a genuine relativism that has clear repercussions for discussions concerning the legal system and its essential variability.[72]

The absence of a hierarchy of rules in the Athenian *polis* throughout the century of Pericles, along with the laws' inherent lack of authority, led to the problem that if two opposing parties found contradictory laws and presented them at trial, the δικασταί (*dikastai* or judges) had to decide which of them was applicable.[73]

Many modern authors who concern themselves with ancient Greek law have been tempted to differentiate the ideas of *nomos* and ψήφισμα (*psephisma*, "decree").[74] It is usual to conclude, however, that—at least in the period under discussion—no difference in principle between the one and the other can be identified,[75] even though in works dating from after the year 411 some authors claim to notice a difference between the two concepts. On balance, it seems clear that, after the period between 410 and 399, during which the laws were revised, the distinction is better defined: *nomos*, as a technical term, was limited to rules of a general character and a certain permanence, while *psephisma* would refer to all those regulations of a transitory and particular character. One can infer from the words of Andocides (1.87), one of the first great Attic orators, that at this time a hierarchy is already evident: no *psephisma* was able to overturn a *nomos*.[76]

3 *Nomothesia*: The Act of Legislating

The enormous importance of unwritten rules, founded *discursively* in the backing of divine justice, doubtless conditioned democratic institutions with

72 On the scope of this sophistic conventionalism and its effects in contemporary sources, see Buis (2013a).

73 Todd (1996: 24) suggests that, since the Athenians had not developed the general principles, as in Roman law, that *lex posterior derogat priori* and *lex specialis derogat generali*, they may quite possibly have opted for the converse system, preferring the oldest legal rule on the grounds that its authority was based on tradition.

74 Cf. Quass (1971).

75 Hansen (1978), Thomas (1996: 18).

76 In regard to its consequences, "… no *psephisma* could override a *nomos*, and *nomoi* could no longer be changed by simple majority vote, but only by means of *nomothesia*, an elaborate and time-consuming procedure in which the assembly had no final say" (Todd, 1996: 123).

respect to the creation of laws. From its earliest beginnings, Athenian democracy established a strong system of checks and balances, based on the idea of ἰσονομία (*isonomia*, "equality of rights") among all its citizens, in order to avoid any possibility of legislative power falling into the hands of the few.[77] The intention was to establish a communal decision-making process.

Throughout the classical period, popular participation in Athens manifested itself in various ways in different facets of public life. The legislative procedure (known in Greek as νομοθεσία, *nomothesia*) demonstrates how Athenian citizens expected ample opportunities to initiate legislation in the Assembly or Ἐκκλησία (*Ekklesía*).[78] If a citizen felt that it made sense to pass a new law or to alter some feature of the legal system, he needed only to exploit the civic spaces of the *polis* to convince the other citizens that his proposal was appropriate.[79]

As Demosthenes points out in his oration *Against Timocrates*,[80] what someone interested in proposing a new law needed to do was to put it in writing and publish it next to the statues of the Eponymous Heroes, so that anyone who might be interested would be able to see it (ἐκθεῖναι πρόσθεν τῶν ἐπωνύμων γράψαντα σκοπεῖν τῷ βουλομένῳ).[81] If the proposal should be authorized, the Council (Βουλή, *Boule*)[82] was to inform the *Ekklesia* of this decision and set a date for a meeting to discuss the proposal in depth (this was done through what was known as a προβούλευμα, *probouleuma*).[83]

During the fifth century, a vote of the *Boule* and *Ekklesia* was sufficient for passage of a law, and, in order to secure passage, it was necessary for whoever proposed the law to present publicly his arguments for approval.[84] A more complex scheme was implemented, however, by the Decree of Teisamenos (403). In this new arrangement, a set of officials called *nomothetai* (νομοθέται) was cre-

---

77 On *isonomia*, cf. Hirzel (1907: 240–251).

78 All adult Athenian citizens could take part in the *Ekklesia*; cf. Herodotus 5.97.2; Lysias 13.32; Lysias 19.31; Xenophon, *Hellenica* 1.7.9; Isocrates 15.190; Demosthenes 18.169; 21.2; 21.180; 21.194; 24.48; 25.95; 58.45; Aeschines 2.13; 3.125. On the Assembly, see the passages collected in Hansen (1983).

79 I focus here on the examination of legislative proposals presented by individual citizens and not on those situations in which the Assembly itself proposed changes in the existing laws or the introduction of new ones, nor on the taking of the initiative by certain public officials (the archons, to whom I will refer below).

80 In this speech, Demosthenes charges his opponent of having introduced a illegal proposal (the form of public action initiated by the orator was called *graphe paranomon*).

81 Demosthenes 24.17–18. The Greek text follows the edition of Butcher (1903).

82 On this body, see the excellent work of Rhodes (1972).

83 Demosthenes 24.27; 24.48; Aeschines 3.39.

84 MacDowell (1986 [1978[1]]: 44–45).

ated, dedicated exclusively to the control and oversight (δοκιμασία, *dokimasia*) of the mechanisms for the creation and revision of laws.[85] The increasing importance of the figure of the *nomothetes* deserves to be taken into account, since on the basis of their activity a true collective system for the adoption of new legal rules was gradually achieved.[86]

Despite the introduction of this position, the process of legislation itself did not undergo substantial change. The citizen could still submit a law for approval or propose the modification of a particular rule.[87] According to evidence from the Demosthenic corpus, the *nomothetai*—chosen from among Athenian citizens who had taken the dicastic oath, that is, the oath required for them to serve as judges[88]—reviewed the proposal after it had been submitted in writing[89] and had been read several times in the context of the *Ekklesia*. If anyone came forward to argue the necessity for modifying a particular law, he was invited to propose in the Assembly a text to replace the one that was being criticized.[90] In fact, no proposal was accepted if not accompanied by a draft of the new law.[91] Thus, the benefits that a particular law might offer were expressed in a public and open fashion so that the citizens could understand its contents and its desirability. After this, and if the Assembly decided that the proposal had sufficient merit,[92] the *nomothetai* expressed their judgment through a public vote: they raised their hands if they were in favor of the proposal. Their decision was final.[93] Once a decree had been drafted and approved, it was inscribed on stone so as to be publicly available.[94]

---

85 This procedure, however, in practice became so complicated that a few decades later (sometime before 370) a new standard for legislation was implemented. On this new law, and the related laws such as the "Review Law," see the critical study by Rhodes (1984).

86 Dupont (1983: 271). Cf. Quass (1971: 44–72), who refers to this "Entwicklung der Gesetzgebungstechnik".

87 This is one of the three tasks reserved to the *nomothetai*. The other two were (i) the revision of the laws at the direct request of the Assembly (Demosthenes 24.20) and (ii) the scrutiny of the laws at the request of the six archons called *thesmothetai* (Aeschines 3.38).

88 Demosthenes 24.27; Demosthenes cites the text of this oath at 24.149–151.

89 Demosthenes 24.23.

90 Demosthenes 24.33.

91 Demosthenes 20.89–94; 24.21.

92 Demosthenes 24.21; 3.10–13; Aeschines 3.39.

93 Demosthenes 20.89–99; 20.91; 24.20–23; cf. MacDowell (1975: 73).

94 Athenian democracy was based, fundamentally, on the idea that citizens should be informed. Publication in the form of inscriptions was the simplest way to make the content of the laws known to the people (Meritt 1940: 89–93). See Hedrick (1994) for the various points of view on this subject. According to Hansen (1987: 164–165), there were so many

We can observe a logic in the legislative procedure that runs through the different political arrangements of the fifth and fourth centuries. Both before and after the institution of the *nomothetai*, there is participation by the citizen body in the Assembly. Every legislative project was based on the defense of a particular position, which frequently resulted in reactions on the part of those who took a different view of the content of the proposed law. We have considerable evidence that in these cases there was a genuine debate between opposing views. In fact, we know that the Assembly, during its first session of each year, chose five citizens who would be charged from then on with defending those laws whose repeal or amendment was proposed.[95]

Thus, in a clearly defined space and with the formalities appropriate to the public institution of the *Ekklesia*,[96] a real confrontation was arranged in which opposing positions were set forth and defended. As third parties, the *nomothetai* would then decide by their vote which of the two positions should be supported.

In the context of ancient Greece's fundamentally agonistic culture, based on dialectical confrontation between parties with generally opposed opinions and interests, the work of legislation is not an isolated phenomenon. On the contrary, it is interesting to situate this *nomothesia* in relation to other public and civic spectacles that shared its structural logic and fundamental ideology, in particular the theater and the judicial activity of the courts.

4 Dramatic Competitions and Athenian Festivals

For centuries, the Greek theater has been a fruitful field of study. Its performative context has frequently attracted the attention of philologists and historians.[97] Even today, however, the origins of Greek tragedy and comedy remain obscure, seemingly traceable to primitive religious rituals, ancient dithyrambic choruses, and phallic songs in honor of the god Dionysus.[98] Despite the difficulties, there exist good sources that permit us to infer the major features of

laws in Athens from the fourth century onwards that, instead of being inscribed on stone, they were written on softer media and kept in the city's public archive, known as the Metroon.

95 Demosthenes 24.23; 24.36.

96 Hansen (1987).

97 On the distinctive features of Greek drama, see Arnott (1967) and Ley (1991).

98 According to Aristotle, *Poetics* 3–4, these two genres were, respectively, the foundation of tragedy and comedy. In his understanding, tragedy seemed to derive from the ancient

the genre. Plays were performed in an open-air theater by a chorus and three actors who performed the main roles while dressed in special tunics and masks. Tragedy generally exploited these resources to stage stories with an almost exclusively mythological background, whereas Old Comedy was characterized, to a greater extent, by an effort to burlesque contemporary figures and situations.[99]

The plays that have survived display common features which reflect their performance in theaters with particular physical characteristics; these characteristics in turn reflect the society and culture of the Greek people. Architecturally, the most typical feature of the Greek theater is the ὀρχήστρα (*orkhestra*) or dance floor. This was a very simple circular space where the chorus stood. The design may have been related to the origins of the drama in local festivals featuring song and dance.

The location of the stage on a hill- or mountainside permitted a large number of spectators to have a wide view over the *orkhestra*.[100] The σκήνη (*skene*), which hung or stood behind the dance floor, was a facade behind which the actors could change their clothes to represent other characters. In the classical period, the playwrights had already begun to employ a stone wall with projecting sides. To its right and left were entrance corridors for the chorus, called πάροδοι (*parodoi*); these flowed directly into the *orkhestra*.[101]

The actors placed themselves either in the *orkhestra* with the chorus or, failing that, on the steps leading to the doors in the *skene*. The protagonist, deuteragonist, and tritagonist—chosen and employed by the city-state—played the various roles, although it was possible for non-speaking actors to be used when the plot required a fourth character to appear on the stage. All the actors were men, and the use of masks had a twofold purpose: on the one hand, it allowed spectators to identify the age, sex, and social status of the different characters; on the other hand, it enhanced the audibility of the speakers.

The members of the chorus—twelve and later fifteen in tragedy, double that number in comedy—were coached by the poet in the performance of his work.

---

epics while comedy was based on ancient iambic poetry. On the controversial origins of Greek theater, see Pickard-Cambridge (1927) and Burkert (1966).

99 We may note that, in contrast to this *arkhaia komoidia*, there emerged in the fourth century the so-called New Comedy, which aimed to portray conflicts of a private character; the central objective of attacking politicians and officials was thus set aside.

100 Arnott (1991: 3) explains that around most of the sides of the orchestra "tiers of seats were built into the convenient hillside, so that the audience could look down onto the stage."

101 This description follows Arnott (1991).

Once the *khoreutai* entered through the *parodoi*, the chorus began to interact with the characters, mainly through its leader or *koryphaios*. They also sang and danced the *stasima*. In examining the typical features of Athenian drama and the way in which it responded to the requirements of a theater that was especially interested in the spoken word, we notice that one of its defining characteristics is the is on-stage debate, either between the protagonist and the chorus or between the different characters. In both comedy and tragedy, debate plays a vital role, sometimes even drawing attention away from the main line of the plot. This argumentative tendency—which, as we shall see in the next section, also characterizes the activity of the Athenian courts—is quite noticeable in these plays.

The audience as well constituted an essential element in dramatic performance. In the *theatron*, the seats were carefully assigned according to social rank. The front row of seats was reserved for members of the Council and the young conscripts who were receiving military training. The citizens occupied the middle rows, and foreigners and women (if the latter attended the performances, which remains in doubt) were placed in the last two rows of the theater.[102] Most historians agree that all citizens had the right to attend dramatic festivals, although it is possible that in practice many lacked the means to pay for entry.[103] Nevertheless, there were very few occasions when plays were performed, so that it seems safe to affirm that the spectacle was essentially open, popular, and democratic. Plays were only performed in Athens on two occasions during the year.[104] Both were festivals of Dionysus, the god of wine, fertility, and the theater. The Greater Dionysia took place for six days in the month of *Elaphebolion* (roughly corresponding to March),[105] while the Lenaea lasted for four days during *Gamelion* (around January).[106] It is likely that both religious festivals were held in the Theater of Dionysus, next to the Acropo-

102 Dover (1972: 17): "… when the adult male citizens had seated themselves women, children, foreigners and slaves saw as much of the plays as they could."

103 Although the issue is debated, we have evidence—discussed by Csapo and Slater (1994: 288)—that in classical times the price never exceeded two obols. By the end of the fourth century, however, this was changed and the cost increased considerably to five drachmas (equivalent to thirty obols).

104 MacDowell (1995: 6). On Athenian festivals, see the excellent works of Pickard-Cambridge (1968) and Parke (1977). Smaller rural festivals took place in other locations.

105 On this civic importance of this festival, see Goldhill (1990).

106 Two other festivals in honor of the god were held annually at Athens: the Lesser Dionysia in December and the Anthesteria in February. Dramatic performances apparently were not performed in Athens during these celebrations.

lis.[107] The plays that were performed competed to win the prize for the best work. After a first day of religious processions and two days of dances (known as dithyrambs) in praise of Dionysus, the plays were performed as an integral part of the festivities.

The poets who were authorized to stage their works were chosen by an archon, the magistrate who was in charge of the festival. Only three playwrights were chosen, each of whom had to present a tetralogy of three tragedies plus a satyr play. The festivals were wholly financed by wealthy Athenians, who paid all expenses related to the competition. Some citizens were chosen by the archon to finance and supervise the dramatic performance; this was part of a system of public services or "liturgies" that were carried out for the benefit of the community. These *khoregoi* had to procure costumes and masks, pay the actors and musicians, hire a director or διδάσκαλος (*didaskalos*) and provide all the necessary support for the preparation and training of the chorus.[108]

Playwrights participated in these competitions in hopes of emerging victorious. In order to choose a winner, a number of judges were selected a few days before the performances. First, a long list of possible judges (κριταί, *kritai*) was agreed upon at sessions of the *Boule*. All the names proposed were written on balls and sealed in special containers. During the presentation of the plays, the list was shortened: it was believed that this was an effective way to reduce the corruption of the judges and the payment of bribes, something which nevertheless is frequently mentioned. Only ten judges were finally chosen from the containers, and it was they who wrote their individual verdicts on tablets after all the plays had been performed. We know that the archon then chose five of the tablets at random and counted those votes to determine who had won first prize.

Some aspects of this voting procedure, however, remain unclear, and have aroused the interest of scholars of the ancient theater. There is still debate, for example, about how the system of selecting judges was ultimately implemented. Csapo and Slater (1994) call attention to the problems involved in choosing only five of ten votes for purposes of determining the order of the prizes. This poses an insoluble problem and they therefore propose that more votes would be used in the event that the ranking could not be established with those five alone. In any case, it was desirable to use fewer than ten votes so as to minimize the possibility of partiality.

---

107 Pickard-Cambridge (1946).

108 On the civic importance of *khoregia*, see Wilson (2000).

The *kritai* of the contest were central figures in the organization of the dramatic festivals, because theirs was the responsibility for selecting the winning plays. We can clearly see that these festivals were characterized by competitiveness, and thus were an active manifestation of political agitation and open debate, in which citizenship became operational and publicly visible.[109] In this respect, there are many similarities between the Athenian dramatic competitions, legislative participation in the Assembly, and the administration of justice. The particular features of the theater can lead us to examine the close connection between law and drama in the democratic world of the *polis* and thus to understand the scope of the civic "rules" that regulated all areas of community life.

5 Justice as Spectacle in Athens: Judicial *praxis*

Although the institutional complex of the Greek city-states prefigures characteristics of the autonomous political units of the Later Middle Ages and Renaissance, it is not generally believed that Greek law—as a normative order—has plainly had an influence upon later legal systems.[110] In the classical period, however, the various *poleis* had succeeded in creating true legal systems, frequently in connection with questions of religion or ritual, in which they attempted to render justice in the face of actions that the community condemned.

Greek law has been preserved only in fragmentary form,[111] and strictly juridical sources are lacking, with the exception of a small number of epigraphic documents. Moreover, we need to recognize the difficulty of conceiving of "Greek law" as a single system of regulations in the way that we now think of "Roman law." The multiplicity of *poleis*, which were organized over time through intricate networks of alliances and enmities, produced a variety of legal systems.[112]

In keeping with the information supplied by our literary sources (mainly oratory), it is clear that in Athens—for which, again, we have the greatest

109 "As festivals were a stage for the performance of citizenship, so that performance becomes restaged as a factor in the contestation of status and the politics of self-representation that constitutes public life in democracy" (Goldhill, 1999: 23). Cf. Osborne (1993).

110 Todd (1993: 3).

111 MacDowell (1986 [1978¹]: 8).

112 The adoption of common institutions, as a basis for examining the existence of a uniform Greek legal experience among the different *poleis*, has been studied by Talamanca (1981: 5–7).

quantity of information, compared to other cities—[113] the exercise of justice took form in the orality of public debate. The litigiousness of the Athenians, which Aristophanes made it his business to expose and criticize, was supported by a culture of dialectical struggle.[114]

The judicial system of the Athenians endeavored to resolve public and private disputes through the establishment of a process in which the community of citizens were participants. Ever since the creation of the classical legal system by the lawgivers Draco and Solon, one of its notable features was that the job of those charged with putting an end to disputes was never professionalized. The absence of lawyers in the Greek context is a peculiarity that has often been pointed out. Facing a jury, litigants often showed themselves to be unfamiliar with procedural issues, and they frequently accused their opponents of being experienced orators practiced in trickery and sophisticated techniques of argumentation. To present oneself as someone who was not characterized by enthusiasm for litigation became itself a popular rhetorical pose among the Athenians.[115]

Even the judges were not professional, and most of them came from the rural classes, who could not be considered rich or poor but who met the requirements of an economic middle class.[116] Periodically, a huge number of judges was chosen. The short length of time in office, as well as the large size of juries, which could reach six thousand members, always with an odd number to avoid ties in the final verdict, made it nearly impossible for a magistrate to acquire the technical competence of an expert. As for the compensation that they received, the judges collected three obols daily for their service. During the classical period, this was about one third of what a skilled craftsman could earn for a day's work.

The procedure for the selection of judges was well organized. Any citizen, or πολίτης (*polites*), over thirty years of age could be registered in one of the ten tribes (φυλαί, *phylai*) into which the city was divided ever since the reforms of Cleisthenes. The judges were chosen at random.[117] An allotment machine

---

113 "Obwohl das athenische Recht das bekannteste und ruhmvollste der griechischen Rechte ist ..." (Triantaphyllopoulos, 1985: 2). Cf. Selb (1993: 89). Paoli (1976: 4) argues that the lack of information about the other cities makes it impossible to reconstruct the operation of other Greek legal systems.

114 See the thesis of Johnstone (1999), for whom Athenian law is essentially rhetorical.

115 Cf. Ober (1989), Hesk (1999).

116 Todd (1990).

117 We have numerous pieces of evidence, many of them mutually inconsistent, concerning the point in Athenian history at which judges began to be chosen by lot: cf. Hansen (1990).

decided—among all members of the same tribe or *phyle*—whether they would serve at that time as judges and, if so, within which court. The need for juries to be fully manned during the period when trials were taking place had a practical consequence: every adult Athenian citizen, at least at one time during his life, was part of a court. During the fifth century, each judge served in a particular court for a term of one year.

The Athenian judicial system was arranged into various courts.[118] While less important offenses could be tried by lesser courts, the most important crimes, such as homicide, fell under the jurisdiction of courts such as the Areopagus, the Palladium, the Delphinium, the Prytaneum, and the court "in Phreatto."[119] Each court had been created to deal with particular issues. The Areopagus, for example, had the exclusive task of judging those accused of intentional homicide.[120] The Palladium was reserved for cases of unintentional homicide,[121] the Delphinium examined cases of justifiable homicide,[122] while the Prytaneum was the court charged with homicides committed by animals, inanimate objects, or persons unknown.[123] Although there are controversies surrounding its existence and proper name, the sources also mention a court "in Phreatto" (ἐν Φρεαττοῖ, ἐν Φρεάτου). Located perhaps in the port of Piraeus, this court was charged with prosecuting those who, having already been exiled for unintentional homicide, were now charged with intentionally committing a violent crime.[124]

After the reforms introduced by Ephialtes, the power and jurisdiction of the Areopagus were diminished, and various panels of judges, or δικαστήρια (*dikasteria*) were introduced to represent the people (δῆμος, *demos*) as a whole.[125]

Judicial proceedings could be initiated by a magistrate or—more commonly—by a private citizen, who had to bring his opponents before the jury to present his accusation. An oral summons was pronounced in the presence of the alleged offender, and he was notified of when he had to appear in court.

---

118 On the administration of justice in Athens, see the two-volume general presentation of Bonner and Smith (1930–1938).

119 On the judicialization of homicide in Athens from Draco to the fourth century, see the recent work of Pepe (2012). Boegehold (1995) investigates the ancient sources regarding the multiplicity of courts.

120 Cf. MacDowell (1963: 39–47).

121 MacDowell (1963: 58–69).

122 MacDowell (1963: 70–81).

123 Demosthenes 23.76; cf. MacDowell (1963: 85–89).

124 Demosthenes 23.77; cf. MacDowell (1963: 82–84).

125 Ostwald (1986: 47–77).

When that day came, and the plaintiff had paid the appropriate fees, the magistrate who accepted the case initiated a preliminary hearing called an ἀνάκρισις (*anakrisis*) before transferring the matter to a court for final adjudication. If the case was accepted, each party to the dispute had to assemble all the available evidence so as to present it before the jury. Ordinarily, litigants had to present themselves before the court of the magistrate who had accepted the case, together with their witnesses and supporters.

The general public could stand in the space around the court to hear the litigants' arguments. The case began with speeches by the respective parties, each of which was subject to a time limit, to ensure equal opportunities to both sides. The duration of the pleadings was determined by a waterclock or κλεψύδρα (*klepsydra*). Each litigant had to present his case in person and attempt to convince the jury that he did not have courtroom experience. Thus, it was essential to present simple explanations using language stripped of technical artifice.

The role of public prosecutor did not exist in Athens, so the case had to be decided based solely on the speeches delivered by the opposing parties. The contest between the complainant and the accused took the form of persuasive arguments and counter-arguments intended to win the support of those charged with resolving the dispute. The authority of rhetoric was incontestable, and its skilful use was decisive for the trial's outcome: the speaker knew that he had to convince his audience if he was to win.[126] The delivery of the speeches was so important that, in the event that a participant could not speak for himself in a forceful manner, it was permitted for others to assist him during the course of the trial.[127] Although it was legally prohibited, it was possible in practice to hire well-known speechwriters—λογόγραφοι (*logographoi*)—to prepare a client's prosecution or defense.

126 "In seeking to persuade the audience, speakers attempted to appear authoritative, yet the institutional context of litigation limited the intrusion of external, social sources of authority (...) When a litigant faced a jury, all but the most famous must have been largely unknown to most of the jurors. Minimizing possible sources of external authority and local knowledge made juries more impartial, but it left jurors with little basis on which to trust the words of a speaker other than those words themselves" (Johnstone, 1999: 1–2).

127 Rubinstein (2000). We should not underestimate the role played by Athenian political clubs: they had great importance for the legal system. The influence of these clubs' activities on litigation was enormous; for instance, it was common for a defendant to arrange for a fellow member of his club to initiate actions against the complainant and thus pressure him into dropping his case or—by a contrary tactic—to bring a new charge against the defendant for the purpose of weakening the original suit.

The judges received two official "stones" (ψῆφοι δημόσιαι, *psephoi demosiai*), one concave and one convex. These objects, which had the shape of a wheel, were used to cast one's vote. Thus, if the judge believed that the accused was innocent, he voted with the solid stone. On the other hand, if he accepted the complainant's case, he used the hollow one. During the fifth century, however, two urns were used to receive the votes in favor of the prosecutor or the defendant, respectively.[128] In both systems, a simple majority of the votes was needed to determine the outcome of the trial. Four judges were chosen at random to count the votes. The results of the voting and the verdict would then be read aloud.[129]

Although the judicial procedure in Athens seems clear—at least according to the written sources that survive—we may note that judicial *praxis* does not seem to constitute a technical and autonomous field of law distinct from other forms of social regulation. In fact, it has been argued that the administration of justice was no more than the continuation of communal, political, or ideological disputes by other means.[130] Pursuant to this, it should be said that in ancient Athens *nomos* (which, as I have said, has the various meanings of abstract law, a specific statute, or social convention) does not perhaps constitute the central element of the legal system but rather represents only a form of evidence that could be invoked in the course of legal proceedings. In stark contrast to the modern world, in which the concept of "law" implies (even for those who have no professional familiarity with jurisprudence) a fixed, binding, and detailed text for the regulation of behavior, the *nomos* in Athens was not imposed in any direct fashion. A *nomos* is not "applied" to a specific case to provide a solution to the dispute (which resolves itself simply based on the existence and interpretation of the relevant legislation); rather, it serves to supply a set of standards, more or less solid, that can be used to reinforce the arguments and counter-arguments that are presented in the courts. The regulatory

128 Boegehold (1963).

129 Although no explanation was given for the judges' votes, this does not mean that they were quiet during the course of the trial, nor that they did not actively intervene in the proceedings: "Athenian juries were not like the silent juries of many modern courts. But in courts where no cross-examination was possible and a prosecutor could only counter an argument by anticipating it, interjections might help to discourage outrageous claims" (Sinclair, 1988: 207).

130 Cohen (1995: 23–34) has argued persuasively, as his book's central thesis, that "[c]ourts, rather than finally resolving conflicts, may provide yet another arena where they are pursued."

regime was based much less on the substance (or content of the applicable law) than on the procedural forms available to the contending parties.

In Book 2 of his *Rhetoric*, Aristotle distinguishes non-artificial or non-technical proofs (πίστεις ἄτεχνοι, *pisteis atekhnoi*)—those that exist outside the speaker—from those which are artificial or technical (πίστεις ἔντεχνοι, *pisteis entekhnoi*)—i.e., those which a speaker can prepare. The former are useful, as the text says, for "inventing the latter" (1355b):

τῶν δὲ πίστεων αἱ μὲν ἄτεχνοί εἰσιν αἱ δ' ἔντεχνοι. ἄτεχνα δὲ λέγω ὅσα μὴ δι' ἡμῶν πεπόρισται ἀλλὰ προϋπῆρχεν, οἷον μάρτυρες βάσανοι συγγραφαὶ καὶ ὅσα τοιαῦτα, ἔντεχνα δὲ ὅσα διὰ τῆς μεθόδου καὶ δι' ἡμῶν κατασκευασθῆναι δυνατόν, ὥστε δεῖ τούτων τοῖς μὲν χρήσασθαι, τὰ δὲ εὑρεῖν.[131]

As for proofs, some are artificial, others inartificial. By the latter I understand all those which have not been furnished by ourselves but were already in existence, such as witnesses, tortures, contracts, and the like; by the former, all that can be constructed by system and by our own efforts. Thus we have only to make use of the latter, whereas we must invent the former.[132]

Although the *nomoi* are employed in forensic oratory with a narrative of their own and are referred to repeatedly,[133] Aristotle defines them as a non-technical legal proof (*pistis atekhnos*), together with the testimony of witnesses, the torture of slaves, or contracts. On the other hand, the most important *pistis entekhnos* is rhetorical argumentation, i.e., the logical construction of a persuasive discourse.

In other words, what was essential in an argument was not the identification of a law that could encompass the alleged criminal conduct, but rather the argumentative elaboration of a line of reasoning that could lead the jury to a vote in one's favor. Thus, there is reason to doubt the direct translation of *nomos* as "law" and to prefer instead, within its semantic range, the connotation "norm." This understanding of the character of *nomos* is rewarding because it allows us to relate the administration of justice to other social norms. This is consistent with the fact that in classical Athens the courts of justice became an essential arena for reproducing and negotiating the city's values and beliefs.[134]

What pertains strictly to the legal sphere needs to be complemented by the complex system of social constructs that condition and explain it.

131 The Greek text follows the edition of Ross (1959).

132 Translation by Freese (1926).

133 This has been demonstrated by Wohl (2010).

134 Wohl (2010: 21).

If law is thus insufficient for a full understanding of the "justice" of the Greek *polis*, it becomes necessary to study our sources from more global perspectives that adjust the size and shape of the judicial. Here, I take the view that the studies of the concept of "normativity" that have been done in recent years are conducive to understanding jurisprudence in the Athenian context because they permit us to transcend the limited framework offered by law (and its idea of individual laws as the regulatory system appropriate to the institutions of the *polis*) and to replace it with an understanding centered on the existence of a system of principles/rules/codes (all these ideas are contained in the word *nomos*) that provides sustenance and order (κόσμος, *kosmos*) to communal life.

The concept of "normativity" can be extrapolated from social anthropology as well as legal and moral philosophy[135] and, if we replace the idea of the narrowly "legal" with the broader concept of "legitimate" or socially acceptable, it can constitute a useful theoretical tool for surveying the social ties reflected in the written documents of the classical Greek world.[136] This in turn allows us to interrelate the idea of *nomos* as a rule of conduct with the ritualized spheres of the Assembly and the theater.

6 The Assembly, the Theater, and the Courts: Performative Activities of Democracy

It is apparent that, in democratic times, civic action could occur through the staging of public speeches in the spaces available to the public. As we have noted, the Assembly, theater, and courts are, in this sense, clearly connected areas within the territory of political activity.[137] Legislation and trials can be

135 Cf. Stocker (1990), Brandom (1994), Korsgaard (1996), Esfeld (2001), Steup (2001), Cuneo (2001), *inter alios multos*.

136 Concrete applications of this idea to the study of Greco-Roman antiquity demonstrate its usefulness for the study of the classical world: see Meyer (2004) and, more recently, Darbo-Peschanski (2010). When I speak of ancient "law" in this book, then, I am in fact thinking of a broad normative web.

137 This relationship did not exist only in antiquity; in fact, there may be much to learn from a comparison between the theater and the modern practice of law: "... drama itself is a vital part of the tissue of experience that develops our ideas and expectations of justice" (Larner, 1998: 17); cf. the work of Laster (2000). Although tragedy is probably the dramatic form most closely connected with the administration of justice, we cannot ignore comedy in drawing the parallel between the two spheres: "The action of a civil society is what on stage is known as comedy—that form of drama which displays how individuals grow and

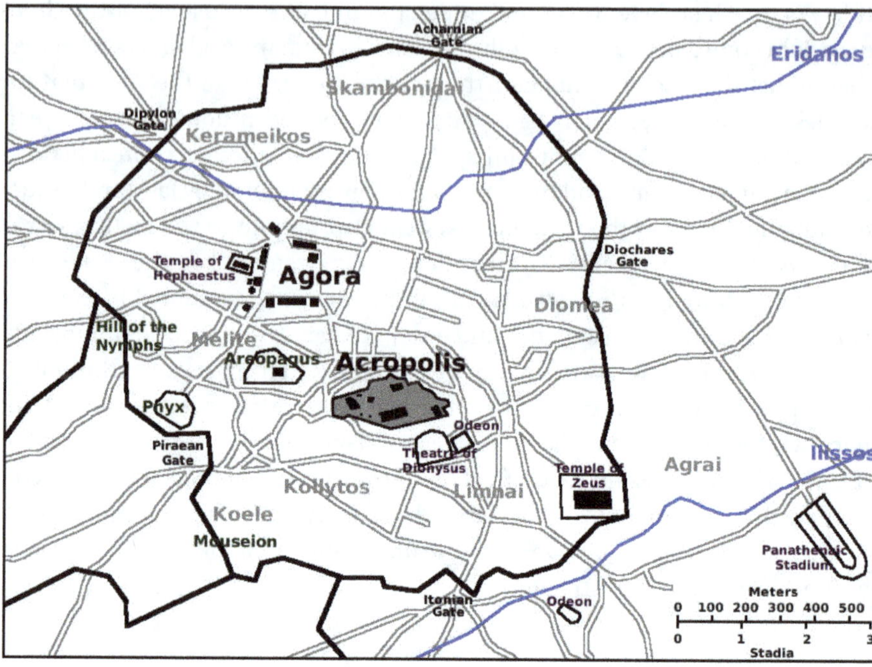

MAP 2 *Classical Athens*

seen as a dramatic spectacle and, in this sense, they are channels for a political message—understanding "political" in a broad sense—which, more or less indirectly, is oriented to the audience.[138]

The text of a play or a legal argument are conceived in terms of their transference from the inscribed paper to the acting space, where it will be realized in front of others: both become social instances of performance. In the center of the debate, the legislators/litigants/actors play their roles.[139] In these

learn, and how societies integrate youth and age, the conventional and the rebellious, the ordinary and the odd, into community" (Larner, 1999a: 209–210); "… we see how integral the development of cultural conceptions of justice are to the very fabric and essence of the drama, and how, for more than two thousand years, we have found the essential forms of those ideas in the tissues of our drama where its tragic and comic sensibilities collide, conflict, and connect" (Larner, 1999b: 429).

138 Thus Garner (1987: 97): "… these legal and dramatic verbal contests shared various details of procedure and administration which suggested their equivalence to democratic audiences. Some of the resemblances were elaborately specific."

139 It is interesting to note here that the Latin word for a character in drama (*persona*) is also

agonistic character-driven games,[140] an entire public dimension is brought into existence and made relevant: the *Ekklesia*, the theater, and the courts are means of embodying collective and symbolic events in the public sphere. The three spectacles operate as social rituals.[141] Certain conventional elements that they all share[142] make them—in some sense—ceremonies which from a formal point of view are deeply structured; this in turn means that as experiences they remain close to their religious origin.

A ritual is a codified complex of systematic and repeated behaviors:[143] the norms that give the ritual its origin and continuation have as their object the recreation and promotion of a set of essential values within the context of a given society. The legislative mechanism and judicial procedure, therefore, become secular rituals *par excellence*, insofar as they tend to enshrine a conservative order, impose the traditionally supported power structure, and reaffirm the reigning ideology.[144] Dramatic performances also constitute examples of ritual: they are ceremonies where each person occupies a particular place, where the actors and the public appear clearly separated and identified on a prepared stage where the spaces are solemnly arranged.[145] The dividing line between the two groups, which produces the dramatic illusion, serves as the border between ordinary reality and the logic of the plot. From this point of view, ritual is basically a performative activity.[146]

It is possible then to find a much more representative link between judicial practice and the literary phenomenon of drama. We should identify an appropriate parameter of comparative analysis by surveying argumentative strategies, structural organization, and the performative dimension.

---

the term used in law to express that a certain individual is invested with legal personality. In this sense, every litigant plays a predefined role before his judges, in the same way that an actor portrays a masked character before the audience.

140 "The significance of storytelling in the courtroom is grounded in an important parallel between our system of jurisprudence and fables: both are driven by a personal and thematic 'protagonist vs. antagonist' structure. The common law system is adversarial; parties square off against one another seeking victory, not compromise" (Stachenfeld and Nicholson, 1996: 904).

141 On the importance of the community and the theater as "a public event par excellence," see Longo (1990).

142 On theatrical conventions, see Dedoussi (1995).

143 Kertzer (1988: 9).

144 Cf. Foucault (1975), Garapon (1985), Garland (1990).

145 Duvignaud (1965).

146 Rappaport (1976: 175–176), Bell (1992: 37–46), Jameson (1999: 321).

During the fifth and fourth centuries, law and theater in Athens formed privileged areas for political argumentation. In the Assembly, in the courts, and on the stage, the Athenians employed their persuasive skills to attract their audience and their judges. In the three arenas, the introduction of a certain social representation led to the performance of particular actions intended to gain conviction, i.e., to motivate one's hearers to adopt a particular sort of behavior. From this it follows that the effort to persuade the people concerning the advantages of a law, the forensic interaction of legal arguments, and the agonistic debates between characters before an audience are all equally characterized by argumentative devices, insofar as they are all built around a logical and deliberate presentation of opposing ideas.[147]

The organization of these spectacles may also display some similarities, given that tragedies derived part of their formal structure from legislative debates and the courts. In general, we have two individuals confronting one another, each of whom delivers a speech of approximately equal length. Moreover, other similarities between public hearings in the legislative-judicial sphere and performances for citizens in the theater have also been noticed.[148] Legislative proposals, trials, and dramatic festivals were seen and heard[149] by a large public of spectators/listeners, who would even become involved in the dynamism of the action,[150] and in all three shows the performative devices of the litigant/actor are intended to attract and convince a majority of the jury.

The speeches spoken in the courts were essentially dramatic because they were delivered as if performed on a stage: the actors and litigants needed to rehearse in advance, memorizing the speech and then pretending to speak it extemporaneously. The plaintiff and the defendant, standing on two platforms in view of the public, were involved in a "process of self-dramatization."[151] Based on these performances as described, the relation between law and theater can be conceived of as twofold: if, on the one hand, it is reasonable to state that the courts functioned as dramatic spectacles, it must also be recog-

147 Pardo (1996 [1992[1]]: 117), Ducrot (1982 [1972[1]]: 12). On the nature of the argumentation, its function, and its limits in legal discourse, see the first chapter of Rybacki and Rybacki (2000) ("What is Argumentation?").

148 Hall (1995), Wiles (2000: 131), Ober and Strauss (1990: 237).

149 Wallace (1997), proposing an interpretation of the cultural importance of the public in social performances such as drama, speaks of a "theatrocracy" in Athens.

150 In the theater, the audience were identified—in certain situations—with the court, since they were involved in the dramatic fiction through the civic activity of the *choreutai* (Calame, 1999: 149).

151 Wiles (2000: 57).

nized that the tragedies and comedies can be seen not only as literary fictions but as an open political space in which mutually contradictory opinions are democratically presented and the disagreements are brought to a resolution. In the classical period, we see democratic power brought to bear and the political authority of the *demos* made manifest.[152]

The close relation between legal and dramatic spaces is well-known: the legislators/actors/litigants are discursively interconnected in a bilateral debate or ἀγών (*agon*) before the judges who must choose the winner and the watchful gaze of the audience around the Assembly/court/stage. These popular activities constitute the nature of the performance, insofar as they are marked as spaces for the creation of a civic frontstage—differentiated from a private backstage—in which the role of the *politai* is performed.[153] Framed within the institutional system, these attitudes and practices, which were an integral part of Athenian society, illustrate the culture of the democracy.[154]

We cannot agree with the view of Wise (1998) when he argues that the problems and limitations involved in staging plays in Athens resulted in corruption of the works' original texts. Even if it is true that the original form of the drama was written, we cannot forget that the theater is—in its truest sense—that which ends up being represented on the stage. In Athens, where the transition from an oral community to a literary culture was a lengthy process, a play was composed not to be read but to be performed. The use of non-verbal forms of communication in both the courts and the stage performances, as part of a spectacle that was acted as well as spoken, can be understood as another performative feature that they share.[155]

---

152 "Above all, both institutions [law-courts and theatre] were means of gaining status and authority within the political realm of the city, and thus such performances became key instruments of power. The political subject is constituted in and by performance, and citizens require self-conscious manipulation of performance in the pursuit of power" (Goldhill, 1999: 25). For these ideas, Goldhill draws heavily on Ober (1989).

153 On the theory behind performance as a new field of study, see Dolan (1933), Schechner (1977), Zarilli (1986), Diamond (1996), and Carlson (1996), among others. Goffman (1959) introduced the concept of "frontstage" as a means of explaining, in terms of dramaturgy, the phenomenon of staging an individual's performance in the social realm.

154 Goldhill (1999: 1).

155 "As in the court-room, the clustering of signs in the theatre challenges the centrality of the word with signs other than the text contributing to the making of meaning. Although academically we read law as a text, in the court-room law is also a collection of images, performances, signs that influence if not determine the outcome. In this con-text, rather than text, the 'word' may be made to mean something different through the intervention and disruption by other linguistic and non-linguistic signs. In the theatre as in the court-

Law and drama are domains of the word, but if they were limited to it they would lose much of their essence: performance is fundamentally visual.[156] Numerous physical features of the associated architecture aided the spectators in identifying the participants and differentiating them from the judges. The spatial arrangement creates the different roles; it separates them and, thus, opposes them. In keeping with their placement, the plaintiffs and defendants are visible, and the actors and the chorus are separated in a *mise en scène* that is specially designed so that they are heard and seen.[157] A work of tragedy or comedy is no more than the lively interplay of words and gestures; a trial or a debate in the *Ekklesia* is not only a dialectical process that develops in a predetermined place; it is also the image and the sound produced by that process. Drama is performance in all its senses, and so too is justice.[158]

Ultimately, the dramatic, legislative, and judicial competitions should be analyzed as platforms of performance. Theatrical spectacles are structured as a lawsuit, where a written charge (the text) is acted out and then judged by a mass audience.[159] The legislative debates in the ritualized context of an *Ekklesia* meeting, in which the citizens position themselves for or against a particular change in the judicial system's current body of laws, find their logic in the same antagonistic framework.

Once performance has been understood as a cultural value, it becomes a key instrumental concept for explaining and understanding the modalities according to which subjects relate to social norms within a community. The recognition of this subjective dimension in Athens reveals that both theater and law must be perceived as public creations and socially dynamic: drama,

---

room, musical, pictorial and gesticular forms, the choice of actors, the choice of audience, stage-sets, costumes, lightings, not only illustrate, decorate or accompany the written text but can disrupt the text, reveal its fragility, and deliver a different message. The performance of the text can explore, exceed, and even explode the text, and even dislocate the meanings suggested by any reading. It can explore the margins and limits of the text and of classical theatre, and in the process demystify, even kill the text and the author and his author-ity" (Aristodemou, 2000: 77). Cf. Hibbits (1992).

156 Kavoulaki (1999: 294): "… processional ritual shares with theatrical performances—performances par excellence—an explicitly declared emphasis on viewing."

157 Seeing and hearing are the two essential aspects of the dramatic experience as a whole (Green and Handley, 1995: 11–13). Voice was, without a doubt, one of the most important elements: "A performer, whether actor or orator, with an outstanding, professionally trained voice could give intense pleasure to large audiences in open-air theatres and places of assembly …" (Easterling, 1999: 160).

158 Hall (1995).

159 Wiles (2000: 135).

festivals, formal institutional gatherings, rites and spectacles are all cultural platforms[160] played out according to pre-set scenarios before an audience that shares with their protagonists a common ideology which serves to reinforce the power of the *demos*. Performative rituals are oriented toward the reproduction and discussion of those values by the citizens, renewing their consciousness and beliefs in the interactions of voices and the polyphony of characters.

Only within the framework of this subjective interaction is it possible to evaluate the legislative, judicial, and dramatic platforms, and the individuals who participate in them. And it is in this framework that the idea of performance is a significant theoretical tool for presenting—as I shall do in the following chapters—the regulation of conduct and behavior in times of war.

Summation: Democracy as Performative Ritual

On the basis of our discussion, it can be seen that in classical Athens the participation of the citizen in the framework of the process of the adoption of legal rules is the fundamental element. It is not possible to give an account of legislative activity in an isolated way; rather, one must present it within the framework of a logic and an overarching socio-cultural structure on which it depends and of which it forms a part. In the Athenian case, the existence of a community based on an agonistic structure means that the Assembly, the theater, and the administration of justice all constitute areas of political activity marked by a performative dimension.[161] The identification and study of these democratic experiences, to which I will add the performance of warfare, require a global analysis that takes account of the civic and sociological patterns in which it is rooted.

Upon this particular cultural basis—sustained by the direct participation of citizens in the public spectacles of the city-state—chapter 2 will proceed to the idea of "subjectivity" and the political implications of the intervention of the city-state in the international sphere. Beginning in chapter 3, reflections on "performativity" will be used to identify the models and patterns of behavior of the Greek *poleis* in their military confrontations.

160 Cf. MacAloon (1984).

161 On the agonistic character of Greek society, see, recently, Lebow (2010:170).

CHAPTER 2

Greek *poleis* and International Subjectivity

ἄνδρες γὰρ πόλις, καὶ οὐ τείχη οὐδὲ νῆες ἀνδρῶν κεναί.

For men are the *polis*, and not walls or the ships empty of men
THUCYDIDES, *History of the Peloponnesian War* 7.77.7

The concept of "subject"—understood as the center of imputation of the rules that compose a legal system[1]—is a creature of law and it is closely related to the personal scope of a given legal system: a body of rules exists precisely because it is applicable to certain individuals or entities, whom such a body vests with a number of rights and duties that come into play as a result of social interaction. Paradoxically, then, thinking about law entails identifying its "subjects" (who consequently must pre-exist law itself). At the same time, the consideration of who has subjectivity is determined by (and it is therefore a result of) the existence of a legal system.[2] "Subject" has become a technical term of the legal discipline.[3]

Modern international law, as mentioned in the previous chapter, takes into account these considerations, albeit with some peculiarities characteristic of its nature. Unlike domestic legal systems, international law is—according to the Westphalian system—decentralized and horizontal, so the notion of subjectivity acquires a new meaning. By this I mean that, when the treaties of the Peace of Westphalia set forth the principle of legal equality of the European monarchies, a political community was constituted in which States recognized each other on an equal footing of sovereignty. Therefore, international law could only be created by the mutual consent of those States, provided that there was no superior entity or institution that could impose

1 This Kelsenian definition of subjectivity is used in this work for heuristic purposes. Note that, as explained below, it is a legal concept whose full understanding depends on different legal schools of thought.

2 "Il soggetto di diritto è una creazione dell'ordinamento" (Schiavone, 2003: 175).

3 Duff (1971 [1938¹]: 1).

 | DOI: 10.1163/9789004363823_004

international laws, sanction non-compliance or enforce the decisions made by international organizations. Overall, the early modern period was characterized by the idea that the creators of international law—based on the mutual equality of their legal nature—were, at the same time, its subjects. Thus, States not only precede the law, but also build it and use it to recognize themselves as its main subjects.

Because of that feature, due to which some schools of thought considered international law a self-regulated system, international law has been deemed a much less developed system in terms of content and structure when compared to domestic law. The rationale behind these interpretations, equally frequent and erroneous, is that "developed" law (i.e., domestic law) involves both a degree of hierarchy and a centralization in which a third party is responsible for establishing rights and duties for dependent subjects. The latter are then forced to abide by the imposed system under penalty of sanction in case of non-compliance. In domestic systems, unlike international ones, this theory assumes enforcement procedures derived from the *imperium* wielded by States in their own territories and in respect of their own subordinate subjects.

Hence, if our starting point is this general opinion on the "primitive" nature of the self-regulating role of States at the international level, the question that opens the discussion in this chapter concerns the identification of the "subjects" of international law in the ancient world.[4] In my view, a historical interpretation of international law provides a useful tool for rethinking its conceptual bases. Following this approach, as mentioned before, this work will analyze the framework of interstate relations among Greek cities in the classical period. The case study is relevant as the Hellenic world preceded the Roman concept of *persona*, according to which the *ius civile* is the grounds for the legal conception of subjectivity that law would develop over time. The first part of this chapter will focus on the discussions about a concept of legal personality in ancient Greek law. This will let me introduce an approach to the groups and associations that, despite their not being defined as subjects, is relevant in legal terms. Secondly, I will deal with opinions concerning the nature of classical *poleis* in order to proceed to the specific study of certain

4 Naturally, this is part of a wider line of thinking that tries to develop a historical conception of international law which, more in accord with practice, is no longer based on institutions and criteria created to explain domestic or state law (which is strikingly different in its fundamentals and scope). Whereas in this case only the concept of "subject" is relevant, we can also also suggest a similar reasoning with regards to other institutions that are characteristic of law, such as the concepts of "sources" or "responsibility", which may not always be of much help in fully understanding international law.

Greek treaties. Reading clauses and provisions from agreements between *poleis* will allow us to notice how the parties are identified and the potential effects of this in accepting the existence of an international legal system without a theory recognizing them as its "subjects."

1 Toward an Archaeology of the Subject: Did Fictional Entities Have a Legal Personality in the Greek World?

1.1 *Subjects as an Object of Study: A Modern Concept*

A subject is typically defined in legal terms as "an entity that has at least one right or one duty by virtue of a positive legal rule".[5] Naturally, this is a theoretical conceptualization whose conceptual origin is modern rationalism which provides that individual subjects are on an equal footing.[6] In contrast, Roman law did not put forward a coherent theory about legal personality as it is known today,[7] to the point that the use of the term *persona* frequently involved all living human beings,[8] including slaves and those who did not actually have capacity in the legal field.[9] Nevertheless, as a consequence of this classification of non-free individuals as *iure naturali*,[10] legal authorities started to make a progressive identification of the concept's legal scope. This distinguished it from a term like *homo*, which was never used in the legal language[11] and covered the biological condition instead.[12] Still, the notion of *persona* is essential to the theoretical grounds of law, as Hermogenian states when noting that he should begin his introduction of the *ius civile* as "the law is constituted by men".[13] The terminology adopted by law shows it as a representative institution: "persona" is in fact the Latin word for the masks actors used in theaters (from *per-*

5 They are the "direct addressees" of a legal system. Cf. Cheng (1991: 25).

6 Schmidlin (2008: 107), Brutti (2011: 94).

7 Nicholas (1962: 60). In this regard, see the excellent study of sources performed by Duff (1971 [1938[1]]) to reach that conclusion.

8 Gaius 1.121. As regards the notion of *persona* here, see Agnati (2009).

9 The word *caput* (head, then individual), often used to refer to slaves and animals, is assigned the meaning of "capacity" in Justinian's *Institutes* (Schiavone 2003: 177).

10 Buckland (1912: 15–16).

11 Schmidlin (2008: 105).

12 Although both terms are commonly used as synonyms in the sources (cf. Gaius 1.9), "person" has acquired a more abstract nature over time (Brutti, 2011: 98–99).

13 "Cum igitur hominum causa omne ius constitutum sit, primum de personarum statu ac post de ceteris ... dicemus" (D. 1,5,2).

sonare, "to make noise through")[14] to create their "characters".[15] Being a person involves performing and playing a role in front of others,[16] and is therefore a fiction that goes from the dramatic level to the formal level of the legal field. It is in this sense that "legal capacity" began to be granted only to a small number of individuals.[17] This having been said, it is worth mentioning that the Romans failed to acknowledge the legal personality of associations (artificial persons) as subjects derived from natural persons. However, they did identify their distinctive features, developed their spheres of action in practical terms and in some cases used the concept to refer to those entities.[18]

It has long been considered that the law in force in the Greek world was similar to Roman law as to its content and main characteristics.[19] The progress achieved in the discipline, however, soon evidenced that it was a methodological mistake to apply the knowledge of the Roman world anachronistically to understand a clearly different social field, marked by distinctive features that significantly differ from those determining the legal substratum of other civilizations.

The concept of subjectivity is also exposed to these generic observations. Hence, in order to ascertain whether this notion was used by the Greeks to define the role of those who participated in the legal system, we should analyze

14 Cf. Dunand and Pichonnaz (2010: 128).

15 The term *persona*, generally used to refer to a mask in literary sources (e.g. Phaedrus, *Fables* 17 or Cicero, *De oratore*, 2.193), is also used with that meaning in some strictly legal sources such as Ulpian (D. 19.1.17.9).

16 It refers to someone who is able to "jouer un rôle dans la vie juridique" (Monier, 1947: 207).

17 This explains the importance of the description of the different Roman legal *status*, namely *civitatis, societatis* and *familiae*.

18 As regards this issue, cf. Ortesano (1968), du Plessis (2010). The Romans did not accept the existence of *personae fictae* (Buckland 1913: 16). In their opinion, artificial persons had capacity to act because they were inherently natural persons who had established a given relationship (Nicholas, 1962: 61). Nonetheless, they used the metaphor to refer to them as *personae*: "È una metáfora già presente nel linguaggio dei romani e, come vendremo, destinada ad avere fortuna e rilievo nella tradizione e nelle culture giuridiche dell'Occidente" (Brutti, 2011: 96). As to the practical possibility of considering the *populus Romanus*, priestly *collegia* and small political communities (such as *coloniae* and *municipia*) as public artificial persons or considering professional *collegia* or associations for religious purposes (*sodalites*) as private legal entities, see Duff (1971 [1938(1)]) and Corbino's synthesis (2010: 222–231).

19 For instance, the first studies and monographs on Athenian law suffered from a strong Romanization; such is the case of the monumental works by Beauchet (1897) and Lipsius (1905).

the original primary sources. Nevertheless, tracing the distinctive features of subjectivity back to pre-Roman antiquity entails discussing what this term means from a legal perspective in the first place. Only after understanding the meaning of "subject" will we be able to analyze its existence in a given socio-cultural context. In this regard, certain legal authors have held that being a subject only means having rights and duties (I will identify this as opinion A), although there is a difference of opinion regarding the number or nature of the rights and duties necessary to create subjectivity. According to other authors, whose position is more restrictive, a subject exists only when having a real possibility of gaining access to the judicial system to enforce its rights (*ius standi*), which means that there is no legal personality if the legal system fails to provide an institutional body where claims can be submitted (opinion B).[20] In contrast, some authors assert that an individual or entity is a subject provided he/she or it can be taken to the courts to determine his/her or its liability (standing to be sued) (opinion C). Lastly, a more extreme approach to the existence of subjects claims that they can only be deemed as such if, apart from fulfilling the above-mentioned requirements, they can make legal rules in the heart of the legal system (law-making capacity) (opinion D).[21]

The legal literature that describes subjectivity in the context of domestic law generally draws a distinction between the existence of original subjects (natural persons or individuals) and other derived subjects (as in the case with artificial persons or legal entities, created by natural persons). The distinction between the former and the latter means that artificial persons—associations, foundations, businesses and organizations—are legal entities with rights and duties (limited in accordance with their capacity) that differ from those granted to their original subjects. That is how, for example, the official incorporation of a corporation entails the creation of an entity different from the

20 This is what the International Court of Justice held in its advisory opinion of 11 April 1949, on "Reparation for Injuries Suffered in the Service of the United Nations," where it concluded that the United Nations is an "international person" as it performs duties and has rights that can only be grounded on "the possession of a large measure of international personality and the capacity to operate upon an international plane" (p. 179).

21 Cf. Brownlie (2003: 57). It goes without saying that this is the most restrictive opinion, as it limits the international legal personality of States (which are the law-makers of international law) or even interstate organizations in those cases in which they can create rights and duties for themselves and others.

shareholders who decided its constitution. From this perspective, it has been argued that the original subjects of international law are States (which were the only entities that had rights and duties in the late nineteenth century in that field). At the same time, these States gradually supported the creation of derived subjects (like international organizations or individuals), whose capacity is limited to the provisions of the international instruments that set out their rights and/or duties.[22] From this starting point, and following the aim stated at the beginning of this chapter, I will proceed to analyze ancient texts to identify allusions to the creation—at the domestic level, particularly in Athenian law—of derived institutions and organizations, in order to extend those observations to the logic of the constitution of the *polis* as a potential state organization. Then, I will examine its role in international relations.

1.2 *Groups and Associations in Athenian Law*

The case of Athens is perhaps the most relevant to the present chapter. During the fifth and the fourth centuries, it is possible to identify in Athens an interesting number of groups of citizens who were involved in activities related to the private and the public sphere.[23] Firstly, the existence of religious associations has been widely recorded, including *orgeones* (ὀργεῶνες), *thiasotai* (θιασῶται) and *eranistai* (ἐρανισταί).[24] Similarly, there are records of partisan groups (ἑταιρεῖαι, *hetaireiai*),[25] as well as political and economic associations (κοινόν, *koinon*; κοινωνία, *koinonia*).[26] What is more, after Cleisthenes' urban and demographic reforms in 508–507, citizens were divided into territorial and family

22 It is noteworthy that what domestic law considers a derived person (the State, which is clearly an entelechy and has been created by human beings) becomes the original subject of the international legal system, where human beings end up being derived persons after decisions embodied in treaties establish that they should have inherent rights (i.e., human rights, developed during the mid-twentieth century). Hence, in this passage from the domestic order to the international legal system, it is interesting to analyze the subjectivity of artificial persons (particularly of the State) in order to understand how personality is consolidated in international law.

23 A comprehensive approach to these groups (including relevant terminology, their membership conditions, purposes and activities) was already developed by Ziebarth (1896), who, however, was not interested in the legal aspect of their participation.

24 Cf. Arnaoutoglou (2003), Vondeling (1961).

25 Whibley (1889), Croiset (1906).

26 On the Achaean *koinon*, as an outstanding example of these associations, see Harter-Uibopuu (1998).

groups of 139 δῆμοι (*demoi*, demes or local units) grouped into 10 φυλαί (*phylai*, tribes), which were subdivided into φρατρίαι (*phratriai*, phratries).[27]

A passage from the *Digest* of Justinian (47.22.4) contains a text attributed to Gaius' commentaries on the Twelve Tables (4 *ad legem XII Tabularum*) about a law on associations in force in Athens: *Sodales sunt, qui eiusdem collegii sunt: quam graeci ἑταιρείαν vocant.* ("'*Sodales*' are those who belong to the same *collegium*; what the Greeks call '*hetaireia*'").[28] Curiously, Gaius then points out that, according to the passage, the law of the Twelve Tables translates a *nomos* attributed to Solon and quotes it directly in its original text in Greek:

ἐὰν δὲ δῆμος ἢ φράτορες ἢ †ἱερῶν ὀργίων ἢ ναῦται† ἢ σύσσιτοι ἢ ὁμόταφοι ἢ θιασῶται ἢ ἐπὶ λείαν οἰχόμενοι ἢ εἰς ἐμπορίαν, ὅτι ἂν διαθῶνται πρὸς ἀλλήλους κύριον εἶναι, ἐὰν μὴ ἀπαγορεύσῃ δημόσια γράμματα.	If a *demos* or *phratriai* or *orgeones* of heroes or *naukrariai* (?) or those who eat together or those who are buried together or *thaisotai* or those who go off for plunder or for trade, whatever they agree with one another shall be valid unless it is forbidden by public documents.[29]

Although we cannot know for sure whether the text is the original Greek legal rule, it is relevant for our purposes due to several reasons.[30] Firstly, because it uses a very specific terminology to refer to a series of social groups which evidence the richness of the associative phenomenon in the Hellenic world.[31] Secondly, because the end of the paragraph is a significant record of these associations' capacity to establish their own law (what "they agree" πρὸς ἀλλήλους),

27 [Aristotle] *Constitution of the Athenians* 20; Herodotus 5.66–69. Cf. Whitehead (1986), Lambert (1993). This Cleisthenean division of Attica was made in response to the need for an organizational structure that could carry out state activities; especially the citizen army and the Council of 500 (cf. Anderson, 2003). As regards the importance of the division into demes and trittyes, cf. Milchhoefer (1892) and Siewert (1982). Needless to say, it was not just an administrative reorganization since new rights and duties arose for the inhabitants of every deme, as is well shown by Scheid-Tissinier (2011: 276).

28 Ciulei (1967).

29 Greek text and translation by Leão and Rhodes (2016: 133–134), fr. 76a.

30 This is not the only part of the *Digest* that refers to the participation of these associations; a compilation of sources can be found in Ascough, Harland and Kloppenberg (2012: 269–275).

31 Sartori (1958) deals with the lack of a generic notion of "association" in the Greek world. The word *hetaireiai* (similar to the Roman concept of *sodales*), however, seems to exclude political groups (generically called συνωμοσίαι, *synomosiai*).

the limit of which is given by the superior legal system of the city-state ("public regulations," δημόσια γράμματα).[32] Nevertheless, the document does not exactly explain how the law-making capacity of these groups was exercised (reference is made to the fact that "members" may draw up rules and not the groups themselves), and neither does it shed light on the potential differences in how rules could be formulated by each of these associations. On the whole, this Solonian legislation reflects an increasing interest on the part of the *polis* in establishing rules authorizing the free will of citizens subject to certain limitations. These norms aimed at ensuring the political stability of these groups—which play an intermediate role between individuals and authorities—,[33] the plurality and diversification of existing groups, as well as their multiplicity of purposes. The information provided in the passage, however, does not contribute to the understanding of their practical aspects or their operating methods.[34]

Indeed, Greek texts do not lead us to definite conclusions about the mentality related to these social or community groups, but they do provide certain noteworthy perspectives that assist us in their interpretation. For one thing, our attention is drawn to the great number of types of associations—which go from family and religious to commercial types—[35] and the emphasis given to their purposes, which generally respond to social interests aimed at mutual support in social, legal or financial assistance.[36] Aristotle, for instance, described associations as voluntary agreements between peers (ὁμολογία, *homologia*), which contributed to the idea of the *polis* as a large community of interests shared by equals (*Nicomachean Ethics* 8.12.1, 1161b15–16):

32 Cf. Ismard (2007a).

33 Jones (1999).

34 This is unmistakably clear in the recent compilation of records of groups in the Greco-Roman world edited by Kloppenborg and Ascough (2011).

35 In the Roman world there is a clear evolution in the types of citizen associations, which go from *collegia* to corporations; cf. de Robertis (1938). Kloppenborg (1996) identifies in Rome two types of associations. On the one hand, public groups (which included associations and sacred sodalities, established by the Senate and composed of well-off classes); on the other hand, private groups (constituted by non-elite individuals and tolerated but not endorsed by the system). More recently the author draws a distinction between these social groups based on their nature: family groups (like phratries), religious groups and those related to ethnical, neighborhood or commercial criteria (Kloppenborg 2006). Regarding the specific case of the Greek world, Schmitt-Pantel (1990) establishes four categories: civic groups, worship groups, age groups and partner companies.

36 Leiwo (1997).

ἐν κοινωνίᾳ μὲν οὖν πᾶσα φιλία ἐστίν, καθάπερ εἴρηται. ἀφορίσειε δ' ἄν τις τήν τε συγγενικὴν καὶ τὴν ἑταιρικήν. αἱ δὲ πολιτικαὶ καὶ φυλετικαὶ καὶ συμπλοϊκαί, καὶ ὅσαι τοιαῦται, κοινωνικαῖς ἐοίκασι μᾶλλον· οἷον γὰρ καθ' ὁμολογίαν τινὰ φαίνονται εἶναι.	All friendship, as we have said, involves community; but the friendship between relatives and between members of a comradeship may be set apart as being less in the nature of partnerships than are the friendships between fellow-citizens, fellow-tribesmen, shipmates, and the like; since these seem to be founded as it were on a definite compact (*homologían*).[37]

In some epigraphic texts, reference is made to the fact that these groups could become holders of their own rights and duties under certain circumstances (cf. Opinion A in the previous section). Thus, for example, an Athenian inscription of Piraeus dated 330/324 (*IG* II[2] 1361) contains the text of a sacred decree of the *orgeones* of Bendis,[38] which read as follows:

[ἐὰ]ν δ[έ τι]ς [ε]ἴπ[ηι] ἢ ἐπιψηφίσηι παρὰ τόνδε τὸν νόμον, ὀφειλέτω :: δραχμὰς τῆι [θεῶι] ὅ τ[ε εἰπὼν καὶ] ὁ ἐπιψηφίσας καὶ μὴ μετέστω αὐτῶι τῶν κοινῶν. ἀναγράφειν δ-[ὲ αὐτὸν ὀφείλο]ντα τῆι θεῶι τοῦτο τὸ ἀργύριον εἰς τὴν στήλην τοὺς ἐπιμελητά[ς].	If someone should move or introduce a motion in violation of this law, they will owe 50 drachmae to the goddess—both the one who formulated the motion and the one who moved it—and let them not participate in the common activities (*ton koinon*) and the supervisors (*epimeletaí*) are to inscribe on a stele the names of these persons who owe this money to the goddess (lines 13–16).[39]

This is a specific example of a rule establishing the requirement to pay a debt as a sanction for infringing a rule created by an association, and the association itself is—by virtue of divinity—entitled to receive that fixed amount.[40] A later text from the second century, which is not from Attica—it is a decree issued

37 Translation by Rackham (1934).

38 *Orgeones* seem to have been private organizations of individuals, whose membership was probably hereditary, aimed at conducting rites for a given god or hero.

39 Translation by Kloppenborg and Ascough (2011: 35).

40 Kloppenborg and Ascough (2011: 36). As regards the importance of this law, see Jones (1999: 260).

by the *koinon* of Dionysian actors in Ionia and the Hellespont—, is also interesting as it offers a similar case in which the artistic *troupe* is legally entitled to receive a sacred sum of a thousand drachmae consecrated to a divinity (ἀποτεισάτω τῶι κοινῶι τῶν περὶ τὸν Διόνυσον τε-/χνιτῶν Ἀντιοχ[εί]ας δραχμὰς χιλίας ἱεράς, *I. Iasos* 152, lines 21–22).[41]

Groups could also participate as such in commercial transactions such as buying, selling and leasing land.[42] As to the courts before which they could defend their rights—a capacity which, according to Opinion B, was required for subjectivity to exist—, there are records of certain specific actions between the members of organizations (δίκαι κοινονικαί, *dikai koinonikai*).[43] The *Constitution of the Athenians*, attributed to Aristotle, contemplates disputes that could arise between family groups (γένη, *gene*) which had to be resolved by a magistrate, the archon *basileus*.[44] A passage from the same text also talks about the participation as a litigant of a group of members representing the entire deme[45] in actions filed with popular courts against their district ([Aristotle] *Constitution of the Athenians* 42.1):

41 As regards this particular record, see Arnaoutoglou (2003: 155). Regarding this association of actors, cf. Le Guen (2001).

42 In this regard, for instance, we can quote inscription *IG* II² 1241, whereby phratry-members Callicles, son of Aristides from Myrrhinous, and Diopeithes, son of Diophantus from Myrrhinous, and the community (*koinon*) of Dialeis have leased a piece of land (κατὰ τάδε ἐμίσθωσαν τὸ χωρί[ο]-/ν τὸ Μυρρινοῦντι ο[ἱ] φρατρίαρχοι Κα[λλ]-/ικλῆς Ἀριστείδου Μυρρινούσιος κα[ὶ Δ]-/ιοπείθης Διοφάντου Μυρρινούσιος [κα]-/ὶ τὸ κοινὸν Δυαλέων τὴν Σακ(ι)νην καλ[ου]-/μένην ..., lines 4–9). By the same token, see the stele presented by Rhodes and Osborne (2003), No. 36, lines 16–23 and 30–34, or the decree of the *orgeones* from Bendis and Deloptis on the lease of property for worship (*Agora* I 4143, *SEG* 19.125, 41.103; cf. Woodhead [1997], No. 329).

43 They are actions "entre associés"; cf. Beauchet (1897: 353).

44 "Public actions for mercilessness and disputes as to the obtaining of hereditary priesthood are brought before him [the *basileus*]. He settles controversies between family groups (*tois genesi*) and between priests in all cases involving the obtaining of privileges" (γραφαὶ δὲ λαγχάνονται πρὸς αὐτὸν ἀσεβείας, κἄν τις ἱερωσύνης ἀμφισβητῇ πρός τινα. διαδικάζει δὲ καὶ τοῖς γένεσι καὶ τοῖς ἱερεῦσι τὰς ἀμφισβητήσεις τὰς ὑπὲρ τῶν ἱερῶν ἁπάσας οὗτος, *Constitution of the Athenians*, 57.2).

45 The term *deme* (δῆμος), already mentioned, is used to refer to each of the territorial subdivisions in the city of Athens and its surroundings, i.e. the neighborhoods of the Attica region. Demes exercised considerable powers over their inhabitants and—in that sense—operated as an archive and civil registry. I will come back to this concept in section 1.3 when I discuss the *polis* and the debates about its legal nature.

ἔπειτ' ἂν μὲν ἀποψηφίσωνται μὴ εἶναι ἐλεύθερον, ὁ μὲν ἐφίησιν εἰς τὸ δικαστήριον, οἱ δὲ δημόται κατηγόρους αἱροῦνται πέντε ἄνδρας ἐξ αὑτῶν, κἂν μὲν μὴ δόξῃ δικαίως ἐγγράφεσθαι, πωλεῖ τοῦτον ἡ πόλις· ἐὰν δὲ νικήσῃ, τοῖς δημόταις ἐπάναγκες ἐγγράφειν.	After this, if the vote as to free status goes against him, he appeals to the jury-court, and the demesmen (*demotai*) elect five men from among themselves to plead against him, and if it is decided that he has no claim to be registered, the state (*polis*) sells him, but if he wins, it is compulsory for the demesmen (*demotais*) to register him.[46]

Oddly enough, in this case, the juxtaposition between the neighborhood and its members—note the use of the demonym *demotai*—prevents us from distinguishing whether it was possible to file an action against the deme itself (and, therefore, whether the deme was something different from its members) or against its members instead.[47] Nonetheless, other testimonies seem to cast some light on the feasibility of bringing an association or a group to trial (a requirement of Opinion C); this is what Dionysius of Halicarnassus suggests in one of his passages (*Isaeus* 16.4) when he mentions that the Attic deme of Erkhia had been put on trial by one of its inhabitants who claimed to have been deprived of his civic rights (τὸν Ερχιέων δῆμον εἰς τὸ δικαστήριον προσκαλεῖταί τις τῶν ἀποψηφισθέντων ὡς ἀδίκως τῆς πολιτείας ἀπελαυνόμενος).

The members of a *genos* could also participate jointly in trials as witnesses. Demosthenes, for instance, mentions a case where the members of the *genos* called Brytidae (τῶν γεννητῶν οἳ καλοῦνται Βρυτίδαι) were summoned to give testimony of what had happened when a citizen's son was introduced to the clan (59.61). The analyzed documents prove that associations—as entities different from the individuals who constitute them—could exercise specific powers and participate in the judicial field independently. The distinction between personal liability and joint liability (according to which all of the members of an association would be held liable jointly) is clear-cut in one of Aeschines' speeches (3.18) in which the case of a religious group is described:

46 Translation by Rackham (1952).

47 In the next section I will analyze the reason for the use of these demonyms instead of the geographical term.

οἷον τοὺς ἱερέας καὶ τὰς ἱερείας ὑπευθύνους εἶναι κελεύει ὁ νόμος, καὶ συλλήβδην ἅπαντας καὶ χωρὶς ἑκάστους κατὰ σῶμα, τοὺς τὰ γέρα μόνον λαμβάνοντας καὶ τὰς εὐχὰς ὑπὲρ ὑμῶν πρὸς τοὺς θεοὺς εὐχομένους, καὶ οὐ μόνον ἰδίᾳ, ἀλλὰ καὶ κοινῇ τὰ γένη, Εὐμολπίδας καὶ Κήρυκας καὶ τοὺς ἄλλους ἅπαντας.

For example, the law directs that priests and priestesses be subject to audit, all collectively, and each severally and individually—persons who receive perquisites only, and whose occupation is to pray to heaven for you; and they are made accountable not only separately, but whole priestly families (*ta gene*) together (*koinei*), the Eumolpidae, the Ceryces, and all the rest.[48]

Lastly, what can we say about Opinion C, which further requires law-making capacity in order for subjectivity to exist? Ancient Greece provides examples of several citizen associations with law-making capacity in classical and post-classical Athens. In this regard, an Attic document from the Piraeus from the late fourth century (*IG* II^2 1275) mentions the case of legislation agreed upon at the heart of a religious group (θίασος, *thiasos*):

ἐπειδὰν δὲ κυρώσωσι τὸν νόμ-/ον οἱ θιασῶται, μηθὲν εἶναι τοῦ νόμου κυριώτερ-/ον· εἰὰν δέ τις παρὰ τὸν νόμον ἢ εἴπει ἢ πράξει, κα-/τηγορίαν αὐτοῦ εἶναι τῶι βουλομένωι τῶν θιασωτῶ-/ν, καὶ ἂν ἕλει αὐτὸν τιμάτωσαν αὐτὸν καθότι ἂν δο-/κεῖ τῶι κοινῶι.

Whenever the thiasos-members (*hoi thiasotai*) ratify the law, may nothing prevail over it. If someone should say or do something contrary to the law, there will be an accusation against him for anyone so wishing of the thiasos-members, and if he convicts him, they will fix the penalty as seems good to the association (*toi koinoi*) (lines 12–17).[49]

Lastly, another supplementary Athenian text dated only shortly after (from the mid-third century) refers to the common rules of an ἔρανος, *eranos* (*IG* II^2 1291):[50]

48 Greek text and translation by Adams (1919).

49 Translation by Budin (2013: 302).

50 The term *eranos* was originally used, in Homeric times, to refer to group meals. As time went by, its meaning changed. In the mid-fifth century, that semantic value starts to coexist with a new meaning connected with loans. Therefore, in classical times, *eranistai* were private associations, dinner clubs, all of which had multiple functions, including providing loans; cf. Millett (1992: 155–156) and Thomsen (2015).

καὶ δικαί[ως διεχείρισε τὸ ἀ]-/[ρ]γύριον τ[ὸ] κοινὸ[ν ὃ παρακατέθεν?]-/το αὐτῶι οἱ ἐρανιστ[αὶ κατὰ τοὺς νό]-/μους τοὺς κοινοὺς τ[ῶν ἐρανιστῶ]-/ν καὶ τὸν ἔρανον.	… having managed accurately and fairly the common (*koinon*) money, which the *eranistai* had entrusted him in accordance with the laws of the *eranistai*, and the *eranos* (lines 3–7).[51]

Altogether, this selection of sources—small but still representative of the epigraphic accounts preserved—indicates that the ancient Greeks were acutely aware of potential collective actions and their role in groups, companies or divisions within the city. When faced with these items of evidence, legal historians have not always been of the same opinion as to the legal status of these groups.

In the early twentieth century, some scholars, perhaps biased due to a late Romanist view of ancient rights, argued that these associations had a specific legal personality.[52] According to a second opinion, artificial persons have never had their own subjectivity (since this notion did not exist); thus, natural persons were the only ones who were able to be subjects.[53] Nonetheless, this interpretation also assumes the concept of "subject" and, in this sense, it does not correspond to the sources either, which in fact show a practice on the part of people, sometimes individually and sometimes collectively, with no significant legal implications.[54] Truth be told, as discussed above, we may notice that these groups of citizens as such have certain rights and duties, a hint of collective liability and, in some isolated cases, even a certain law-making capacity. Yet, the distinction between the group and its members (the ones who have decision-making power) is not clear and, if it were, we still could not identify individuals as subjects in the modern sense of the word.

All things considered, we may imagine a kind of "flawed fiction" whereby an association "joins" its members, thus blurring the boundaries between the former and the latter.[55] At the most, we could agree with those who lean towards the existence of something like a "quasi-legal phenomenon"[56] in some cases, as

51 Translation by Thomsen (2015).

52 For example, Radin (1910).

53 Cf. San Nicolò (1913–1915), Jones (1999).

54 Arnaoutoglou (1998) denies the existence of legal personality in the Greek associations of that time.

55 This is Ismard's opinion (2007b).

56 Arnaoutoglou (2003).

with religious associations, which created a sort of associative property exceptionally identified with divinity.[57] In any case, this differs significantly from our current notion and is far from constituting an example of legal subjectivity.

1.3 *The* polis *as State and Its Legal Representations*

The foregoing sections have discussed certain useful sources to lay down the issue of private and public groups' activities at the domestic level in classical and post-classical Athens. The fact that the legal personality of these associations had not been conceptualized will now lead me to take these reflections to the field of international relations. Indeed, the ways in which the Greeks thought of collective agents within the city's borders provide a good starting point for considering the idea they had of their *polis* in relation to other city-states.

In a work such as this, it would be impossible to cover in detail the interesting counterpoints found in the most recent historiography about the possibility or convenience of imagining the classical *polis* in terms of the idea of the State.[58] It will be useful, however, to derive from certain authors some of the features that the Greek themselves considered as typical of their conception of a *polis* for the purpose of discussing the characteristics of the city-state from the point of view of international legal subjectivity.

It has been held that the *polis* was a "society without a State" as there were neither political institutions separated from the community of citizens (therefore, there was no distinction between governors and governed), nor mechanisms designed to enforce the rules, such as police or security forces.[59] However, this interpretation has been roundly criticized for several reasons[60]

---

57 Hatzopoulos (1973). This quasi-legal nature does not affect the normative implications involved.

58 It should be enough for interested readers to see the contributions of Khazanov (1978), Morris (1991), Faraguna (2000), Berent (2000a, 2000b, 2004, 2006), Grinin (2004), van der Vliet (2005, 2008), Miyazaki (2007), Gallego (2011) and Paiaro (2011), *inter alios*. As regards the composition of state structures in the ancient world, see Scheidel (2013)—with updated bibliography—for further details.

59 See Berent's staunch defense of this interpretation from his doctoral thesis onwards (1994, 2000a, 2000b, 2004). By the same token, Cartledge (1999: 468) argues that "(t)he State, an entity distinct from both the wider community as a whole and its chosen rulers or government, cannot be found either in ancient Greek actuality or in ancient Greek terminology".

60 Van der Vliet (2005: 133) has criticized the *polis* as a "society without a State." This argument entails imposing upon the ancient world a state definition marked by Hobbesian influences. Grinin (2004: 101), on the other hand, has also opposed the theory

and the studies pursued by the Copenhagen Polis Centre in the last decades have shown that in the ancient Greek city the *arkhontes* and the *arkhomenoi*—those who had provisional political positions and the rest of the *politai*—were clearly different groups, even in democratic times. Moreover, citizens would not take the law into their own hands precisely because there were organs in charge of making or enforcing decisions.[61]

Perhaps the problem with considering the *polis* as a "State", a "non-State" or a hybrid and *sui generis* entity[62] lies, ultimately, in the fact that the Greeks used the very same term *polis* with different meanings (sometimes even simultaneously). The same word was used to refer to a physical place and the community of people who lived there.[63] Nevertheless, it is worth highlighting that, out of the two elements typical of the classical *polis* (which are actually, together with the government, the key constituents that modern political theory has identified in the definition of State), territory was considerably less important than population.[64] Thus, even when it was strictly a question of the geography or topography of the *polis*, it was inconceivable for the Greeks to think of a city without its social element. This distinctive feature of the *polis* is pointed out in Thucydides when he recounts how, in the middle of war, Nicias decided to encourage the Athenians by telling them it is in the human factor, and nowhere else, that the idea of city lives: "For men are the *polis*, and not walls or the ships empty of men" (ἄνδρες γὰρ πόλις, καὶ οὐ τείχη οὐδὲ νῆες ἀνδρῶν κεναί).[65]

---

stating that it does not sufficiently account for the democratic nature of Greek *poleis*. Berent (2006) has responded to these severe critics, not always with the required nimbleness.

61 Hansen (2002).

62 This last line of thinking was developed by Anderson (2009), who argues that the *polis* is at the same time a "State" and a "city."

63 Both meanings converge in many cases. In its first meaning, *polis* appears in ancient texts as a synonym for *acropolis* (the fortified heart of the city, located on a height), *asty* (downtown), *ge* or *khora* (urban and rural territory). In contrast, in its personal meaning, *polis* refers to words like *politai* (citizens), *Ekklesia* (the popular assembly) or *koinonia* (political community); cf. Hansen (1998: 17–34).

64 As regards the importance of the population element, cf. Ténékidès (1956: 500–504, reproduced in 1993: 256–260), Davies (1978: 26), Hansen (1991: 58) and Dabdab Trabulsi (2006: 56).

65 Thucydides 7.77.7. The Greek text from Thucydides, in this quotation and the following ones, was taken from Jones and Powell's edition (1942). As regards the importance of this figure and the city of men, cf. Longo (1975: 87–113).

By the second half of the fifth century, the *polis* is a community of citizens or *politai*,[66] if by citizens we mean the free men of age born to Athenian parents.[67] It is a political, military, male, clearly institutionalized organization where public activity was the fundamental aspect—its inherent feature—in the context of a complex and deliberate rational construction based on a feeling of belonging and an active role in the civic sphere.[68] In this regard, it cannot possibly be denied that the *polis* is nothing but its citizens collectively.[69] As it is closely related to the body politic, it must not be considered as an abstract entity that imposes itself upon others.[70] Rather, it should be deemed a natural extension of the individuals who confer meaning upon it.

Yet, this convergence of citizens with the *polis* itself does not set aside the conceptualization of the collective universe as an entity somehow different from the individual elements that give rise to it. This is how the first references found in Greek texts about the "political community" were interpreted in generic terms. By way of example, in *Crito* 50a Plato's Socrates makes reference to the "laws and the *polis* as a whole" (οἱ νόμοι καὶ τὸ κοινὸν τῆς πόλεως),[71] a twist that has been regarded as an example of the conceptual progress towards the acknowledgment of a "personality" different from the people and built through the imposition of a rule of law.[72]

---

66 Jackman (2005: 133).

67 This link is so tight that in the Greek world one could only become a *polites* of a single *polis*; cf. Hansen (1998: 114–115, 122–123). The requirement of being born to an Athenian mother and an Athenian father is an innovation of the citizenship law proposed by Pericles in 451/0.

68 Murray (1997), Hansen (2000: 165–173), Murray (2000: 241–242). When the *polis* refers to the political field, it is said that it is a "male" organization of citizens, as women, foreigners and slaves are excluded. This does not mean, however, that in a wider sense—especially when the word is used to talk about the economic or social order—*polis* does not cover all its inhabitants. In this regard, Hansen (1993) indicates that, whereas the institutional atom of the *polis* is the citizen (*polites*), its economic, social and cultural atom is the family (οἰκία, *oikia*). The word ἀστός, *astos* (and its feminine form *aste*) is used to refer to citizenship in a social rather than political sense, instead of the (almost always) masculine noun *polites*.

69 "The polis was the state of the *politai*, the citizens", as Ehrenberg (1969: 88) puts it.

70 Paiaro (2012: 63–64).

71 The expression also appears in Xenophon, *Anabasis* 5.7.18 and in Herodotus 1.67.

72 Burnet (1924: 2000) explains in his edition that the phrase "marks at least the beginning of the idea that the State as such was a juristic personality or corporation, a view not as a rule clearly grasped by the Athenians or the Greeks generally." In Lysias 16.18 the expression is compared to the ἰδιῶται (*idiotai*, "particular citizens"). According to Emlyn-Jones (1999:

Truth be told, it would seem to be more productive to think of this interplay of "subjectivities" not in terms of a gradual progression toward the establishment of a more elaborate notion of the body politic, but in terms of a certain logic aimed at understanding the convergence (and thus, the interchangeability) of personal and social interests in public affairs. The term *demos* (people) is equivalent to the *koinonia* (community), and the political regime (the so-called *politeia*) is exercised by citizens through representative bodies, which are in essence the citizens themselves. The heading formulas used in decrees and provisions issued at different administrative levels in the *polis* refer to the whole group as a decision-making body: ἔδοξε τῇ βουλῇ (*edoxe tei boulei*, "The Council has decided"), the typical phrasing used in Athenian decrees,[73] or δεδόχθαι τοῖς δημόταις (*dedokhthai tois demotais*, "The district inhabitants have decided"),[74] are examples of linguistic structures that, by way of synecdoche, represent through a partial subject (a body or a subgroup of the community) the legal decisions deriving from the whole social plexus involved.[75]

2 The Role of the *polis* in the Conclusion of Treaties during the Peloponnesian War

We have just dealt with how in classical times the *polis* was regarded as an *alter ego* of citizenship, an entity that replicates and reproduces the very same *politai* as if it were nothing but themselves. This immediate resemblance seems natural in the organization of civic affairs resulting from the democratic exercise of power, especially given the representativeness that the selection of authorities in participatory regimes involves within each *polis*. But, is it the same when the

---

75), this passage from *Crito* seeks to provide a wide conception of the Laws as they are "the embodiment of the legal, social and cultural authority of the *polis*." As regards the rule of law and the sovereignty of the *nomos* that starts to develop in the late fifth century, cf. Ostwald (1986).

73 The decrees passed in the Council begin with the phrase ἔδοξε τῇ βουλῇ; cf. Rhodes and Lewis (1997: 19). According to Henry (1977: 1–4) the "formula of enactment" generally used in classical Attic epigraphy is precisely ἔδοχσεν τει βōλει καὶ τōι δέμοι. This formula is parodied in Aristophanes, *Thesmophoriazusae* 372, among other passages.

74 Regarding internal rules created in the *demos*, Ismard (2007b: 61) highlights the importance of the plurality associated with the identification of the group. As we will see, I am of the opinion that here lies the same intent that leads to the definition of *poleis* based on their citizens ("Athens" is presented as "the Athenians," οἱ Ἀθηναῖοι).

75 "Each of the various institutional 'parts' of the citizen body (*ekklesia, dikasteria, nomothetai, boule*) could stand for and refer to the whole citizen body" (Ober, 1996b: 118–119).

polis phenomenon is interpreted from an external dimension? What happens with the image of itself that every *polis* builds abroad? In other words, how does the political community picture itself in its interaction with "other" peers? Of course, this leads us to ask ourselves about the possibility of conceptualizing the *polis* internationally as an independent subject in its international negotiations, in order to analyze whether or not there are changes concerning its identification between the domestic and the inter-*polis* level.

The steps I will follow in order to answer these questions include, again, the documentary analysis of historical sources, especially the way in which *poleis* are presented when it comes to their international participation. In order to investigate the conception of the *polis* in agreements from classical times, I will study the names given to the negotiating parties and the parties to the treaties signed during the Peloponnesian War. After an introduction to the nature of treaties as sources of inter-*polis* law, the following examples will be discussed: (a) the bilateral treaties entered into by Athens with Rhegium and Leontinoi in 433–432; (b) the multilateral treaty entered into by Athens, Argos, Mantineia and Elis in 420; and (c) the three treaties signed by Sparta and the Achaemenid Empire in 412/1.[76]

2.1 *The Classical Greek Treaties*

Very simply put, in modern international law a treaty can be defined as a voluntary agreement between the subjects of the international legal order.[77] Taking this into account, by treaty we mean a source of international law, as it is an instrument used to define legal rules that may give rise to rights and duties. The Greeks had a very specific conception of the existence of conventions between different cities and, in many cases, it is clear—at least from the

76 The treaties included in (a) and (b) have been chosen because they have the advantage of having been transmitted by a literary source (Thucydides) that can be compared to contemporary material of different origin (i.e., inscriptions involving the same parties). Naturally, this will allow us to compare the use of terminology in epigraphy and historiography. Regarding (c), it is a corpus of texts presenting (together with the Greek *poleis* led by Sparta) the Persian Empire as a party. This will be interesting in political terms as it will allow us to have a better understanding of the presentation of formulas for each negotiating party (Greeks and non-Greeks).

77 A more restrictive definition can be found in the Vienna Convention on the Law of Treaties (1155 U.N.T.S. 331), signed in May 23, 1969, and in force from January 27, 1980. In article 2, the Convention makes it clear that, for the purposes of the conventional text itself, "'treaty' means an international agreement concluded between States in written form and governed by international law, whether embodied in a single instrument or in two or more related instruments and whatever its particular designation."

drafting of their clauses—that treaties were of a bilateral nature. Reciprocal obligations were often balanced, leading us to infer that the parties were on an equal footing. Such is the case with the first agreement preserved directly (and not through indirect transmission), the treaty between Elis and Heraea in Western Arcadia, which might date from 500 (*IvO* 9):[78]

ἀ ϝράτρα τοῖρ Ϝαλείοις : καὶ τοῖς Ἐρ-
ϝαόίοις : συνμαχία κ' ἔα ἐκατὸν ϝέτεα :
ἄρχοι δέ κα τοῖ : αἰ δέ τι δέοι : αἴτε ϝέπος αἴτε ϝ-
άργον : συνέαν κ' ἀλ(λ)άλοις : τά τ' ἄλ(λ)⟨α⟩ καὶ πα-
ρ πολέμō : αἰ δὲ μὰ συνέαν : τάλαντόν κ'
ἀργύρō : ἀποτίνοιαν : τοῖ Δὶ Ὀλυνπίοι : τοὶ κα-
(δ)δαλέ̄μενοι : λατρειόμενον : αἰ δέ τιρ τὰ γ-
ράφεα : ταῖ κα(δ)δαλέοιτο : αἴτε ϝέτας αἴτε τ-
ελεστὰ : αἴτε δᾶμος : ἐν τἐ̄πιάροι κ' ἐνέχ-
οιτο τοἰνταυτ' ἐγραμ(μ)ένοι.

The *rhetra* of the Eleans and the Heraeans. The alliance shall be for a hundred years, and shall begin this [year]. If there is need either of word or of deed, they shall combine with each other, in other matters and especially in war. If they do not combine, the offenders shall pay a talent of silver consecrated to Olympian Zeus. If anyone offends against these writings, whether private citizen or official or state (*demos*), he shall be held in the sacred penalty written here.[79]

In this example, we can see that the declaration of independence of each of the *poleis* implied as a corollary a kind of formal equality between the city-states. When we analyze literary testimonies (and not only the legal texts preserved in epigraphic form), the language used is homogeneous. In the *Phoenician Women*, staged in Athens in the late fifth century, Euripides described the value of justice by putting into Jocasta's mouth a reference to the need to honor equality (ἰσότης) between friends (φίλους … φίλοις), cities (πόλεις … πόλεσι) and allies (συμμάχους … συμμάχοις) (vv. 535–538). Significantly, equality is treated in the passage as a feature regulating the personal relations between citizens, and as such it projects itself onto international relations, whether with allied communities or not.[80]

78 *StV* 110; van Effenterre, H. and F. Ruzé (1994, No. 52). Ténékidès (1954: 19, No. 3) classifies it as a "sur pied d'égalité" treaty. For a detailed study of the text, Baltrusch (1994: 9–10).

79 Translation by Rhodes (2007: 264–265).

80 Indeed, that is the only way in which we may understand the distinction made in the text between people, cities and "allies" in combat. Some authors even point out that in the Greek world, an image of natural equality already existed, grounded on divine

At the interstate level, some authors have recognized a general principle under which equals should not be injured (μὴ ἀδικεῖν τοὺς ὁμοίους).[81] From this point of view, appealing to equality is useful for obviating the difficulties of conceiving in theory what would be an unfair distinction between dominant and dominated city-states.

The Greeks themselves classified cities into big and small ones,[82] and the former had reserved powers that were denied to the latter.[83] Nonetheless, in practice, they interacted with each other symmetrically; at least that is what historiographical, epigraphic and literary sources indicate. In his *History of the Peloponnesian War* (5.77.5–7), Thucydides describes the clauses of the treaty concluded by Spartans and Argives in 418. According to the text, the cities located in the Peloponnese, whether big or small (καὶ μικρὰς καὶ μεγάλας), would be all independent (αὐτονόμος), pursuant to ancient customs (καττὰ πάτρια).[84] Pursuant to this principle, which is presumed to be customary due to the reference to previous habits, it was also determined that, in case of territorial invasion from abroad, the parties to the treaty would join to repel the attack and the allies from Sparta and Argos would be on an equal footing with each other.[85]

---

law. The progressive incorporation in the law of nations of equality was a logical consequence of the fictional analogy created between natural persons and derived international subjects or artificial persons. The frequent use of body or material metaphors to designate organizations created by men has its origin in the ancient view of the world and was fully developed during the medieval period, as Dickinson (1917) argues.

81 Thucydides, 1.42. Glotz (1915: 98) speaks of the importance of equality between city-states when he mentions that "entre Grecs, le droit des gens se fondait sur les principes du respect qu'on se doit entre égaux ..."

82 This comparison, according to Savalli-Lestrade (2013: 118), is omnipresent in Greek historiography and history, and, in many cases, it was perceived by the ancients themselves. Although this classification is not explicit in epigraphy (Ma, 2013: 67), it does appear frequently in literary sources. However, it is also worth mentioning that many *poleis* did not fall into either of the categories. In practical terms, they belonged to a rather intermediate rank.

83 Amit (1973).

84 Cf. also 5.79.1. Calabi (1953: 72) argues that, although this was not a legal distinction, there is a relationship of greatness related to the individual "potenza" of certain *poleis* in terms of interstate relations. This is connected with the adjective "first" (*protos*), which, for instance, Thucydides uses to refer to the "main cities" (*ton proton poleon*) in 2.8.1.

85 Following Graves' commentary (1891: ad loc.), we must point out that these equal provisions were essentially aimed at limiting the influence of the powers located outside the

Thus, the insistence on the fact that bigger cities with higher population levels as well as smaller and weaker cities were all independent, at least until the mid-fourth century, should not take us by surprise.[86] *Poleis* totally different in power and influence can be found signing tidily symmetric agreements.[87] For instance, the recognition of the sovereignty of all the cities (the signatories and the third parties) is frequently used to express legal equality in the framework of bilateral conventions. In the context of the Peace of Antalcidas (signed in 386 with Persia, by which the cities of Asia Minor were sacrificed to preserve Sparta's control of Greece), Xenophon writes that King Artaxerxes thought that the Asian cities belonged to him, together with Clazomenae and Cyprus, while the rest of the Greek cities, both big and small (καὶ μικρὰς καὶ μεγάλας), would continue to be independent (αὐτονόμους).[88]

When Pericles decided to call for a pan-Hellenic congress in the mid-fifth century to restore the temples destroyed by the barbarians, fulfill the vows made to the gods and adopt safety measures at sea, he convened the big and the small cities.[89] The congress' failure, probably due to the profound differences between the communities,[90] does not negate the fact that *poleis* had equal bargaining power, as expressed in the very same oration.[91]

Peloponnese, particularly Athens. That is, the parties' "equality" is expressly presented as balancing actual inequality with the third *polis*.

86 It may be true that, in many respects, all *poleis*—either big or small—could enter into agreements, send and receive delegations and issue decrees on the same terms as Ma (2003) indicates when analyzing the relations between cities in Hellenistic times. Notwithstanding, multiple testimonies show the differences that, in practical terms, there must have been: "City-states varied in size. The extent of their independence differed: some colonies accepted their mother city's choice of annual magistrates, for instance, and some small cities, while independent, are not likely to have been able to pursue foreign policies distinct from the foreign policy of a large neighbouring city" (MacKechnie, 1989: 1).

87 "Treaties between cities of manifestly different strengths were symmetrical" (Hunt, 2010: 103).

88 Xenophon, *Hellenica* 5.1.31; Diodorus Siculus, 14.110.3.

89 Plutarch, *Life of Pericles* 17.1. As regards this proposal for a congress as a precedent for what will be the Common Peace (*Koine Eirene*) in the fourth century, cf. Hampl (1938). Giovannini (2007: 100, n. 50), following Seager's arguments (1969), states that Pericles' proposal was certainly a late invention. On this general peace, see also Ryder (1965) and Jehne (1994).

90 According to McGregor (1987: 74), the convention failed because Sparta refused to acknowledge the Athenian leadership in religious matters and common policy.

91 In the case of συμπολιτεῖαι, *sympoliteiai* (i.e., a formal union of *poleis*) where a smaller

Similarly, when Demosthenes states that the Greeks concluded two treaties with the Persian king, one signed by Athens (praised by everyone) and another one by Sparta (condemned by everyone), he particularly criticizes the inequality between the parties and argues for their formal equivalence. According to what he says in a speech from the year 351, the definition of rights is different in both treaties: in each city, legislation confers common and equal participation upon each party (κοινὴν τὴν μετουσίαν ἔδοσαν καὶ ἴσην), be it strong or weak (καὶ τοῖς ἀσθενέσιν καὶ τοῖς ἰσχυροῖς), whereas at the international level it is only the powerful parties that establish the rights of the weak ones (οἱ κρατοῦντες ὁρισταὶ τοῖς ἥττοσι γίγνονται).[92] Nevertheless, Isocrates clearly explained how international treaties should be drafted using egalitarian clauses instead of unilateral impositions (*Panegyricus* [4], 176):

ἃ χρῆν ἀναιρεῖν καὶ μηδὲ μίαν ἐᾶν ἡμέραν, νομίζοντας προστάγματα καὶ μὴ συνθήκας εἶναι. τίς γὰρ οὐκ οἶδεν ὅτι συνθῆκαι μέν εἰσιν, αἵ τινες ἂν ἴσως καὶ κοινῶς ἀμφοτέροις ἔχωσι, προστάγματα δὲ τὰ τοὺς ἑτέρους ἐλαττοῦντα παρὰ τὸ δίκαιον;	Though we ought to have expunged them [the assymetric provisions] and not allowed them to stand a single day, looking upon them as commands (*prostagmata*), and not as compacts (*synthekas*); for who does not know that a compact is something which is fair and impartial to both parties (*isos kai koinos amphoterois ekhosi*), while a command is something which puts one side at a disadvantage unjustly (*ta tous heterous elattounta para to dikaion*)?[93]

city was "absorbed" by a bigger city, the difference between both negotiating parties was substantial. However, Mack (2013: 107–108) has held that, throughout the discussions concerning its constitution, there was an attempt to reach a mutual and voluntary agreement in the interests of both communities. Such an interpretation—naïve, to say the least—must be revised as, strictly speaking, the sources indicate that only successful *sympoliteiai* actually convey an effective rhetoric on the part of the beneficiary communities to lead the other community to the conviction that the agreement is convenient.

92 Demosthenes, *On the Freedom of the Rhodians* (15) 29. Cf. Dawson (1996: 82).

93 Translation by Norlin (1980). The expression *ex epitagmaton* ("from impositions") can also be found in Andocides, *On the Peace* (8) 11. On the importance of Isocrates for understanding the logic of international relations in the fourth century, cf. Bouchet (2014).

In practice, military treaties (of friendship or alliance) are made on the delicate boundary between the false coordination between equals and the inevitable subordination of the weaker ones, and in that sense language has a key role.[94]

Against this background, it is worth mentioning that bilateral treaties generally insist on expressing in writing that the agreement is negotiated and entered into by the parties on equal terms.[95]

This purpose is often noticeable in offensive agreements through the inclusion of a provision whereby both parties must have the same friends and enemies.[96] For instance, in 433 Corcyra offered the Athenians a proposal for an offensive alliance in which both would have "the same friends and enemies" (τοὺς αὐτοὺς ἐχθροὺς καὶ φίλους) but the latter rejected it and ended up making a defensive alliance based on mutual assistance (τῇ ἀλλήλων βοηθεῖν) in case of attack.[97] In addition, the Corinthians decided to keep a previous defensive agreement (grounded on the sending of mutual help, ἀλλήλοις βοηθεῖν) and did not sign an offensive agreement with Mantineia and Argos whereby the three would "combat and make peace with the same people" (τοῖς αὐτοῖς πολεμεῖν καὶ εἰρήνην ἄγειν).[98] Even though the equality of the parties is repeatedly and explicitly mentioned in the texts, the final determination of the type

94 Fernández Nieto's book (1975) covers war agreements (monomachy, truce, armistice). Alonso Troncoso (2001) has already demonstrated that we still need an equivalent corpus and systematic study of alliance treaties (*symmakhiai*) to distinguish their main features.

95 That is the meaning of the expression "*epi tois isois kai homoiois*" (Xenophon, *Hellenica*, 7.1.13). When describing the stages of an agreement proposed by the Persian King Cyrus, the historian states that "when they heard the proposal, both parties gave their consent and said that this was the only way in which peace could be effective; and, under those circumstances, they exchanged trust guarantees (τὰ πιστά) and agreed that each party would be independent (ἐλευθέρους) from the other, that there would be a right to mutual marriage, as well as a right to work and to pasturage in both territories and that there would be a defensive alliance (ἐπιμαχίαν ... κοινήν) should any of the parties be damaged" (*Cyropædia*, 3.2.23).

96 Regarding this clause, cf. Giovannini (2007: 241–242). The concept of φιλία (*philia*) is critical in structuring bilateral international relations of reciprocity in the Greek world, as pointed out by Panessa (1999), Mitchell (1997), Low (2007: 33–76) and Scheibelreiter (2013: 91–97).

97 Thucydides, 1.44.1 and 1.45.3.

98 Thucydides, 5.48.2. Defensive alliances were sometimes referred to by the Greek term ἐπιμαχία (*epimakhia*) implying a limited defense of the allied territory. Oddly enough, defensive treaties from classical times were frequently drafted with such ambiguity that they could also justify aggressive military actions; see Alonso Troncoso (1997: 28).

of alliance (offensive or defensive) to be signed ultimately lies with the most powerful city-state.

This superior bargaining power of the most influential *poleis* sometimes derives directly from the provisions agreed upon in the treaty itself. There are documents showing the existence of a true hierarchy between subjects, commonly offensive treaties in which a strong city imposes itself upon its weak counterpart. Sparta made its privileged position count during most of the fifth century: in 403, by way of example, it imposed overwhelming conditions upon the Athenians in an unequal treaty, thereby making them destroy their walls, hand over almost all of their fleet and "have the same friends and enemies as the Spartans" (τὸν αὐτὸν ἐχθρὸν καὶ φίλον νομίζοντας Λακεδαιμονίοις), whom they even had to follow wherever it was necessary.[99] An identical duty to have the same friends and enemies (τὸν αὐτὸν ... ἐχθρὸν καὶ φίλον Λακεδαιμονίοις νομίζειν) and follow them as allies is included in the treaty imposed by the Spartans upon the Olynthians in 379, taking advantage of the widespread famine affecting them.[100] Likewise, the Athenians included a parallel provision in the treaties they had the Corcyraeans[101] and the Thurians[102] sign: in both cases, Athens tried to impose an alliance urging them to have the same friends and enemies as the Athenians (τοὺς αὐτοὺς ἐχθροὺς καὶ φίλους τοῖς Ἀθηναίοις νομίζειν).[103]

The subtle textual difference between treaties tending to establish an equal relation between the parties on the one hand, and those clearly evidencing the hegemonic position of one of the parties on the other hand, lies in a subtle change in the formula under discussion, which, as in the examples above, promotes a notorious imbalance by excluding mutual duties. Indeed, the fact that both parties must "have the same friends and enemies" substantially differs from specifying that one must "have the same friends and enemies" *as the*

---

99 Cf. Rhodes (2007: 249). Xenophon, *Hellenica*, 2.2.20. Pistorius (1985: 184–185) identifies both provisions, which are typical of this kind of treaties, such as "Freund-feindklausel" and "Heeresfolgeklausel" respectively. Cf. also Scheibelreiter (2013: 91–136). Bonk (1974: 63–65) also analyzes the content and value of the formulas that establish the duty to have the same friends and enemies.

100 Xenophon, *Hellenica*, 5.3.26.

101 Thucydides, 3.75.6.

102 Thucydides, 7.33.6.

103 A very similar situation is that of the unequal treaty entered into by Athens and Bottiaea (*Syll.*³ 89), in which, apart from the equal provisions, there are two additional duties detrimental to the Macedonians: to have the same friends as the Athenians and to favor Athens' enemies neither with money nor with any other means; cf. Martin (1940: 373–374).

other. However, in the eyes of inattentive readers, the syntactic resemblance of both expressions represents an interesting formal mechanism to hide the deep underlying differences in seemingly neutral language at the time of negotiation.

Another case where we can accurately appreciate the tension between independence and subordination in international relations between Greek cities is the gradual creation of international organizations in which *poleis* necessarily participated with different degrees of interest and commitment. Such organizations included religious associations (ἀμφικτυονίαι, amphictyonies) and military associations (known as συμμαχίαι, *symmakhiai*).[104] Greek history reveals how the sovereignty of city-states was progressively compromised in practice, from the mid-fourth century, by the creation of these actual federal systems: at that time, we can see a growing conflict between a centripetal will to unify into suprastate bodies and an impulse for centrifugal resistance by *poleis* as autonomous entities.[105] Although associations between allied cities observed and guaranteed the formal equality and independence of each member, at the same time they ensured that one of the associated *poleis* had effective supremacy in practice.[106] Confederations and leagues were *de facto* under control of a ἡγεμών (*hegemon*) or leader,[107] who, in his implicit capacity as such, was entitled to decide what actions should be taken by the organization as a whole.[108]

104 As regards the legal nature and operation of these associations, see Tausend (1992) and, more specifically, Baltrusch (1994). On amphictyonies, see Calabi (1953: 11–49).

105 Barker (1927: 509). As for the relation between cities and the federal system, between local laws (*politeia*) and the common laws of the federal structure, see Bearzot (2004). Cf. Beck (1997: 9–29) and Johnston (2008: 198–199).

106 A way to obscure and at the same time highlight a *polis*' supremacy over its allies is determined by the "Dualitätsklausel," which, for instance, connected in the same phrase "Athenians and their allies" (οἱ Ἀθηναῖοι καὶ οἱ σύμμαχοι) in that order. In this regard, see Pistorius (1985: 183). Some authors draw a distinction between coordination and subordination organizations; cf. Bonk (1974: 67–68).

107 Van Wees (2004: 7) points out that this informal position of the *hegemon* was also called ἀρχή (*arkhe*), which is usually translated in certain contexts as "empire." As regards *hegemonia* as a complex institution from the perspective of international law, see Alonso Troncoso (2003). Regarding the Greek term *arkhe* and its lexical variations indicating Athenian supremacy in the fifth century, cf. Low (2008: 9).

108 In these cases, as mentioned above, there is a clear voluntary limitation of sovereignty, but we must admit that there are several types and degrees of relation between city-states. A synthetic chart helps Ténékidès (1954: 179) identify three association methods among which the Greek federalism of that time fluctuated: *confederations* (constituted by

Again, the actual inequality is disguised in legal instruments. For instance, Aeschines says that, in the Delphic Amphictyonic League, each city, both big and small, had a single vote in the council (ἕκαστον ἔθνος ἰσοψῆφον γιγνόμενον τὸ μέγιστον τῷ ἐλαχίστῳ), when it was actually obvious that some *poleis* were at the helm of the affairs to be dealt with.[109] An example used by Thucydides illustrates the rationale behind the division of powers at the international level in cases of confederations: when in 431 Sparta demands that Athens return *autonomia* (αὐτονομία) to its allies,[110] the Athenians answer that the Spartans should also do that and reciprocrate with their people.[111] The discussion, which on first thoughts could be said to be about recognizing the value of independence for all *poleis* (big or small) and the importance of legal equality of every city-state, is to a certain extent really about less abstract issues. In the expressions used by the Athenians and Spartans, autonomy as a concept is used rather as a useful argument so that each *hegemon* can distinguish itself from rival hegemonies.[112] Once again, we find discourse in favor of the most important cities.

One may infer from the texts that, in practice, a *polis* could act as a *hegemon* in a given organization with special privileges that were seldom questioned.[113] For example, Athenian regulations show that, in the case of the Delian League led by Athens, less important allied cities gradually relinquished their legal independence (their *autodikia*), so their own citizens were often tried by the courts of the main *polis*.[114] The case of Melos, once again, shows the

---

autonomous States), *empires* (in which one *polis* directs the group's foreign policy) or *fake confederations* (in which one of the members arrogates to itself *de facto* executive powers, although each member's sovereignty is respected *de iure*). To this complex scene, we may add the phenomenon of colonialism; contrary to what one may expect, in the Greek world the relation between metropolis and colony did not entail a single central State and a subordinate territory, but a linkage of forces similar to those of political associations, where both parties behaved as independent cities. As Graham (1964: 5) indicates, although the metropolis enjoyed a sort of indefinite hegemonic position, "… most Greek colonies were founded to be self-sufficient Greek *poleis* …"

109 The passage is quoted by Calabi (1953: 73).

110 Thucydides, 1.139.3.

111 Thucydides, 1.144.2.

112 Giovannini (2007: 102).

113 At that time, the consolidation of State federations did not result from multilateral agreements, but essentially from bilateral agreements generally promoted by the *hegemon* wishing to increase his number of allies (Ehrenberg, 1969: 107 and 112).

114 As regards the Athenian hegemony in the League, see Alonso Troncoso (2002) and Blanchet (2013: 162). Balcer (1978: 119–144) has proposed the existence of an "Athenian judicial decree," in force since 412, which imposed local justice upon the *politai* from allied cities.

counterpoint between hegemonic strategy and the need to respect the independence of subordinate cities: while Athens proposed an alliance treaty unilaterally conditioned, the Melians preferred to stabilize mutual relations by means of a jointly negotiated peace agreement.[115]

By the mid-fifth century, the consolidation of a true maritime "empire," as historians call Athens' expansionist regime of domination over its allies on the islands, accounts for the separation, more and more evident, between politically unequal cities.[116] The discourse that started to gain traction, however, is often critical of imperialism,[117] but nevertheless favorable to a democracy with expansionist desires. However, the political narrative never endorses the existence of a superior authority or sets up the existing inequality between powerful and weak cities as a paradigm.[118]

115 Martin (1940: 355–356). In this concealment of the imbalance existing behind apparently symmetric patterns, there is room, however, for suspicion on the part of less privileged cities: "Interference of some sort in the domestic politics of the allied city was undoubtedly a widely feared consequence of an alliance with a leading state ..." (Ryder, 1965: 24). Ostwald (1982) and Karavites (1982b) are of the opinion that *autonomia* worked in these cases as a guarantee or effective mechanism for small cities to ensure their independence against the political advance of hegemonic States.

116 In chapter 1, I have analyzed the political scope of dramatic spectacles. Athenian festivals played a key role in the promotion of this hegemony of the *polis*, especially if we bear in mind that in the Great Dionysia the allies' ambassadors went to the theater to pay their taxes there; cf. Evans (2010: 200). The performative and visual meaning of this tax payment is clear-cut: the image of a powerful city-state acquires its full symbolic significance there.

117 Pericles himself, promoter of Athenian hegemony, seems to have confessed that the power Athens exercised over the allies was not lawful; cf. Thucydides 2.60, 2.63, cf. 1.42.

118 There seem to have been considerable feelings of suspicion when it came to demonstrating the supremacy of a city over another one, as Hunt (2010: 102) very well argues: "In addition, hegemonic powers bound their subject allies by bilateral treaties or more commonly through a treaty organization such as the Delian League. They tended to emphasize their benefactions to justify their rule over their subject allies. (...) On the other hand, there were various ways that even these obvious superiors tried to obscure their own power. The reason for this obfuscation was the unacceptability of subordinating relationships among states." Indeed, in ancient times, the imperialist logic, albeit frequent, was already questioned: "'Imperialism' has become a term of abuse, implying unjust or oppressive rule or control of one people by another. These pejorative connotations are central to the meaning of the word as it has been interpreted by numerous historians of antiquity, with the result that it has been all but eliminated from their accounts of interstate relations" (Garnsey and Whittaker, 1978: 1). These authors state that, due to that negative connotation, many historians have decided to talk about "hegemonic" instead of "imperialist" tenden-

2.2 *Three Examples as Case Studies*

In this work, I analyze all the agreements transmitted (either by epigraphic means or by literary reference) during the Peloponnesian War period. Appendix 1 includes a chart summarizing each of these agreements, the documentary sources in which they are mentioned and the type of agreement in terms of features and purpose. This study includes three cases that are relevant for my analysis. The conclusions I shall reach after examining these agreements may be expanded and generalized for the comprehensive understanding of the phenomenon of treaty-signing in that time.

2.2.1 The Treaties of Athens with Rhegium and Leontinoi

Toward the beginning of the events that gave rise to the Peloponnesian War, the Athenians concluded several *symmakhiai* in the summer of 433/2, including alliances with the Ionian cities of Rhegium in Italian territory and Leontinoi in Sicily.[119] The signature of the agreements—considered as an act of war against the interests of Syracuse (Corinth's western ally)—[120] is mentioned by Thucydides, who explains that Rhegium and Leontinoi appealed to the existence of such agreements[121] to claim assistance from Athenians around 427 (Thucydides 3.86.3–5):

ἐς οὖν τὰς Ἀθήνας πέμψαντες οἱ τῶν Λεοντίνων ξύμμαχοι κατά τε παλαιὰν ξυμμαχίαν καὶ ὅτι Ἴωνες ἦσαν πείθουσι τοὺς Ἀθηναίους πέμψαι σφίσι ναῦς· ὑπὸ γὰρ τῶν Συρακοσίων τῆς τε γῆς εἴργοντο καὶ τῆς θαλάσσης.	The Leontines and their allies sent an embassy to Athens and urged them, both on the ground of an earlier alliance and because they were Ionians, to send them ships; for they were being excluded from both the land and the sea by the Syracusans. And the Athenians sent

cies to define the political attitudes of the big Greek *poleis*; for the purposes of this work, despite the differences, both terms will be used interchangeably to refer to the desire for interstate supremacy.

119 On the historical context of these two treaties, cf. Cataldi (1990: 27–65).

120 The Syracusans, of Dorian origin like most of the Western Greeks, supported Sparta; cf. Rhodes (1994: 240–241). On the other hand, the Leontinians were Ionian (since they originally came from Chalcis, in the Aegean island of Euboea, just as the Rhegians). Thus, it was logical that Athens—considered as the mother city of the Ionian Greeks—would offer to sign alliances; Rutter (1996: 18).

121 According to Smart (1972: 144–146), the reference made to an "ancient alliance" (παλαιὰν ξυμμαχίαν, without a definite article in the text) does not involve former agreements—which in his opinion were never renewed—but the "general solidarity between Athens and the Ionians." In this regard, see Hornblower (1991: 493).

καὶ ἔπεμψαν οἱ Ἀθηναῖοι τῆς μὲν οἰκειότητος προφάσει, βουλόμενοι δὲ μήτε σῖτον ἐς τὴν Πελοπόννησον ἄγεσθαι αὐτόθεν πρόπειράν τε ποιούμενοι εἰ σφίσι δυνατὰ εἴη τὰ ἐν τῇ Σικελίᾳ πράγματα ὑποχείρια γενέσθαι. καταστάντες οὖν ἐς Ῥήγιον τῆς Ἰταλίας τὸν πόλεμον ἐποιοῦντο μετὰ τῶν ξυμμάχων. καὶ τὸ θέρος ἐτελεύτα.

them ships; professedly on the ground of their relationship, but really because they wished to prevent the importation of grain from Sicily into the Peloponnesus, and also to make a preliminary test whether the affairs of Sicily could be brought under they own. So they stablished themselves at Rhegium in Italy and proceeded to carry on the war in concert with their allies. And the summer ended.[122]

As typical in the case of Thucydides, the appearance of smaller cities always seems to work in the light of the fundamental antithesis (of the great bipolar dichotomy) that his work sets up between Athenians and Spartans.[123] In linguistic terms, it is worth highlighting the fact that the parties to the ancient treaty (Athens and Leontinoi) are referred to in the text as "the Athenians" (οἱ Ἀθηναῖοι) and "the Leontinians" (τῶν Λεοντίνων), respectively, and their enemies are referred to as "the Syracusans" (τῶν Συρακοσίων, instead of "Syracuse"). In fact, when action verbs are used, *poleis* are generally referred to by their citizens (the demonym is used instead of the abstract name of the city), whereas topographic names ("Athens," "Peloponnese," "Rhegium") are exclusively reserved to refer to the city or region in its physical dimension or its condition of object: thus, allies go to Athens (ἐς … τὰς Ἀθήνας), attempts are made to control the wheat taken to the Peloponnese (ἐς τὴν Πελοπόννησον), Athenians arrive at Rhegium (ἐς Ῥήγιον).

Possibly, the original treaties mentioned in Thucydides, which date from 433/2 in the archonship of Apseudes at Athens, are the ones contained in two inscriptions preserved in stone (*IG* I^3 53 and *IG* I^3 54, respectively) that transmit the beginnings of two military treaties. It is presumed that, as critics point out, these agreements entailed the renewal of formerly concluded conventions.[124] The texts are also extremely significant for my purposes because,

122 Translation by Smith (1894).

123 When comparing Syracuse (and the Dorian cities) with Leontinoi (and the colonies of Chalcis), "Thucydides wishes to present the basic nature of this struggle as a part of the conflict between two superpowers"; cf. Konishi (2008: 963).

124 Smith (1894: 200). Accame (1935 and 1952: 127–136) dates the original treaty with Rhegium near 460. On the other hand, Meritt (1946: 85–91) argues that, although the ancient alliance had been agreed upon indefinitely, its renewal was still deemed appropriate around 433.

as they are a direct legal source, they provide the original text of the agreements and invite us to draw conclusions about the way in which the contracting *poleis* were mentioned and referred to.

The inscription containing the alliance with Rhegium (*IG* I³ 53), preserved at the British Museum in London,[125] shows the tenor of the diplomatic arrangements agreed upon in the following terms:

[θεοί· πρέσβες ἐκ Ῥεγίο *h*]οὶ τὲν χσυμμαχίαν
[ἐποέσαντο καὶ τὸν *h*όρκ]ον Κλέανδρος
Χσεν-
[........19........]τίνο, Σιλενὸς Φόκο,
[......15...... ἐπ' Ἀφ]σεύδος ἄρχοντος κ-
[αὶ τε̂ς βολε̂ς *h*ε̂ι Κριτιά]δες προ̂τος ἐγραμ
[άτευε vv ἔδοχσεν τε̂ι βο]λε̂ι καὶ το̂ι δέμοι·
Ἀ-
[καμαντὶς ἐπρυτάνευε, Χ]αρίας
ἐγραμμάτευ-
[ε, Τιμόχσενος ἐπεστάτ]ε, Καλλί-
[ας εἶπε· χσυμμαχίαν εἶν]αι Ἀθεναίοις καὶ
[Ῥεγίνοις· τὸν δὲ *h*όρκο]ν ὀμοσάντον Ἀθενα-
[ῖοι *h*ίνα ε̂ι τὰ πάντα πι]στὰ καὶ ἄδολα καὶ *h*-
[απλᾶ παρ' Ἀθεναίον ἐς ἀί]διον Ῥεγίνοις,
κα-
[τὰ τάδε ὀμνύντες· χσύμ]μαχοι ἐσόμεθα πισ-
[τοὶ καὶ δίκαιοι καὶ ἰσ]χυροὶ καὶ ἀβλαβε̂ς
[ἐς ἀίδιον Ῥεγίνοις καὶ] ὀφελέσομεν ἐ[άν τ]-
[ο δέονται---------------]

Gods. Envoys from Rhegion who made the alliance and the oath: Kleandros son of Xen–,—son of –tinos, Silenos son of Phokos; [—son of –]. In the archonship of Apseudes and the Council for which Kritiades was first secretary. The Council and the People decided. Akamantis was in prytany. Charias was secretary. Timoxenos was chairman. Kallias proposed: that there shall be an alliance between the Athenians and the Rhegians. Let the oath be sworn by the Athenians, so that everything may be faithful and without deceit and straightforward on the part of the Athenians for all time towards the Rhegians, swearing as follows: 'We shall be faithful allies, just, strong and unharmful for all time to the Rhegians, and we shall help if they need anything …'[126]

The treaty with Leontinoi (*IG* I³ 54), meanwhile, presents a similar structure, beginning with a divine reference, the identification of the diplomats in charge of the negotiation and the oath, and the Athenian bodies involved in its approval, before introducing the exact purpose of the agreement (lines 1–27):

---

125 *GIBM* 5. A picture of the inscription is reproduced in Appendix B (No. 1).

126 Translation by Lambert and Rhodes (*Attic Inscriptions Online*, available at: www.atticinscriptions.com). Access to the full text is available in Fornara (1977: 173–174), No. 124; a comprehensive commentary can be found in Meiggs and Lewis (1969: 171–175), No. 63.

[θε] οἱ [] {θεοί } πρέσβες ἐγ Λεον[τ]-
ίνον *h*οὶ τὲγ χσυμμαχί-
αν ἐποέσαντο καὶ τὸν *h*-
όρκον Τιμένορ Ἀγαθοκ-
λέος, Σôσις Γλαυκίο Γέ-
λον Ἐχσεκέστο, γραμμα-
τεὺς Θεότιμος Ταυρίσ-
κο· ἐπ' Ἀφσεύδος ἄρχοντ-
ος καὶ τε̑ς βολε̑ς *h*ε̑ι Κρ-
ιτιάδες ἐγραμμάτευε·
ἔδοχσεν τε̑ι βολε̑ι καὶ
τôι δέμοι· Ἀκαμαντὶς ἐ-
πρυτάνευε, Χαρίας ἐγρ-
αμμάτευε, Τιμόχσενος
ἐπεστάτε, Καλλίας ε-
ἶπε· τὲμ μὲν χσυμμαχία-
ν εἶναι Ἀθεναίοις καὶ
Λεοντίνοις καὶ τὸν ὅρ̣-
κον δôναι καὶ δέχσασ-
[θαι· ὀμόσ]αι δὲ Ἀθεναί-
[ος τάδε· σύ]νμα[χ]οι ἐσόμ-
[εθα Λεοντ]ίν[οις ἀί]δ̣ιο-
[ι ἀδόλος κ]αὶ [ἀβλα]βôς·
[Λεοντίνο]ς ὁ[μôς ὀ]μόσ-
[αι· σύνμαχοι ἐσόμ]εθα
[Ἀθεναίοις ἀίδιοι] ἀδό-
[λος καὶ ἀβλαβôς· π]ερὶ

Gods. The envoys from Leontinoi who made the alliance and the oath: Timenor son of Agathokles, Sosis son of Glaukias, Gelon son of Exekestos; secretary Theotimos son of Tauriskos. In the archonship of Apseudes and the Council for which Kritiades was secretary. The Council and the People decided. Akamantis was in prytany. Charias was secretary. Timoxenos was chairman. Kallias proposed: that there shall be the alliance between the Athenians and the Leontinians, and they shall give and receive the oath. The Athenians shall swear as follows: 'We shall be allies of the Leontinians for all time, without deceit and unharmfully.' The Leontinians shall swear likewise: 'We shall be allies of the Athenians for all time, without deceit and unharmfully.' Concerning ...[127]

The apparent parallelism between both—equally fragmentary—documents demonstrates the repetition of formulas that are presumed to have characterized the set of treaties concluded by Athens around the time of the Peloponnesian War. As for the second inscription, the full text of the main purpose of the agreement has been preserved: "An alliance shall be established between Athenians (Ἀθεναίοις) and Leontinians (Λεοντίνοις), and an oath shall be taken and administered".[128] Just as in Thucydides' passage, it is undeniable here that,

127 Translation by Rhodes (*Attic Inscriptions Online*, available at: www.atticinscriptions.com). Cf. Fornara (1977: 174–175), No. 125, as well as the complete commentary in Meiggs and Lewis (1969: 175–176), No. 64. A picture is reproduced in Appendix B (No. 2).

128 As regards the importance of oaths in the negotiation of treaty clauses and the entry

when it comes to determining the core of the duties contained in the treaty, the parties are mentioned using the citizens' ethnic identification instead of each city's abstract name. Also apparent is the use of the demonym "Athenians" (Ἀθεναίοις) in the treaty with Rhegium when reference is made to the main purpose of establishing a *symmakhia*. Hence, we can easily agree with epigraphists on the inference of the expression "the Rhegians" (and not Rhegium itself) as signatory: Ῥεγίνοις.[129]

Taking into account my analysis in the previous section, it is not surprising that in these (literary and legal) passages, reference is made to *poleis* by mentioning their body of citizens. The assimilation of a city (understood in its political scope) into its population is also a practice at the international level. On the one hand, this convergence of the individual and the plural perspective typical of political unity[130] seems to explain a lot about the way in which Greeks perceived international relations. As a matter of fact, unlike our representation of the international field, in the Greek world the idea of a *polis* as the main participant is blurred by the constant introduction of the individual field, the human and private sphere.[131] The analysis of other conventional instruments will allow us to go deeper into this line of thinking.

---

into force of their provisions, see Phillipson (1911, i: 389), who considers that treaties are the underpinning of the whole body of the ancient law of nations. Likewise, Bederman (2001: 61) argues that, in the ancient world, treaties themselves were essentially an exchange of oaths between the parties.

129 The reader may see the deterioration of both inscriptions: the words in brackets in the Greek text are interpolations by scholars often based (as in this case) on the presence of similar formulas in other inscriptions. What is not in brackets is therefore the only thing that can be read in each document just as it was transmitted.

130 When Zumbrunnen (2008: 83) talks about the Mytilene debate, he considers that the constant plural reference to the Athenians (οἱ Ἀθηναῖοι) in a context of deliberative action is not random and responds to a literary figure or *tropos* that connects the plurality of the discussion with the unity of the measure taken.

131 "Slippage between representations of individuals and states as actors in interstate politics is, generally, a prominent feature of discussions of Greek interstate relations—much more so than in accounts of contemporary international politics, where the use of the state as the basic unit of analysis is more firmly established" (Low, 2007: 59).

2.2.2 The Quadripartite Treaty of Athens with Argos, Mantineia and Elis

The inscription containing the treaty known as the "Quadruple Alliance," signed by Athens, Argos, Mantineia and Elis in 420, confirms my hypothesis to a great extent.[132] It is a very fragmentary piece, engraved on Pentelic marble, which was discovered in the spring of 1876 (CE) during the excavations of the southern slope of the Acropolis of Athens.[133]

Unlike the Athenian treaties with Rhegium and Leontinoi, in this case the text in Thucydides (5.47.8–12) is almost identical in form and content to the version found in the inscription. In fact, the text has proven useful in supplying readings for missing portions of the inscription.[134] For classical philology and ancient history, it is one of the very rare cases in which literary testimonies find an echo in what is known from direct legal sources.[135]

Although I have discussed Athens' superiority over the other three *poleis*,[136] and I have even mentioned the possibility that the Athenians might have imposed unilateral agreements upon each of the cities instead of a single multi-

---

132 As regards the situation of international politics after 421, cf. Seager (1976).

133 *IG* I^2 86 = *IG* I^3 83. Epigraphical Museum of Athens, EM 6813. The text was first published the year after its discovery by Kirchhoff (1877). A picture of the inscription is reproduced in Appendix B (No. 3).

134 As regards the connections between *IG* I^3 83 and Thucydides 5.47, cf. Kirchhoff (1895: 86–102) and Meyer (1955: 56, No. 1).

135 According to Canfora (1990: 202), "i due testi concidono perfettamente, se si prescinde di qualche meccanico salto di parole nella tradizione manoscritta tucidideana." Gomme, Andrewes and Dover (1970: 54–55) are also in accord that the differences between both versions are not important. Cohen (1956) suggests some differences in the heading and the first clause. However, these are minor changes that do not alter the strong connection between the two texts. Should it be true that "(t)he match between the inscription and Th[ucydides] is one of the best proofs of his accuracy over detail," as Hornblower (2008: 109) indicates, it is not futile to think that Thucydides may have copied an original document he had before him. For various reasons, Clark (1999) argues that Thucydides must have actually consulted a copy in Olympia. That is impossible to demonstrate, but Hornblower (2008: 111) makes it clear that, as the most likely scenario is that this version of the treaty was written in Elian dialect, not Attic, it is more reasonable to think that Thucydides must have seen the Athenian version or a copy of it.

136 At the beginning (in Thucydides 5.47.1–2), the unusual word order suggests an attempt to separate Athens from the other three cities (in the first part, Athens even appears separated from the other three cities in the parallel provisions), but the distinction between Athens and the "others" is not used later in the text of the treaty; cf. Gomme, Andrewes

lateral instrument,[137] the fact is that the concordant clauses of the inscription and Thucydides' passage unmistakably show the use of demonyms tidily alternated with references to *poleis* in general terms. Here is the passage in full (Thucydides 5.47.1–7):

σπονδὰς ἐποιήσαντο ἑκατὸν Ἀθηναῖοι ἔτη καὶ Ἀργεῖοι καὶ Μαντινῆς καὶ Ἠλεῖοι ⟨πρὸς ἀλλήλους⟩, ὑπὲρ σφῶν αὐτῶν καὶ τῶν ξυμμάχων ὧν ἄρχουσιν ἑκάτεροι, ἀδόλους καὶ ἀβλαβεῖς καὶ κατὰ γῆν καὶ κατὰ θάλασσαν. [2] ὅπλα δὲ μὴ ἐξέστω ἐπιφέρειν ἐπὶ πημονῇ μήτε Ἀργείους καὶ Ἠλείους καὶ Μαντινέας καὶ τοὺς ξυμμάχους ἐπὶ Ἀθηναίους καὶ τοὺς ξυμμάχους ὧν ἄρχουσιν Ἀθηναῖοι μήτε Ἀθηναίους καὶ τοὺς ξυμμάχους ⟨ὧν ἄρχουσιν Ἀθηναῖοι⟩ ἐπὶ Ἀργείους καὶ Ἠλείους καὶ Μαντινέας καὶ τοὺς ξυμμάχους, τέχνῃ μηδὲ μηχανῇ μηδεμιᾷ. [3] κατὰ τάδε ξυμμάχους εἶναι Ἀθηναίους καὶ Ἀργείους καὶ Μαντινέας καὶ Ἠλείους ἑκατὸν ἔτη. ἢν πολέμιοι ἴωσιν ἐπὶ τὴν γῆν τὴν Ἀθηναίων, βοηθεῖν Ἀργείους καὶ Μαντινέας καὶ Ἠλείους Ἀθήναζε, καθ᾽ ὅτι ἂν ἐπαγγέλλωσιν Ἀθηναῖοι, τρόπῳ ὁποίῳ ἂν δύνωνται ἰσχυροτάτῳ κατὰ τὸ δυνατόν· ἢν δὲ

The Athenians, Argives, Martineians and Eleans have made a treaty with one another for a hundred years, on behalf of themselves and the allies over whom they have authority respectively, to be observed without fraud or hurt both by land and sea. [2] It shall not be allowed to bear arms with harmful intent, either for the Argives, Eleans, Mantineians and their allies over whom the Athenians have authority, or for the Athenians and the allies over whom the Athenians have authority against the Argives, Eleans, Mantineians and their allies, by any art or device. [3] The Athenians, Argives, Eleans, and Mantineians shall be allies for a hundred years on the following terms: If an enemy invade the territory of the Athenians, the Argives, Eleans and Mantineians shall bring aid to Athens, according as the Athenians may send them word, in whatever way they can most effectually, to the limit of their power; but

and Dover (1970: 55). As a matter of fact, the text talks about "allies within the domain" of each one and not just the Athenians' *symmakhoi*, as Welwei (1996) has clearly pointed out.

137 There has been debate on whether Athens proposed the signature of separate agreements (but with identical content) to each of the parties, or whether it was a single treaty approved by the four parties instead. The doubt arises from the use of the term ἑκάτεροι ("each of two parties") instead of ἕκαστοι ("each of several parties"); Hornblower (2008: 112) leans towards the second possibility in his commentary, arguing that multilateral treaties were unusual in that time, and therefore, they must have frequently contained expressions typical of bilateral agreements, which were much more ordinary.

δῃώσαντες οἴχωνται, πολεμίαν εἶναι ταύτην τὴν πόλιν Ἀργείοις καὶ Μαντινεῦσι καὶ Ἠλείοις καὶ Ἀθηναίοις καὶ κακῶς πάσχειν ὑπὸ ἁπασῶν τῶν πόλεων τούτων· καταλύειν δὲ μὴ ἐξεῖναι τὸν πόλεμον πρὸς ταύτην τὴν πόλιν μηδεμιᾷ τῶν πόλεων, ἢν μὴ ἁπάσαις δοκῇ. [4] βοηθεῖν δὲ καὶ Ἀθηναίους ἐς Ἄργος καὶ Μαντίνειαν καὶ Ἦλιν, ἢν πολέμιοι ἴωσιν ἐπὶ τὴν γῆν τὴν Ἀργείων ἢ τὴν Μαντινέων ἢ τὴν Ἠλείων, καθ' ὅτι ἂν ἐπαγγέλλωσιν αἱ πόλεις αὗται, τρόπῳ ὁποίῳ ἂν δύνωνται ἰσχυροτάτῳ κατὰ τὸ δυνατόν· ἢν δὲ δῃώσαντες οἴχωνται, πολεμίαν εἶναι ταύτην τὴν πόλιν Ἀθηναίοις καὶ Ἀργείοις καὶ Μαντινεῦσι καὶ Ἠλείοις καὶ κακῶς πάσχειν ὑπὸ ἁπασῶν τούτων τῶν πόλεων· καταλύειν δὲ μὴ ἐξεῖναι τὸν πόλεμον πρὸς ταύτην τὴν πόλιν ⟨μηδεμιᾷ τῶν πόλεων⟩, ἢν μὴ ἁπάσαις δοκῇ [ταῖς πόλεσιν]. [5] ὅπλα δὲ μὴ ἐᾶν ἔχοντας διιέναι ἐπὶ πολέμῳ διὰ τῆς γῆς τῆς σφετέρας αὐτῶν καὶ τῶν ξυμμάχων ὧν ἄρχουσιν ἕκαστοι, μηδὲ κατὰ θάλασσαν, ἢν μὴ ψηφισαμένων τῶν πόλεων ἁπασῶν τὴν δίοδον εἶναι, Ἀθηναίων καὶ Ἀργείων καὶ Μαντινέων καὶ Ἠλείων. [6] τοῖς δὲ βοηθοῦσιν ἡ πόλις ἡ πέμπουσα παρεχέτω μέχρι μὲν τριάκοντα ἡμερῶν σῖτον, ἐπὴν ἔλθωσιν ἐς τὴν πόλιν τὴν ἐπαγγείλασαν βοηθεῖν, καὶ ἀπιοῦσι κατὰ ταὐτά· ἢν δὲ πλέονα βούληται χρόνον τῇ στρατιᾷ χρῆσθαι, ἡ πόλις ἡ μεταπεμψαμένη διδότω σῖτον, τῷ μὲν ὁπλίτῃ καὶ ψιλῷ καὶ τοξότῃ τρεῖς ὀβολοὺς Αἰγιναίους τῆς ἡμέρας ἑκάστης, τῷ δ' ἱππεῖ δραχμὴν Αἰγιναίαν. [7] ἡ δὲ πόλις ἡ μεταπεμψαμένη ⟨τῇ στρατιᾷ⟩ τὴν ἡγεμονίαν ἐχέτω, ὅταν ἐν τῇ αὐτῆς ὁ πόλεμος ᾖ· ἢν δέ ποι δόξῃ ⟨ἁπάσαις⟩ ταῖς

if the invader shall have ravaged the land and gone, that city shall be hostile to the Argives, Mantineians, Eleans, and Athenians, and shall suffer ill at the hands of all these states; and to discontinue hostilities against that state shall not be allowed to any one of these states, unless all agree. [4] Likewise the Athenians shall bring aid to Argos and to Mantineia and Elis, if an enemy comes against the territory of the Eleans or that of the Mantineians or that of the Argives, according as these states send word, in whatever way they can most effectually, to the limit of their power; but if the invader shall have ravaged the land and gone, that city shall be hostile to the Athenians, Argives, Mantineians, and Eleans, and shall suffer ill at the hands of all these states; and to discontinue hostilities against that state shall not be allowed to any one of these states, unless all agree. [5] It shall not be permitted to pass under arms with hostile intent through their own territory or that of the allies over whom they severally have authority, nor by sea, unless passage shall have been voted by all of these states, Athenians, Argives, Mantineians, and Eleans. [6] For the relieving force the state which sends for them shall furnish provisions for thirty days after their arrival in the state which sent for succour, and in like manner on their return; but if they wish to use the army for a longer period, the city which sends for it shall furnish provisions for heavy-armed or light-armed troops or bowmen, three Aeginetan obols per day, and for a cavalryman one Aeginetan drachma. [7] The state which sent for the troops shall have command whenever the war is in its territory. But if it shall

πόλεσι κοινῇ στρατεύεσθαι, τὸ ἴσον τῆς ἡγεμονίας μετεῖναι ἁπάσαις ταῖς πόλεσιν.	seem good to all the states to make a joint expedition anywhere, all the states shall share the command equally.[138]

The full text[139] reveals—just as in the Attic-Rhegian and Attic-Leontinian treaties examined—the frequent reference to the four *poleis* involved by mentioning their citizens: the Athenians (Ἀθηναῖοι), the Argives (Ἀργεῖοι), the Mantineians (Μαντινῆς) and the Elians (Ἠλεῖοι), not necessarily always in the same order. If, as I have argued, the rationale behind the use of the demonym is connected with political factors (since a city is defined as the men who constitute it), the text very well reflects the fact that the four parties had democratic systems of government in that time.[140]

While going through the passage, the reader may note that, instead of referring to citizens as a group, cities are sometimes identified with their generic name (in their nature as "*polis*"), the toponymic names, or the generic word *polis*, both in singular and plural. Cities are mentioned with the toponyms "Athens" (Ἀθῆναι), "Argos" (Ἄργος), "Mantineia" (Μαντίνεια) and "Elis" (Ἦλις) in two parallel situations (5.47.3 and 5.47.4), when the provisions concerning the assistance to be provided to each city are introduced. The grounds underly-

138 Greek text and translation by Smith (1921) with minor corrections.

139 A picture of the epigraphic text of *IG* I³ 83, which replicates this passage, has been included in Appendix B (No. 3). For the sake of brevity, the text of the inscription has not been included herein as it has nothing to contribute and its clauses have been reconstructed precisely from Thucydides' text to a great extent; cf. Hornblower (2008: 110). Despite its fragmentary preservation—there is only a maximum of three words for each of the 28 transmitted lines—the use of demonyms to refer to the contracting *poleis* is explicit (Mantineians are mentioned in lines 4, 8, 9 and 11 and Argives are mentioned in line 14). The word *polis* appears in lines 20 and 22, which is significant for the analysis of the treaty and its drafting methods that I propose next.

140 Hornblower (2008: 117–118) also draws that conclusion due to the reference, at the end of the text, to the political bodies involved in the administration of oaths in each case. According to Bolmarcich (2007: 35), this four-party agreement is the last epigraphic example of the mention of oaths in treaties until 375. Bayliss (2013: 323–325) adds that oaths like this have played a significant role in the evolution of Greek interstate relations, especially the passage from a foreign policy endorsed by aristocratic leaders in archaic times to the creation of two clearly different blocs by the end of the fifth century. Although this sort of oath is meant to enforce compliance, the fact is that Athens would violate the treaty by not preventing the Lacedaemonians from arriving at Epidaurus by sea (Thucydides 5.56.1–2) and the Argives, in breach of the agreement, would enter into their own agreement with Sparta (Thucydides 5.61.2).

ing this exceptional mention of the toponyms become clear in the introduction of a context where *poleis* are deemed to be mere objects of protection (βοηθεῖν) and not active subjects with a certain behavior. In fact, in contrast to this identification of the cities to be helped as passive objects, in both cases the ethnic name is—not surprisingly—used to refer to the party who must provide assistance.

As for the frequency of the term *polis* to designate cities, it is worth highlighting that this occurs where (a) the four parties must be referred to collectively, namely, situations where the noun is accompanied by the determiner "all" (πᾶσαι), the pronoun "none" (μηδεμία) and/or the demonstrative pronoun "this" (αὕτη) modifying the noun; (b) an unknown city that may invade the territory of some party must be identified; (c) one of the four cities is to be identified by their possible behavior. In this case, as we do not know which of the four *poleis* may be in the situation prescribed by law, generic and undefined forms are used to identify it, such as "the city that sends" (ἡ πόλις ἡ πέμπουσα), "the city that required" (ἡ πόλις ἡ ἐπαγγείλασα) or "the city that requested" (ἡ πόλις ἡ μεταπεμψαμένη).[141]

141 Whitehead (1996: 4–7) reviews and lists all the recorded cases where the toponym is used to refer to a city instead of the ordinary ethnic name. He concludes his analysis by indicating that, unlike what one might imagine, toponyms often designate personal entities: "enough evidence has been presented here to disprove, in any formal sense, any categorical distinction between (as Finley had it) *polis*-toponyms as mere 'geographical place-names' and *polis*-ethnika as 'political communities'" (1996: 10). According to this author, that is so because Greeks had various rules. Although that is possible, my opinion is that, in fact, the examples gathered are exceptions, many of which can even be explained. I invite the reader to consider the anomalous cases found by Hansen (1996: 192–193, No. 127) in which a city is called by its name and my explanation in each case: (1) Κόρινθος (Xenophon, *Hellenica* 4.4.6)—here the passage presents the city as fatherland and it is mentioned right after stating that, once the territory is devastated, there would be nothing left in the city;—(2) Σπάρτη in Aristophanes, *Birds* 814–815—in this case, there is a lexical game with the name of the city, similar to what happens in Cratinus' fragment 117; cf. Dunbar (1995: 489–490); (3) Σπάρτη again, but this time in Herodotus 7.234.5—the expression used here is Σπάρτη πόλις ἀνδρῶν, its phrasing suggests that *polis* is considered as a group of human beings, so that ethnic identity would no longer be necessary; cf. Macan (1895: 344); (4) Τεγέα in Thucydides 5.32.3, 5.62.1 y 5.64.1—here, Hornblower (2008: 168) explains that, as the author wishes to show that the city is in danger, it is a "personification of the city." In connection with the first reference, he clarifies that "here it is Th[ucydides] himself, not just his translators, who speaks of 'Tegea' as the entity to be 'detached', 'won over', etc." Hornblower (2008: 77); (5) Ἄργιλος, Στάγιρος, Ἄκανθος, Σκῶλος, Ὄλυνθος y Σπάρτωλος when referring to the Peace of Nicias (Thucydides 5.18.5)—in this case, the explanation is not provided by Hornblower (1996: 476–478), as he

Hence, except in these situations, the use of plural demonyms is the norm in the quadripartite treaty. That evidently corresponds to the usual manner in which cities are presented as interacting entities that agree on international conventions, and reflects the way in which the Greeks expressed political configurations.

As explained above, in order to understand the nature of the *polis* as a particular city-state, it is essential to take into account its typical ethnic identification.[142] Moreover, treaties are signed between entities which are also mentioned in terms of their human factor.[143] In contrast, any reference to the cities by their geographical name entails a merely physical, passive image of the city's location.[144]

---

remains silent. Rather, Gomme (1956b: 669) argues that the episode translates a "mutual bargaining" of small populations between Athens and Sparta: the *poleis* are presumed to have been called by their toponyms as they were mere objects of transaction, with no decision-making powers in political terms. All in all, this exercise demonstrates that references made to a city using its toponym may have an explanation. Defining a city as its group of citizens is still the rule.

142 "Alors que l'État romain est surtout territorial et que ce fait est marqué par la formule qui sert à le désigner, car on dit *Roma, Urbs, ager Romanus*, l'État grec est essentiellement humain car aucun texte officiel n'a jamais dit 'Lacédémone', 'Corinthe' ou 'Athènes' mais toujours 'les Lacédémoniens', 'les Corinthiens', 'les Athéniens', 'la cité des Athéniens', 'le peuple des Athéniens'" (Ténékidès, 1956: 501, 1993: 257). "An ancient Greek could only express the idea of Athens as a political unit by saying 'the Athenians'; the single word 'Athens' never meant anything but a spot on the map, a purely and narrowly geographical notion. One travelled to Athens; one made the war against the Athenians", Finley (1963: 35). In a similar manner, Finley (1984: 10) and, with more radical thoughts, Hampl (1939). Numismatic testimonies are concordant: even in coins, the *poleis* are recognized through the national adjective, sometimes abbreviated, in plural genitive, as stated by Guarducci (1969: 615–705).

143 Hansen (1996: 193) says that "(a)lmost all treaties are concluded between parties identified by ethnics" and soon after that "… every *polis* seems to have used the plural of the city-ethnic as the name of the state and conversely, whenever the plural of an ethnic can be identified as a city-ethnic and is used as the name of a political community, this community must have been a *polis*". Pursuant to these criteria, any war-related matters involve identifying the opposing parties also through the demonym: "It was never Athens and Sparta that went to war but always 'the Athenians' and 'the Lakedaimonians'" (Hansen, 1991: 58).

144 Schachermeyr (1953: 32) held that, while in Greece the prevalence of ethnic names refers to the State's personal support and as such represent the State, names such as "Athens" or "Corinth" "représentent uniquement des paysages qui n'ont jamais eu le moindre rapport avec ce que représente l'État".

How could we explain that in the international arena (currently marked by the State's omnipresence, clearly differentiated from its inhabitants) the ancient Greeks had resorted to an image that, instead of showing the *polis* as a independent autonomous entity, explained its nature on the basis of a group image of its members?

On the one hand, it should be noted that Greek diplomatic language shows a consistent projection of individual relations onto the international level. Hence, institutions such as friendship (φιλία, *philia*) or kinship (συγγένεια, *syngeneia*), with clear interpersonal implications, were used in the international arena to characterize diplomatic relations as collective and emotional networks.[145] Thucydides connects the private level and foreign policy by pointing out that friendship among individuals and alliances among cities cannot be permanent unless they are composed by those who recognize each other as honorable and who think alike in other respects (3.10.1).[146] Since the city is by extension a communion of its members, it should not surprise us that each of them has special personality features, and that the differences among the *poleis* are presented in terms of natures (*physeis*) like those of individual people.[147]

Thucydides' war narrative incorporates a large amount of metaphor about the comparison and the relation between citizens and cities, between *idiôtai* and *poleis*.[148] Through that constant analogy, there seems to be a transfer of the intra-political model (aimed at solving problems among citizens within society) to the solution of controversies among *poleis*.[149]

Therefore, if I have suggested an explanation for the almost unanimous identification of the *polis* with its citizens in a context of representative democracy,

145 Bolmarcich (2010).

146 εἰδότες οὔτε φιλίαν ἰδιώταις βέβαιον γιγνομένην οὔτε κοινωνίαν πόλεσιν ἐς οὐδέν, εἰ μὴ μετ' ἀρετῆς δοκούσης ἐς ἀλλήλους γίγνοιντο καὶ τἆλλα ὁμοιότροποι εἶεν.

147 Mattaliano (2012: 109–115). Hence, while the quality of the Spartans (and, therefore, of their city) is slowness and tranquility, speed and anxiety is characteristic of the Athenians (and of Athens) (Thucydides 1.70.2).

148 Thucydides 1.82.6, 1.124.1, 1.144.3, 2.64.6, 3.45.3, 3.82.2, 6.85.1. Cf. Morrison (2006: 103–108).

149 Morrison (2006: 113). Similarly, Low (2007: 129–174) analyzes the construction of an international ethic (or interstate interests) based on domestic morality, through the application of language related to interpersonal links. It is precisely based on these similarities that, according to the author, we can explain why the Greeks did not feel the need to theorize on international relations. On the use of domestic legal language to describe the regulation of interstate affairs, cf. Lauterpacht (1927) and a critical view in Bottici (2004).

the opposite situation should command our attention. In other words, when decisions within a city are no longer made through egalitarian deliberation, the collective subject is replaced in the presentation of the *polis* by the individual figure of a leader. Another example from Thucydides is relevant as a description of the interesting relationship between the people and their leader (mentioned in the singular): in the words of the Spartans, the Athenian general Pericles is described as "the most powerful (…) operator of public affairs" (δυνατώτατος … καὶ ἄγων τὴν πολιτείαν) and the person who "entirely confronted the Spartans" (ἠναντιοῦτο πάντα τοῖς Λακεδαιμονίοις, 1.127.3). The Spartan denigration of the Athenians' actions, seen as a despotic measure rather than as the result of internal dialogue, leads them to present Athens in terms of the (unique) character of Pericles rather than in terms of the plurality of the *demos*.[150]

A final example reinforces these considerations: a speech, included in Book 2 of Thucydides' history as pronounced by Pericles in the first person. This speech reflects a political rupture (2.60–64) as the Athenians change their attitude towards their general: after having followed him in the confrontation with Sparta, they now realize that this caused a plague and then provoked the Lacedaemonian invasion of Attica. Accordingly, the citizens accused Pericles of being responsible for the war and the cause of all their misfortunes (καὶ τὸν μὲν Περικλέα ἐν αἰτίᾳ εἶχον ὡς πείσαντα σφᾶς πολεμεῖν καὶ δι ἐκεῖνον ταῖς ξυμφοραῖς περιπεπτωκότες, 2.59.2). In view of this general feeling, Thucydides says that Pericles called an Assembly (ξύλλογον ποιήσας, 2.59.3) and addressed his compatriots with words that definitively fractured the plural body of the *polîtai*, opening a gap between the ruler and those ruled.[151] Only at the end will the discourse recover a comprehensive second person in the plural, when Pericles states that the power of the Athenians is so great that their ships can go wherever they want, "and the King (of Persia) or any other nation will not be able to prevent it" (ὑμᾶς οὔτε βασιλεὺς οὔτε ἄλλο οὐδὲν ἔθνος τῶν ἐν τῷ παρόντι κωλύσει, 2.62.2). Pericles, "the most powerful" (δυνατώτατος) according to the Spartans, will return to the path of collective will in order to persuade his audience that the Athenians, as a whole, are "the most sovereign" (κυριωτάτους, 2.62.2).

---

150 Brown Ferrario (2013: 184–185) highlights here that "the historian re-articulates the Spartans' perspective using stronger language that represents Pericles as the Spartans' personal, individual enemy". That tyrannical role of the Athenian στρατηγός (*strategos*) can be clearly seen with the inclusion of a superlative in the singular.

151 In the entire passage, there is a contrast between "I" and "you", personal pronouns that become the axes of the discourse as a whole (Connor, 1984: 65).

2.2.3 The Treaties between Sparta and the Achaemenid Empire

While it seems clear that undemocratic regimes are assimilated to individual figures and affect the normal nexus that leads to conceiving each *polis* as the sum of its citizens, that idea gains greater purchase with the description of the Persian political system. An analysis of the Spartan-Persian agreements will provide the clearest evidence that there are political considerations behind a preference for ethnic denominations—rather than topographical ones—in the presentation of the parties to the treaties of the time.

Thucydides mentions in Book 8 three agreements signed between the Spartans and the Achaemenid empire in the years 412 and 411 (described in 8.17.4–18, 8.37 and 8.58.2, respectively). Even though the actual nature of these instruments and their condition as true treaties is in fact debated,[152] a reading of the three passages together may give rise to some reflections on the image that circulated among the Greeks regarding the exercise of monarchical power by the Persian empire.

The first two treaties, in the summer of 412 and winter of 412/1, provide incomplete information regarding their content and their provisions,[153] and are interpreted as mere drafts without legal content.[154] Unlike other examples in Thucydides, which described in detail how agreements were negotiated and signed,[155] interstate negotiations are mentioned here more lightly, without reference to external or formal elements.

152 "Without the formal backing of the King and of the home government at Sparta, no one of these documents could have more than local and provisional validity" (Gomme, Andrewes and Dover, 1981: 143). Indeed, in Thucydides 8.29 we notice that Tissaphernes (who signed on behalf of the Persians) had to consult his King (ἕως ἂν βασιλέα ἐπέρηται) before making certain decisions derived from the agreement.

153 As regards the first, which clearly favored the Persian side, see Kirchhoff (1895: 128–152), Meyer (1955: 66–92), Lewis (1977: 83–106), Lévy (1983), Debord (1999: 210) and Hornblower (2008: 800–802). The second treaty, which seems more thorough, realistic and equitable, even though it was not as advantageous to Sparta as expected, entailed a significant improvement compared with the prior one given the inclusion of more evenhanded clauses; see Lewis (1977: 93), Lévy (1983: 224), Debord (1999: 211), Heitsch (2006), Kallet (2001: 257) and Hornblower (2008: 854–857).

154 Cawkwell (2005: 149), who also adds that the first of the three treaties seems to be a preliminary arrangement by the armed forces in the course of belligerent operations.

155 For example, the other agreements, which are gathered at the end of Book 4 and in Book 5—such as annual truce of 423/2, the Peace of Nicias and the Spartan-Athenian

The third agreement, approved in the winter of 412/1, does include the solemnities inherent to official arrangements.[156] Its wording precisely defines the mutual obligations of both negotiators (8.58.1–7):

τρίτῳ καὶ δεκάτῳ ἔτει Δαρείου βασιλεύοντος, ἐφορεύοντος δὲ Ἀλεξιππίδα ἐν Λακεδαίμονι, ξυνθῆκαι ἐγένοντο ἐν Μαιάνδρου πεδίῳ Λακεδαιμονίων καὶ τῶν ξυμμάχων πρὸς Τισσαφέρνην καὶ Ἱεραμένη καὶ τοὺς Φαρνάκου παῖδας περὶ τῶν βασιλέως πραγμάτων καὶ Λακεδαιμονίων καὶ τῶν ξυμμάχων. [2] χώραν τὴν βασιλέως, ὅση τῆς Ἀσίας ἐστί, βασιλέως εἶναι· καὶ περὶ τῆς χώρας τῆς ἑαυτοῦ βουλευέτω βασιλεὺς ὅπως βούλεται. [3] Λακεδαιμονίους δὲ καὶ τοὺς ξυμμάχους μὴ ἰέναι ἐπὶ χώραν τὴν βασιλέως ἐπὶ κακῷ μηδενί, μηδὲ βασιλέα ἐπὶ τὴν Λακεδαιμονίων χώραν μηδὲ τῶν ξυμμάχων ἐπὶ κακῷ μηδενί. [4] ἢν δέ τις Λακεδαιμονίων ἢ τῶν ξυμμάχων ἐπὶ κακῷ ἴῃ ἐπὶ τὴν βασιλέως χώραν, Λακεδαιμονίους καὶ τοὺς ξυμμάχους κωλύειν· καὶ ἤν τις ἐκ τῆς βασιλέως ἴῃ ἐπὶ κακῷ ἐπὶ Λακεδαιμονίους ἢ τοὺς ξυμμάχους, βασιλεὺς κωλυέτω. [5] τροφὴν δὲ ταῖς ναυσὶ ταῖς νῦν παρούσαις Τισσαφέρνην παρέχειν κατὰ τὰ ξυγκείμενα μέχρι ἂν αἱ νῆες αἱ βασιλέως ἔλθωσιν· [6] Λακεδαιμονίους δὲ καὶ τοὺς ξυμμάχους, ἐπὴν αἱ βασιλέως νῆες ἀφίκωνται, τὰς ἑαυτῶν ναῦς, ἢν	In the thirteenth year of the reign of Darius the King, when Alexippidas was Ephor at Lacedaemon, a treaty was made in the plain of the Maeander between the Lacedaemonians and their allies on the one hand, and Tissaphernes, Hieramenes, and the sons of Pharnaces on the other, touching the interests of the King, and of the Lacedaemonians and their allies. [2] All the King's country which is in Asia shall continue to be the King's, and the King shall act as he pleases in respect of his own country. [3] The Lacedaemonians and their allies shall not go against the King's country to do hurt, and the King shall not go against the country of the Lacedaemonians and their allies to do hurt. [4] If any of the Lacedaemonians or their allies go against the King's country and do hurt, the Lacedaemonians and their allies shall interfere: and if any of the dwellers in the King's country shall go against the country of the Lacedaemonians and their allies and do hurt, the King shall interfere. [5] Tissaphernes shall provide maintenance for the number of ships which the Lacedaemonians have at present, according to the agreement, until the King's ships arrive. [6] When they have arrived, the

alliance, the quadripartite agreement and the alliance between Sparta and Argos—are referred to with "fedeltà e compiutezza per così dire diplomatica", Canfora (1990: 201–202).

156 Cartwright (1997: 281).

βούλωνται, τρέφειν ἐφ᾽ ἑαυτοῖς εἶναι. ἢν δὲ παρὰ Τισσαφέρνους λαμβάνειν ἐθέλωσι τὴν τροφήν, Τισσαφέρνην παρέχειν, Λακεδαιμονίους δὲ καὶ τοὺς ξυμμάχους τελευτῶντος τοῦ πολέμου τὰ χρήματα Τισσαφέρνει ἀποδοῦναι ὁπόσα ἂν λάβωσιν. [7] ἐπὴν δὲ αἱ βασιλέως νῆες ἀφίκωνται, αἵ τε Λακεδαιμονίων νῆες καὶ αἱ τῶν ξυμμάχων καὶ αἱ βασιλέως κοινῇ τὸν πόλεμον πολεμούντων καθ᾽ ὅτι ἂν Τισσαφέρνει δοκῇ καὶ Λακεδαιμονίοις καὶ τοῖς ξυμμάχοις. ἢν δὲ καταλύειν βούλωνται πρὸς Ἀθηναίους, ἐν ὁμοίῳ καταλύεσθαι.

Lacedaemonians and their allies may either maintain their own ships, or they may receive the maintenance of their ships from Tissaphernes. But in this case the Lacedaemonians and their allies shall at the end of the war repay to Tissaphernes the money which they have received. [7] When the King's ships have arrived, the ships of the Lacedaemonians and of their allies and of the King shall carry on the war in common, as may seem best to Tissaphernes and to the Lacedaemonians and their allies: and if they wish to make peace with the Athenians both parties shall make peace on the same terms.[157]

The specificities of this agreement and the commitments undertaken by the signatories will not be described here in detail.[158] Instead, it is my intent to reassess the manner in which the parties to the agreement are mentioned. While the Greeks are identified with a reference to their ethnic group ("the Spartans", οἱ Λακεδαιμόνιοι), it is striking that the Persians are never mentioned using the plural. Indeed, at the beginning, mention is made of the monarch's representatives, and then the text points directly to the ruler of the empire, the King (βασιλεύς). The reference to the hierarchical power of the supreme authority takes the place of possible toponyms like "Persia" or ethnic references like "the Persians" in the stipulations.

This use of language certainly says much about the Hellenic perspectives on the ideology[159] and practice of one-man political leadership, since monarchical imposition represents the counter-side—the opposite end, in other words—of the characteristic horizontality of civic practice in Greek *poleis*.[160] The Persian

157 Translation by Jowett (1881).

158 As regards these aspects, see Kirchhoff (1895: 139–142), Meyer (1955: 84–92), Lewis (1977: 103–107), Lévy (1983), Debord (1999: 212), Kallet (2001: 265) and Hornblower (2008: 924–932).

159 As regards the complex (and often inconsistent) images of monarchy in classical Greek sources, cf. Fowler and Heckster (2005: 9–38).

160 "... we could say that the very notion of an individual ruler clashed with non-negotiable portions of the system of values and norms that characterize Greek political culture (...)

King represents a fear of the most obvious risks represented by a tyranny to democratic eyes: the displacement of a *koinonia* of *politai* by a vertical command structure supported by the submission of all to a one-man rule.[161]

The identification of Persia with the role of the King could, under these circumstances, be associated with the "public-private" analogy used by Thucydides when speaking of despotic cities as opposed to democratic *poleis*. Hence, the Corinthians refer to Athens twice as "tyrant-city": in 1.122.3, for instance, they declare that they are "permitting the establishment of a tyrant-city, and yet we believe that monarchy in a single city must be dissolved" (τύραννον δὲ ἐῶμεν ἐγκαθεστάναι πόλιν, τοὺς δ ἐν μιᾷ μονάρχους ἀξιοῦμεν καταλύειν), while in 1.124.3 they state:

καὶ τὴν καθεστηκυῖαν ἐν τῇ Ἑλλάδι πόλιν τύραννον ἡγησάμενοι ἐπὶ πᾶσιν ὁμοίως καθεστάναι, ὥστε τῶν μὲν ἤδη ἄρχειν, τῶν δὲ διανοεῖσθαι, παραστησώμεθα ἐπελθόντες, καὶ αὐτοί τε ἀκινδύνως τὸ λοιπὸν οἰκῶμεν καὶ τοὺς νῦν δεδουλωμένους Ἕλληνας ἐλευθερώσωμεν.	The tyrant city which has been set up in Hellas is a standing menace to all alike; she rules over some of us already, and would fain rule over others. Let us attack and subdue her, that we may ourselves live safely for the future and deliver the Hellenes whom she has enslaved.[162]

Like the Achaemenid monarchy, the *polis tyrannos*—a true institutional fright—is a logical cause of concern for the Greek mind, as it de-naturalizes the citizen basis of every political community. This is the only way to explain that when, instead of the ethnic denomination, the individuality of the Persian "enemy" is defined as a separate, unattached unit, isolated from its components and only linked to the exclusive power of the king/tyrant, it represents an image of danger that could undermine the collective spirit of the democratic city-state.[163]

Individual decisions binding for the whole political community and substracted to the public eye were therefore doubly inacceptable" Luraghi (2013).

161 "Tyranny was the antithesis of the *polis*. It is no accident that most tyrants are credited with centralizing state power" (Morris, 1991: 48). Like Persian kings, Greek tyrants and Macedonian monarchs also swore an oath to ratify treaties on behalf of their people. The recognition of these individual "others" (and their anti-democratic regimes) reflects the true universal nature of Greek interstate law.

162 Translation by Jowett (1881).

163 Whitehead (1996) observed that, when the question at stake was not territorial, *poleis* were only rarely designated by toponyms. In such cases, the city designated by the toponym was

Summation: International Subjectivity in Ruins

Since the agreed-upon origins of modern public international law, the State has shown a progressive consolidation as an autonomous construct, as a legal subject in its own right. Such development was gradual, but unstoppable. In Francisco de Vitoria (1485–1546), the State was still a perfect structure of free men led by a prince capable of creating law, while for Hugo Grotius (1583–1645), who was imbued with the principles of natural law, the true subject could not be other than the individual. Only after the contractualist guidelines established by Thomas Hobbes, who nevertheless links the State and the prince; Samuel Pufendorf, who confuses the State and its bodies while notoriously differentiating it from the people that compose it;[164] and, especially Christian Wolff, who considers the State as a sovereign—though that sovereignty is "held" by the ruler—, did Emmerich de Vattel (1714–1767) define for the first time international law as an interstate system.[165] From that point on, it is difficult to stop thinking about a fiction of the State as a legal subject different from the citizens who compose it or the authorities governing it,[166] because only the States create international law and define it to its full extent.[167]

often involved in rebel activities. In Thucydides, for example, the toponym is used when there is a reference to "revolt": "Again and again, when *poleis* in Thucydides either (A) revolt (intransitive; *polis* the subject) or (B) are induced to revolt (transitive; *polis*, the object)". Hence, the political profile of these designations cannot be doubted.

164 In view of Hobbes's preliminary developments, Aufricht (1943: 218–210) considered that Pufendorf could be the source of the idea of the State as a moral person-group, different from the biological beings that composed it.

165 "Though adapting to the new political and social circumstances, International law in the tradition from Vitoria to Grotius was still conceived as an overarching law of all men including rulers and private individuals (...) Only after Grotius, in the second half of the seventeenth and the first half of the eighteenth centuries, did international law begin to be regarded as an interstate law [with Vattel]" (Portmann, 2010: 35).

166 Remec (1960).

167 de Vattel (1758) argues in *Preliminaires* § 6: "Hence, the rules of Natural Law must be applied to the nations in order to discover their rights and obligations. Consequently, the law of nations is originally nothing but the law of nature applied to nations. (...) A Civil Society, a State, is a subject remarkably different from a human individual: by virtue of natural laws, in many cases that results in quite different rights and obligations, since the same general rule applied to two subjects cannot lead to similar decisions as those subjects are not the same. Also, a particular rule, though fair for one subject, may not be suitable for another subject whose nature is completely different" (personal translation).

In this context, the debate among jurists as to whether something is or is not a subject under the international order is the basis of the legal construction of the law *inter nationes*. Hence, it seems difficult to avoid the idea of a preexisting concept—i.e., the "subject"—that helps us understand the personal scope of a given regulatory system. After restricting the definition of law to those who are its subjects, any discussions regarding what should be included and what should be excluded from its content, who is or is not a subject to it, end up in pointless (and endless) arguments.

Ultimately, is it reasonable in this context to think about the idea of a "subject" before the law? It is often said that the concept is essential because possession of international legal personality enables an entity to engage in actions whose effects must conform to international law.[168] However, setting aside such abstractions, the reality is an international system where various participants (either state or non-state, local or transnational) play active roles, broadly and specifically participating in networks of interaction.

In order to deal with the perplexing phenomenon of the growing number of participants at the international level[169] and the apparent failure by the "subject" category to embrace them, ultimately three alternatives seem possible: (i) readapting the concept of "subject", broadening its scope to adjust to new realities; (ii) replacing the idea of "subject" with a more effective category to meet current needs; or (iii) setting aside the concept of "subject" and any other substitute, after concluding that enshrining a theory of subjectivity is not essential for international law to exist.

In current times, when the Westphalian paradigm is deeply questioned, when new voices criticize State-centered approaches and the State's sovereign voluntarism, the first alternative is widely supported by those who propose new interpretations that overcome the subject/object distinction and that are aimed at incorporating other entities intervening in current relationships as legal persons.[170] This contributes to a more realistic perspective on the international phenomenon, even though—given its broad scope and ubiquity—it will inevitably lead to challenging the concept of the "subject". The second position has been sustained by Higgins, among others, who advocates for the

168 Pérez Bernárdez (2009: 133).

169 Schreuer (1993: 449–450), proposes replacing the State-centered logic of international law by recognizing a "multi-layered reality consisting of a variety of authoritative structures" (1993: 455).

170 Parlett (2011: 38–40).

replacement of the idea of the "subject" by a more flexible concept: the "participant".[171] This proposal is undoubtedly interesting, though it ultimately offers a mere partial and temporary solution, especially considering that, should said replacement succeed in academic fields, the discussion will abandon the idea of "person" or "subject" and introduce a new concept. Hence, it would give rise to new considerations regarding what it means to "participate" in international law (in turn, sooner or later this would bring about challenges very similar to those existing today: we should afterwards analyze whether a given entity falls in the "participant" category, for instance). Therefore, this second alternative would lead to an *ad infinitum* regression. In view of those obstacles, the examples analyzed in the Greek world would suggest that the third solution is the most adequate (and most radical) alternative, i.e., that it is not necessary to start from subjectivity in order to conceive a law of nations.[172]

Indeed, the case of classical Greece provides sufficient historical basis to support the conclusion that international law may exist even before the theorizing of its "subjects", as it reveals a context of fruitful interstate relations between Greek *poleis* that, nevertheless, do not in fact involve "legal" persons distinct from their citizens. That is to say, the fifth century offers a series of sources of law—e.g., treaties—that have effects upon the parties, giving rise to courses of action and conditioning conduct, without building a theory that identifies "subjects" within *poleis* with roles different from those played by the human beings who make up their population.

In contrast to what happened with public and private legal entities in the domestic law of each Greek city—which, as discussed in section 1.2, would reflect a quasi-legal phenomenon of autonomy of action—, in the wake of our discussion of the possible personality of the *polis* (section 1.3), there appear

---

171 "It is more helpful, and closer to the perceived reality, to return to the view of international law as a particular decision-making process. Within that process (which is a dynamic and not a static one) there are a variety of participants, making claims across state lines, with the object of maximizing various values. Determinations will be made on those claims by various authoritative decision-makers—Foreign Office Legal Advisers, arbitral tribunals, courts. Now, in this model, *there are no 'subjects' and 'objects', but only participants.* Individuals are participants, along with states, international organisations (...), multinational corporations, and indeed private non-governmental groups not" (Higgins, 1995: 50).

172 Such a statement undoubtedly deserves further analysis and would be an interesting topic for future research in the field.

juridical elements that condition its (internal and external) performance in the light of its identification or overlapping with the individuals who make decisions.

Rather than expanding the category of "subjects" or switching to a name that is less conditioned by modern legal tradition, the literary and epigraphic sources discussed suggest the possibility of envisioning an international law whose existence does not depend on the identification of "subjects" who define it. It rather depends on organized groups of individuals who act beyond certain political borders in order to negotiate with neighbors and third parties. Thus, the lesson learnt from the Hellenic case is useful.

Even without being described as a subject, in practical terms the *polis* operated as a true city-state, an institutional entelechy that, in a given cultivated territory (χώρα, *khora*), had a population of free men politically organized under certain bodies of government seated in the fortified center of the city (ἄστυ, *asty*). It was clearly an entity of an independent nature, even to the extent that concepts such as αὐτονομία (*autonomia*) or ἐλευθερία (*eleutheria*, freedom)—used in the sources of the time to indicate the features inherent to each *polis*—[173] reflect an idea similar to what is currently understood as "sovereignty".[174] However—as I concluded—such independence is determined by the independent status of its citizens.

Nijman suggested that emerging participants should be *listened* to and argued that, when discussing the issue of legal personality, it was already time to move from the mask (*persona*) to the vocal cords.[175] The fact that the Greeks explained the *polis* on the basis of the *politai*, that they preferred the factual reality of the ethnic group rather than the toponymic abstraction of the city should perhaps move us to rethink current criteria, which were laid down by the passage of time and uncritical repetition. Escaping from the "person" simply entails putting aside the masks of legal subjectivity—the emerging labels of fiction and artifice—in order to give space to true

173 Together with the adjective *autonomos*, terms such as *autopolis* (able to individually decide on a particular foreign policy), *autoteles* (autonomous with respect to taxation) or *autodikos* (judicially independent) are frequently used to emphasize the independence of *poleis*. Under expressions such as *eleutheroi te kai autonomoi* ("free and independent", Thucydides, 3.10.5) or *eleutherotate* ("very free", Thucydides, 6.89.6, 7.69.2), independence is one of the essential features of cities, even under panhellenic customary law. Cf. Ténékidès (1954: 17–19).

174 Giovannini (2007: 98).

175 Nijman (2004: 448).

faces.[176] Faces of individuals who—under the protection of collective interests in which their own identity is involved—respond to an energetic, living, human reality that among the Greeks was undoubtedly more suitable for representing the passions of international praxis than the cold and calculated staging of empty legal entelechies, devoid of intensity and actual commitment to the community's social values.

Based on such an active conception of inter-*polis* connections and the identification of conventional *nomoi* under a legal code, the following chapters of this study are aimed at examining this "international" praxis of Greek city-states with regard to the regulation of the use of force and war. Even though, as explained below, in the Greek world there are very few specific treaties on the limitation of hostilities,[177] it is possible to notice in the conduct of *poleis* (and in the awareness of the compulsory nature of such conduct) interesting rules that determine the scope of their international action.[178] Thus, our goal is to show the legal nature of those rules regarding *ius ad bellum* and *ius in bello*, in order to trace the customary basis of many of the legal provisions currently in force back to ancient times.

---

176 At this point, we should move away from Anderson (2009: 17–18), who claims that references to *poleis* in the sources based on their toponyms or their demonyms are indiscriminate, given that both are entities that are neither material nor observable, since "they all referred to rather a discursive construct, a fictitious corporate person, the ultimate source of political power in numerous Greek polities". Indeed, it has been shown that, by representing political entities as a group of citizens instead of a generic denomination ("the Athenians" instead of "Athens"), the Greeks avoided the problem of dealing with excessively abstract conceptualizations about a "legal subject" and exposed the inextricable relationship—inherent to a democratic ideology—between the human community, its collective identity, its common interests and its modes of representation towards the outside.

177 Gaurier (2014: 67) admits that "il exista fort peu de conventions écrites" regarding the regulation of war, even though he identifies a list of applicable rules.

178 As regards the prevalence of custom over signed agreements as sources in the Greek world, cf. Lanni (2007: 4, n. 4).

PART 2

The Rules

CHAPTER 3

The Outbreak of War and Its Limits in Inter-*polis* Law

> We must begin by acknowledging the hard truth that we will not eradicate violent conflict in our lifetimes. There will be times when nations—acting individually or in concert—will find the use of force not only necessary but morally justified (...) The instruments of war do have a role to play in preserving the peace (...) To begin with, I believe that all nations—strong and weak alike—must adhere to standards that govern the use of force. I—like any head of state—reserve the right to act unilaterally if necessary to defend my nation.
>
> BARACK H. OBAMA, "Nobel Peace Prize Acceptance Speech", Oslo, 10-12-2009

•••

> οὕτω τις οὔτ' ἄν ποτε πολιτικὸς γένοιτο ὀρθῶς, πρὸς τὰ ἔξωθεν πολεμικὰ ἀποβλέπων μόνον καὶ πρῶτον, οὔτ' ἂν νομοθέτης ἀκριβής, εἰ μὴ χάριν εἰρήνης τὰ πολέμου νομοθετοῖ μᾶλλον ἢ τῶν πολεμικῶν ἕνεκα τὰ τῆς εἰρήνης.
>
> That man will never make a genuine statesman who pays attention primarily and solely to the needs of foreign warfare, nor will he make a finished lawgiver unless he designs his war legislation for peace rather than his peace legislation for war.
>
> PLATO, *Laws* 628d–e (tr. BURY)

∴

In the first part of this work, reference has been made to the importance of *nomos* as the essential regulatory basis in the Greek world, capable of regulating multiple aspects of social life within *poleis*. In the context of a debate on the subjectivity and modes of creating international law in classical city-states, I have discussed the legal scope of a series of regulations that determine the rights and obligations of *polis* citizens in the field of international relations. The purpose of the second part of this research is to move that "legal" aspect to the realm of war—as a regulated act—, paying special attention to certain

 | DOI: 10.1163/9789004363823_005

patterns of conduct and the definition of limits for initiating or participating in an armed conflict.

It should be noted that the natural condition of war, although an omnipresent phenomenon throughout classical Greek history and an opportunity for glorification of power, is often chacterized negatively in ancient sources.[1] In his narrative of the Peloponnesian War, Thucydides, for example, puts in the mouths of certain historical characters real arguments in favor of peace. According to his account, for instance, in the allied congress at Sparta in the year 432, the Corinthians spoke of the "delightful tranquility of peace" (τῷ ἡσύχῳ τῆς εἰρήνης ἡδόμενον).[2] Two years later, according to the same author, waging war was described by Pericles, in Book 2, as "the greatest folly" (πολλὴ ἄνοια πολεμῆσαι)[3] and in 424 in Gela we are reminded that, for Hermocrates, the fact that war is evil is an idea so familiar to all that it would be tedious to develop it (καὶ περὶ μὲν τοῦ πολεμεῖν ὡς χαλεπὸν τί ἄν τις πᾶν τὸ ἐνὸν ἐκλέγων ἐν εἰδόσι μακρηγοροίη).[4]

Along with Thucydides, Attic drama contributed to a negative image of the consequences of war. With no fear of exaggeration, it could be argued that without the Peloponnesian War as a background, those literary works would certainly have not existed as such.[5] Almost half of the thirty-two complete tragedies that have survived to the present day were produced in times of war or develop a wartime theme.[6] Tragedies by Euripides such as *Children of Heracles* (c. 430), *Suppliants* (423) or *Helen* (412) are a sort of anti-war propaganda. Other works by him—such as *Andromache* (c. 425), *Hecuba* (424) or *Trojan Women* (415)—resort to the myths of the Trojan cycle to present the dramatic effects of the war, suggesting similarities that the public could promptly associate with contemporary reality.[7] Aristophanes' comic output—eleven complete plays and more than a thousand fragments—also includes a notoriously contemptuous treatment of war, to such an extent that the main characters of the *Acharnians* (425), *Peace* (421) and *Lysistrata* (411) decide to promote peace through a series of humorous plans whose rationales were certainly understood by the Athenian audience of that time.[8]

---

1 These literary and philosophical texts reveal some optimism in view of the excessive cruelty of conduct in times of war; cf. Rebuffat (2000: 194–199).

2 Thucydides 1.120.3.

3 Thucydides 2.61.1.

4 Thucydides 4.59.2.

5 Raaflaub (2007: 117).

6 Millett (2013: 52).

7 Gregory (1991) shows the didactic profile of these tragic performances in a war context.

8 Perrin-Saminadayar (1999: 151), Crowley (2012: 88). More specifically, it deals with the impor-

In such a context of intellectual hatred and denunciation of the constant reality of war,[9] it should not surprise us that the use of force is accompanied by a more or less explicit justification that arouses feelings of support for the military enterprise.[10] Hence, this chapter will particularly analyze the manners in which hostilities commenced in the Greek world and the schemes for justifying an armed incursion, usually associated with a long-term tradition that was based on considering war as "holy" or "fair".

War is a reality that occurs in specific socio-cultural contexts as a consequence of unfulfilled needs.[11] Its causes are deeply rooted in economic, social, and political necessities.[12] Since it responds to the needs of specific contexts, war can only be conceived in archaic societies in terms of the methods of representation created by a given community to reflect it. Evidently, the complex phenomenon of war (and its opposite, peace, which is described as the absence of violence) is only understandable insofar as it is analyzed in the light of records obtained from historical anthropology and the history of mentalities, which take into account social memory and collective consciousness.[13] However, given that these are "mental" projections reflected and transmitted through discourse, this work will attempt to examine written documentary sources to explore the foundations of this shared construct. I am not interested in defining a social "reality" of war—which is impossible—, but rather in considering the "representation" (or "representations") of war: the task is to analyze these forms of discourse where war emerges as a phenomenon. These discourses reveal perspectives that may be contrary to practice or to other attempts to present reality. In any event, these transmitted voices reveal the

---

tance of war in the Aristophanic comedy, Newiger (1980). In fact, the eleven complete comedies we know today deal, more or less explicitly, with the question of armed conflict.

9 "Les auteurs athéniens font connaître des crimes de guerre commis pendant ces années" (Vial, 1999: 139).

10 "Naturally, moral imperatives and ethical niceties could be, and indeed often were, swept aside by *Realpolitik*, but the Greeks preferred, where possible, to offer pretexts or justifications before recourse to arms" (Crowley, 2012: 90).

11 Ciccotti (1971: 145–153) explained that in the Greek world, war responds to the needs of productive forces.

12 In a large-scale study on the origins of war in ancient times, Gillespie (2013: 239) focused on the economic justification. He considered that, even if the control of resources was the main motivation for warfare, "it was rare to find justifications for war based purely on material or social reward". The reason behind hostilities is not always the alleged cause of war.

13 Loreto (2006: 218–219).

forms adopted by the regulatory impulse, the "rules" imposed to counteract the excessive display of armed force.

It is therefore necessary to establish that, in these representations, there is no unanimous concept of what should be understood as a "just war". From a discursive perspective, "just wars" reflect a normativity that is (re)defined depending on the context. It is perhaps in this permanent semantic fluctuation that the history of the concept has always consisted. In a sinuous path bordering law, morality, religion and politics, speaking of "just wars" involves, in fact, two different and (to some extent) opposite acts. Based on an extrapolation of categories derived from Koskenniemi's philosophical approach, we can speak of a double dimension of the "just war" issue.[14] On the one hand, we could identify a "utopian" dimension, programmatically intended to radically limit the existence of armed conflict to those conflicts that meet the ethical criteria shared by the community.[15] This is the use given to the term by most international law philosophers, who have supported a "theory" of just war with the aim of introducing an ethical element into decision-making in connection with the beginning of armed conflict (*ius ad bellum*) and the way in which hostilities are conducted (*ius in bello*).[16] Under this programmatic perspective, associated with some sort of "ought" (*iustitia ferenda*), any belligerent act that fails to meet certain moral standards would be excluded from any justification and, therefore, should not be considered lawful.[17] Walzer is probably the main author in the twentieth century who readdresses the tradition of just war: he holds that everyone wants to act morally and that deciding on war's justness is a job for humanity as a whole, not just the armed forces (i.e., the State).[18] Taking into account the existence of legal and extra-legal elements inherent to the concept, Bellamy identified three sub-traditions within the just war tradition

---

14 Koskenniemi (1989).

15 The concept of ethics appears to be inherent to the political aspect; Elshtain (2001: 4).

16 "Just war tradition developed on the basis of the principles of *jus ad bellum* and *jus in bello* which determine justified recourse to war and put restraints on the waging of war" (Johnson, 1991: 5).

17 As mentioned above, law itself seems insufficient to encompass the debate over just war; hence, politics or religion often step in to define the usefulness and operation of the category in a given context.

18 Walzer's book (1992 [1977]), based on a leftist theoretical position that sought to expose the illegality of the Vietnam war, represented a turning point in incorporating the element of morality into armed conflict (both in the *ius ad bellum* and in *ius in bello*). However, the value of "justice" and the programmatic-ethical level that operates throughout the

(positive law, natural law and realism), depending on the values that are to be protected in abstract terms.[19]

On the other hand, it is useful to identify an "apologetic" dimension, which seeks to use the language of just wars as part of a rhetoric of justification in contexts in which the use of force is not clearly lawful.[20] This is a more political perspective on the "doctrine" of just war that, based on a realistic principle, is concerned with respecting the existing justice (*iustitia lata*) in specific situations in order to provide solid support to the international conduct of States.[21] At least at a general level, it seems that the utopian theory of just war gives rise to a theoretical discourse regarding the present and the future (what should happen to avoid future armed confrontation), while the apologetic doctrine attempts to understand past conduct in a practical way in order to endorse specific military actions. The establishment of the discourse or rhetoric of justification is based on the need to proclaim a defense that, in most cases, does not precede decision-making, but ratifies it *a posteriori*.[22]

In this chapter, I offer a diachronic study of *ius ad bellum* based on a complex approach to just war that will account for its apologetic use, in order to show how the contributions of legal philosophy and political discourse con-

---

text is relativized in the author's subsequent production and presented in rhetorical terms rather than in terms of reality as shown below.

19 Bellamy (2010: 26), on the other hand, proposes an innovative theory where legitimacy is the result of the balance of the three sets of values contained in the different sub-traditions.

20 As regards the existence of a *lex rhetorica* of war, cf. Ansah (2003).

21 In an article published one year after the attack on the Twin Towers and included in a more recent volume, Walzer (2004: 11) reviews the history behind his own thinking and introduces the rhetorical level ("apologetic", in the reading here suggested) of the doctrine to explain its validity and use: "But does this mean that it [war] has to be more just or only that it has to look more just, that it has to be described, a little more persuasively than in the past, in the language of justice? The triumph of just war theory is clear enough; it is amazing how readily military spokesmen during the Kosovo and Afghanistan wars used its categories, telling a causal story that justified the war and providing accounts of the battles that emphasized the restraint with which they were fought".

22 In general terms, in the current world, both discourses are so permeable that it is even possible to observe a political-juridical "institutionalization" of the apologetic dimension. This happens, for example, when the Charter of the United Nations, through the right to veto granted to the five great powers which were victorious in 1945, gives a *carte blanche* of "justification" for their future wars.

verged throughout history. In particular, I will call attention to this legitimizing aspect of "just war" in classical Greece, which is expressed in discourse through appeals to motivation that leave no room for a rejection of the rules in force.

Some preliminary comments should be made in order to understand how, although the historical context is remarkably different in terms of the law applicable to the use of force, providing a justification for armed attacks is still a surprisingly valid strategy. In the contemporary world, following the prohibition of the use of force (or threat of use of force) in the Charter of the United Nations (Article 2.4), the concept of "just war" has been largely reduced to self-defense[23] (the only exception States are expressly granted under the treaty, as set forth in Article 51).[24] The situation in the ancient world seems to be different since conquest was a legitimate means for attaining the public purposes of city-states. Indeed, far from being prohibited, among cities in the Greek world the use of force was a suitable mechanism for conflict resolution or territorial expansion[25] and on many occasions violence was considered an efficient tool to achieve economic prosperity. Yet, it is possible to find various examples where

---

23 Johnson (1984: 3), Flint and Fallah (2004: 1384). Walzer (1992 [1977]) argues that in the twenteeth century, there is a reductionist notion of "just war", since issues such as intervention in defense of the innocent, punishment of wrongdoers and sacred wars no longer fall within its scope.

24 Under a State-centered international law, such as that enshrined in the modern age and supported by the Westphalian myth of legal equality of the States, self-defense stands as an "inherent" right of States that—if exercised in accordance with established positive rules (both conventional and customary)—does not entail a violation of the prohibition of the use of force (see below, n. 65). The other two "exceptions" to Article 2.4 traditionally agreed upon by legal authorities (i.e., the action of the Security Council under Article 42 of the Charter and the fight carried out by the peoples who confront their rulers or occupiers to enforce their right to self-determination) do not involve conduct or actions at the level of the State. This is so even though Chapter VII of the Charter undoubtedly allows decision-making by the Security Council as an obvious delegation upon this body of an exercise of power that the States deny themselves through the Convention.

25 For example, when in the year 112 a group of Magnesian magistrates were called to settle a dispute about boundaries between the Cretan cities of Hierapytna and Itanus, a long arbitration award (about one hundred verses) was rendered, recognizing the ancestral dispute and, almost as some sort of *obiter dictum*, the valid methods of territorial acquisition were made explicit: "… Men hold property rights on land either because they received the land themselves from their ancestors, or because they bought it for money, or because they gained it with the sword, or because they received it from some mighty one …" (*IC* III.IV.9, v. 133–134: [… ἄν] θρωποι τὰς κατὰ τῶν τόπων ἔχουσι κυριείας ἢ παρὰ προγόνων π[αραλαβόν]

confrontation is claimed to be fair; that explains the fact that the expression "just wars" finds fertile ground—in political, religious, ethical and legal terms—and authorizes interstate violence.

The idea underlying this section of my research is that, even though since archaic times the Greek worldview was characterized by *polemos* and its express recognition as a legal act, contrary to what the majority position in historiography maintains, it is not a question of accepting uncontrollable violence without a response. Indeed, in case of conflict a peaceful settlement was always available[26] but—when fighting was chosen—various sources allow us to infer the necessity of identifying a *casus belli*, in terms not so different from those prevailing today.

The purpose here will be to survey the constant presence, at a discursive level, of motivations for the use of force and a clear intention to prove that no contribution was made to the outbreak of war. In order to do so, I will examine some key examples that will give an account of the ways in which the Greeks perceived the need to find a discourse of justification for their military incursions. It is worth mentioning that, besides the apparent economic or political reasons to conduct an attack, there is an explicit search for the grounds of self-defense in illegal actions by others, which justifies a true legal exercise of retaliation rather than a mere discretionary onslaught.

In this chapter, when considering how war against the enemy was conceived in Greece as "just" (δίκαιος, *dikaios*) in religious and political terms, I will focus on revealing the legal issue of *legitimacy* of war actions. We can glimpse—prior to the legal systematization of *ius ad bellum*—an interesting conceptual basis for thinking about the customary grounds that, from ancient times, allow us to appraise public discourse aimed at justifying the outbreak of violence.

τες αὐτοὶ [ἢ πριάμενοι] / [κατ'] ἀργυρίου δόσιν ἢ δόρατι κρατήσαντες ἢ παρά τινος τῶν κρεισσόν[ων σχόντες·); Guarducci (1942). For a legal analysis of the passage in relation to the acquisition of land, cf. Chaniotis (2004: 185–187). On this affair, see also Kallet-Marx (1996: 177–184).

26 With regards to arbitral settlements in ancient Greece, see Westermann (1907), Raeder (1912), Calabi (1953: 91–124) and more recently Carty (2017). On arbitral decisions, see below in chapter 4 (section 5).

1 The Rhetoric of the Use of Armed Force in the Greek World

While some authors have claimed that any consideration of just war should be traced back to Saint Augustine and not to the classical period,[27] other voices have risen to seek earlier origins of the concept in the Roman world.[28] Bellamy finds the theoretical foundations of *bellum iustum* in Ciceronian works,[29] and he draws attention to interesting prior works that examine the solemnities for declaring war required by the fetials in Rome.[30] However, it should be remarked that the most distant precedent for the regulation of just war is not the wars carried out under the *ius fetiale*: in the universe of Greek cities, there was already a consciousness of the need to limit military action to those cases explicitly considered fair.[31]

To begin with, there is specific vocabulary in the Greek world to refer to the beginning of hostilities: the most frequently used verbs—τίθεσθαι (*tithesthai*, "place"), εἰσιέναι (*eisienai*, "go towards"), καθίστασθαι (*kathistasthai*, "to establish, to enter")—show that the idea of the creation of a new, previously nonexistent state of affairs underlies the declaration of hostility.[32] Hence, war is perceived as an act which, despite its prevalence, entails a decision and an action that gives rise to its declaration. This act of embarking upon *polemos* therefore requires an explanation that justifies adopting the measure, a previous hostile act upon which terminology confers a negative connotation. "Raising" or "awakening" a warlike confrontation (ἀναίρεσθαι, *anairesthai*; αἴρεσθαι, *airesthai*) as a result of no previous attack expresses an onus associated with injustice.[33] On the other hand, the sources usually have a positive attitude toward defensive combat: the protection of the *polis* itself usually works as a solid argument for exerting violence.[34]

---

27 Mattox (2006: 2).

28 Burkert (1986: 82) explicitly indicates that before Rome, there was no concept of "just war" among the Greeks.

29 See the works on the subject and a study of the supplementary positions in Calore (2003), who discussed the relation between *bellum iustum* and *causa iusta belli*. Cf. also Loreto (2001).

30 This idea has also been analyzed in books on Roman law; cf. Albert (1980), Bacot (1989), Mantovani (1990).

31 Bederman (2001: 212).

32 du Bouchet (2012: 69–70), who thoroughly surveys the vocabulary appearing in the sources.

33 du Bouchet (2012: 70).

34 "Au ve siècle, le schéma d'une guerre opposant les 'patriotes' défendant leur territoire et

Despite the realism that usually seems to characterize the Greek world (as, for example, in Thucydides), a passage in Isocrates' *On Peace* clearly reveals that, in fact, the Athenians believed that it was unfair for the most powerful to govern the weakest (οὐ δίκαιόν ἐστι τοὺς κρείττους τῶν ἡττόνων ἄρχειν, 8.69).[35] Likewise, in his speech to the Cypriot King Nicocles, Isocrates recommended being bellicose in the understanding of war, but a pacifist by avoiding any struggle that is contrary to law (πολεμικὸς μὲν ἴσθι ταῖς ἐπιστήμαις καὶ ταῖς παρασκευαῖς, εἰρηνικὸς δὲ τῷ μηδὲν παρὰ τὸ δίκαιον πλεονεκτεῖν, 3.24).[36] Similarly, in a minor Platonic dialogue the character of Alcibiades argued that "even if someone considers it necessary to go to war against peoples who behave justly, he would not admit it" (εἰ γὰρ καὶ διανοεῖταί τις ὡς δεῖ πρὸς τοὺς τὰ δίκαια πράττοντας πολεμεῖν, οὐκ ἂν ὁμολογήσειέν γε); acting otherwise would be considered illegal and improper in Socrates' view (109c1–3).[37] The injustice of beginning an armed conflict would lie in fighting against those who have not caused any harm.[38] However, the practice of discourse clearly shows that whether confrontation is considered as "just" depends, in many instances, on a justificatory argument that is sometimes presented to explain the need to carry out hostilities against the enemy. The Funeral Oration assigned to Demosthenes acknowledges that the Athenians always claimed not to have committed unjust acts against other Greeks or the barbarians (ἠδίκησαν μὲν οὐδένα πώποτ' οὔθ' Ἕλλην' οὔτε βάρβαρον, 60.7), and even sought to punish those who committed acts of injustice against foreigners (τιμωρίαν ὑπὲρ ὧν τοὺς ἄλλους ἠδίκουν ἐπέθηκαν, 60.11).

Having noticed that there are almost no works aimed at exploring the scope of just war in ancient Greece,[39] my aim in this chapter will consist in: firstly (1.1), surveying the existence of specific terminology intended to reflect the atten-

---

leur ville, aux autres, les 'honteux' qui agressent les premiers et pour ce faire n'hésitent pas à quitter leur terre, est semble-t-il particulièrement efficace" (Sebillotte Cuchet, 2006: 226).

35 The Greek text corresponds to the edition by Norlin (1980).

36 Cf. Dawson (1996: 66) and Sidebottom (2004: 55). The same expression is repeated word-for-word in 8.136.

37 As regards the political scope of this passage in the core of the dialogue, see Parra (2010: 32–34).

38 Plato expressed a similar position in his *Republic* (464e–465b).

39 Indeed, there are no comprehensive studies on the subject except for a few recent contributions: an article by Bertoli (2009) that is limited to a few passages by Thucydides, the brief doctoral thesis by Hugsby (2009)—which deals briefly with only four authors (Herodotus, Thucydides, Plato and Aristotle)—, some pages in Christopher (2004: 9–11) and a chapter by Dewald (2013). Mention must be made of the interesting work by Clavadetscher-Thürlemann (1985), which—despite its title—is mostly focused on tracing

tion paid to the "origins", "causes" and "motivations" (either actual or alleged) for the initiation of hostilities. Secondly, (1.2) discovering some instances where reference is made to a given circumstance as motivating military action, in order to assess the rhetorical devices used for disclaiming one's own responsibility and, in turn, imposing it upon others. These first two sections will refer to the Peloponnesian War; however, special emphasis will be given to other great wars in the Greek world which are constantly mentioned in the classical period and offer a valid basis for comparison in terms of legitimacy: the Trojan War (with Helen's abduction) and the Greco-Persian Wars (particularly the Persian justification). Thirdly, I will try (1.3) to analyze the specific case of self-defense as representative of the whole discourse that condemns war initiated by the enemy and, consequently, legitimizes the speaker's position. Lastly, I will attempt to demonstrate (1.4) the legal nature of the principle of self-defense in the context of Greek interstate law.

2 The Vocabulary of the Grounds: The Spoken and the Unspoken in Thucydides

When Thucydides addressed the origins of the Peloponnesian War, he immediately expressed the need to explain the grounds for the armed conflict between Athenians and Spartans (1.23.5–6):

διότι δ' ἔλυσαν, τὰς αἰτίας προὔγραψα πρῶτον καὶ τὰς διαφοράς, τοῦ μή τινα ζητῆσαί ποτε ἐξ ὅτου τοσοῦτος πόλεμος τοῖς Ἕλλησι κατέστη. τὴν μὲν γὰρ ἀληθεστάτην πρόφασιν, ἀφανεστάτην δὲ λόγῳ, τοὺς Ἀθηναίους ἡγοῦμαι μεγάλους γιγνομένους καὶ φόβον παρέχοντας τοῖς Λακεδαιμονίοις ἀναγκάσαι ἐς τὸ πολεμεῖν· αἱ δ' ἐς τὸ φανερὸν λεγόμεναι αἰτίαι αἵδ' ἦσαν ἑκατέρων, ἀφ' ὧν λύσαντες τὰς σπονδὰς ἐς τὸν πόλεμον κατέστησαν.

Why they broke it [i.e., the Peace] and what were the grounds (*aitias*) of the quarrel I will first set forth, so that in time to come no man may be at a loss to know what was the origin of this great war. The real (*alethestaten*) though unavowed (*aphanestaten*) cause (*prophasin*) I believe to have been the growth of the Athenian power, which terrified the Lacedaemonians and forced them into war; but the reasons (*aitiai*) publicly (*es to phaneron*) alleged on either side which led to the dissolution of the treaty and the breaking out of the war were as follows.[40]

Greek philosophical precedents to explain the Roman conception of *bellum iustum* rather than in the conceptualization of πόλεμος δίκαιος (*polemos dikaios*).

40 Translation by Jowett (1881) with corrections.

Thucydides' passage is relevant as it lets us survey the lexical plurality regarding the grounds for armed conflicts: thus, the quoted text develops terms such as αἰτία (*aitia*, "cause") or πρόφασις (*prophasis*, "excuse"): based on their semantic content and their etymological origins, we can infer that while the noun *aitia* refers to the factual origin of conflict (i.e., what produces it), *prophasis* would be limited to discourse, i.e., what is said openly (the term is composed of the prefix *pro-* "forward", and a noun derived from the verb φημί, *phemi*, "to say").[41] Nevertheless, Thucydides seems to disarticulate that contrast between the actual and the declared, insofar as he believes in the existence of an actual *prophasis* in the Peloponnesian War that contradicts what is articulated orally (in discourse, in *logos*). Hence, his intention is to unveil the actual motivations for conflict, which are due to a considerable power imbalance between Athens and Sparta.[42] Indeed, what motivates war is δύναμις, *dynamis*, "power" (1.8), but this does not appear clearly at the discursive level. Instead, the historian takes an apparently objective stance from which he attempts to reveal the true reason rather than the one proclaimed by the contending parties.[43]

Later in his work, however, there is an explanation of the reasons that led to confrontation, using the first person singular. In 417/6, the Athenians wanted the island of Melos to join the Delian League, but the Melians refused. In Book 5, Thucydides tells how the Athenian generals Cleomedes and Tisias sent ambassadors to justify their intention to attack the Melians.[44] In the text,

41 As regards the concept of "grounds" for war and its terminology (in particular, regarding the difference between the terms *prophasis* and *aitia*), cf. among many others, Deichgräber (1933), de Romilly (1947: 23), Pearson (1952), Kirkwood (1952), Schuller (1956), Andrewes (1959), Momigliano (1966), Schäublin (1971), de Ste. Croix (1972), Pearson (1972: 52–58), Rawlings (1975), Sealey (1975), Nikitas (1976), Robert (1976), Heubeck (1980), Pouncey (1980), Rhodes (1987), Ostwald (1988: 1–2), Garlan (1989), Richardson (1990), Rood (1998: 208–210), Rawlings (2007: 13–16).

42 Polybius seems to make a similar terminological distinction and states (3.6–7): διόπερ αἰτίας μὲν τὰς πρώτας ῥηθείσας ἡγητέον τοῦ πρὸς τοὺς Πέρσας πολέμου, πρόφασιν δὲ τὴν δευτέραν, ἀρχὴν δὲ τὴν Ἀλεξάνδρου διάβασιν εἰς τὴν Ἀσίαν ("Here we have, first the grounds [*aitias*] for making war against the Persians; second, the reasons [*prophasin*]; lastly, Alexander's expedition to Asia as its origin [*arkhe*]"). However, the meaning of *prophasis* here is different and Thucydides does not speak about *arkhe*.

43 On the other hand, note that when mentioning Athens' power and the alarm this caused in Sparta as the actual reason, Thucydides sees the war as inevitable, the result of impersonal factors that reflect the *anangkai* or the necessities of war. This interpretation is offered by Dawson (1996: 89).

44 Walzer (1992 [1977]: 5–12) deals with the event from a realist perspective, in terms of the concept of "need".

they argue that there is a rule accepted by gods and men that provides for the imposition of the strongest over the weakest (5.105.2):

ἡγούμεθα γὰρ τό τε θεῖον δόξῃ τὸ ἀνθρώπειόν τε σαφῶς διὰ παντὸς ὑπὸ φύσεως ἀναγκαίας, οὗ ἂν κρατῇ, ἄρχειν· καὶ ἡμεῖς οὔτε θέντες τὸν νόμον οὔτε κειμένῳ πρῶτοι χρησάμενοι, ὄντα δὲ παραλαβόντες καὶ ἐσόμενον ἐς αἰεὶ καταλείψοντες χρώμεθα αὐτῷ, εἰδότες καὶ ὑμᾶς ἂν καὶ ἄλλους ἐν τῇ αὐτῇ δυνάμει ἡμῖν γενομένους δρῶντας ἂν ταὐτό.	For of the Gods we believe, and of men we know, that by a law of their nature wherever they can rule (*kratei*) they will. This law (*nomon*) was not made by us, and we are not the first who have acted upon it; we did but inherit it, and shall bequeath it to all time, and we know that you and all mankind, if you were as strong (*dynamei*) as we are, would do as we do.[45]

The power (κράτος, *kratos*) to carry out a conquest is in this passage interpreted by the Athenians as an established law (*nomos*). Note that the invasion of Melos (which, indeed, ended in the total destruction of the island) is justified under a legitimizing discourse: the rule that allows the most powerful to exercise its dominion—it is alleged—was not created by the Athenians themselves, but rather previously accepted by others in accordance with religious standards. At least in Thucydides' reconstruction of the diplomatic speech, the Athenians claim not to have been the first to apply that rule. The argument whereby the Melians would behave in the same way if they were the most powerful should also be taken into account, as it exempts the Athenians from specific responsibilities and, instead of isolating them in their decision, puts them in a position where a series of precedents support the intended action. Even though it is known that the strongest can impose upon the less powerful, it is also true that the Athenians feel the need to clarify that this principle was not drafted by them for their private benefit, but resulted from a continuous historical tradition.[46]

45 Translation by Jowett (1881).

46 As mentioned above, I will later analyze self-defense. I will show that the claim that the other party has attacked first is put forward in Greek sources with remarkable consistency.

3 Considerations on Guilt, Responsibility, Motivation and Encouragement: Helen's Case

In the early legendary period described by the Trojan epic cycle, Homeric references to the barbarism of warfare (e.g., the bloody episodes occurring as the Argive army fights the forces of King Priam) are very frequent. However, this apparent excess in acts of war does not exclude the existence of formal regulations and mechanisms designed to regulate (and mitigate) the effects of hostilities. From their earliest origin, confrontations were discursively preceded by a solemn unilateral statement about the opening of conflict, as well as by an explanation of the reason that motivated the beginning of war. This is especially evident in the first great epic of Western literature: the *Iliad* (attributed to the poet Homer) and, in particular, in the discussion about Helen's abduction and its aftermath as the origin of a legitimate war conducted by the Greek cities against Troy.[47]

It could be held that the concern for finding a logical explanation for the origins of hostilities is present in the first texts of the Hellenic civilization. In narrating the events related to the ninth year of the siege of the city of Troy by the Achaean army, the *Iliad* focuses on responsibility for war. The confrontation between Greeks and Trojans was mythically conceived to have been brought about by the abduction of Helen—wife of Menelaus, King of Sparta—carried out by Paris—son of Priam, monarch of Troy. The epic story reveals the uncertainties that surrounded female guilt.[48] Whereas Helen is found guilty by the Trojan elders at the Scaean Gates—not so much for her actions as for her beauty—, shortly afterwards the Trojan sovereign addresses the girl to absolve her of any responsibility whatsoever (3.161–165):

ὣς ἄρ' ἔφαν, Πρίαμος δ' Ἑλένην ἐκαλέσσατο φωνῇ·
δεῦρο πάροιθ' ἐλθοῦσα φίλον τέκος ἵζευ ἐμεῖο,
ὄφρα ἴδῃ πρότερόν τε πόσιν πηούς τε φίλους τε·

So they said, but Priam spoke, and called Helen to him: "Come hither, dear child, and sit before me, that thou mayest see thy former lord and thy kinsfolk and thy people—thou art nowise to blame (*aitie*) in my eyes; it is the gods, methinks, that

47 A recent survey of opinions on Helen's responsibility can be found in Gómez Seijo (2017: 9–45).

48 Cf. Roisman (2006).

οὔ τί μοι αἰτίη ἐσσί, θεοί νύ μοι αἴτιοί εἰσιν οἵ μοι ἐφώρμησαν πόλεμον πολύδακρυν Ἀχαιῶν·	are to blame (*aitioi*), who roused against me the tearful war of the Achaeans …".[49]

In any case, Helen's exoneration from guilt (*aitia*) does not entail a lack of motivation for the outbreak of war. On the contrary, through a single verse, Priam liberates her from responsibility only in order to identify those he considers the true promoters of the armed struggle: the divinities. The grounds for conflict are no longer human but divine, and there remains the urgent need to find some sort of explanation.

The evidence of the *Iliad* is not isolated, and literary opinions about Helen's responsibility are not rare. Thus, in a lyrical fragment dated around the early sixth century, the poet Alcaeus from Lesbos said that "as the story (λόγος, *logos*) points out, due to bad actions, the bitter curse fell on Priam and his sons for your sake, Helen".[50] Furthermore, in the fifth century, the sophist Gorgias of Leontinoi produced an interesting rhetorical exercise—the so-called "Encomium of Helen"—, where he aimed to present different arguments to release Menelaus' wife from guilt for having caused the Greek-Trojan confrontation. The power of the word (*logos*) as a legitimating element is of the utmost importance from the beginning of the speech.[51] Inasmuch as there is a condemning discourse for Helen, Gorgias drafts a counterargument seeking to "release this woman of bad reputation from responsibility" (τὴν μὲν κακῶς ἀκούουσαν παῦσαι τῆς αἰτίας, 2) and trying to identify reasons to put her in a special position of vulnerability and inaction.[52] In any event, guilt—or lack thereof—is determined by the strength of the discourse and created by *logos*.[53]

As regards the origin of the Greco-Persian Wars in the early fifth century, Herodotus turned once again to the famous story about Helen in order to show

49 Translation by Murray (1924).

50 Fr. 42 (Voigt, 1971).

51 This text includes an explicit explanation of the relation between discourse and the truth, alleging that false words give rise to disorder in the city; fr. 11 (1); cf. Diels and Kranz (1952).

52 Gorgias contends that Helen was abducted by Paris because of fate, because of the decision of the gods, because of persuasion of words or the power of love. In any event, she is exempted from guilt. Note that, when Helen is released from responsibility, guilt must be rhetorically based upon other factors; cf. the analysis of the text by MacDowell (1982).

53 Regarding the literary tradition on the character of Helen, see Calame (2000: 145–168).

to what extent the Persian kings mocked the reasons traditionally given by the Greeks to justify their attack (1.4.1–4):[54]

τὸ δὲ ἀπὸ τούτου Ἕλληνας δὴ μεγάλως αἰτίους γενέσθαι· προτέρους γὰρ ἄρξαι στρατεύεσθαι ἐς τὴν Ἀσίην ἢ σφέας ἐς τὴν Εὐρώπην. [2] τὸ μέν νυν ἁρπάζειν γυναῖκας ἀνδρῶν ἀδίκων νομίζειν ἔργον εἶναι, τὸ δὲ ἁρπασθεισέων σπουδήν ποιήσασθαι τιμωρέειν ἀνοήτων, τὸ δὲ μηδεμίαν ὤρην ἔχειν ἁρπασθεισέων σωφρόνων· δῆλα γὰρ δὴ ὅτι, εἰ μὴ αὐταὶ ἐβούλοντο, οὐκ ἂν ἡρπάζοντο. [3] σφέας μὲν δὴ τοὺς ἐκ τῆς Ἀσίης λέγουσι Πέρσαι ἁρπαζομενέων τῶν γυναικῶν λόγον οὐδένα ποιήσασθαι, Ἕλληνας δὲ Λακεδαιμονίης εἵνεκεν γυναικὸς στόλον μέγαν συναγεῖραι καὶ ἔπειτα ἐλθόντας ἐς τὴν Ἀσίην τὴν Πριάμου δύναμιν κατελεῖν. [4] ἀπὸ τούτου αἰεὶ ἡγήσασθαι τὸ Ἑλληνικὸν σφίσι εἶναι πολέμιον.

So far it was a matter of mere seizure on both sides. But after this (the Persians say), the Greeks were very much to blame; for they invaded Asia before the Persians attacked Europe. [2] "We think," they say, "that it is unjust to carry women off. But to be anxious to avenge rape is foolish: wise men take no notice of such things. For plainly the women would never have been carried away, had they not wanted it themselves. [3] We of Asia did not deign to notice the seizure of our women; but the Greeks, for the sake of a Lacedaemonian woman, recruited a great armada, came to Asia, and destroyed the power of Priam. [4] Ever since then we have regarded Greeks as our enemies".[55]

The text clearly recapitulates, in Persian terms, the use of women's abduction as a reason for war, which is understood as an act of folly, injustice and lack of prudence. Herodotus' text explains Persian enmity, which was conceived from ancient times as the result of the destruction of Trojan power; again the underlying idea is that the construction of responsibility falls, once again, within the realm of discourse (*logos*).

On the other hand, Herodotus suggested that the reasons for Persia's going to war were reducible to Atossa's words, which persuaded her husband—King Darius—to attack the Greek cities (3.134.1–2):

54 Husby (2009: 31) holds that "This judgment implies that for Herodotos there was a rubric for judging the justifications for war and that the Trojan War had failed it".

55 Translation by Godley (1920).

ὦ βασιλεῦ, ἔχων δύναμιν τοσαύτην κάτησαι, οὔτε τι ἔθνος προσκτώμενος οὔτε δύναμιν Πέρσῃσι. οἰκὸς δὲ ἐστὶ ἄνδρα καὶ νέον καὶ χρημάτων μεγάλων δεσπότην φαίνεσθαί τι ἀποδεικνύμενον, ἵνα καὶ Πέρσαι ἐκμάθωσι ὅτι ὑπ' ἀνδρὸς ἄρχονται. ἐπ' ἀμφότερα δέ τοι συμφέρει ταῦτα ποιέειν, καὶ ἵνα σφέων Πέρσαι ἐπίστωνται ἄνδρα εἶναι τὸν προεστεῶτα, καὶ ἵνα τρίβωνται πολέμῳ μηδὲ σχολὴν ἄγοντες ἐπιβουλεύωσί τοι.

O King, although you have so much power you are idle, acquiring no additional people or power for the Persians. The right thing for a man who is both young and the master of great wealth is to be seen aggrandizing himself, so that the Persians know too that they are ruled by a man. On two counts it is in your interest to do this, both so that the Persians know that their leader is a man, and so that they be occupied by war and not have time to plot against you.[56]

In this passage—which echoes the Athenians' arguments regarding the attack on Melos—, Atossa assumes that wars of conquest are natural and fair, and she explains that war against the Greeks is inevitable. The king had to display power to his own population in order to divert attention and guarantee his dominance. Almost in Machiavellian terms, the queen's speech is striking: on the one hand, it is one of the only instances in which Greek sources convey women's opinion about the justification of war. On the other hand, it is pronounced in the privacy of a palace context. That fact suggests emphatic criticism by Herodotus, who again played with the opposition between alleged *causae belli* and true intentions. By situating these real arguments in a domestic environment, without Greek presence, the historian revealed the actual basis for war: when the grounds are not openly stated in public, but rather concealed behind apparently more tolerable motives, historiographical fiction can clearly present in the first person the less diplomatic (but more accurate) reasons for Persian expansion through the Aegean Sea.

In the last quarter of the fifth century, in the midst of the Peloponnesian War, the playwright Aristophanes resorted to a comic appeal to female guilt in order to provide a humorous justification for the confrontation between the Athenians and Spartans. In verses 523–529 of *Acharnians* (staged in 425), the origin of the fearsome confrontation between the most powerful *poleis* of the time is found in the abduction—not of Helen—but of some women of profligate life:

56 Translation by Godley (1920).

καὶ ταῦτα μὲν δὴ σμικρὰ κἀπιχώρια,
πόρνην δὲ Σιμαίθαν ἰόντες Μεγαράδε
νεανίαι κλέπτουσι μεθυσοκότταβοι·
κᾆθ' οἱ Μεγαρῆς ὀδύναις πεφυσιγγωμένοι
ἀντεξέκλεψαν Ἀσπασίας πόρνα δύο·
κἀντεῦθεν ἀρχὴ τοῦ πολέμου κατερράγη
Ἕλλησι πᾶσιν ἐκ τριῶν λαικαστριῶν.

Now that, to be sure, was trivial and purely local; but then some cottabus-playing young rakes went to Megara and stole a whore named Simaetha. After that the Megarians, garlic-stung by the smart, stole two whores of Aspasia's in retaliation. And from that broke forth the origin (*arkhe*) of the war upon all Greeks: from three prostitutes.[57]

In a strategy inherent to the comic genre, the traditional legitimating discourse (and the reference to the Megarian decree, which possibly caused the Peloponnesian War)[58] is subverted by the presence of a vulgar tone that parodies political justifications for hostile acts carried out by the Greeks. Also in *Birds*—a comedy that (in the year 414) puts on stage an armed fight for supreme power between birds and the gods—, Aristophanes makes fun again of those who try to initiate a war inspired by female characters: "Are we going to make war for one single woman?" (ἡμεῖς περὶ γυναικὸς μιᾶς πολεμήσομεν;, 1639). It is striking that in this passage, the numeral μιᾶς appears to indicate that it would be only one single woman: indeed, what the comedy ultimately criticizes in a ridiculous manner is that war is declared here because of a specific woman, instead of many women, as if a greater number of them would stand as more effective grounds for hostilities. It is, undoubtedly, staunch criticism of discourse legitimating war.[59]

In that work, in a spirit of profound irreverence, the confrontation between Cloudcuckooland (*Nephelokokkygia*) and Olympus is presented as a sacred war that could break out as a result of the enemy's failure to stop and think (554–556):

57 Translation by Sommerstein (1980).

58 This Athenian decree prevented Megarians from accessing imperial ports and Attic markets; cf. Thucydides 1.139. As regards its true relevance in the origin of war, see Thucydides 1.67. On these references and their parody in Aristophanes, see Rebuffat (2000: 20).

59 For a study of the ways in which comedy makes fun of legalistic discourse in wartime diplomacy during the Peloponnesian War, cf. Buis (2008).

κἄπειτ᾽ ἢν τοῦτ᾽ ἐπανεστήκῃ, τὴν ἀρχὴν τὸν Δί᾽ ἀπαιτεῖν· κἂν μὲν μὴ φῇ μηδ᾽ ἐθελήσῃ μηδ᾽ εὐθὺς γνωσιμαχήσῃ, ἱερὸν πόλεμον πρωὐδᾶν αὐτῷ …	And when that's set up, you demand the rulership back from Zeus; and if he says no and is unwilling and doesn't immediately concede defeat, you proclaim a holy war (*hieron polemon*) against him …[60]

Hence, it is possible to establish that the sources progressively build an argumentative approach aimed at conceiving the justice of war. Focusing the debate on Helen's (voluntary or forced) action with respect to the origin of the Trojan War poses the question as to the pervasiveness of the need to explain the causes of military action (or reject them) through a discourse (*logos*) that is religiously and politically effective.[61]

4 Exoneration from Responsibility for the Attack: The Adversary's Fault

Greek sources insist on emphasizing that all parties to a conflict sought to escape responsibility for declaring war.[62] Thus, in *Politics*, Aristotle described several reasons for considering hostilities commenced, then explained how responsibility could be escaped (Book 7, 1333b37–1334a2):

τήν τε τῶν πολεμικῶν ἄσκησιν οὐ τούτου χάριν δεῖ μελετᾶν, ἵνα καταδουλώσωνται τοὺς ἀναξίους, ἀλλ᾽ ἵνα πρῶτον μὲν αὐτοὶ μὴ δουλεύσωσιν ἑτέροις, ἔπειτα ὅπως ζητῶσι τὴν ἡγεμονίαν τῆς ὠφελείας ἕνεκα τῶν ἀρχομένων, ἀλλὰ μὴ πάντων δεσποτείας· τρίτον δὲ τὸ δεσπόζειν τῶν ἀξίων δουλεύειν.	The proper object of practising military training is not in order that men may enslave those who do not deserve slavery, but in order that first they may themselves avoid becoming enslaved to others; then so that they may seek suzerainty for the benefit of the subject people, but not for the sake of world-wide despotism; and thirdly to hold despotic power over those who deserve to be slaves.[63]

60 Translation by Sommerstein (1987).

61 The discourse about war and its legitimation is ubiquitous in classical Athens, as shown by Raaflaub (2001).

62 Adcock and Mosley (1975: 202). See also Dewald (2013: 38–40).

63 Translation by Rackham (1944).

Setting aside the reference to slavery (considered by Aristotle and his contemporaries as a natural phenomenon), we can detect in the passage a series of legitimate justifications for war. The first argument is concerned with the need to defend against an imposition by others. Instead of attacking in order to put enemies in a servile position, Aristotle restricted war to counter-attack in case of external aggression. The second argument, which is related to territorial expansion and the establishment of dominance, could echo Atossa's words when she claimed that Darius needed to consolidate his hegemony. However, the Aristotelian discourse does not focus on the rulers' interest in perpetuating their dominance over their subjects. Hegemony is rather understood in terms of the realization of the common good.[64] War is made as long as it benefits the community as a whole. The third argument is concerned with an imperative of nature: given that certain men are to be slaves, masters must impose themselves through the use of force.

If we take into account the careful organization of the Aristotelian argument, it should not surprise us that justification by defensive war—mentioned in the passage—ranks first. Indeed, Aristotle privileges hostilities that are justified in terms of a retaliation for a prior attack.[65]

In *Birds*, Aristophanes showed Peisetaerus' interest in making it clear that it was not he who initiated hostilities, expressing this in a speech (1596–1601) that establishes a criterion for determining what is just (*dikaion*):

64 At the beginning of *Politics*, Aristotle conceived the *polis* as a community (*koinonia*) of interests united in the pursuit of the common good (1252b–1253a). Man is a political animal to the extent that he takes part in that common good and seeks to achieve it for the benefit of all.

65 Note that Resolution No. 3314 XXIX of the United Nations General Assembly states at the beginning of Article 2 that "the *first use* of armed force by a State in contravention of the Charter shall constitute *prima facie* evidence of an act of aggression". Regarding the conditions that must apply in order to consider a "first strike" as an act of aggression, see May (2008: 93). Article 51 of the Charter allows a State to respond to an earlier use of force in the following terms: "Nothing in the present Charter shall impair the inherent right of collective or individual self-defense if an armed attack occurs against a member of the United Nations, until the Security Council has taken the measures necessary to maintain international peace and security." We might suppose that the fact that it is an "inherent" right allows it to be conceived as an "earlier customary international law right" (Gray, 2000: 86) and, therefore, to claim its existence since archaic times.

ἀλλ᾽ οὔτε πρότερον πώποθ᾽ ἡμεῖς ἤρξαμεν πολέμου πρὸς ὑμᾶς, νῦν τ᾽ ἐθέλομεν, εἰ δοκεῖ, ἐάν τι δίκαιον ἀλλὰ νῦν ἐθέλητε δρᾶν, σπονδὰς ποιεῖσθαι. τὰ δὲ δίκαι᾽ ἐστὶν ταδί, τὸ σκῆπτρον ἡμῖν τοῖσιν ὄρνισιν πάλιν τὸν Δί᾽ ἀποδοῦναι …	Well, in the beginning we never initiated hostilities against you, and now we are willing, if you wish, to make a peace treaty—if, that is, you are prepared, even so late, to do what is right. And what is right is the following: that Zeus should restore the sceptre to us, the birds, again.[66]

The passage is significant as it points out the need not to be identified as the originator of the belligerent situation. However, perhaps the clearest example of the operation of the discourse of self-defense can be found in historiography, rather than in Athenian theater. The initial part of Thucydides' history of the Peloponnesian War includes a discursive confrontation between the Corcyraeans and Corinthians about the siege of Epidamnus and the origin of the conflict between them.

Thucydides relates (1.23–43) that Epidamnus—a city of Illyria founded by the Corcyraeans—was threatened by exiled aristocrats. Its inhabitants asked Corcyra for support, but their claim was unsuccessful. Therefore, they immediately asked for Corinthian help, since the Corinthians had also played a role in the establishment of the city. When the Corinthians showed up to assist them, the Corcyraeans, who had previously refused to intervene, sent twenty-five ships to demand readmission of the exiles by the Epidamnians. With their ships at the port, they were ready to begin hostilities (1.26.5):

προσκαθεζόμενοι δὲ τὴν πόλιν προεῖπον Ἐπιδαμνίων τε τὸν βουλόμενον καὶ τοὺς ξένους ἀπαθεῖς ἀπιέναι: εἰ δὲ μή, ὡς πολεμίοις χρήσεσθαι. ὡς δ᾽ οὐκ ἐπείθοντο, οἱ μὲν Κερκυραῖοι -ἔστι δ᾽ ἰσθμὸς τὸ χωρίον- ἐπολιόρκουν τὴν πόλιν …	They sat down before the city, and made proclamation that any Epidamnian who chose, and the foreigners, might depart in safety, but that all who remained would be treated as enemies. This had no effect, and the Corcyraeans proceeded to invest the city, which is built upon an isthmus.[67]

Hence, the Epidamnians were besieged by the Corcyraeans. As a result, the Corinthians devoted themselves to preparing a military expedition to free the city. After learning about those preparations, Corcyra chose to send a diplo-

66 Translation by Sommerstein (1987).

67 Translation by Jowett (1881).

matic embassy to Corinth in order to request withdrawal of their troops, claiming that Epidamnus "was none of their business". They offered to submit the matter to arbitration in order to define who the colony belonged to, making it clear that, should the Corinthians reject this solution, there would be sufficient grounds for possible military action (1.28.3):

πόλεμον δὲ οὐκ εἴων ποιεῖν· εἰ δὲ μή, καὶ αὐτοὶ ἀναγκασθήσεσθαι ἔφασαν, ἐκείνων βιαζομένων, φίλους ποιεῖσθαι οὓς οὐ βούλονται ἑτέρους τῶν νῦν ὄντων μᾶλλον ὠφελίας ἕνεκα.	But they deprecated war, and declared that, if war there must be, they would be compelled by the Corinthians in self-defence to discard their present friends and seek others whom they would rather not, for help they must have.[68]

The Corinthians, however, sent a herald to declare war (1.29) in the year 435 and confrontation occurred on the high seas, facing the promontory of Leucimna; the Corcyraeans were victorious and controlled the sea. Defeated, the Corinthians intensively devoted themselves to shipbuilding in order to organize a counter-attack. The citizens of Corcyra were frightened by those preparations and, since they had signed no agreement with either the Athenians or the Spartans at that time, they submitted to the former a proposal for a defensive alliance. Upon learning this, the Corinthians sent an embassy to Athens as well. Thucydides presents two opposing speeches before the Athenian Assembly. Both speeches contain interesting ideas about the nature of "just war", as each of the parties to the conflict tries to justify its actions and, at the same time, to characterize any action by the enemy as illicit. Once again, there is an effective rhetorical use of *ius ad bellum*.

The Corcyraeans appealed to the desirability of helping the victims of aggression (1.32.5–1.33.1):

ἐπειδὴ δὲ μείζονι παρασκευῇ ἀπὸ Πελοποννήσου καὶ τῆς ἄλλης Ἑλλάδος ἐφ' ἡμᾶς ὥρμηνται καὶ ἡμεῖς ἀδύνατοι ὁρῶμεν ὄντες τῇ οἰκείᾳ μόνον δυνάμει περιγενέσθαι, καὶ ἅμα μέγας ὁ κίνδυνος εἰ ἐσόμεθα ὑπ' αὐτοῖς,	But now they are on the point of attacking us with a much greater force which they have drawn together from the Peloponnesus and from all Hellas. We know that we are too weak to resist them unaided, and may expect the worst if we fall into their hands. We are

68 Translation by Jowett (1881).

ἀνάγκη καὶ ὑμῶν καὶ ἄλλου παντὸς ἐπικουρίας δεῖσθαι, καὶ ξυγγνώμη εἰ μὴ μετὰ κακίας, δόξης δὲ μᾶλλον ἁμαρτίᾳ τῇ πρότερον ἀπραγμοσύνῃ ἐναντία τολμῶμεν. γενήσεται δὲ ὑμῖν πειθομένοις καλὴ ἡ ξυντυχία κατὰ πολλὰ τῆς ἡμετέρας χρείας, πρῶτον μὲν ὅτι ἀδικουμένοις καὶ οὐχ ἑτέρους βλάπτουσι τὴν ἐπικουρίαν ποιήσεσθε …

therefore compelled to ask assistance of you and of all the world; and you must not be hard upon us if now, renouncing our indolent neutrality which was an error but not a crime, we dare to be inconsistent. To you at this moment the request which we are making offers a glorious opportunity. In the first place, you will assist the oppressed and not the oppressors …[69]

When an illicit action is characterized by the verb ἀδικέω (*adikeo*, "to commit an injustice"), the distinction between the active voice (that which is rejected and attributed to the enemy) and the passive voice (used to recognize oneself as the object of an injustice: *adikoumenois*) is essential for constructing a polarity that defines the opposing "us"/"them" in terms of "fair"/"unfair", of "aggressor"/"victim".[70] Self-justification is supplemented by the ascription to enemies of reprehensible actions. The Corcyraeans claimed that their opponents, instead of resorting to a peaceful solution to the controversy such as the one proposed, immediately chose to launch an unreasonable attack (1.34.2):

ὡς δὲ ἠδίκουν σαφές ἐστιν· προκληθέντες γὰρ περὶ Ἐπιδάμνου ἐς κρίσιν πολέμῳ μᾶλλον ἢ τῷ ἴσῳ ἐβουλήθησαν τὰ ἐγκλήματα μετελθεῖν.

And the injustice of their conduct to us is manifest: for we proposed an arbitration in the matter of Epidamnus, but they insisted on prosecuting their quarrel by arms and would not hear of a legal trial.[71]

The Corinthian response to the accusations of Corcyra's envoys is brief and it answers the accusation of having initiated an unjustified war; the Corinthians say it is the Corcyraeans who are guilty of injustice (again, the verb *adikeo*) (1.37.1):

69 Translation by Jowett (1881).

70 Debnar (2011) rhetorically analyzes this passage and arrives at the conclusion that "responsibility belongs to the implied agent of the passive participle and verb" (2011: 122–123).

71 Translation by Jowett (1881).

ἀναγκαῖον Κερκυραίων τῶνδε οὐ μόνον περὶ τοῦ δέξασθαι σφᾶς τὸν λόγον ποιησαμένων, ἀλλ᾽ ὡς καὶ ἡμεῖς τε ἀδικοῦμεν καὶ αὐτοὶ οὐκ εἰκότως πολεμοῦνται, μνησθέντας πρῶτον καὶ ἡμᾶς περὶ ἀμφοτέρων οὕτω καὶ ἐπὶ τὸν ἄλλον λόγον ἰέναι, ἵνα τὴν ἀφ᾽ ἡμῶν τε ἀξίωσιν ἀσφαλέστερον προειδῆτε καὶ τὴν τῶνδε χρείαν μὴ ἀλογίστως ἀπώσησθε.	Since these Corcyraeans have chosen to speak, not only of their reception into your alliance, but of our misdoings and of the unjust war which has been forced upon them by us, we too must touch on these two points before we proceed to our main argument, that you may be better prepared to appreciate our claim upon you, and may have a good reason for rejecting their petition.[72]

The Corinthians explain the true reason for the Corcyraeans' prior refusal to make an agreement[73] and justify their actions also on the basis of self-defense and the underlying principle of proportionality: "We did not send an extraordinary army against them without having been injured in an extraordinary way" (οὐδ᾽ ἐπιστρατεύομεν ἐκπρεπῶς μὴ καὶ διαφερόντως τι ἀδικούμενοι, 1.38.4). It is noticeable that the discourse around Epidamnus (both the Corcyraeans' and Corinthians') focuses on the justification of each side's own acts as intended to respond to an earlier injustice on the part of the other. These arguments allow us to understand that the explicit appeal to "just war" was probably frequently used as an apologetic resource at the time.

The resort to a claim of self-defense also appears, for instance, when Thucydides puts a prayer in the mouth of Archidamus—the Spartan king—before the attack on Plataea (2.74). His prayer includes a specific attempt to prevent his army from being seen as the aggressor:

θεοὶ ὅσοι γῆν τὴν Πλαταιίδα ἔχετε καὶ ἥρωες, ξυνίστορές ἐστε ὅτι οὔτε τὴν ἀρχὴν ἀδίκως, ἐκλιπόντων δὲ τῶνδε προτέρων τὸ ξυνώμοτον,	O ye Gods and heroes who possess the land of Plataea, be our witnesses that our invasion of this land in which our fathers prayed to you when they conquered the Persians, and which

72 Translation by Jowett (1881).

73 "They pretend that they have hitherto refused to make alliances from a wise moderation, but they really adopted this policy from a mean and not from a high motive. They did not want to have an ally who might go and tell of their crimes, and who would put them to the blush whenever they called him in." (φασὶ δὲ ξυμμαχίαν διὰ τὸ σῶφρον οὐδενός πω δέξασθαι: τὸ δ᾽ ἐπὶ κακουργίᾳ καὶ οὐκ ἀρετῇ ἐπετήδευσαν, ξύμμαχόν τε οὐδένα βουλόμενοι πρὸς τἀδικήματα οὐδὲ μάρτυρα ἔχειν οὔτε παρακαλοῦντες αἰσχύνεσθαι, 1.37.2).

ἐπὶ γῆν τήνδε ἤλθομεν, ἐν ᾗ οἱ πατέρες ἡμῶν εὐξάμενοι ὑμῖν Μήδων ἐκράτησαν καὶ παρέσχετε αὐτὴν εὐμενῆ ἐναγωνίσασθαι τοῖς Ἕλλησιν, οὔτε νῦν, ἤν τι ποιῶμεν, ἀδικήσομεν· προκαλεσάμενοι γὰρ πολλὰ καὶ εἰκότα οὐ τυγχάνομεν. ξυγγνώμονες δὲ ἔστε τῆς μὲν ἀδικίας κολάζεσθαι τοῖς ὑπάρχουσι προτέροις, τῆς δὲ τιμωρίας τυγχάνειν τοῖς ἐπιφέρουσι νομίμως.	you made a propitious battle-field to the Hellenes, has thus far been justified, for the Plataeans first (*proteron*) deserted the alliance; and that if we go further we shall be guilty of no crime (*adikesomen*), for we have again and again made them fair proposals and they have not listened to us. Be gracious to us and grant that the real authors (*proterois*) of the iniquity (*adikias*) may be punished, and that they may obtain revenge who lawfully (*nomimos*) seek it.[74]

Our sources reveal the rhetoric of justification.[75] However, at this stage, at least two questions may be raised: Is it possible to draw conclusions regarding the need to justify the use of force based on accounts that reflect authorial invention, on texts that make no explicit mention of the concept of "just war"? And, even if we accept these texts as evidence of contemporary practice, can we reach any definite conclusions despite the lack of a theoretical discourse on the means of justifying war in ancient Greece?

As regards the first question, it should be stated that—even though these historiographical passages embody a plausible discourse—it is not possible to take their content as a reflection of a specific international political reality. However, based on the literary-fictional nature of these *logoi*, it is possible to detect a justification of wartime conduct at the level of language and, therefore, to obtain interesting data. As regards the second question, widespread opinion holds—on reasonable grounds—that these isolated passages would not allow us to infer a concept of "just war" in the Hellenic world; at least not to the same extent as in Cicero's works or later with Saint Augustine. However, we may note an extremely interesting passage in the *Rhetorica ad Alexandrum*. This treatise—which lacks a specific date but whose style and format suggest beyond doubt its connection with the Aristotelian school—may suggest that the Greek language already contained specific vocabulary to identify *causae belli* and the main grounds for beginning war. Indeed, a passage in Book 2, 1425a10–21, offers an idea of the sort of justification that must be resorted to when seeking the population's support by rhetorical means:

74 Translation by Jowett (1881).

75 On revenge as another "motivator" of violence, cf. Lendon (2000: 1–3), Nevin (2017: 175).

Προφάσεις μὲν οὖν εἰσι τοῦ πόλεμον ἐκφέρειν πρός τινας αὗται· δεῖ πρότερον ἀδικηθέντας νῦν καιρῶν παραπεπτωκότων ἀμύνασθαι τοὺς ἀδικήσαντας, ἢ νῦν ἀδικουμένους ὑπὲρ ἑαυτῶν πολεμεῖν ἢ ὑπὲρ συγγενῶν ἢ ὑπὲρ εὐεργετῶν, ἢ συμμάχοις ἀδικουμένοις βοηθεῖν, ἢ τοῦ τῇ πόλει συμφέροντος ἕνεκεν ἢ εἰς εὐδοξίαν ἢ εἰς εὐπορίαν ἢ εἰς δύναμιν ἢ εἰς ἄλλο τι τῶν τοιούτων. Ὅταν μὲν οὖν ἐπὶ τῷ πολεμεῖν παρακαλῶμεν, τούτων τε τῶν προφάσεων ὅτι πλεῖστα συνακτέον, καὶ μετὰ ταῦτα δεικτέον, ἐξ ὧν ἔστι περιγενέσθαι τῷ πολέμῳ, ὅτι τὰ πλεῖστα τούτων τοῖς παρακαλουμένοις ὑπάρχοντά ἐστιν.[76]

The pretexts (*prophaseis*) for making war on another state are as follow: when we have been the victims (*adikethentas*) of aggression, we must take vengeance on those who have wronged us (*amynasthai tous adikesantas*), now that a suitable opportunity has presented itself; or else, when we are actually being wronged (*adikoumenous*), we must go to war on the behalf of our kindred or benefactors; or else we must help our allies when they are wronged (*adikoumenois*); or else we must go to war to gain some advantage for the city, in respect either of glory, or of resources, or of strength, or of something similar. When we are exhorting any one to go to war we must collect as many of these pretexts (*prophaseon*) as possible, and afterwards show that those whom we are exhorting possess most of the advantages which brings success in warfare.[77]

The passage—a suggested repertoire of excuses—[78] reproduces the same terminology contained in the texts we have considered, leading us to suppose the existence of a well-established customary discourse in belligerent rhetoric: it is necessary to rely on as many elements as possible to strengthen the argument and be released from responsibility.[79] The value of constructing effective motivations for initiating war is clear, and the attempt to delineate "just" causes for attack may reflect real incentives that remain unspoken (glory, wealth, or power). A speech by the orator Andocides (*On the Peace*, 3.13) can be useful in comparative terms as it also departs from specific considerations to provide information on what should be thought of as a just act of war:

---

76 The Greek text corresponds to Bekker's edition (1837).

77 Translation by Forster (1924).

78 Garlan (1989: 20) also defines it as an armory of disparate justifications.

79 The issue here is one of harmonizing what is fair and what is advantageous, two very frequent concepts in the sophistical debate around diplomacy and war; cf. Dawson (1996: 81–83).

φασὶ δέ τινες ἀναγκαίως νῦν ἡμῖν ἔχειν πολεμεῖν· σκεψώμεθα οὖν πρῶτον, ὦ ἄνδρες Ἀθηναῖοι, διὰ τί καὶ πολεμήσωμεν. οἶμαι γὰρ ἂν πάντας ἀνθρώπους ὁμολογῆσαι διὰ τάδε δεῖν πολεμεῖν, ἢ ἀδικουμένους ἢ βοηθοῦντας ἀδικουμένοις.	Now it is argued by some that present circumstances oblige us to continue fighting. Let us begin, then, gentlemen, by considering exactly why we are to fight. Everyone would agree (*pantas anthropous homologesai*), I think, that war is justified only so long as one is either suffering a wrong oneself or supporting the cause of another who has been wronged (*boethountas adikoumenois*).[80]

Here, Andocides recognizes the validity of self-defense or defense of third parties as an explanation for the conduct engaged in.

5 A 'Legal' Rhetoric of Self-Defense?

I have already examined Greek sources and their recourse to self-defense as a common mechanism in belligerent discourse. It is now time to prove that appealing to self-defense, based on considerations of a non-legal nature, was nevertheless among the Greeks the result of normative principles. We should start with a passage by Thucydides, where the Plataeans address the Spartans to explain their enmity with Thebes (3.56.2):

πόλιν γὰρ αὐτοὺς τὴν ἡμετέραν καταλαμβάνοντας ἐν σπονδαῖς καὶ προσέτι ἱερομηνίᾳ ὀρθῶς τε ἐτιμωρησάμεθα κατὰ τὸν πᾶσι νόμον καθεστῶτα, τὸν ἐπιόντα πολέμιον ὅσιον εἶναι ἀμύνεσθαι, καὶ νῦν οὐκ ἂν εἰκότως δι᾽ αὐτοὺς βλαπτοίμεθα.	They came, not only in time of peace, but at a holy season, and attempted to seize our city; we righteously and in accordance with universal law (*ton pasi nomon*) defended ourselves and punished the aggressor; and there is no reason why we should now suffer for their satisfaction.[81]

What is the meaning of this "universal right" mentioned by the Plataean representatives that sets forth the principle that one can defend against an aggressor? A series of recent studies, which have attempted to reassess the complex nature of interstate relations in the Greek world,[82] has succeeded in demon-

80 Translation by Maidment (1968).

81 Translation by Jowett (1881).

82 *Inter alia*, we may emphasize the preliminary works by Phillipson (1911), Martin (1940),

strating that the conduct of foreign relations and the creation of a close network of legal connections with other cities constituted one of the elements that most clearly characterized sovereign power in classical *poleis*,[83] and that this activity adhered to specific legal regulations. Indeed, the existence of genuine customary "inter-*polis*" or "panhellenic" legal practices, capable of regulating permitted conduct among organized Greek communities and proscribing improper behavior, reveals a normative order. Such an order was more general than that of domestic systems (each *polis*' legal regime) so, *mutatis mutandis*, it was not so different from modern international law. Hence, when the sources employ expressions such as the "law of the Greeks" (νόμος τῶν Ἑλλήνων, *nomos ton Hellenon*), "common law" (νόμος κοινός, *nomos koinos*) or the "law of all men" (νόμος πάντων τῶν ἀνθρώπων, *nomos panton ton anthropon*),[84] they are describing a legal system similar in many aspects to what the Romans will identify as *ius gentium*.[85]

In the next chapter, I will thoroughly discuss the scope of the concept of "common law" by studying the legal rules applicable to armed conflict. It will suffice here to say that the use of force has its regulatory basis in the classical Greek period, given that self-defense is presented in numerous passages as theoretically supported by a legal framework rooted in a shared legal system. For example, when the Corinthians concluded their speech before the Athenians, they said that their arguments (including references to self-defense) were formulated pursuant to that common legal basis (1.41.1):

Tenekides (1956 and 1993), Bickerman (1950), Mosley (1972 and 1973) and Adcock and Mosley (1975), most of whom have already been mentioned. Supporting a broader perspective on the phenomenon, Low (2007) points out the presence of a conceptual framework of legal rules, beliefs and expectations that underlay the development of interstate relations among Greek cities.

83 "Each independent polis had its own territory, its own citizenry and government, and its own defense capacity; each, in theory at least, pursued its own foreign policy, and claimed to enjoy an ostensibly equal standing to other States in the Hellenic community. That community, in turn, was constituted not only by a common culture, but by an intricate web of legal relationships" (Sheets, 1994: 53). As regards the "international" feature of such a system, see Ago (1982). On the complexity of these foreign policy links in classical times, especially after the development of a polarity between Athena's democratic regime and Sparta's oligarchy, see MacMullen (1963).

84 Cf. Bonucci (1903). Wogasli (1895) has dealt particularly with the general issue raised by these expressions, though to a large extent his conclusions have been overtaken by historiographical criticism and new philological studies. On this vocabulary, see Ilari (1980: 101–103).

85 Phillipson (1911, i: 57–58), Bederman (2001: 38). This idea is enlarged by Buis (2012) and will be discussed more emphatically in the next chapter of this work.

δικαιώματα μὲν οὖν τάδε πρὸς ὑμᾶς ἔχομεν ἱκανὰ κατὰ τοὺς Ἑλλήνων νόμους …	Such are the grounds of right which we urge; and they are sufficient according to the laws of the Greeks.[86]

Similarly, when addressing the Spartans in the year 427, Plataea's envoys hold that taking aggressive action without having previously been a victim of an attack is contrary to "inter-*polis*" law (3.59.1):

οὐ πρὸς τῆς ὑμετέρας δόξης, ὦ Λακεδαιμόνιοι, τάδε, οὔτε ἐς τὰ κοινὰ τῶν Ἑλλήνων νόμιμα καὶ ἐς τοὺς προγόνους ἁμαρτάνειν οὔτε ἡμᾶς τοὺς εὐεργέτας ἀλλοτρίας ἕνεκα ἔχθρας μὴ αὐτοὺς ἀδικηθέντας διαφθεῖραι.	These things, O Lacedaemonians, would not be for your honour. They would be an offence against the common laws of the Greeks (*ta koina ton Hellenon nomima*) and against your ancestors. You should be ashamed to put us to death, who are your benefactors and never have done you any wrong, in order that you may gratify the enmity of another.

In view of other sources, this passage from Thucydides allows us to conclude that self-defense was evidently safeguarded by law and accepted under the legal system then in force.

Summation: Restraining the Use of Armed Force

In Book 1 of Plato's *Laws* (626a), Cleinias states that peace, in its common usage, is nothing but a mere name (ὄνομα, *onoma*) since nature dictates that the ordinary behavior of a city towards all other *poleis* is that of "undeclared war" (πόλεμος ἀκήρυκτος, *polemos akeryktos*).[87] The passage reveals that very often the situation was one of unspoken aggression, veiled (by rhetoric) under

86 Translation by Jowett (1881) with minor corrections, both here and in the next passage.

87 ἣν γὰρ καλοῦσιν οἱ πλεῖστοι τῶν ἀνθρώπων εἰρήνην, τοῦτ' εἶναι μόνον ὄνομα, τῷ δ' ἔργῳ πάσαις πρὸς πάσας τὰς πόλεις ἀεὶ πόλεμον ἀκήρυκτον κατὰ φύσιν εἶναι. However, it should be said that the Platonic passage reflects a position that the dialogue itself disarticulates; cf. Sidebottom (2004: 56). Literally, a *polemos akeryktos* is an armed conflict that begins without any herald announcing it (Corvisier, 2014a: 62). As regards the concept of "undeclared war with no truce" (πόλεμος ἄσπονδος)—about which evidence is scarce—, we should also take into account Herodotus 5.81 (in relation to the attack of the Aeginetans against the Athenians) and Demosthenes 18.262. For the particular meaning of the concept in the Greek context, and a thorough analysis of all its appearances in texts, see Stouder (2006: 210–213).

the name of peace (*eirene*).[88] However, when open confrontation occurs, war must be "spoken", thus resulting in the need to translate it into words in order to describe its nature, causes and effects. Recognition of the "just" status of conduct is, therefore, a discursive artifice that legitimizes one's own rational conduct through reference to others' excesses.[89]

If, as argued by some authors, "just war" is indeed a legitimating myth,[90] that is so in the most archaic sense of the term. It is a myth because it constitutes a foundational account for the origins of violence, becoming a discursive creation that—mediated by religious and political aspects—manages to convey an argument or a position. While myths are always political and religious, the timeless and legendary account of "just war" in the context of the ancient Greek cities is also legal, because it results from an interpretation of a normative order. Hence, even though there was no prohibition against the use of armed force in the Hellenic world, city-states had to vest their acts with legitimacy, justifications and divine support.

The object in this chapter has been to examine different sources from classical Greece in order to understand that in the sixth and fifth centuries there already existed genuine discursive strategies designed to legitimize military action in defensive terms. Ultimately, it seems certain that ancient sources develop a true apologetic *logos*, which serves as a precedent for current uses.

We should not be surprised that this continuity in justifying the decision to wage war—despite notorious differences between classical panhellenic law and post-Westphalian international law—will allow us to expand some lines of thought regarding the functionality of the "just war" concept, its rhetorical efficacy, its apologetic role and its strategic use as supportive discourse at a political-legal level.

The Greek example presents us with a situation in which, in the case of interstate armed conflicts, if something does not seem to conform to law, it must at least be persuasively constructed and presented through language as fair. If in the area of "just war", as mentioned above, the last shall be the best (one should

88 As regards the semantic scope of the concept of *eirene*, see Algarza Roldán (1998: 123–152) and Santi Amantini (1985: 45–68).

89 In the Greek world, Sidebottom (2004: 56) states that the recourse to war is "unproblematic" as long as there was always a justification for such actions: the enemy had certainly committed an unfair act against one's *polis* or the allies, and that constituted sufficient grounds to legitimate an armed incursion. See also Neff (2005: 35).

90 Gordon Fiala (2008).

never admit having been the *first*), the principle is reversed in historical terms and the *first* are those who established the final basis for legitimacy. Indeed, it seems that, since the records left by the Greeks (the first people in Western civilization to have resorted to a specific legitimation of armed conflict), little progress has been made in terms of *ius ad bellum* for pragmatically establishing the grounds that would "authorize" armed attacks against those who are identified as enemies. Therefore, there is a great apologetic continuum that unites the past and the present under the same language and—even more disturbing—subserves the same unaltered and permanent will to conceal the true intentions of the powerful and to use the *logos* for strengthening the ultimate foundations of their authority.

Complementing these sources, the next chapter will explain that the abovementioned regulation of the use of force (*ius ad bellum*) should be supplemented with a series of rules used for defining *ius in bello*. Many sources from classical Greece reveal that *poleis* regulated interstate violence through common legal principles, such as proportionality and distinction, which are precisely those sustaining contemporary international humanitarian law.

The Conduct of War and Its Limits in Inter-*polis* Law

ἔνθά κ' ἔτι μείζων τε καὶ ἀργαλεώτερος ἄλλος
πὰρ Διὸς ἀθανάτοισι χόλος καὶ μῆνις ἐτύχθη,
εἰ μὴ Ἀθήνη πᾶσι περιδείσασα θεοῖσιν
ὦρτο διὲκ προθύρου, λίπε δὲ θρόνον ἔνθα θάασσε,
τοῦ δ' ἀπὸ μὲν κεφαλῆς κόρυθ' εἵλετο καὶ σάκος ὤμων,
ἔγχος δ' ἔστησε στιβαρῆς ἀπὸ χειρὸς ἑλοῦσα
χάλκεον· ἣ δ' ἐπέεσσι καθάπτετο θοῦρον Ἄρηα·

Then would yet greater and more grievous wrath and anger have been stirred between Zeus and the immortals, had not Athena, seized with fear for all the gods, sped forth through the doorway, and left the throne whereon she sat, and taken the helm from the head of Ares and the shield from his shoulders; and she took from his strong hand the spear of bronze, and set it down, and with words rebuked furious Ares.

HOMER, *Iliad* 15.123–127 (tr. MURRAY)

∴

In light of our discussion in the previous chapter, it seems impossible to deny that the negotiation of agreements among various city-states or political units proved to be an effective means of regulating the many economic and commercial connections that developed throughout Mesopotamia and the Mediterranean Sea. In fact, given the profusion of interstate relationships that we can discern among the peoples of the Near East and among the Greek *poleis*, it was always necessary to have recourse to written instruments and longstanding customs in order to establish the expected rules of conduct for parties acting in good faith and, ultimately, to control the actions of allies or potential enemies by delineating predictable rules of behavior.[1] Although some works on

1 Chaniotis (2004) reaches this conclusion after examining evidence on the modes of territorial acquisition in Greek antiquity. See also Johnston (2008: 188).

 | DOI: 10.1163/9789004363823_006

this topic mention the importance of these regulations but fail to make use of the original documents, we have seen that a precise understanding of the ancient legal norms requires a survey of the primary sources, many of which reveal the theoretical understanding that the ancient peoples themselves had of the nature and scope of their "international law".

As I have said, it is far from the case that relations between Greek political communities were structured exclusively around the uncontrolled imposition of physical force, and a number of recent studies have sought to reassess the complex nature of interstate relations in the Greek world and to define their legal aspects. As a result of such investigations, it now seems clear that the conduct of foreign relations and the creation of a dense network of legal ties between States was one of the most conspicuous expressions of the sovereign power of the classical *polis*: there was not merely limitless cruelty and a lack of constraints.[2] In many cases, however, the restrictions on warfare were not an obstacle to hegemonic ambitions, insofar as a respect for ethical formulas was not necessarily incompatible with the exercise of power.[3]

In chapter 1, I discussed in some detail the performative character of the process of law-making and its relationship to the judicial and theatrical spheres: we saw that they were all examples of mass spectacles that operated as creators of civic consciousness and opportunities for the exercise of citizenship. In this chapter, that same perspective will be extended to the military sphere; here too we shall find definite rules and models of regulatory behavior.

In order to understand the institutional character of military activity, I must begin by noting the presence of social rituals related to war. Armed conflict was shaped by a series of formalities ranging from the military service of the young ἔφηβοι (*epheboi*)[4] to the organization of the Athenian forces under ten generals (στρατηγοί, *strategoi*) and the division of the army into battalions or τάξεις (*taxeis*, each under the leadership of a taxiarch).[5]

As in other cities, the military forces of Athens were based on the presence of the heavily-armed citizen-infantryman called the hoplite (ὁπλίτης, *hoplites*).[6]

2 On the political-legal bonds between city-states as a precedent for modern diplomatic limitations, see Gómez Mampaso and Sáenz de Santa María Gómez Mampaso (2001: 25).

3 Dawson (1996: 72).

4 Cf. Vidal-Naquet (1991: 123–207).

5 Most writers believe that the the *taxis* was a military unit similar to a modern regiment, internally cohesive and conducive to a sense of equality among its members. A minority group, recently represented by Crowley (2012: 79), has begun to argue that in fact it was a temporary organization, tactically advantageous but unable to produce solidarity among those who constituted it.

6 Cf. Windrow (1985). On the debates concerning its origin, see Sage (1996: 27).

The hoplite originated in the seventh century, apparently as a result of the prosperity of farmers who began to claim greater participation in the affairs of the city; in fact, the hoplite corresponds to a definite social reality and a particular civic ideology.[7]

The existence of hoplites as the military force *par excellence* gave rise—in the era when the civic organization of the *polis* was emerging—to the particular model for the conduct of hostilities that we see in Greek military history. In this new social context there appears a very distinctive type of land combat, in which battles (subject to a regime of strict discipline) reproduce a collective dynamic of predictable formalities whereby the staging of war becomes a scrupulously detailed ritual.[8] Many books have been dedicated to describing the establishment of this new military reality, beginning with a "hoplite revolution" at the beginning of the seventh century.[9] A change in the status of infantry and an increasing sophistication among the population of small farmers would have been the factors that made this new state of affairs possible.[10]

The idea of the phalanx (φάλαγξ, *phalanx*)—a rectangular formation of soldiers advancing together with spears and shields—is connected to the development of hoplite armament[11] and demonstrates the level of tactical organization involved in the conduct of warfare.[12] With the institution of combat between phalanxes, the battle became a true theater of operations: it required rehearsal in advance and it was strictly regulated[13] and planned according to a pre-established arrangement.[14] It is possible to imagine the deployment of troops in the presence of the enemy as a ritualized competition between equiv-

7 On the hoplite as a citizen and his social context, cf. Ridley (1972: 508–548). On his importance for the *polis*, see Cartledge (1997: 11–27), Salmon (1977: 84–101), Holladay (1982: 94–103), Cawkwell (1989: 375–389) and Mitchell (1996: 87–105).

8 The testimonies are numerous: Thucydides 5.66–70; Herodotus 6.111–112, 7.104, 9.31, among others. On this hoplite "tactical" order, see Anderson (1970: 94–110).

9 Regarding this "hoplite revolution," one may consult Ducrey (1986: 45–79). Some have spoken out against this characterization: Hanson (1999: 235) maitains that there was neither a revolution nor a reform but the speeding-up of a gradual transition from Homeric to hoplite warfare. Krentz (2002: 23–39), meanwhile, has maintained that hoplite ideology developed only in the fifth century.

10 Cf. Salmon (1977: 95). On the characteristics of these warriors, see Gillespie (2011, 1: 16).

11 On this topic, see Snodgrass (1965: 110–122) and Hanson (1991a: 63–84). One may also consult the work of van Wees (1994: 1–18 and 131–155).

12 Cf. Detienne (1968: 119–142).

13 Ober (1996[a]: 56–60). See also Dayton (2006).

14 Cf. Pritchett (1971: 134–143).

alent forces that, in its practiced harmony, left little room for the element of surprise.[15] Aristotle pointed out that hoplites became useless outside a formation (ἄνευ μὲν γὰρ συντάξεως ἄχρηστον τὸ ὁπλιτικόν, *Politics* 4.1297b) and that this new military reality corresponded to an extension of political and citizen rights to the middle class.[16]

In the line of development that runs from primitive disorganization to the establishment of good order (εὐταξία, *eutaxia*) within a formation, the standardization of face-to-face combat in units—a sort of aggregation of individual combats—in place of aristocratic personal confrontation constitutes one of the aspects of the emergence of the hoplite model.[17]

We have recently come to understand to what extent battle in the Greek world was governed by rituals both military and religious.[18] On the basis of an anthropological reading of the phenomenon of war, it has been argued that the celebration of military success was produced by rituals, monuments, and ideological concepts, with the aim of generating emotional participation and solidarity through certain common normative values.[19] Despite the current polyvalence of the term "ritual," which is criticized in some fields as an imprecise theoretical concept, it cannot be denied that war was marked by a continuous progression of routine stages determined by formalized moments and gestures that were coherent, often religious, and sometimes subject to variation in different parts of the Greek world.[20] Among these regular and uniform actions, the sources clearly mention the habitual recourse to oracles and the military prayer before the beginning of a campaign; the sacrifices and the "challenge" or duel for the commencement of hostilities;[21] and the dedication of enemy armor, the distribution of spoils, the burial of the fallen, and the final

15 Garlan (1999: 27), Raaflaub (1999: 140–141).

16 Debate has arisen concerning the actual connection between the appearance of the hoplite and the political change in the rights of citizens. Scholars such as van Wees (1995: 170–171) have denied this link. On this issue, cf. Rawlings (2013: 18–19), who presents the various theoretical perspectives on the logic underlying the "hoplite revolution."

17 Krentz (1985a). The system was based on τιμή (*time*), "honor".

18 "In particular the Greek sources mention an institution of notable interest: the formally arranged battle as a means of resolving disputes" (Whitman, 2012: 31). See also Lonis (1979: 7–8). On the religious nature of these rituals, see Parker (2016: 130).

19 Hölscher (2003: 13–14). Burkert (1984: 47), for his part, conceives of military ritual as self-affirmation by a masculine society in search of survival strategies. This point of view has been developed by Connor (1988), who identifies war as a type of symbolic expression.

20 Tompkins (2013: 527).

21 Herodotus 6.110; Thucydides 6.63.3, 7.3.1, to take just a few examples.

sacrifice at the conclusion of combat. The setting-up of a trophy in the event of victory is also part of these ritualized displays.[22]

In the balanced system of *poleis*, the contending powers confronted one another in war in the same way that litigants presented their arguments in court or actors played their roles in the theater, in a true discursive dispute or ritualized *agon*.[23] In this "Greek way of war" the performance of hostilities is structured by a respect for definite legal norms, formal or informal.[24] This military *agon* has been examined in terms of a symbolic competition.[25] The operation of this performative isomorphism in Greek culture is remarkable. Thus, for example, the accuser in a court case is typically represented as a combatant, and vice versa. This can be seen even in the vocabulary that is used: "to accuse," in Greek, is represented by the verb διώκειν (*diokein*, "pursue"), "to defend oneself" is φεύγειν (*pheugein*, "flee"), and "to be convicted" can be expressed by ἁλίσκεσθαι (*haliskesthai*, "to be captured").[26] It is clear that the metaphors of the military and judicial *agones* overlap to create an omnipresent image of combat and that these two conflicts are, in that respect, shaped by similar models of action. If the male citizen who participates in the city's public activities such as the Assembly and the courts is, in essence, the soldier of the *polis*, then it should not be surprising that masculinity (which turns a man into the lord or *kyrios* of his family and thus into a political subject in his own right) is constructed on the basis of meritorious and honorable conduct on the battlefield.[27] Bravery (ἀνδρεία, *andreia*) is a value associated with the male (ἀνήρ, *aner*) and it conditions the rules of his behavior in the public sphere, both in peacetime and in the (more common) times of war.[28] Thus, we see the affirmation of a code of honor in which citizenship itself is implicated.[29] This explains why the natu-

---

22 A ritual appropriation of spaces for military remembrance can also be noted; cf. Monaco (2015: 153–175).

23 An extensive bibliography on the analysis of Greek culture's performative logic was presented in chapter 1.

24 Lombardo (2002: 43–67).

25 Hanson (1991b), Connor (1988: 3–29).

26 du Bouchet (2012: 66).

27 Crowley (2012: 87, 92).

28 Shipley (1993: 13) adapts a famous dictum of Clausewitz and argues that war is the continuation of the symposium (συμπόσιον) by other means: we must bear in mind that the symposium in the Greek world was a highly ritualized institution based on interactions among male aristocrats. On the symposium as an institution based upon strict ties of sociability, see Murray (2009: 508–523), Vetta (1999: 96–105) and Osborne (2014: 34–60).

29 Robinson (2006: 11–34).

ralized violence of the masculine finds definite limits in respect for the rule of law, to the point where any aggression against a citizen could be—and should have been—channeled into the alternative sphere of legal proceedings.[30]

From certain pieces of evidence, we can infer that a considerable number of informal "rules of engagement"[31] were recognized and eventually applied in intra-Hellenic conflicts—i.e., those in which the barbarians did not play a role—and remained part of the institutional practice of war until at least the middle of the fifth century. These were a result of the consolidation of the archaic social hierarchy and the underlying logic of the hoplite combat formation based on the class of small peasants: we can perceive a Greek code of honor that sought victory through shared social norms[32] that were designed to protect the interests of the hoplite class.[33] It has been pointed out that the prevailing *nomoi* in the archaic period sought to protect the farmers by preventing others from taking part in combat and by reducing, by means of limitations on the nature and duration of the fighting, the costs associated with large military campaigns.

But can we say in all cases that these rules were expressed as positive obligations in law? Some authors have sought to stress that even in pre-classical times there were no "rules" in the legal sense but only military tactics and religious considerations which had no legal significance[34] and which were systematically violated after the appearance of democratic regimes. Others, by contrast, have attempted to demonstrate the existence of a set of rules of conduct.[35] Many of the latter, such as Ober (1994), have argued for the presence, in the seventh and sixth centuries, of normative limits on war as a result of the generalization of the hoplite model—because the need for military discipline justified the suppression of acts of violence. Many of these scholars, however, are of the opinion that these rules were abandoned during the second half of the fifth century.[36] This occurred as a consequence of the elimination of social inequalities, the exceptional character of the two great adversaries in the Peloponnesian War, the asymmetry of the armies that met in battle, and the impres-

30 Cf. Demosthenes 21.71–75; see Fisher (1998).

31 Ober (1994).

32 Lanni (2007: 17).

33 Ober (1994: 13). Hanson (1989) speaks of a "hoplite ideal".

34 Krentz (2002), van Wees (2004: 115–150). On religion, see Verzijl (1978: 130).

35 "Battles were intense and bloody affairs, but governed by extensive rules" (Lebow, 2010: 188).

36 For Gondicas and Boëldieu-Trevet (1999: 84), it was in this era that "la structure générale de la 'guerre selon les règles' fut brisée et ne fut jamais ressucitée."

sion made by military confrontations on a grand scale.[37] It has been argued that the great clash in the last quarter of the fifth century pitted two different concepts of war against each other: if the Spartans favored "classic" conflicts of brief duration characterized by the collision of hoplite phalanxes and managed according to traditional rules, the Athenians (who, aiming at empire, employed their naval power in addition to their army) pursued a military strategy that, in the words of Pericles, alienated them from respect for "common" norms (Thuc. 1.140–144).[38]

As we have mentioned, the purpose of the present investigation is to show that war in the classical Greek world was—in spite of excesses in practice—frequently understood and mentioned within a framework of definite limits.[39] Even after the hoplite era, normative restrictions on excessive violence in armed conflicts persist,[40] based perhaps on the progressive development of ideas of panhellenic brotherhood that began in the sixth century and lasted until the fourth.[41]

In this chapter, I submit that an examination of the classical sources—principally from the end of the fifth century—demonstrates that the limited effectiveness of the legal regime (revealed in frequent references to criminal acts in armed conflicts mentioned by authors such as Herodotus, Thucydides, and Xenophon) can by no means be understood as negating the recognition of genuine legal rules and an awareness of moral obligations that can be discerned even in the behavior of both the Athenians and Spartans during the Peloponnesian War.

Below, I present some of the ancient evidence that allows us to identify stable norms—norms considered "common" among the Greeks—and I offer an interpretation in which the identification of explicit references to rules allows us to recognize the "international" character of those rules and their underlying ethical-religious origins. Moreover, it is my objective to show how—at least from the perspective of the theory that underlies these ancient texts—these

37 Hanson (2005: 90). On the new styles of combat that prevailed during the fourth century, see Ober (1985: 37–50).

38 Gondicas and Boëldieu-Trevet (1999: 82), Prost (1999: 81).

39 "En somme, l'effort continu pour tempérer les pratiques guerrières et les effets de la violence serait l'une des facettes du 'miracle grec'. Quoi qu'il puisse se dérouler d'extrême, la guerre est un univers de seuils, de limites." (Payen, 2012: 95).

40 As has been mentioned, this is precisely the thesis of Krentz (2002).

41 Cf. Kiechle (1958). Demosthenes (9.47–51) criticizes the new methods employed by Philip II and Polybius (13.3) feels sorrow for the disappearance of the old rules of pitched battles. Cf. Alonso Troncoso (2007: 218).

laws of war in the Greek world became effective tools of social regulation in accordance with the customary role of *nomos*, the religious basis of its content, and the value that the Greeks accorded to honor (τιμή, time) and social status.[42]

In the following pages, I shall first examine regulations for the performance of armed conflict by looking at speeches that appeal to certain uniform, broadly restrictive normative limits. From there, I shall focus on a number of institutions in order to determine the scope of the common *nomoi*, recognized by the *poleis*, that constrained the escalating violence which threatened to sully the practice of war.[43]

1 Greek Warfare between Military Necessity and Limitation

The language of our texts presents the confrontations between *poleis* as expressions of antagonism, as attacks against an enemy and not as opportunities for cooperation. Verbs such as προσβάλλειν (*prosballein*) and προσφέρεσθαι (*prospheresthai*) mean "attack" and express unidirectional, generally hostile motion; in both cases the prefix προσ- (*pros-*) marks the offensive orientation of one party *against* another. On the other hand, the prefix συν- (*syn-*) means "together with" and is reserved for an ally (σύμμαχος, *symmakhos*, literally "one who fights together with") and never used for enemies.[44]

We cannot deny that various sources recount acts of extreme violence during the Trojan War, and these have led to interpretations that postulate a lack of limits in the conduct of hostilities. In a similar vein, we see the profound dehumanization that resulted from the bloody clashes during the Peloponnesian War,[45] regarded by many as a clear-cut case of "total war."[46] It is usual

---

42 According to Lanni (2007: 2), these are the three factors that explain their effectiveness.

43 Shipley (1993) has maintained that warfare in Greek antiquity—marked by ritual—must be understood within a larger spectrum of organized social violence; from this perspective, as we have seen, the rules of military clashes were similar in meaning to those that were imposed on the celebration of rituals like the symposium.

44 du Bouchet (2012: 70), who also points out that when describing an attack it is usual to employ verbs with the prefix ἐπι- (*epi-*), which lets us see the aggression directed by the attacker *upon* the enemy. This is the case with verbs like ἐπιφέρειν (*epipherein*) and ἐπιεἶναι (*epieinai*).

45 One may mention, by way of example, Thucydides 2.5.7, 2.67.4, 3.32.1, 3.68, and 4.116.3, in addition to the longer descriptions we find in 4.3–41, 7.19–28 and 7.72–87.

46 "… the Peloponnesian War was an ancient equivalent of a 'total war', fought with every means available, affecting virtually the entire Greek world, depriving most communities

to point out, as an example of unconstrained violence, the legendary Spartan fierceness that, according to Thucydides, led them, at the war's outset, to execute as enemies all those whom they captured at sea, whether they were Athenians or Athenian allies or even neutrals (πάντας γὰρ δὴ κατ' ἀρχὰς τοῦ πολέμου Λακεδαιμόνιοι ὅσους λάβοιεν ἐν τῇ θαλάσσῃ ὡς πολεμίους διέφθειρον, καὶ τοὺς μετὰ Ἀθηναίων ξυμπολεμοῦντας καὶ τοὺς μηδὲ μεθ' ἑτέρων, 2.67)—this despite Sparta's supposed preference for traditional, normatively regulated hoplite warfare. In many cases this was answered by the Athenians with cruel acts like the murder of Spartan ambassadors, mentioned in the same passage.

If we read such passages carefully, we may detect the presence of two of the fundamental principles, rooted in tradition, that today sustain the international law regulating armed conflicts: these are the principles of *distinction*—i.e., the need to identify combatants and distinguish them from those who are not participating in hostilities, and to distinguish military objectives from the property of civilians[47]—and of *proportionality*—the conduct of hostilities using means that do not exceed the aim of the conflict, which should be simply to neutralize the enemy, rendering him unable to wage war.[48]

The violation of these limits can be seen in Thucydides' accounts of the taking of women as captives (4.47–48) and the murder of adversaries who supplicate (3.81). There are, of course, several examples of the violent irrationality of the Athenians during the Peloponnesian War, the most notorious of them in the year 416 when, after the surrender of Melos, the Athenians decided to massacre all the men and enslave the women and children (οἱ δὲ ἀπέκτειναν Μηλίων ὅσους ἡβῶντας ἔλαβον, παῖδας δὲ καὶ γυναῖκας ἠνδραπόδισαν), repopulating the land with five hundred settlers (τὸ δὲ χωρίον αὐτοὶ ᾤκισαν, ἀποίκους ὕστερον πεν-

even of the possibility of remaining neutral, displacing tens of thousands of persons, and causing untold miseries. Its after-effects, visible not least in armies of refugees and hordes of unemployed mercenaries, plagued the Greek world for decades to come" (Raaflaub, 2007: 111).

47 Cf. Gutiérrez Posse (2014: 71–73).

48 Gutiérrez Posse (2014: 74–77). It is sufficient to recall here that this principle of proportionality has been recognized since the very beginning of the multilateral codification of the rules of modern humanitarian law, as we can see in the text of the 1868 St. Petersburg Declaration, which prohibited the use of explosive projectiles of less than 400 grams. The text establishes that "the only legitimate object which States should endeavour to accomplish during war is to weaken the military forges of the enemy"; this object "would be exceeded by the employment of arms which uselessly aggravate the sufferings of disabled men, or render their death inevitable" (points 2 and 4).

ταχοσίους πέμψαντες, 5.116.4).[49] A second example comes from the summer of 428 when, after Mytilene revolted and subsequently surrendered, the Athenians held a debate concerning the future of its inhabitants. Initially, the Athenian Assembly ordered the mass execution of all the men.

Both of these wartime events, however, must be considered in context. Our sources suggest that many of the Melian men were allowed to escape and that therefore there were fewer deaths than might have been expected.[50] With respect to Mytilene, the Athenians reversed themselves the following day and revoked the sentence when they saw that what they had decided was savage and excessive (καὶ τῇ ὑστεραίᾳ μετάνοιά τις εὐθὺς ἦν αὐτοῖς καὶ ἀναλογισμὸς ὠμὸν τὸ βούλευμα καὶ μέγα ἐγνῶσθαι, Thucydides 3.36.4).[51] Even for the most serious atrocities we have evidence indicating that there was still some circumspection; it is not surprising, therefore, that it was necessary to produce definite reasons justifying the exercise of violence.

The sophisticated philosophy underlying international humanitarian law today is based on a precise balance between the criteria of humanity, on the one hand, and military necessity, on the other.[52] Similarly, in the context of armed conflict between *poleis* in the second half of the fifth century, there existed a need to explain attacks in terms of *necessity*.[53] Indeed, we may affirm that the

49 This has been described as a documented example of the commission of genocide in antiquity; cf. Chalk and Jonassohn (2010: 98–108).

50 For this reason Bosworth (2012: 21–22) has argued that one cannot call this a massacre in the strict sense of the word. Moreover, Bosworth (1993) had already shown that the Melian dialogue is not only about the Athenians' realism in imposing their power at all costs but also expresses sympathy for the vulnerability of a small city-state confronted by the logic of imperialism. From this perspective, even one of the most violent passages in Greek literature has a "humanitarian" side.

51 "It looks as though the Athenians had little experience of collective executions, and tended to back away when faced with the reality" (Bosworth, 2012: 23). The lively debates on the actions to take are interesting: one faction, led by Cleon, proposed the execution of the Mytilenean men and the enslavement of their women and children (Thucydides 3.37–40), while the other faction, led by Diodotus, suggested, more moderately, that only the city's leaders should be condemned (3.42–48).

52 Schmitt (2010: 796–805).

53 Despite its extreme vagueness—convenient, to be sure, for the States invoking it—military necessity is a key principle of the international law of armed conflict today and functions as an exception to humanitarian norms. Concerning its scope, characteristics, and limitations, cf. Hayashi (2010).

proof that the Greek world had developed a real notion of the rules of war lies precisely in the elaborate arguments from necessity that we see being used in our texts to justify the flouting of the expected guidelines in particular cases.[54] Here again, we see fertile ground for the *rhetorica bellica*.

The behavior of both parties at Delium in the year 424 may illustrate the prevailing mindset. The Athenians under Hippocrates had captured a Boeotian temple (Thucydides 4.76.4), which they converted into a fortification by means of a rampart (4.90). This alteration made an attack on the temple permissible, since property that was civilian in nature was now fulfilling a military function:[55] in the speech of Pagondas, urging the Boeotians to attack the Athenians, there is a clear allusion to the "legality" of this operation (ἀγῶνα ποιεῖσθαι, a phrase that, to return to our performative interpretation, combines judicial and military implications in referring to the confrontation in the same terms as a forensic *agon*).[56] The issue is one of military occupation: we read that the Athenians "crossed the border of our territory to attack us and have built a walled fort; they are, of course, our enemies, wherever we encounter them and from whatever quarter they attack" (τὴν γὰρ Βοιωτίαν ἐκ τῆς ὁμόρου ἐλθόντες τεῖχος ἐνοικοδομησάμενοι μέλλουσι φθείρειν, καὶ εἰσὶ δήπου πολέμιοι ἐν ᾧ τε ἂν χωρίῳ καταληφθῶσι καὶ ὅθεν ἐπελθόντες πολέμια ἔδρασαν, 4.92.1). Encouraged by their general, the Boeotians capture the temple and the Athenians flee (4.96.6–9); a Boeotian herald proclaims, using "a direct legally formulated accusation," that the occupation of the temple was contrary to law.[57]

Among the violations mentioned is the Athenians' contamination of the sacred water in the temple. The Athenian response, which is critical for understanding the means by which wartime actions were vindicated, is that their

54 Bederman (2001: 246).

55 The idea of a "military objective" can be found in current law, in which, according to Article 52.2 of Additional Protocol I to the Geneva Conventions (which reflects traditional international law), "military objectives are limited to those objects which by their nature, location, purpose or use make an effective contribution to military action and whose total or partial destruction, capture or neutralization, in the circumstances ruling at the time, offers a definite military advantage."

56 Allison (2011: 134) examines the use, throughout this episode, of a vocabulary relating to private disputes among neighbors but transposed to the level of international relations: "The Delium episode is thus threaded quasi-metaphorically with elements from a dispute over territory to suggest that what might have been negotiated or arbitrated by neigboring states is rent apart by war" (Allison, 2011: 144).

57 Allison (2011: 139), Corvisier (2000: 104). Later I shall examine the reference in this passage to transgression of the law of the Greeks: ὅτι οὐ δικαίως δράσειαν παραβαίνοντες τὰ νόμιμα τῶν Ἑλλήνων (Thucydides 4.97.2).

act was justified by necessity, since they were compelled to defend themselves from the Boeotians, who had previously invaded their territory (ὕδωρ τε ἐν τῇ ἀνάγκῃ κινῆσαι, ἣν οὐκ αὐτοὶ ὕβρει προσθέσθαι, ἀλλ' ἐκείνους προτέρους ἐπὶ τὴν σφετέραν ἐλθόντας ἀμυνόμενοι βιάζεσθαι χρῆσθαι, 4.98.5).[58] Interestingly, both parties resort to the concept of rules of war that should be respected.[59]

At this point, questions of *ius ad bellum* are interwoven with a genuine justification of the acts permitted *in bello*.[60] The Athenians claim to have done no wrong voluntarily (τῶν ἀκουσίων ἁμαρτημάτων, 4.98.6); they claim that it is only possible to speak of an act contrary to law (παρανομία, *paranomia*) in cases where "evils do not arise from necessity" (ἐπὶ τοῖς μὴ ἀνάγκῃ κακοῖς ὀνομασθῆναι, 4.98.6). In this speech, the Athenians are exonerated from responsibility for the deeds committed during the hostilities: the appeal to military necessity allows the Athenians to justify the occupation and sacrilege in legal terms.[61] Using similar language, Pericles himself will declare to the Athenians that (in Thucydides' words) "one must know that the war is a necessity" (εἰδέναι δὲ χρὴ ὅτι ἀνάγκη πολεμεῖν, 1.144.3).

Force is commonplace in the examples of invasion and conquest recorded by our sources.[62] Since acquisition of territory by force was lawful, it was usual in cases of military occupation to regard the conquered territory as belonging to the occupying power. According to Xenophon (*Cyropaedia* 7.5.73), King Cyrus asserted that there was a permanent law among men to the effect that, when a city was taken from an enemy, both the inhabitants and their property belonged to the conquerors; such acquisition of ownership was just, to the extent that allowing one's enemy to keep something was a result of goodwill rather than legal right (νόμος γὰρ ἐν πᾶσιν ἀνθρώποις ἀΐδιός ἐστιν, ὅταν πολεμούντων πόλις ἁλῷ, τῶν ἑλόντων εἶναι καὶ τὰ σώματα τῶν ἐν τῇ πόλει καὶ τὰ χρήματα.

58 It is interesting that, although the episode may be thought of as an "example of the gradual departure from traditional *nomoi* of conventional warfare" (Evans, 2010: 137), the Athenian justification represents a manipulation of military narrative intended to legalize acts carried out as part of a military strategy.

59 Nevin (2017: 41–47).

60 Of course, the distinction between *ius ad bellum* and *ius in bello*, which is now clear in terms of regulatory *corpora* and responsibility did not exist as such in the ancient Greek world. As I argued in the last chapter, limitations on wartime behavior, which aim at ensuring a "just" struggle, arise from practices connected with the legality of initiating hostilities and with the restriction of the hostilities themselves.

61 "So the occupation and sacrilege and the rest, were committed under conditions of war" (Allison, 2011: 141).

62 Cf. Guizzi (1997) and Chaniotis (2004).

οὔκουν ἀδικίᾳ γε ἕξετε ὅ τι ἂν ἔχητε, ἀλλὰ φιλανθρωπίᾳ οὐκ ἀφαιρήσεσθε, ἥν τι ἐᾶτε ἔχειν αὐτούς).[63] Contrary to such attitudes, however, are some examples in our texts where the rules of the occupied territory are respected: when the Athenian commander Timotheus took possession of Corcyra, instead of subjecting its inhabitants to slavery he allowed them to preserve their own laws (οὐ μέντοι ἠνδραποδίσατο οὐδὲ ἄνδρας ἐφυγάδευσεν, οὐδὲ νόμους μετέστησεν, *Hellenica* 5.4.68).

But to what extent was the nature of war regulated by definite limits at the international level? Another (late) passage reveals in broader terms the debate surrounding the legality or illegality of wartime behavior. In speaking of the Macedonian attack against Thermus in the year 218, Polybius sets forth a new classification of the actions taken by the army of Philip V, giving special attention to the various interpretations to which they are subject (5.9):

καὶ ἕως μὲν τούτου πάντα κατὰ τοὺς τοῦ πολέμου· νόμους καλῶς καὶ δικαίως ἐπράττετο· τὰ δὲ μετὰ ταῦτα πῶς χρὴ λέγειν οὐκ οἶδα. λαβόντες γὰρ ἔννοιαν τῶν ἐν Δίῳ καὶ Δωδώνῃ πεπραγμένων τοῖς Αἰτωλοῖς, τάς τε στοὰς ἐνεπίμπρασαν καὶ τὰ λοιπὰ τῶν ἀναθημάτων διέφθειρον, ὄντα πολυτελῆ ταῖς κατασκευαῖς καὶ πολλῆς ἐπιμελείας ἔνια τετευχότα καὶ δαπάνης. οὐ μόνον δὲ τῷ πυρὶ κατελυμήναντο τὰς ὀροφάς, ἀλλὰ καὶ κατέσκαψαν εἰς ἔδαφος. ἀνέτρεψαν δὲ καὶ τοὺς ἀνδριάντας, ὄντας οὐκ ἐλάττους δισχιλίων· πολλοὺς δὲ καὶ διέφθειραν, πλὴν ὅσοι θεῶν ἐπιγραφὰς ἢ τύπους εἶχον· τῶν δὲ τοιούτων ἀπέσχοντο (…) καὶ μεγίστη δὴ καὶ παράστασις ἐπὶ τούτοις εἶχε τόν τε βασιλέα καὶ τοὺς περὶ αὐτὸν φίλους, ὡς δικαίως ταῦτα πράττοντας

Up to this point everything was right and fair by the laws (*nomous*) of war; but I do not know how to characterise their next proceedings. For remembering what the Aetolians had done at Dium and Dodona, they burnt the colonnades, and destroyed what were left of the dedicated offerings, some of which were of costly material, and had been elaborated with great skill and expense. And they were not content with destroying the roofs of these buildings with fire, they levelled them to their foundations; and threw down all the statues, which numbered no less than two thousand; and many of them they broke to pieces, sparing only those that were inscribed with the names or figures of gods. Such they did abstain from injuring. And in fact the king and his staff were fully convinced that, in thus acting, they were obeying the dictates of right and justice (*dikaios*), by retaliating upon the Aetolians with the same impious

63 On the scope of this "règle éternelle dans toute société humaine," cf. Ilari (1990: 100).

καὶ καθηκόντως, ἀμυνομένους τοῖς ὁμοίοις τὴν τῶν Αἰτωλῶν περὶ τὸ Δῖον ἀσέβειαν. ἐμοὶ δὲ τἀναντία δοκεῖ τούτων.

outrages as they had themselves committed at Dium. But I am clearly of an opposite opinion.[64]

Although considerably later than the period of the Peloponnesian War, the passage is significant because it lets us see that, in contrast to certain actions that are considered justified in the context of an armed conflict according to the laws of war (κατὰ τοὺς τοῦ πολέμου· νόμους καλῶς καὶ δικαίως ἐπράττετο), there are other illegal acts that even Polybius does not know how to describe.[65] Interestingly, the text shows us how an outrage committed on the battlefield and strongly characterized as contrary to prudence (σωφροσύνη, *sophrosyne*) goes beyond both legality and discourse: just as there are no legal rules capable of encompassing these behaviors, there are also no words that describe them. They are unspeakable, and therefore are systematically excluded from any mention in laws (*nomoi*) and discourse (*logoi*).

In similar language—which may even suggest intertextual influence—[66] Diodorus (30.18.2) observes that:

πᾶς γὰρ πόλεμος ἐκβεβηκὼς τὰ νόμιμα καὶ δίκαια τῶν ἀνθρώπων, ὅμως ἔχει τινὰς ἰδίους καθαπερεὶ νόμους, οἷον ἀνοχὰς μὴ λύειν, κήρυκα μὴ ἀναιρεῖν, τὸν δὲ σῶμα αὑτοῦ πρὸς τὴν τοῦ κατισχύοντος πίστιν τιμωρεῖσθαι.

For though all warfare is an exception to humane standards of law and justice, even so it has certain quasi-laws of its own: a truce, for example, may not be broken; heralds must not be put to death; a man who has placed himself under the protection of a superior opponent may not be visited with punishment or vengeance.[67]

The term *nomos*—which, as we have seen in the first chapter, is semantically quite imprecise—is used in these passages specifically to express the legal character of standards in question. In the following pages, I shall examine

64 Translation by Shuckburgh (1889).

65 Ilari (1990: 101–102).

66 "La différence entre les deux passages n'est peut-être pas suffisante pour réfuter l'hypothèse d'une dérivation polybienne du passage de Diodore, mais il fallait la mettre en évidence" (Ilari, 1990: 102).

67 Translation by Walton (1957).

to what extent these *nomoi* that Polybius and Diodorus regard as restrictions on all armed conflict are connected to the modern institutions of international humanitarian law.

For the time being, we should understand the extensive diplomatic interactions between the classical *poleis* via networks of political negotiation as an active mechanism designed to avoid the violence of war.[68] Efforts to avoid war, or to stop it once it had begun, show that there existed in the Greek world a willingness to set limits to conflicts and to resolve disputes by peaceful means.[69] The Greek world was familiar with effective diplomacy via envoys. In contrast to the traditional heralds (κήρυκες, *kerykes*) of the archaic period, the *poleis* began from the late sixth century onward to delegate the conduct of their foreign relations and their negotiations with other cities and peoples to special representatives, originally called πρέσβεις (*presbeis*).[70] Etymologically, the name refers to their advanced age,[71] and these ambassadors—as non-professionalized diplomatic agents—[72] were a legal-political institution essentially characterized by the virtues of prudence and wisdom.[73] We possess abundant evidence (epigraphic and literary) from the classical period that allows us to evaluate the significance and rhetorical features of diplomatic contacts by means of these agents.[74] We usually read that the embassies had the

68 According to Rebuffat (2000: 190), the objective of diplomacy is to create the appearance of justice in a sphere characterized by the imposition of force.

69 Raaflaub (2006: 17–18), Buono-Coro Varas (2012: 15) points out that *ius in bello*, in diplomatic law, has the aim of preventing the commission of abuses.

70 Jones (1999: 20). On its general characteristics and the peculiarities of its language, see the interesting contributions of Piccirilli (2001 and 2002).

71 Adcock and Mosley (1975: 152–153).

72 Mosley (1971: 320–321) calls attention to the amateur nature of diplomatic work.

73 "Aux côtés des hérauts ne tardèrent cependant pas à figurer des envoyés, chargés de persuader et de convaincre. De ceux-ci on attendait surtout qu'ils fissent preuve de souplesse et de prudence …" (Garlan, 1972: 27).

74 "Literary and epigraphic evidence from the classical period highlights the fact that the numerous Greek city-states realized the importance of mantaining diplomatic relations among themselves in order to safeguard their interests" (Missiou-Ladi, 1987: 336). Among non-legal texts, historiography may be the privileged genre for the transmission of the lexicon of these diplomatic relations, as Cresci, Gazzano and Orsi (2002) have shown with respect to Herodotus, Thucydides, and Xenophon. Thus, despite the absence of a specialized diplomatic language—as noted by Grant (1965: 262) and Mosley (1971: 320–321)—the literary sources do permit us to identify, in the speeches of ambassadors and envoys, certain relatively stable patterns of behavior (cf. for the fourth century Demosthenes, who describes the qualities required of a good ambassador in his attack on Aeschines in 343

function of making an approach to an enemy and that those who took part in them (usually in groups of three[75]) had to give an account of their mission to the authorities who had appointed them and had to consult their decision before accepting or rejecting a proposal; in the absence of such consultation, they risked severe sanctions.[76]

In spite of their formal obligations and the institutional control over their activity, ambassadors did not always fulfill their role as peacemakers effectively and armed conflicts were common. In the context of actual hostilities, an important consideration is respect for the distinction between those who are directly involved in the fighting and those who, on the other hand, belong to the civilian population and therefore have to be protected from the effects of conflict. Some texts stress the need to fight clearly-defined battles so as to avoid more widespread fighting that could have unjustifiable consequences for innocent people. Herodotus relates that, in the case of a territorial dispute between Sparta and Argos, an agreement was reached: instead of waging a full-scale campaign, they resolved to designate three hundred men to fight on each side, with the understanding that the territory would belong to the victorious party (ἐνθαῦτα συνέβησαν ἐς λόγους συνελθόντες ὥστε τριηκοσίους ἑκατέρων μαχέσασθαι, ὁκότεροι δ᾽ ἂν περιγένωνται, τούτων εἶναι τὸν χῶρον, 1.82.3). In a similar fashion, when the Athenians and Tegeans disputed the position on the left wing of the battle line at Plataea, the latter remembered that one of them, Echemus, had killed Hyllus—the son of Heracles—in a duel after Hyllus had proposed a single combat with fixed conditions in lieu of risking two armies in battle (Herodotus 9.26).[77] The creation of a "theater of operations" away from urban centers can likewise be seen as a way to arrange a military confrontation that does not endanger civilians. Herodotus attributes to Mardonius, who is speaking to King Xerxes as the latter prepares to invade Greece, an interesting description of how the Greeks conduct themselves in battle (Herodotus 7.9):

[19.4–5]). Theater often presents scenes in which actors, appearing in the roles of heralds and envoys, subvert the supposed rules of diplomacy. The literary-dramatic function of such allusions is evident, as is the way in which they play with expectations; cf. Gastaldi (2007) for the case of Euripides' *Children of Heracles* and Buis (2008) with respect to Aristophanes' *Acharnians*.

75 Mosley (1965).

76 Lonis (1969: 66), Bederman (2001: 102) explains: "All Greek envoys were subject to an audit upon return to their homes and any misstep (a lavish gift received, the appearance of collusion, or a promise made in excess of instructions) was severely punished."

77 These passages in Herodotus are among only a few examples of bilateral accords intended to limit the level of violence in armed conflict; cf. Lanni (2007: 4, n. 4).

καίτοι γε ἐώθασι Ἕλληνες, ὡς πυνθάνομαι, ἀβουλότατα πολέμους ἵστασθαι ὑπό τε ἀγνωμοσύνης καὶ σκαιότητος. ἐπεὰν γὰρ ἀλλήλοισι πόλεμον προείπωσι, ἐξευρόντες τὸ κάλλιστον χωρίον καὶ λειότατον, ἐς τοῦτο κατιόντες μάχονται, ὥστε σὺν κακῷ μεγάλῳ οἱ νικῶντες ἀπαλλάσσονται· περὶ δὲ τῶν ἑσσουμένων οὐδὲ λέγω ἀρχήν· ἐξώλεες γὰρ δὴ γίνονται· τοὺς χρῆν ἐόντας ὁμογλώσσους κήρυξί τε διαχρεωμένους καὶ ἀγγέλοισι καταλαμβάνειν τὰς διαφορὰς καὶ παντὶ μᾶλλον ἢ μάχῃσι·	Yet the Greeks are accustomed to wage wars, as I learn, and they do it most senselessly in their wrongheadedness and folly. When they have declared war against each other, they come down to the fairest and most level ground that they can find and fight there, so that the victors come off with great harm; of the vanquished I say not so much as a word, for they are utterly destroyed. Since they speak the same language, they should end their disputes by means of heralds or messengers, or by any way rather than fighting.[78]

Despite the annihilation of the enemy (which clearly would violate the principle of proportionality mentioned earlier), the passage suggests an apparent respect for the principle of distinction: the selection of an isolated plain indicates an attempt to "close off" the physical location of the battle, setting limits to its geographic scope.[79] In light of my reflections in chapter 1 concerning the performative nature of participation in citizenship, this passage seems to refer to genuine examples of "ritual combat," which we may set beside other agonistic contests.[80] We also see mention of a preference for peaceful methods rather than violence as a way of settling disputes: we may be reminded of current legal standards which, since the Kellogg-Briand Pact of 1928, have proscribed war as a means of resolving disputes at the international level.

We should also note that the institution of capitulation (which, as a solemn ritual, formally ended the state of war and limited the effects of hostilities) became commonplace in the Hellenic world. Arising from moral considera-

78 Translation by Godley (1920).

79 There is even textual evidence concerning the identification of combat areas, the existence of neutral zones (such as Delphi, under the protection of the Amphictyonic Countil), and undefended sites (such as Alalcomenae, in Boeotia, which was respected out of reverence for Athena and which was always protected from armed attack; this city was never destroyed, despite being unwalled, as Strabo 9.2.36 relates).

80 Debidour (2002: 60).

tions and unwritten law, capitulation served, for example, to avoid the disastrous consequences of a city's destruction.[81]

In a similar fashion, the institution of the truce (σπονδαί, *spondai*) served to enforce certain temporary immunities in times of armed conflict; this was theoretically done under the sanction of religion but it was motivated by considerations of a political nature.[82] A clear example of this phenomenon was the famous Olympic law (ὁ Ὀλυμπιακὸς νόμος) decreeing that it was illegal to attack military objectives during the celebration of the various panhellenic games.[83] In the year 420 the Eleans excluded the Spartans from the temple at Olympia during the Olympic games because they refused to pay the fine imposed upon them for having attacked the fortress of Phyrcon and sent soldiers into Lepreum in the period of the truce (οὐκ ἐκτίνοντες τὴν δίκην αὐτοῖς ἣν ἐν τῷ Ὀλυμπιακῷ νόμῳ Ἠλεῖοι κατεδικάσαντο αὐτῶν φάσκοντες ⟨ἐς⟩ σφᾶς ἐπὶ Φύρκον τε τεῖχος ὅπλα ἐπενεγκεῖν καὶ ἐς Λέπρεον αὐτῶν ὁπλίτας ἐν ταῖς Ὀλυμπιακαῖς σπονδαῖς ἐσπέμψαι, Thucydides 5.49). The Spartans, however, objected that the truce had not yet been proclaimed at Sparta when their troops entered Lepreum (λέγοντες μὴ ἐπηγγέλθαι πω ἐς Λακεδαίμονα τὰς σπονδάς, ὅτ' ἐσέπεμψαν τοὺς ὁπλίτας) and they claimed that the hostilities had ceased as soon as the truce was proclaimed.

To summarize, formalities for the initiation and conclusion of hostilities (whose legality or illegality I examined in the previous chapter), interruptions for religious reasons such as truces, and the designation of agreed-upon combat zones confirm the indications in our sources that there were extensive normative restrictions to the exercise of armed violence, setting limits to it both spatially and temporally. But to what extent do the rites described in the literary sources have a legal basis? How can we say that the formalities and rules that had to be respected actually imply a law that governed behavior in cases of *polemos*, or armed conflict?

---

81 Ducrey (1985: 237–239). The detailed study of Karavites (1982a: 90), however, shows that we cannot conclude that every capitulation meant the deliberate employment of a policy of moderation by the Greek city-states. Such agreements may instead reflect a calculated assessment of diplomatic interests.

82 Bederman (2001: 252), Nail (2014: 15). On the relationship bewteen truces and the active exercise of diplomacy, cf. Fernández Nieto (1995).

83 Ostwald (1982: 51), Gaurier (2014: 68). Phillipson (1911, ii: 286) explains that "… the institution of the great games, the Olympian, the Isthmian, the Nemean, the Pythian, together with the convening of the solemn general assembly, πανήγυρις, to which all Greek States had access, each sending its representative (θεωρός), did much to promote pacific relationships between the various Hellenic communities, and at the same time to mitigate the rigours of warfare."

2 The Legal Matrix: The Foundations of "Common," "Universal," Inter-*polis*, and Panhellenic Law

In order to answer the question of the legal nature of the limits imposed in wartime, we must briefly look, for purposes of comparison, at the case of Rome; later, we can return to our examination of Greek sources, which are much less widely used in historical studies of law.[84]

The Romans sharply distinguished between *ius civile*, applicable to relations among citizens, and a *ius gentium* whose provisions regulated relations between Romans and foreigners, or even those between Rome and the other peoples—nearby or distant—with whom it came into contact.[85] Perhaps the best evidence for how the Romans themselves understood the distinction between these two branches of law can be found in a well-known passage of Gaius. At the beginning of his *Institutes* (possibly the first manual for the study of Roman law, dating from the second half of the first century CE), the jurist explained that (1.1):

Omnes populi qui legibus et moribus reguntur partim suo proprio, partim communi omnium hominum iure utuntur; nam quod quisque populus ipse sibi ius constituit, id ipsius proprium est uocaturque ius ciuile, quasi ius proprium ciuitatis; quod uero naturalis ratio inter omnes homines constituit, id apud omnes populos peraeque custoditur uocaturque ius gentium, quasi quo iure omnes gentes utuntur. Populus itaque Romanus partim suo proprio, partim communi omnium hominum iure utitur.[86]

The laws of every people governed by statutes and customs are partly peculiar to itself, partly common to all mankind. The rules established by a given state for its own members are peculiar to itself, and are called *ius civile*; the rules constituted by natural reason for all are observed by all nations alike, and are called *ius gentium*. So the laws of the people of Rome are partly peculiar to itself, partly common to all nations.[87]

It is interesting to note that, in this division presented by Gaius with evident didactic intent, *ius gentium* formed an integral part of the law applicable by

84 This is because, traditionally, research into legal history has traced the origin of the modern-day continental legal system to the opinions of the Roman jurists as compiled by Byzantine scholars in the time of Justinian.

85 Cf. Heuss (1933), Frezza (1938–1939), Ziegler (1972), Zack (2001) and Grotkamp (2009).

86 The edition of Poste and Whittuck (1904) is used for the Latin text.

87 Translation by Poste (1904).

Rome and constituted a "common" law that, by its nature, superseded the laws in force in each individual city.[88] Strikingly, it was a legal system whose rules were created by the *urbs* itself—through the institution of the *praetor peregrinus*, a magistrate charged with dispensing justice outside Rome or in cases where outsiders were involved—for the sake of legislating their own relations with foreign populations; the *ius gentium* was, therefore, a sort of common law that did not, however, originate in an accord between different subjects as an expression of shared desire. The expression *ius gentium*, incidentally, appears in a large number of passages,[89] and in many of these it is connected with restrictions in times of war.[90] In the *Digest* of Justinian, for example, an opinion of Pomponius states that "if someone has mistreated an enemy envoy, it is held that this has been done contrary to the law of nations (against *ius gentium*) because envoys are considered sacred."[91]

With this in mind, and coming back to the initial reflections in this book, is it possible to think, *mutatis mutandis*, of a "common" law in force among the city-states and applicable to armed conflicts in the Greek world? The question implies a departure from the historiographic tendencies that for decades have

---

88 Of course, this *ius gentium* was based partially on fetial law, i.e., on the decisions of the *collegium* of fetial priests, whose approval was required in order to declare war. The *ius gentium* lasted until its fusion with the *ius civile* in 212 CE, when the *Constitutio Antoniniana* extended the Roman citizenship to all the inhabitants of the Empire. On *ius ad bellum* in Rome see Buis (2015: 249–274).

89 As Domingo (2010) is concerned to show, another passage in the *Digest* says that Ulpian maintained that "… the law of nations (*ius gentium*) is that by which the peoples are ruled" (D. 1.1.3–4).

90 The book edited by Kingsbury and Straumann (2010), which documents the antecedents of international law in interpretations of the Roman *ius gentium*, shows how these norms acquired new meaning in the theoretical discussions of jurists in early European modernity (sixteenth and seventeenth centuries).

91 D. 50.7.18. The *ius gentium* included a wide range of provisions, which ultimately regulated everything not covered by the laws that formed the *ius civile*: "To this law of nations (*ius gentium*) belong the declaration of war, the separation between different peoples, the foundation of kingdoms, the division of property, the setting of limits to lands, the layout of buildings, commerce, purchases, sales, bids and offers for rent contracts, and the rules governing obligations, except for those that have been introduced by civil law (*a iure civili*)" (Hermogenian at D. 1.1.5). It is clear that, in modern terms, the concept includes provisions specific both to what is defined as public international law (we may mention, for example, *ius ad bellum* and border agreements) and to what is now known as private international law (i.e., the regulation of relations between individuals in which there exists some foreign element, such as in commercial transactions between Romans and foreigners).

led scholars to approach the study of Greek law on the basis of prior familiarity with the Roman legal system. Overcoming the methodological anachronism imposed by Romanist thinking means studying Greek interstate relations according to their own standards and not under the influence of external categories, and this is possible only if we find, among the texts from the Greek period, sources capable of being read so as to suggest a legal regulation of relations between city-states that was conceived of in terms of a "common" law (*nomos koinos*) of the Greeks, an inter-*polis* or panhellenic law.[92]

With respect to *ius in bello*, we should thus determine whether we can identify, from a legal standpoint, common arrangements that establish the traditional rules and rituals relevant to the conduct of hostilities by the armies of the classical *poleis*. To do so, I shall pay special attention to the identification of combatants and the protection of civilians, the treatment of prisoners of war and injured soldiers, the inviolability of religious and other facilities that offer no military advantages, and restrictions on the use of weapons causing unreasonable harm.[93]

Through a survey of the Greek legal norms that refer to a "common law" (rather than local laws) in the matter, I intend to examine not only the consistency of practices among the Greek city-states but also the possible existence of a sense of obligation (*opinio iuris*) with respect to the ancient norms relating to the conduct of hostilities.[94]

3 Geneva in Greece: The *nomos* of the Greeks with Respect to the Protection of Victims and Practices in Wartime

I have considered the theoretical scope of an inter-*polis* law that established a set of rules shared by the Greek city-states; in this section, I shall examine to what extent we find the specific limits defined by *nomos* in the context of the modern institutions defined by the legal corpus known as the "Law of Geneva",

92 Cf. Fernández Nieto (1975: 129, n. 1). Aristotle was aware of the importance of this common legal basis (δίκαιον κοινόν, *dikaion koinon*) in his *Rhetoric* 1.13 (1373b6–9).

93 These are the limitations provided by custom for the rituals of war, according to Debidour (2002: 60–61), but that have strong legal basis: "Cette limitation est juridique: traditionnellement, la guerre doit être motivée, notifiée, et ne peut être menée que dans le cadre de certaines règles ou du moins de certains usages" (Corvisier, 2014b: 93).

94 Alonso Troncoso (2007). For a theoretical approach that enables us to think about the importance of adapting custom to different stages of international relations, one may begin with some reflections offered by Abi-Saab (1987: 53–65).

which protects from attack both non-combatant individuals (i.e., those who are not participating in—or have ceased participation in—hostilities) and civilian property. At present, the protection guaranteed by international humanitarian law—enshrined in the texts of the four Conventions of 1949[95] and the two Additional Protocols of 1977—[96] covers all categories of non-combatants and civilians (especially minors, mothers with small children, journalists, refugees, and religious and medical personnel) as well as those combatants who for some reason have ceased to participate in hostilities (prisoners of war, the injured, the sick, and the shipwrecked).[97]

The principle of distinction, which today is one of the central pillars of international humanitarian law,[98] separates those who are *combatants* from those who are not and protects the latter to the extent that they do not participate directly in hostilities.[99] If dying in battle is, for an ancient Greek citizen, one of the most outstanding acts of virtue (ἀρετή, *arete*) and perhaps the most perfect expression of patriotism,[100] then it should not surprise us that the death of

95 These are the Geneva Convention for the amelioration of the condition of the wounded and sick in armed forces in the field of August 12, 1949 (hereinafter GC-I), 75 U.N.T.S. 31, in force since October 21, 1950; the Geneva Convention for the amelioration of the condition of wounded, sick, and shipwrecked members of armed forces at sea of August 12, 1949 (hereinafter GC-II), 75 U.N.T.S. 85, in force since October 21, 1950; the Geneva Convention relative to the treatment of prisoners of war of August 12, 1949 (hereinafter GC-III), 75 U.N.T.S. 135, in force since October 21, 1950; and, finally, the Geneva Convention relative to the protection of civilian persons in time of war of August 12, 1949 (hereinafter GC-IV), 75 U.N.T.S. 287, also in force since October 21, 1950.

96 These are the first and second Additional Protocols to the Geneva Conventions of August 12, 1949 relating to the protection of victims of international armed conflicts (hereinafter AP-I) and non-international armed conflicts (hereinafter AP-II), respectively 1125 U.N.T.S. 3 and 1125 U.N.T.S. 609. Both treaties entered into force on December 7, 1978.

97 Gutiérrez Posse (2014: 170–198).

98 Cf. Sassòli (2003).

99 According to the Interpretive Guidance developed by the International Committee of the Red Cross (2009), "direct participation in hostilities" must meet the following cumulative requirements: a) the act must be likely to adversely affect the military operation or military capacity of a party to an armed conflict or, alternatively, to inflict death, injury, or destruction on persons or objects protected against direct attack (threshold of harm); b) there must be a direct causal link between the act and the harm likely to result either from that act, or from a coordinated military operation of which that act constitutes an integral part (direct causation); and c) the act must be specifically designed to directly cause the required threshold of harm in support of a party to the conflict and to the detriment of another (belligerent nexus).

100 Cf. Sebillotte Cuchet (2006: 233–242).

enemy combatants did not produce any sort of remorse—a contrast to our modern feelings concerning war.[101] On the other hand, if we leave aside our modern ethical views of the act of killing in combat (which in any case are anachronistic if applied to the ancient world), we can observe that the same Greek sources that describe the deaths of warriors without apparent qualms also condemn almost systematically any attack on those not involved in the conduct of war.[102]

3.1 *Protecting Envoys*

Among formal legal regulations which were based on a clear distinction between the military role and other functions of a logistical or diplomatic nature, we find interesting allusions to the protection of messengers, heralds, and ambassadors. The *keryx* carried a staff and was charged with transmitting messages of peace or war; from Homeric times onward his killing was an extremely grave act.[103] To be sure, such a rule—which has practical effects, in that it allows cooperation and the negotiation of agreements, to the advantage of both parties—[104] has a clear religious basis, insofar as it was believed that envoys were under the protection of Zeus and an attack on them would produce religious consequences.[105] But, to the extent that these two spheres can be separated, a legal dimension must be joined to these religious considerations. An inscription on marble, preserved in two fragments found in the Athenian agora in January, 1937, is significant because it presents us with the legal scope of a precept concerning the good treatment of envoys. The text—which is later than most of our sources but extremely useful—is that of an Athenian decree dating from 367/6 on the subject of diplomatic relations with the Aetolian League; in the decree, it is decided to appoint a representative to demand redress for the illicit detention of some messengers who announced a halt to hostilities for the purpose of celebrating the Eleusinian Mysteries:

101 Crowley (2012: 94–95).

102 To speak of "civilians" in these cases is anachronistic, as Rebuffat (2000: 139) argues; in any case, the old, women, and minors are "ceux qui ne font pas la guerre" and it is appropriate to think of them as "non-combatants."

103 Corvisier (2000: 105). I discussed the role of *kerykes* in p. 153.

104 Lanni (2007: 16), Bryant (2016: 32).

105 According to Pausanias (1.36.3), for example, the Two Goddesses punished the Megarians for having killed the herald Anemocritus when he approached them in order to prevent an armed incursion. On the religious protection of heralds, cf. Sheppard (2005: 921) and Hall (2007: 94).

[Θε]οί / [Δημό]φιλος Θεώρο Κεφαλῆ/[θεν] ἐγραμμάτ[ε]υε *vac.* / ["Εδοξεν τῆ]ι βουλῆι καὶ τῶ[ι] δήμωι· Οἰνηὶς / [ἐπρυτάν]ε[υ]ε· Δημόφιλος Θεώρο Κεφαλῆθε/[ν ἐγραμμ]άτευεν· Φί[λι]ππος Σημαχίδης ἐπ/[εστάτει Π]ολύζηλος [ἦρχ]ε· Κηφισόδοτος ε/[ἶπεν· ἐπει]δὴ Αἰτωλων [τ]οῦ κ[ο]ινοῦ δεξαμέ/[νου τὰς μυ]στηριώτιδ[α]ς [σ]π[ο]νδὰς τῆς Δήμ/[ητρος τῆ]ς ['Ε]λευσινίας καὶ τῆς Κόρης τοὺ/[ς ἐπαγγε]ίλαντας τὰς σπονδὰς Εὐμολπιδ/[ῶν καὶ Κη]ρύκων δεδέκασι Τ[ρ]ιχονείης Πρ/[οφήτην (?) κ]αὶ Ἐπιγένην παρὰ τοὺς νόμους τ/[οὺς κοιν]οὺς τῶν Ἑλλήνων· ἐλέσθαι τὴμ βο/[υλὴν αὐτ]ίκα μάλα κήρυκα ἐξ Ἀθηναίων ἀπ/[άντων ὅστ]ις ἀφικόμενος πρὸς τὸ κοινόν / [τὸ τῶν Αἰτω[λ]ῶν ἀξιώσει τὸς] ἄνδρας ἀφεῖ/[ναι ...[106]

Gods. Demophilus son of Theorus from Cephale was secretary. Resolved by the council and the people. Oeneis was the prytany; Demophilus son of Theorus from Cephale was secretary; Philippus of Semachidac was chairman; Polyzelus was archon (367/6). Cephisodotus proposed: Since the Aetolians of the *koinon* have accepted the truce for the Mysteries of Eleusinian Demeter and of Kore, but those of the Eumolpidae and Kerykes announcing the truce, Promachus and Epigenes, have been imprisioned by the Trichonians, contrary to the common laws of the Greeks (*tous nomous t[ous koin]ous ton Hellenon*), the council shall forthwith choose a herald from all Athenians, who on arrival at the *koinon* of the Aetolians shall demand the release of the men.[107]

In this document—a primary legal source—we plainly see the Athenian desire not to leave unpunished the Trichonians' violation of the physical safety of the peace envoys (σπονδοφόροι, *spondophoroi*), which is presented in the text of the decree as a transgression of universal norms, of those "common" laws that protect sacred messengers (lines 12–13).[108]

As I mentioned in the previous chapter, references in classical-period sources—both literary and epigraphic—to the "law of the Greeks" (*nomos ton Hellenon*), to "common law" (*nomos koinos*), or to "the law of all men" (*nomos panton ton anthropon*) signify something similar to what the Romans will conceptualize as *ius gentium*.[109] Although its content is broad and covers different

106 *Syll.*³ 643 (FD 3.4.75). The Greek text follows the *editio princeps* of Schweigert (1939: 5–7).

107 Translation by Rhodes and Osborne (2003).

108 This is interpreted as a violation of the international law of the period: "This act was a breach of international law, and called forth a formal protest on the part of Athens" (Schweigert, 1939: 8).

109 Allowing, of course, for the relevant differences: while in the Roman world the *ius gentium*

specific situations in the various examples given,[110] the rules in question, established by treaties or—more often—fixed by custom, would have been binding on all *poleis* irrespective of their individual bodies of law.[111]

Our identification of a distinct "international" law in the Greek world is strengthened by an episode in Herodotus's *Histories* related to the Persian Wars. In the passage to which I wish to call attention, the historian emphasizes, in the following terms, the Persian king Xerxes' refusal to resort to retaliation against the Athenians and Spartans who had murdered his heralds (7.136.2):

λέγουσι δὲ αὐτοῖσι ταῦτα. Ξέρξης ὑπὸ μεγαλοφροσύνης οὐκ ἔφη ὅμοιος ἔσεσθαι Λακεδαιμονίοισι· κείνους μὲν γὰρ συγχέαι τὰ πάντων ἀνθρώπων νόμιμα ἀποκτείναντας κήρυκας, αὐτὸς δὲ τὰ ἐκείνοισι ἐπιπλήσσει ταῦτα οὐ ποιήσειν, οὐδὲ ἀνταποκτείνας ἐκείνους ἀπολύσειν Λακεδαιμονίους τῆς αἰτίης.[112]	To this Xerxes, with great magnanimity, replied that he would not imitate the Lacedaemonians. "You," said he, "made havoc of all human law (*ta panton anthropon nomima*) by slaying heralds, but I will not do that for which I censure you, nor by putting you in turn to death will I set the Lacedaemonians free from this guilt."[113]

regulated relations between the *urbs* and foreigners, being imposed by the former upon the latter, the Greek context typically shows us a system of rules created through a balance of power between *poleis* (a *ius inter gentes*) that long precedes the interstate regulation of modern international law. For the Greeks, of course, it was a question of "equality among equals," which entirely excludes barbarians and other non-Hellenic peoples (cf. the habitual reference to "civilized nations" in the world of the late nineteenth and early twentieth century).

110 Ilari (1980: 101–103).

111 Contrary to what many have supposed, these shared rules are, in their character, strictly legal, and are accordingly mandatory; they constitute a law that every city-state must respect if it intends to avoid incurring liability: "En revanche, un système de valeurs cher à un groupe donné, qui se sent différent des autres et supérieur à eux, peut aisément définir un idéal commun. Et, s'il s'agit de corriger la varietés du droit, de cité à cité, s'il s'agit de chercher quelque part, où que ce soit, un ensemble de règles débordant ce cadre, et s'appliquant en particulier aux devoirs simplement humains qui peuvent régir les rapports entre gens de diverses cités, alors on a recours à ce que les auteurs appellent les lois communes des Grecs" (de Romilly, 1971: 39–40). See, in addition, Lanni (2007: 5–6).

112 The Greek text corresponds to the edition of Legrand (1963–1968).

113 Translation by Godley (1920).

These statements, although similar to those in the texts examined in the previous section, are in fact unique. This is because we have here a Greek historian who puts a humane sentiment in the mouth of a barbarian monarch. Xerxes' affirmation that he will not violate "the laws of all men" (*te panton anthropon nomima*)—in contrast to the behavior of the Athenians and Spartans toward the Persian envoys—agrees with the sources already discussed with regard to the existence of universal standards that all Greek city-states are compelled to respect regardless of their domestic constitutions.[114] In this case, however, what is surprising is that the spokesman for these views—in a speech condemning actions taken by Greeks—is a Persian ruler; this is especially remarkable if one takes into account that the "common" law of the Greeks specifically seems to have excluded non-Hellenic civilizations, which were considered to be culturally and politically inferior.[115] There is no simple explanation for this unusual passage: perhaps Herodotus intends a strong criticism of his fellow Greeks. In any case, this passage seems distinct from other references to a "common" law as the legal basis for the rules governing armed conflicts, even if its content does correspond to panhellenic norms.[116] Literary sources usually emphasize a sharp distinction between Greeks and barbarians, often to the point that separation from Hellenic culture implies the absence of law and justice.[117]

Two passages from Euripidean tragedies staged, respectively, at the beginning and end of the Peloponnesian War tend to confirm the idea that barbarian culture is opposed to the law of the Greeks. In *Medea* (431), the character Jason makes it clear to his wife (the play's protagonist) that she is now living in a Greek land and not among barbarians (πρῶτον μὲν Ἑλλάδ᾽ ἀντὶ βαρβάρου χθονὸς / γαῖαν κατοικεῖς); therefore she understands justice and law instead of the power

114 On the treatment and protection of heralds in the Greek world, cf. Lonis (1969: 63–70), Goblot-Cahen (2002). On reprisals and their regulation, cf. Garlan (1972: 22–23).

115 On this construction of the non-Greek foreigner as barbarian, cf. Bacon (1961), Mosley (1971), Dubuisson (2001), Santiago Álvarez (1998). With particular regard to Greco-Persian relations, cf. Picard (1980) and Miller (1997).

116 "... the distinction between 'the laws of the Greeks' and 'the laws of mankind' is not consistently applied, and it is not clear whether there was a shared understanding of precisely which laws applied only to Greeks and which were wider in scope" (Lanni, 2007: 5).

117 A Homeric example is sufficient to demonstrate how the Greeks envisioned this legal deficiency among those who did not share Greek values. In the *Odyssey*, the law of the nascent *poleis* is contrasted with the anarchic world of beasts: the Cyclopes, for example, lack agoras in which to hold councils and make rules; each one of them imposes his own decisions on his children and wives, without regard to the others (9.112–115); cf. the text in the edition of von der Mühll (1962).

of force (καὶ δίκην ἐπίστασαι / νόμοις τε χρῆσθαι μὴ πρὸς ἰσχύος χάριν, 536–538).[118] In his play *Orestes* in 408, Euripides places in the mouth of Tyndareus (485–507) a criticism of Tyndareus's son-in-law Menelaus on the grounds that, having been so long among barbarians, he seems to have forgotten the rules that apply among Greeks: "it is a rule in Greece always to honor a relative" (Ἑλληνικόν τοι τὸν ὁμόθεν τιμᾶν ἀεί, 486).[119] Criticizing Orestes for having killed his mother Clytemnestra instead of bringing her before the law, Tyndareus says (492–495 and 523–525):

εἰ τὰ καλὰ πᾶσι φανερὰ καὶ τὰ μὴ καλά, τούτου τίς ἀνδρῶν ἐγένετ' ἀσυνετώτερος, ὅστις τὸ μὲν δίκαιον οὐκ ἐσκέψατο οὐδ' ἦλθεν ἐπὶ τὸν κοινὸν Ἑλλήνων νόμον; (…) ἀμυνῶ δ', ὅσονπερ δυνατός εἰμι, τῷ νόμῳ, τὸ θηριῶδες τοῦτο καὶ μιαιφόνον παύων, ὃ καὶ γῆν καὶ πόλεις ὄλλυσ' ἀεί.	If right and wrong are clear to all, who was ever more senseless than this man, because he never weighed the justice of the case, nor appealed to the universal law of the Greeks (*ton koinon Hellenon nomon*)? (…) But I will defend the law with all my might, to put an end to this brutal spirit of murder, which is always the ruin of countries and cities alike.[120]

If someone's behavior, like that of the barbarians, is far removed from Greek customs and violates civilized law—the "common" law—this is considered savagery and an attack on society which must be denounced. In these norms there is clearly a close connection with the religious sphere,[121] and it is precisely when certain sacred institutions (such as that of the heralds) are shared among communities that the tissue of common *nomoi* can be revealed in speech.[122] The protection of bonds between communities and the inviolability of protected persons are, ultimately, values that are imposed in the context of conflict, revealing a deep interconnection between religious rituals and military activities.[123] Xenophon explained to his troops that, since they had stoned foreign

118 The Greek text follows the edition of Kovacs (1994).

119 The Greek text is that of Diggle (1994).

120 Translation by Coleridge in Oates and O'Neill (1938) with minor corrections.

121 "Lorsque les Grecs crurent découvrir des lois panhélleniques de la guerre, il est évident que ce fut en fait toujours les lois religieuses qui furent reprises pour s'imposer à tous les Grecs" (Rebuffat, 2000: 188). As we have seen, these obligatory rules of a sacred character incorporate the legal regulations of the time in a shared conception of normativity.

122 Corvisier (2000: 108) says that when these commonalities exist, the differences between the relations among Greek *poleis* and those between Greeks and barbarians disappear.

123 "Battles themselves were of course permeated with religious ritual" (Ager, 2005: 426).

heralds, the punishment would now fall upon them insofar as no one would want to perform the office of a herald after having slaughtered the envoys of others (τίς γὰρ ἐθελήσει κῆρυξ ἰέναι κήρυκας ἀπεκτονώς;, *Anabasis* 5.7.30).[124]

The customary character of these principles—which, as has been mentioned, superseded the effective rules in each city (hence the reference to the Hellenic or panhellenic as an interstate category)—should not be surprising in the context of a legal system in which custom constituted a privileged source of laws;[125] in fact, it allows us to see how natural it was for these principles to be observed.[126] But alongside these customary Greek norms, the example of Xenophon and the attitude of the Persian king in Herodotus indicate clearly that it is also possible to find evidence of a programmatic discourse that protects ambassadors (*presbeis*): even without tracing their origin back to legendary times, we can state that they were frequently attacked; in discursive terms, however, they nevertheless seem to have been protected like heralds under a kind of progressive immunity.[127] Their assimilation to the status of heralds is clear in the *Letter of Philip* that appears in the Demosthenic corpus; in the letter, Philip asserts that "to offend against a herald or ambassadors is an act that everyone considers impious" (καίτοι τὸ παρανομεῖν εἰς κήρυκα καὶ πρέσβεις τοῖς ἄλλοις τε πᾶσιν ἀσεβὲς εἶναι, 12.4).[128] I should stress that the crime's impiety is of a religious nature (ἀσεβὲς, *asebes*), while at the same time the act is defined in the text in legal terms as contrary to *nomos* (τὸ παρανομεῖν).

---

124 Bernand (1999: 375).

125 Cf. Sheets (1994). It is interesting to mention in this connection the notion of "unwritten law" (*agrapta nomima*), established as we have already seen in Sophocles' *Antigone* (454–455), a play in which the protagonist appeals to a universal law that finds its support on the level of the divine: on this theme and its intricacies, see Flumene (1925), Moore (1967) and Ostwald (1986: 164–169). On the importance of custom as a source of law (and therefore of legal obligations) in ancient societies, see Thirlway (2014: 53): "In human societies generally, custom ranking as something amounting to law can be traced back to preliterate societies, where indeed it was virtually the only form of law possible."

126 "For the Greeks, the notion of applying a customary international law based on state practice was familiar and completely uncontroversial. (…) The laws of war were naturally part of the culture and values of constituent states, and as such could more easily encourage compliance than laws whose legitimacy is based purely on a theory of consent or on the fairness of the procedure by which they were enacted" (Lanni, 2007: 2–3).

127 Corvisier (2000: 105). On diplomatic inviolability, see Philipson (1911, i: 328). Mosley (1973: 81–92) concludes that heralds were regarded as inviolate, whereas the status of ambassadors was less clear. See also Johnston (2008: 193).

128 The Greek text is that of Vince (1930).

3.2 *Protecting Civilians*

It is generally recognized that there are vulnerable parts of the population, people who pay the costs of war but who are not the targets of the military operations being conducted. In the Funeral Oration ascribed to Pericles, Thucydides refers to the parents and widows of the dead.[129] Awareness that such innocent victims existed led the *polis* to care for war orphans: in Athens, for example, they were maintained at public expense.[130]

The identification of different groups within society distinguishes the fighting men—organized hierarchically in a definite military structure—from the others, those who passively bear the consequences of hostilities. The geographical distribution of space facilitates the separation of human groups, inasmuch as—according to the Greek conception of a theater of operations—the battlefield is set apart from the interior of the city, whose walls protect the anonymous collective of women, children, and the elderly.[131]

Although it is true that ancient accounts of war regularly record massacres of conquered cities' inhabitants,[132] in general these occurrences are very harshly criticized. In many cases, the texts are concerned to counterbalance this treatment of the most vulnerable groups by opening up a space between fact and discourse, mentioning measures taken by belligerents to protect those who do not participate in hostilities.[133]

129 Thucydides 2.44–45.

130 Rebuffat (2000: 116, 142). The protection of children had probably more to do with their representing the city's future than with compassion for their vulnerability.

131 Bernard (2000: 15–16).

132 Corvisier (2000: 107) offers the statistic that, out of 100 examples between the sixth and second centuries, 25% involved large-scale massacres, 34% involved the subjection of the population to slavery, and 41% saw the siege of the city interrupted by a surrender. On the forms of subjection to slavery in war, cf. Bernard (2000: 66–76).

133 In situations of armed conflict today, civilians and civilian property are protected by conventional international law (articles 48 through 56 of AP-I), as well as by international custom (cf. Henckaerts and Doswald-Beck, 2005, rules 87–105). With respect to the Greek world, Bernard (2000: 64) affirms that "…la pratique guerrière est codifiée, sur le front comme sur ses marges, et la violence à l'égard des non-combattants a ses limites. L'existence de ses règles informelles mais normatives interdit aux guerriers de prendre les populations pour cibles de leur fureur, au nom d'un idéal d'honneur dicté par des principes moraux et religieux". And, regarding the Peloponnesian War, the author concludes that we do not see a break in the applicability of these rules, insofar as civilians were not usually the victims of violence: "les nombreux massacres commis par des soldats grecs frappent essentiellement les belligérants". See also Gillespie (2011, 2: 113).

Some examples from the period of the Peloponnesian War help us to illustrate this division between combatants and those who must be protected because they are not part of the fighting force.[134] In 431, after the attack on Plataea, the Athenians marched there, brought supplies, left a garrison, and decided to take away "the least fit men, the women, and the children" (τῶν τε ἀνθρώπων τοὺς ἀχρειοτάτους ξὺν γυναιξὶ καὶ παισὶν).[135] In 423 the Spartan Brasidas ordered the women and children of the Scioneans and Mendeans to be sent to Olynthus in the Chalcidice, fearing that the Athenians would send ships to attack them.[136] After the capture of Agrigento by the Carthaginians in 406, the Greeks of Sicily also decided to send their families to areas that were fortified or far away from the theater of operations.[137]

Often, however, this binary opposition between combatants and non-combatants does not allow us to perceive the social complexity of the categories employed or the various ways in which society deals with a state of war. On the one hand, we know with certainty that many of "excluded" non-citizens such as metics, slaves, and women sometimes took an active part in the defense of vital parts of the *polis*.[138] Thus, even within categories like women and children, there are cases in which the legal status of individuals (and therefore their appropriate treatment in a wartime context) is uncertain.

Plato, in Book 7 of his *Laws* (806a–b), held that "women do not take part in war, so that if they ever had to fight to defend their city and children they

---

134 For Sidebottom (2004: 55), killing non-combatants was seen in the Greek world as a morally dubious act. For a less optimistic view, see Bryant (2016: 33–24).

135 Thucydides 2.6.4. On this threefold identification of women, children, and the weakest as objects of protection in times of violence, cf. Loraux (2003: 260–264).

136 Thucydides 4.123.4.

137 Diodorus Siculus 12.91.1. Other examples from before the Peloponnesian War reveal a similar attitude; cf. Herodotus 8.40–41.

138 On the contribution of these "others" to the war effort, see Bernard (2000: 22–44). Because of their lack of ability, women clearly belonged in principle to the group of non-combatants, and references in writers such as Plato (*Laws* 806a–b, see below) and Xenophon (*Hellenica* 6.5.28) show that they were excluded. This does not mean that they did not play a significant and surprising role in certain circumstances: we may mention the cases of Tomyris (queen of the Massagetae) in Herodotus 1.205–214, Telesilla of Argos and her women fighting with the Spartans (Plutarch, *De mulieribus virtutibus* 245c–e; Pausanias 2.20.8–9) and, even more clearly, Artemisia of Halicarnassus, allied with Xerxes against the Greeks (Herodotus 8.93). On the ambiguity inherent in these and other "warrior women," feared in antiquity for their extreme masculinity, cf. Gera (1997). In general, women usually functioned on a different but equally important battlefront: the birthing of combatants; cf. Bernard (2000: 42), who takes up the central ideas of Loraux (1981).

could not shoot arrows, as the Amazons do, or employ other projectiles with skill" (τῶν δ' εἰς τὸν πόλεμον μὴ κοινωνούσας, ὥστε οὐδ' εἴ τίς ποτε διαμάχεσθαι περὶ πόλεώς τε καὶ παίδων ἀναγκαία τύχη γίγνοιτο, οὔτ' ἂν τόξων, ὥς τινες Ἀμαζόνες, οὔτ' ἄλλης κοινωνῆσαί ποτε βολῆς μετὰ τέχνης δυνάμεναι).[139] Although in 405 the Gelans decided to evacuate all their children and wives to Syracuse because of the seriousness of the danger they faced (οἱ δὲ Γελῷοι τὸ μὲν πρῶτον ἐψηφίσαντο τέκνα καὶ γυναῖκας εἰς Συρακούσας ὑπεκθέσθαι διὰ τὸ μέγεθος τοῦ προσδοκωμένου κινδύνου),[140] many women pleaded to be allowed to remain there and fight against the Carthaginians, running the same risks as their men.[141] Women frequently take part in hostilities in more or less direct ways; indirectly, they may rebuild the walls that protect a city, as at Gela;[142] at other times, they may jeer at the enemy and pelt them with stones or roof tiles, as happened in Plataea,[143] Corcyra,[144] and Selinunte.[145]

Although these cases seem to show that warfare could be waged by both men and women, such female participation represents a departure from the usual practice in the conduct of hostilities. More unusual, though not nonexistent, are cases of child soldiers in ancient Greece.[146] We hear, for example, of the young Spartan Isadas who, in 362, came naked to join the combatants (διὰ μέσων τῶν μαχομένων) and fight against the Thebans.[147] Our sources tell us that the boy was ultimately punished because he had faced the enemy before being of the proper age and without his city's proper panoply (ὅτι δὲ πρὸ τῆς ἀπαιτουμένης ἡλικίας καὶ μὴ τὰ ἐπιχώρια ἔχων ὅπλα ὥρμησεν ἐς τοὺς ἐχθρούς, ἐζημίωσαν).[148]

Other civilians who were not part of the armed forces could also be found in the vicinity of hostilities. For example, in describing the Spartan army's order of

---

139 The Greek text here is that of Burnet (1967–1968). The situation becomes less clear if we consider that, for Plato, males and females were equally capable of exercising the functions of each species (*Critias* 110b–c).

140 The Greek text is that of Oldfather (1989).

141 It may also be supposed that the women reduced to slavery in Corcyra remained there to provide support for the soldiers (Thucydides 4.48.4). Cf. Bernard (2000: 50).

142 Diodorus Siculus 13.108.8.

143 Thucydides 2.4.2.

144 Thucydides 3.74.1. Cf. Rebuffat (2000: 146–147).

145 Diodorus Siculus 13.55.4–5; 13.56.7. All these cases are mentioned and studied by Powell (2005: 324–325). See also Gillespie (2011, 1: 16).

146 Rebuffat (2000: 141) maintains that "... en règle générale, l'enfant dans le monde de la guerre est le plus souvent du côté des victimes et non des acteurs."

147 Plutarch, *Life of Agesilaus* 34.7.

148 Aelianus Tacticus 6.3.

march, Xenophon mentions, as members of the king's staff, "diviners, doctors, flute-players, army officers, and volunteers who wish to be present" (καὶ μάντεις καὶ ἰατροὶ καὶ αὐληταὶ καὶ οἱ τοῦ στρατοῦ ἄρχοντες, καὶ ἐθελούσιοι ἤν τινες παρῶσιν, *Constitution of the Lacedaemonians*, 13.7).[149] In other cases too, we observe the presence of civilians who voluntarily accompany the armed forces, as in the year 429 when a group of women remained at Plataea to feed the combatants (Thucydides 2.78.3):

Πλαταιῆς δὲ παῖδας μὲν καὶ γυναῖκας καὶ τοὺς πρεσβυτάτους τε καὶ πλῆθος τὸ ἀχρεῖον τῶν ἀνθρώπων πρότερον ἐκκεκομισμένοι ἦσαν ἐς τὰς Ἀθήνας, αὐτοὶ δὲ ἐπολιορκοῦντο ἐγκαταλελειμμένοι τετρακόσιοι, Ἀθηναίων δὲ ὀγδοήκοντα, γυναῖκες δὲ δέκα καὶ ἑκατὸν σιτοποιοί.	The Plataeans had already conveyed to Athens their wives, children, and old men, with the rest of their unserviceable population. Those who remained during the siege were four hundred Plataeans, eighty Athenians, and a hundred and ten women to make bread.[150]

In any case, there was a general consensus that women and children constituted a group of people requiring a certain level of protection in situations of armed conflict so long as they did not take part in combat. Similarly, our texts usually show that the taking of hostages in war was a practice generally condemned;[151] perhaps this explains why there is only a single example of the execution of hostages in the classical Greek world, in the very particular context of a civil war: this was in the year 417, when the Argives killed the hostages given to them by the Athenians.[152]

In our sources, these codes of conduct, religious and humanitarian, extend to the need to ensure the protection of victims and civilian property even for those who are not Greek and do not share the core values that were regarded as the common Hellenic inheritance.[153] For example, a famous passage in Plato's *Republic* (dated between 380 and 360) proposes to extend the existing

149 This shows that armies had "standard non-combatant staff", as Salazar (2013: 265) points out in his examination of the role of doctors in Greek military formations.

150 Translation by Jowett (1881). On civilians fighting in intra-urban warfare, Lee (2010).

151 On hostages in ancient Greece, see Amit (1970), Lonis (1977) and Corvisier (2012).

152 As Corvisier (2000: 106) notes when explaining this unique example, "Nous sommes donc sortis d' un cas de guerre classique."

153 As Bernand (1999: 427) observes, "les lois de la guerre ne permettaient pas de tuer des civils sans défense."

rules already applicable to cases of *stasis* (i.e., to armed conflicts among Greek *poleis*)[154] to cases of war in which Greeks and barbarians confront one another (469b5–471b8):

τί δέ; πρὸς τοὺς πολεμίους πῶς ποιήσουσιν ἡμῖν οἱ στρατιῶται; (…) φαίνεταί μοι, ὥσπερ καὶ ὀνομάζεται δύο ταῦτα ὀνόματα, πόλεμός τε καὶ στάσις, οὕτω καὶ εἶναι δύο, ὄντα ἐπὶ δυοῖν τινοιν διαφοραῖν. λέγω δὲ τὰ δύο τὸ μὲν οἰκεῖον καὶ συγγενές, τὸ δὲ ἀλλότριον καὶ ὀθνεῖον. ἐπὶ μὲν οὖν τῇ τοῦ οἰκείου ἔχθρᾳ στάσις κέκληται, ἐπὶ δὲ τῇ τοῦ ἀλλοτρίου πόλεμος. (…) Ἕλληνας μὲν ἄρα βαρβάροις καὶ βαρβάρους Ἕλλησι πολεμεῖν μαχομένους τε φήσομεν καὶ πολεμίους φύσει εἶναι, καὶ πόλεμον τὴν ἔχθραν ταύτην κλητέον· Ἕλληνας δὲ Ἕλλησιν, ὅταν τι τοιοῦτον δρῶσιν, φύσει μὲν φίλους εἶναι, νοσεῖν δ' ἐν τῷ τοιούτῳ τὴν Ἑλλάδα καὶ στασιάζειν, καὶ στάσιν τὴν τοιαύτην ἔχθραν κλητέον. (…) οὐδ' ἄρα τὴν Ἑλλάδα Ἕλληνες ὄντες κεροῦσιν, οὐδὲ οἰκήσεις ἐμπρήσουσιν, οὐδὲ ὁμολογήσουσιν ἐν ἑκάστῃ πόλει πάντας ἐχθροὺς αὑτοῖς εἶναι, καὶ ἄνδρας καὶ γυναῖκας καὶ παῖδας, ἀλλ' ὀλίγους ἀεὶ ἐχθροὺς τοὺς αἰτίους τῆς διαφορᾶς. καὶ διὰ ταῦτα πάντα οὔτε τὴν γῆν ἐθελήσουσιν κείρειν αὐτῶν, ὡς φίλων τῶν πολλῶν, οὔτε οἰκίας ἀνατρέπειν, ἀλλὰ μέχρι τούτου	But again, how will our soldiers conduct themselves toward enemies? (…) In my opinion, just as we have the two terms, war and faction, so there are also two things, distinguished by two differentiae. The two things I mean are the friendly and kindred on the one hand and the alien and foreign on the other. Now the term employed for the hostility of the friendly is faction (*stasis*), and for that of the alien is war (*polemos*). (…) We shall then say that Greeks fight and wage war with barbarians, and barbarians with Greeks, and are enemies by nature, and that war is the fit name for this enmity and hatred. Greeks, however, we shall say, are still by nature the friends of Greeks when they act in this way, but that Greece is sick in that case and divided by faction (…) They will not, being Greeks, ravage Greek territory nor burn habitations, and they will not admit that in any city all the population are their enemies, men, women and children, but will say that only a few at any time are their foes, those, namely, who are to blame for the quarrel. And on all these considerations they will not be willing to lay waste the soil, since the majority are their friends, nor to destroy the houses, but will carry the conflict only to the point of compelling the guilty to do justice by the

154 This book has not been particularly concerned with studying the regulation of non-international armed conflicts, a more difficult topic than the analysis of cases of *polemos*. It may be said, however, that the vocabulary used to characterize these conflicts in our available evidence is usually inspired by the architypal model of international conflict, or war; cf. du Bouchet (2012: 75). See Introduction, n. 30.

ποιήσονται τὴν διαφοράν, μέχρι οὗ ἂν οἱ αἴτιοι ἀναγκασθῶσιν ὑπὸ τῶν ἀναιτίων ἀλγούντων δοῦναι δίκην. ἐγὼ μέν, ἔφη, ὁμολογῶ οὕτω δεῖν πρὸς τοὺς ἐναντίους τοὺς ἡμετέρους πολίτας προσφέρεσθαι· πρὸς δὲ τοὺς βαρβάρους, ὡς νῦν οἱ Ἕλληνες πρὸς ἀλλήλους.[155]

pressure of the suffering of the innocent. "I," he said, "agree that our citizens ought to deal with their Greek opponents in this wise, while treating barbarians as Greeks now treat Greeks".[156]

This passage, in a work pervaded by the significance of war,[157] is interesting first of all because it sets forth the panhellenic *nomos* relating to the need to protect non-combatants—innocent men, women, and children—from the effects of clashes between *poleis*. In this respect, the text is compatible with the evidence provided, for example, in the treaty signed between Argos and Sparta in which (as Thucydides relates) both cities are obliged, upon the conclusion of hostilities, to return all captured minors (παῖδα ἔχοντι, 5.77.1, 5.77.3). The relationship between "kindred" cities and regions, like those involved in the Platonic *stasis*, has later echoes. Thus, Plutarch will point out in his *Moralia* that the war between the five *komai* of the Megarid was subject to restrictions insofar as they "fought fairly and in a manner befitting their common origin" (δι᾽ ἐπιείκειαν ἡμέρως ἐπολέμουν καὶ συγγενικῶς).[158]

Beyond this, the Platonic proposal is novel in its promotion of the idea that wartime treatment of barbarians should be the same as that received by other Greeks: those who have not participated in hostilities should always be protected. Commensurate with the principle of distinction—which we have already mentioned—the passage proposes that one should not attack the enemy population indiscriminately but should specifically identify those who should be considered enemies and direct violence only against those who are actually combatants. Plato, who in his *Republic* and *Laws* developed a critique of the contemporary Athenian constitution and set forth his own ideal laws in considerable detail, here proposes an expansion of humane considerations and a modification of the prevailing "common" law.[159] Thus we see the beginning

155 The Greek text is that of Burnet (1967–1968).

156 Translation by Shorey (1969).

157 Craig (1994). See also Neff (2005: 24).

158 Plutarch, *Questiones graecae* 295b–c. The Greek text is that of Bernardakis (1889). Cf. Brelich (2009) on the war's outcome.

159 This reading is not incompatible with the possibility of the text being interpreted in terms of the natural inequality between the parties. It could be argued that the passage

of the real theoretical reflection that will follow in Greek thought concerning the need to regulate armed conflicts; little more than two centuries later, the historian Polybius will return to the topic in his analysis of the rise of the Roman Republic and the progressive extension of its power in Greece.[160]

3.3 *Protecting Temples and Religious Facilities and Personnel*

These regulations extend explicitly to the protection of religious spaces in times of armed conflict, and this rule prevailed from Homeric times until the hellenistic period.[161] The Greeks recognized the concept of *asylia* (ἀσυλία), which meant that certain temples could not be subject to robbery, pillage, or acts of reprisal (the verb *sylan*—συλᾶν—means "to despoil" or "to plunder" a sacred space).[162] I have already mentioned the controversy concerning the

---

is concerned with the behavior of the "agents" of the Greek *poleis* toward foreigners, which would remove the Platonic proposal from a *ius inter gentes* and move it toward a discretionary approach to the humane treatment of barbarian enemies. This does not, however, preclude my recognizing the text's critical approach to the rules in force in armed conflicts and their interstate character.

160 It was Polybius who again took up the distinction between lawful acts—connected to the achievement of objectives required to gain a military advantage—and excessive conduct that was forbidden (cf. Bederman, 2001: 246). Polybius (2.58) explained that, when the inhabitants of Mantineia faced those who had revolted from them and submitted to Sparta in order to gain the Spartans' assistance, the resulting conflict involved violations of the "common" laws of men (*ta koina ton anthropon dikaia*): "they ought at least to have spared these men, and to have let every one of them depart under some terms or another: for this much it is the custom by the law of nations to grant even to foreign enemies. But in order to satisfy Cleomenes and the Lacedaemonians of their fidelity in the policy of the hour, they deliberately, and in violation of international law, consummated a crime of the most impious description" (... τῶν γε προειρημένων ἀνδρῶν ἐχρῆν δήπου φεισαμένους ἐᾶσαι πάντας ὑποσπόνδους ἀπελθεῖν. τοῦτο γὰρ καὶ τοῖς πολεμίοις ἔθος ἐστὶ συγχωρεῖσθαι κατὰ τοὺς κοινοὺς τῶν ἀνθρώπων νόμους. οἱ δ' ἵνα Κλεομένει καὶ Λακεδαιμονίοις ἱκανὴν παράσχωνται πίστιν πρὸς τὴν ἐνεστῶσαν ἐπιβολήν, τὰ κοινὰ τῶν ἀνθρώπων δίκαια παραβάντες τὸ μέγιστον ἀσέβημα κατὰ προαίρεσιν ἐπετέλεσαν; cf. Büttner-Wobst [1893–1905]). The translation belongs to Shuckburgh (1889). Another historian who pondered the common laws of the Greeks in the matter of restrictions on war was Diodorus Siculus (13.23–24; 19.63) in the first century; there were many others as well.

161 Thus, for example, there is abundant fifth-century evidence showing that temples and sanctuaries could not be attacked in wartime; cf. Pausanias 10.28.3; Xenophon, *Life of Agesilaus* 10.1; Polybius 5.10. On this subject, see Corvisier (2000: 103–104) and Lanni (2007: 13).

162 Bravo (1980); cf. Jacquemin (1986 and 2000: 130–132), Lonis (1988).

attack on the temple at Delium, when the Boeotians claimed that the Athenians had violated Greek law, since it was a rule established everywhere that one who invades another country should refrain from laying hands on the temple in that territory (πᾶσι γὰρ εἶναι καθεστηκὸς ἰόντας ἐπὶ τὴν ἀλλήλων ἱερῶν τῶν ἐνόντων ἀπέχεσθαι, Thucydides 4.97).[163] According to Diodorus (19.63), this institution also had a legal character, insofar as, according to him, the honor due to the sanctuaries was part of the common laws of the Greeks (κοινὰ τῶν Ἑλλήνων νόμιμα, *koina ton Hellenon nomima*).[164] Thus, the violation of the sacred precincts was conceptualized as both a religious transgression and an interference with the secular nature of temples as neutral sites for the preservation of signed treaties.[165]

The inviolability of the sanctuaries had two fundamental aspects. On the one hand, the pillaging of sacred spaces with the aim of financing a military campaign or obtaining booty was often criticized as an attack on the religious values of a *polis*.[166] On the other hand, care for the temples meant that, by extension,[167] those who took refuge in a temple were themselves protected: in

163 As has been pointed out, in many cases sanctuaries were attacked for practical reasons when they contained riches or were "tactical strong-points" (Sidebottom, 2004: 55). Cf. Corvisier (2000: 104).

164 "… it is difficult to discover recognized lawlike rules of warfare, except perhaps that the protection granted to sanctuaries by amphyctionic treaties were particularly intended for wartime" (Nussbaum, 1950: 15). The best study of the concept of ἀσυλία is still that by Rigsby (1996) which—although focusing on the hellenistic era and therefore outside the chronological scope of the present investigation—is essential for an understanding of the concept's political, religious, and legal nuances.

165 Bederman (2001: 251); see also Bauslaugh (1991) and Gillespie (2011, 2: 217).

166 Miles (2008: 30–44) has studied military infringements on temples in the ancient world as attacks on cultural property. Today, the protection of cultural property in case of armed conflict is guaranteed by the Hague Convention of 1954 and its two Protocols.

167 "I will call this protection asylia, although this term can be used with a variety of meanings in the ancient sources, from the inviolability of every sanctuary and the personal inviolability of an individual guaranteed by a foreign city, to the prohibition of reprisals agreed upon by two communities, or the inviolability of certain sanctuaries recognized by kings, cities, and confederations" (Chaniotis, 1996: 66). Bearzot (2003: 37) expresses it in similar terms: "Ἀσυλία individua l'inviolabilità dei santuari in relazione alla protezione del supplici così come la protezione giuridica concessa ad un singolo individuo da parte di una comunità, l'immunità dal diritto di rappresaglia sancita dall'accordo fra due città così come l'inviolabilità territoriale riconosciuta individualmente ad un santuario o ad una città da parte di diverse autorità (sovrani, città o federazioni): un aspetto, quest'ultimo, che acquista grande rilievo in età ellenistica".

this way, we see anticipated the protection of civilians who, trying to escape the effects of war, could not be seized in religious sanctuaries, which were held to be places for asylum.[168] Illicit entry into a temple, as an act contrary to the laws of war, was specified as ἱεροσυλία (*hierosylia*) and as such was subject to legal sanction.[169] In 427/6, the terrified Mytileneans, knowing that sacred spaces were inviolable, took refuge at their altars before the Athenian army entered their city (μάλιστα τῶν Μυτιληναίων περιδεεῖς ὄντες, ὡς ἡ στρατιὰ ἐσῆλθεν, οὐκ ἠνέσχοντο, ἀλλ' ἐπὶ τοὺς βωμοὺς ὅμως καθίζουσιν, Thucydides 3.28.2). According to Diodorus Siculus, Dionysius of Syracuse found himself unable to prevent his troops from killing their captives when they conquered Motya in western Sicily around 397, and he ordered his heralds to shout instructions to the civilian population to take refuge in the sanctuaries so as to escape the violence of his own soldiers (παρεστήσατο κήρυκας τοὺς μετὰ βοῆς δηλώσοντας τοῖς Μοτυαίοις φυγεῖν εἰς τὰ παρὰ τοῖς Ἕλλησιν ἱερὰ τιμώμενα, 14.53.2). The immunity of priests was connected to the safeguarding of civilians in sacred areas: as a logical corollary, they also had to be protected from attacks.[170]

It was also not possible, in normative terms, for a city to launch an attack while the enemy was celebrating a religious festival or to send out an expedition while they were holding a festival of their own.[171] Thus, for example, Herodotus relates that the Spartans refused to provide immediate assistance to Athens when the Persians landed at Marathon in 490 because they did not want to break their own law (οὐ βουλομένοισι λύειν τὸν νόμον): it was necessary to wait until the cycle of the moon was complete before they could go to war (ἦν γὰρ ἱσταμένου τοῦ μηνὸς εἰνάτη, εἰνάτῃ δὲ οὐκ ἐξελεύσεσθαι ἔφασαν μὴ οὐ πλήρεος ἐόντος τοῦ κύκλου, Herodotus 6.106). Similarly, before the battle of Thermopylae, Sparta decided to delay the dispatch of its forces and only marched out after the end of the Carneia festival in honor of Apollo (μετὰ δέ, Κάρνεια γάρ σφι ἦν ἐμποδών, ἔμελλον ὁρτάσαντες καὶ φυλακὰς λιπόντες ἐν τῇ Σπάρτῃ κατὰ τάχος

168 Corvisier (2000: 105). Sanctuaries could also serve as safe-harbors for fleeing troops, as shown by Nevin (2017: 111–132).

169 A passage from Euripides' fragmentary tragedy *Oedipus* (fr. 1049 N) makes this idea clear by affirming that "when an unjust man sits on an altar, I would take my leave of tradition and, without fearing the gods, I would hale him into court. A terrible man should always suffer terribly".

170 According to a late passage in Plutarch (*Life of Alexander* 11), Alexander the Great separated religious personnel from the rest of the population when he enslaved the inhabitants of Thebes. On the scope of this protection from Homer to Polybius, see Lanni (2007: 14–15).

171 On this subject, cf. Goodman and Holladay (1986: 158–160).

βοηθέειν πανδημεί, Herodotus 7.206).[172] The significance of this customary rule was such that we even have reports that the *polis* of Argos, taking advantage of a difference between calendars, tried in vain to alter the date of a sacred festival to repel a Spartan attack: when Agesipolis, king of Sparta, consulted the oracles of Olympia and Delphi in order to know the validity of the truce declared by the Argives, the two gods replied in succession that "there would be no impiety in not recognizing a truce that was unjustly invoked" (ὅσιον εἶναι μὴ δεχομένῳ σπονδὰς ἀδίκως ὑποφερομένας, Xenophon, *Hellenica* 4.7.2–3).[173]

3.4 *Protecting Captured Enemies*

In the category of protected persons covered by legal-religious considerations, the Greek sources also include express mention of prisoners of war, captives, detainees, and those interned. It is well known that the status of prisoners of war and the conditions of detention are now extensively regulated in international humanitarian law as it applies to armed conflicts. In the wake of the famous work of Ducrey (1968), we can see that in many cases the conduct of a power holding prisoners or detainees was the object of interesting provisions in classical Greece.[174]

The Greeks had a specialized vocabulary for identifying prisoners of war. We find terms such as αἰχμάλωτος (*aikhmalotos*, "taken by the spear," Aeschylus, *Agamemnon* 1440),[175] δμώς (*dmos*, "captive," both in *Iliad* and *Odyssey*),[176] δορίκτητος (*doriktetos*, "slave of war," "booty," *Ilíad* 9.343 and Euripides, *Andromache* 155),[177] δεσμώτης (*desmotes*, "war detainee," usual in historiography when speaking of imprisoned Athenian combatants—Thucydides 5.35.4—or political prisioners, as in Herodotus 3.143),[178] and even ἀνδράποδον (*andrapodon*,

172 Cf. also Thucydides 7.73.2.

173 Corvisier (2000: 104).

174 In international armed conflicts today, they are protected by GC-III. Article 13 states that "[p]risoners of war must at all times be humanely treated. Any unlawful act or omission by the Detaining Power causing death or seriously endangering the health of a prisoner of war in its custody is prohibited, and will be regarded as a serious breach of the present Convention. In particular, no prisoner of war may be subjected to physical mutilation or to medical or scientific experiments of any kind which are not justified by the medical, dental or hospital treatment of the prisoner concerned and carried out in his interest." This protection is part of customary international law (cf. Henckaerts and Doswald-Beck, 2005, rules 106–108).

175 Ducrey (1968: 16–20).

176 Ducrey (1968: 12–16).

177 Ducrey (1968: 20–21).

178 Ducrey (1968: 21–22).

from their liminal condition between human and animal nature).[179] Our sources also allow us to discuss the terminology used for capturing or detaining enemies: verbs such as ζωγρεῖν (*zogrein*, "to capture alive"),[180] αἱρεῖν (*hairein*, "to take")[181] and its synonym λαμβάνειν (*lambanein*),[182] ἄγειν (*agein*, "to lead, to bring"),[183] and, most often in the case of captive women, ἁρπάζειν (*harpazein*, "to seize, to snatch").[184]

Regarding the practices that took shape in Hellenic times, we must begin from the evidence indicating that the conquering *polis* had the option to do with the conquered as they wished.[185] In *Politics* 1.6.1 (1255a), Aristotle distinguished between slaves by nature and by *nomos*—convention and law—and mentioned the example of captives in war as possessions of their captor: "For the law is a sort of agreement according to which things taken in war belong to conquerors" (ὁ γὰρ νόμος ὁμολογία τίς ἐστιν ἐν ᾧ τὰ κατὰ πόλεμον κρατούμενα τῶν κρατούντων εἶναί φασιν).[186]

In Book 5 of Plato's *Republic* (468a–b), Socrates explains the value of justice to the young Athenians and gives the example of rules that apply in wartime:

—τί δὲ δή, εἶπον, τὰ περὶ τὸν πόλεμον; πῶς ἑκτέον σοι τοὺς στρατιώτας πρὸς αὑτούς τε καὶ τοὺς πολεμίους; ἆρ' ὀρθῶς μοι καταφαίνεται ἢ οὔ;—λέγ', ἔφη, ποῖ' αὖ.—αὐτῶν μέν, εἶπον, τὸν λιπόντα τάξιν ἢ ὅπλα ἀποβαλόντα ἤ τι τῶν τοιούτων ποιήσαντα διὰ κάκην ἆρα οὐ δημιουργόν τινα δεῖ καθιστάναι	"But now what of the conduct of war? What should be the attitude of the soldiers to one another and the enemy? Am I right in my notions or not?" "Tell me what notions," he said. "Anyone of them who deserts his post, or flings away his weapons, or is guilty of any similar act of cowardice, should be reduced to the artisan or farmer class, should he not?" "By

179 Ducrey (1968: 23–26).

180 Ducrey (1968: 29–31). This term seems to express the underlying idea of safekeeping, though it appears to have a provisional meaning and in no way specifies the prisoner's ultimate fate; cf. Bonnard (2014: 18).

181 Ducrey (1968: 33–34).

182 Ducrey (1968: 34–36).

183 Ducrey (1968: 39–44).

184 Ducrey (1968: 45–46).

185 See, for instance, Xenophon, *Cyropaedia* 7.5.73 (a passage we have already examined). Cf. also Jacquemin (2000: 124) and Lanni (2007: 18), who concludes that there was no rule which compelled one to show compassion for enemies defeated in battle.

186 Nevertheless, this principle appears to contradict the rule that forbids imposing slavery upon free men.

ἢ γεωργόν;—πάνυ μὲν οὖν.—τὸν δὲ ζῶντα εἰς τοὺς πολεμίους ἁλόντα ἆρ' οὐ δωρεὰν διδόναι τοῖς ἑλοῦσι χρῆσθαι τῇ ἄγρᾳ ὅτι ἂν βούλωνται;—κομιδῇ γε.

all means." "And anyone who is taken alive by the enemy we will make a present of to his captors, shall we not, to deal with their catch as they please?" "Quite so".[187]

From this perspective, it is not surprising that enemies were enslaved. The Athenians did this when Melos was captured (Thucydides 5.116); similarly, the prisoners at Mytilene were about to be massacred, at the instigation of Cleon, after a debate in the Assembly, although the Athenians ultimately decided to spare them (Thucydides 3.36–49). To limit oneself to examples like this, however, will result in an incomplete view of the phenomenon in question and its prevalence in the ancient sources. The passage from Thucydides, for example, suggests that the opinion of the ordinary citizens of Athens favored some sort of restraint in their treatment of prisoners.[188] It is possible to observe that the killing of prisoners was not a normal phenomenon,[189] since our evidence mentions "relaxations" of a practice that was usually considered harsh.[190] Often, when the warring parties could agree to it, it was common for prisoners not to be killed or enslaved.[191] At least in Herodotus, the mutilation of the body of a captured enemy is considered unworthy and inappropriate among Hellenic peoples (with the particular exception of the killing of the Persian governor Artaÿctes by the Athenians).[192] In Xenophon's *Hellenica* (2.1.31–32), a vote in the Athenian assembly to cut off the hands of prisoners of war—an act considered contrary to Greek *nomos*—is treated as deserving of death.[193]

187 Translation by Shorey (1969). Cf. also 470d.

188 Lanni (2007: 21–22). See also Gillespie (2011, 1: 108–109).

189 "Quand il s' agit de simples campagnes ou à la suite de batailles rangées, les Grecs évitaient de mettre à mort leurs prisonniers ..." (Corvisier, 2000: 106–107).

190 Phillipson (1911, ii: 257–259).

191 Ducrey (1968: 112), Rebuffat (2000: 110). See also Pritchett (1971: 81–82).

192 Laurot (1981: 44), Bonnard (2014). Of the twenty-eight cases of bodily mutilation examined by Muller (2014), twenty-four involve acts committed by non-Greeks (mainly Persians): "Pour les Vᵉ et IVᵉ s., les seuls cas de mutilations pratiquées sur des ennemis par des Grecs sont présentés comme des cas exceptionnels, justifiés par des situations extrêmes ou une réciprocité à vocation éducative: faire comprendre aux Barbares l'*hybris* que représentent de telles pratiques" (Muller, 2014: 71).

193 Tritle (2013: 288).

A passage in Xenophon reports that the Spartan general Callicratidas, Lysander's successor, refused to allow the citizens of Methymna to be sold as slaves, and asserted that no Greek would be enslaved while he was in command (ἑαυτοῦ ἄρχοντος οὐδένα Ἑλλήνων εἰς τὸ ἐκείνου δυνατὸν ἀνδραποδισθῆναι, *Hellenica* 1.6.14). In another passage from the same author, Agesilaus reminded his soldiers that their prisoners should not be treated as criminals to be punished but rather as men to be guarded (μὴ ὡς ἀδίκους τιμωρεῖσθαι, ἀλλ' ὡς ἀνθρώπους ὄντας φυλάσσειν, *Life of Agesilaus*, 1.21).

Some texts, moreover, present the killing of captives as an unjustifiable act. When Alcidas, in the year 427, was returning to the Peloponnese, he stopped at Mysonnesus and killed almost all his prisoners, but the massacre provoked immediate protests: the exiled Samians complained that he had murdered men who were not openly hostile to him but who were Athenian allies only out of necessity (Thucydides 3.32.2):

καὶ ἐς τὴν Ἔφεσον καθορμισαμένου αὐτοῦ Σαμίων τῶν ἐξ Ἀναίων ἀφικόμενοι πρέσβεις ἔλεγον οὐ καλῶς τὴν Ἑλλάδα ἐλευθεροῦν αὐτόν, εἰ ἄνδρας διέφθειρεν οὔτε χεῖρας ἀνταιρομένους οὔτε πολεμίους, Ἀθηναίων δὲ ὑπὸ ἀνάγκης ξυμμάχους· εἴ τε μὴ παύσεται, ὀλίγους μὲν αὐτὸν τῶν ἐχθρῶν ἐς φιλίαν προσάξεσθαι, πολὺ δὲ πλείους τῶν φίλων πολεμίους ἕξειν.

Then he anchored at Ephesus, where he was visited by envoys of the Samians who were settled at Anaea, who said that it was an ill way he had of freeing Hellas, to destroy men who were not lifting their hands against him and were not enemies, but were merely allies of the Athenians under compulsion; and unless he abandoned this course he would win few enemies over into friendship and would turn far more friends into enemies.[194]

On other occasions, prisoners of war were exchanged: in 429, for example, the Athenians agreed to such an exchange with the Spartans (Thucydides 2.103) and seven years later did the same with Olynthus (Thucydides 5.3). In 421, the provisions of the famous Peace of Nicias, which was negotiated and agreed upon between the Athenians and Spartans and which ended hostilities for a short time, enjoined a prisoner exchange (Thucydides 5.18): the Athenians had to turn over all the Spartans being held in Athens and in other Athenian-controlled territory (ἀποδόντων δὲ καὶ Ἀθηναῖοι Λακεδαιμονίοις [...] τοὺς ἄνδρας ὅσοι εἰσὶ Λακεδαιμονίων ἐν τῷ δημοσίῳ τῷ Ἀθηναίων ἢ ἄλλοθί που ὅσης Ἀθηναῖοι

194 Translation by Smith (1920) with minor corrections.

ἄρχουσιν ἐν δημοσίῳ), and the Spartans had to do the same with all Athenians—or Athenian allies—in their own hands (ἀποδόντων δὲ καὶ Λακεδαιμόνιοι καὶ οἱ ξύμμαχοι οὕστινας ἔχουσιν Ἀθηναίων καὶ τῶν ξυμμάχων κατὰ ταὐτά).[195] It should be made clear at this point that truces were made specifically for the exchange, ransom, or release of prisoners of war (ὑποσπόνδους ἀπίεναι τοὺς αἰχμαλώτας).[196] The story of how Philip II of Macedon released all his Athenian prisoners after the battle of Chaeronea without demanding ransom is also well known (πάντας ἀπολῦσαι τοὺς αἰχμαλώτους ἄνευ λύτρων, Diodorus 16.87.13).

There is a passage from tragedy which is especially striking because—given the alleged lack of rules in force—it seems to reveal a truly humane outlook. In Euripides' *Children of Heracles*, produced around 430, a slave explains to Alcmene, mother of Heracles, that she may not kill the prisoner of war Eurystheus—who had unsuccessfully attacked the Athenians—because this is contrary to the laws of the city (961–966):

—οὐκ ἔστ' ἀνυστὸν τόνδε σοι κατακτανεῖν.
—ἄλλως ἄρ' αὐτὸν αἰχμάλωτον εἵλομεν;
—ἄλλως, κατακτανεῖν νιν εἰ πρόθυμος εἶ.
—εἴργει δὲ δὴ τίς τόνδε μὴ θνῄσκειν νόμος;
—τοῖς τῆσδε χώρας προστάταισιν οὐ δοκεῖ.
—τί δὴ τόδ'; ἐχθροὺς τοισίδ' οὐ καλὸν κτανεῖν;
—οὐχ ὅντιν' ἄν γε ζῶνθ' ἕλωσιν ἐν μάχῃ.[197]

Servant:—It cannot be that you shall kill this man.
Alcmene:—Is it for nothing that we have taken him prisoner (*aikhmaloton*)?
Servant:—For nothing, if to kill him is your wish.
Alcmene:—But what law (*nomos*) is it that prevents his being killed?
Servant:—It is contrary to the will of those who rule this land.
Alcmene:—What is the meaning of this? Do men here not find it glorious to kill their enemies?
Servant—Not an enemy they have taken alive in battle.[198]

If this passage does not necessarily reflect a *nomos* (there are debates about its precise implications), it at least presents a legal norm imposed by the

195 For Gaurier (2014: 68), fear of reprisals provides the explanation of this provision.
196 Plutarch, *Life of Solon* 9; cf. Phillipson (1911, ii: 280).
197 The Greek text follows the editions of Murray (1913) and Diggle (1994).
198 Translation by Kovacs (1994).

authorities which prevents the killing of the prisoners. A few verses later, Eurystheus himself, having been saved, will say that it was "the laws of the Greeks" (*toisi Hellenon nomois*) that protected him (v. 1010).[199] The expression is significant, since, in the context of the play, the deliberate appeal, in a speech, to the community of Greek peoples rather than to the legal system in force in a particular city, carries a clear implication of the existence of interstate law. This passage, which many scholars have studied as a source of information on proper Athenian conduct toward prisoners,[200] in fact allows us to infer that respect for prisoners of war was mandated on a level that transcended the positive law of the individual city-states.

The situation was very different in the case of spies (κατάσκοποι, *kataskopoi*),[201] who today also have a separate status in that they are not accorded the same treatment as a combatant who is captured by the other side. Currently, the prevailing law establishes that those who are carrying out espionage cannot enjoy the status of a prisoner of war in the event that they are captured by the enemy.[202] This lack of protection was also the rule in the Greek world, as many pieces of evidence attest.[203] In Book 10 of the *Iliad*, for instance, the Achaeans and Trojans dispatch spies to the enemy camps: in a well-known episode, the Trojan spy, Dolon, is ambushed by Diomedes and Odysseus and forced to talk about his night mission before being killed.[204] In classical times, Herodotus relates that three Greek spies[205] arrived at Sardis to obtain information about

---

199 "νῦν οὖν ἐπειδή μ' οὐ διώλεσαν τότε / πρόθυμον ὄντα, τοῖσιν Ἑλλήνων νόμοις / οὐχ ἁγνός εἰμι τῷ κτανόντι κατθανών" (*Children of Heracles*, vv. 1009–1011). Lanni (2007), argues that these passages may represent a species of political propaganda designed to demonstrate Athens' "humanitarian" policy toward prisoners of war.

200 Ducrey (1968: 290), Lanni (2007: 20).

201 Although Greek military intelligence was not professionalized, spies were frequently employed to discover enemies' number, location, and order of battle. Xenophon (*Cyropaedia* 6.1.31–43) even describes their usefulness for generals in the field; cf. Russell (2013: 487–488).

202 Article 46 of AP-I notes in its first paragraph that "notwithstanding any other provision of the Conventions or of this Protocol, any member of the armed forces of a Party to the conflict who falls into the power of an adverse Party while engaging in espionage shall not have the right to the status of prisoner of war and may be treated as a spy". The following paragraphs of the article suggest that, in order to be subject to such treatment, the spy must have been captured while carrying out espionage, which is understood to presuppose acting under false pretexts or in a deliberately clandestine manner.

203 On espionage in the Hellenic world, see Starr (1974) and Richmond (1998).

204 On the "Doloneia", see Merck Davidson (1979).

205 Three was the most usual number for spies, who generally performed their activities while disguised or under the guise of a civilian (Russell, 2013: 487).

Xerxes' forces; having been discovered, they were sentenced to execution by the Persian commanders, but the king, learning of these events, summoned them and, having questioned them, set them free not out of magnanimity but so that the strength of his forces might be revealed to the Greeks (Herodotus 7.146–147). Evidently, it was not a *nomos* but political calculation that protected them. During the Sicilian expedition, according to Lysias (13.64–67), a slave was caught in the act of transmitting information to the enemy by means of fire signals, and he was beaten to death by order of Lamachus (παραφρυκτωρευόμενος τοῖς πολεμίοις ληφθεὶς ὑπὸ Λαμάχου ἀπετυμπανίσθη, 13.65). Likewise, a charge of espionage was brought by Demosthenes against a foreigner, Anaxinus of Oreos; Anaxinus confessed under torture and was condemned to death (Aeschines 3.223–224; cf. Demosthenes 18.137).

Mercenaries represented one of the great revolutions in military *praxis* at the time of the Peloponnesian War.[206] Although the Greeks did not have a word to identify them (the sources generally employ alternatives such as ξένος—*xenos*, "foreigner"—, ἐπίκουρος—*epikouros*, "helper"—and later μισθοφόρος—*misthophoros*, "one who receives payment"),[207] they appear throughout our sources in both classical and hellenistic times. Under current international law, mercenaries, like spies, do not have the right to be considered prisoners of war if they fall into enemy hands: there is no protection for these individuals who fight for money in the army of a foreign power.[208] In the fifth century, contact with the east meant that many Greek hoplites were hired by the kings of

---

206 On the importance of mercenaries, their activities, and the manner in which they were depicted, cf. Bettalli (1995), Trundle (2004) and, most recently, Gómez Castro (2010), English (2012) and Trundle (2013), to whom we refer here.

207 Gillespie (2011, 1: 17), English (2012: xi–xiii), Trundle (2013: 331).

208 This is the rule set forth in article 47 of AP-I: "1. A mercenary shall not have the right to be a combatant or a prisoner of war. 2. A mercenary is any person who: (a) is specially recruited locally or abroad in order to fight in an armed conflict; (b) does, in fact, take a direct part in the hostilities; (c) is motivated to take part in the hostilities essentially by the desire for private gain and, in fact, is promised, by or on behalf of a Party to the conflict, material compensation substantially in excess of that promised or paid to combatants of similar ranks and functions in the armed forces of that Party; (d) is neither a national of a Party to the conflict nor a resident of territory controlled by a Party to the conflict; (e) is not a member of the armed forces of a Party to the conflict; and (f) has not been sent by a State which is not a Party to the conflict on official duty as a member of its armed forces". Moreover, this legal text lays the foundation for the definition provided by the International Convention against the Recruitment, Use, Financing, and Training of Mercenaries, which was approved by the United Nations General Assembly in 1989 as Resolution 44/34 and entered into force in 2001.

Persia, and the *poleis* for their part hired capable foreigners (especially Thracian peltasts).[209] With the passage of time, the presence of these mercenaries changed the conditions of warfare as lighter-armed formations increasingly took part alongside hoplites. Thucydides (7.27) mentions that thirteen hundred Thracian mercenaries could have participated in the Sicilian expedition in 413 if they had not arrived in Athens too late to do so.[210]

Over the course of the fourth century, the hiring of foreign fighters—mainly from the east—became common in the Greek world. This was motivated principally by a desire to separate the soldier from a connection to his homeland and also by an increasing professionalization caused in turn by an alteration of the socio-political order resulting from the enrichment of new citizens in democratic times.[211] During the Peloponnesian War, however, neither Athens nor Sparta, nor their allies, based their military force on the hiring of mercenaries (although this does not mean that they did not use them).[212] Our sources suggest that the presence of these hired troops resulted in an increase in the technical skill of traditional forces and a widening gulf between financially stronger States and those facing economic difficulties. In legal terms, there was clearly an awareness that these mercenaries, motivated by their expectation of wages, acted outside the law, so that no need was felt to provide for their legal protection in case of capture: in general, it remained the case that their fate on any particular occasion would be decided by their captors.[213] Thus, for example, Thucydides relates that a group of Arcadian and barbarian mercenaries sent by Pissuthnes, a Persian satrap, fought together with the pro-Persian faction in the civil war at Notium in 427; these mercenaries were ultimately all massacred by the Athenian Paches, and the leader of the Arcadians, Hippias, was killed by arrows, even though he had been promised that he would be allowed to leave in safety (Thucydides 3.34.2–3).

---

209 Rebuffat (2000: 83–84). The famous Ten Thousand, for instance, was a mercenary force employed by Cyrus the Younger.

210 Baker (1999: 242).

211 Garlan (1999: 38).

212 Bettalli (1995: 123). Cf. English (2012: 44–53).

213 This is a marginal world, parallel to that of ordinary soldiers, "per il quale tuttavia le regole della guerra valgono solo parcialmente" (Bettalli, 1995: 145; also published in French in 1999: 352). So, for example, captured mercenaries could be killed (Thucydides 3.34.3), incorporated into the enemy army (8.28.4–5) or simply set free without further ado (2.70.3, 4.46.2). On the danger of mercenaries, Aeneas Tacticus 10.19–20.

3.5 *Protecting the Sick and Wounded Combatants and Dead Bodies*

The Greek *nomoi* also regulated, in situations of armed conflict, the care and transport of wounded or sick soldiers. Thucydides' description (7.75.2–5) of the feelings of impotence and anguish (ἀπορία, or lack of a way out) resulting from the abandonment of weakened and suffering companions—something he describes as difficult to endure (μὴ ῥαδίως ἀφορμάσθαι)—indicates humane concern for the fate of the combatants.[214] Likewise, we may consider the speech in which Xenophon, defending himself against charges of *hybris* (a physical attack on honor) toward his soldiers, describes how he tried to save a dying solider during the march of the Ten Thousand in 401 (*Anabasis* 5.8.6–11):[215] the use of an argument based on his good intentions toward a comrade is proof of how highly the Athenians valued the protection of those who were hurt or fell in battle.

Beyond these references, we have little information on the treatment of wounds suffered in combat:[216] thus we must take particular notice of those sources that indicate the importance of having doctors who could see to the transport of the injured.[217] A passage in Xenophon tells us that after the defeat at Cunaxa in Asia in 401, the Greeks "appointed eight physicians, since there were many wounded" (καὶ ἰατροὺς κατέστησαν ὀκτώ· πολλοὶ γὰρ ἦσαν οἱ τετρωμένοι, *Anabasis* 3.4.30).

With respect to the treatment of the bodies of dead enemy soldiers, it can be affirmed that honor for the fallen was a rule widely recognized in the Greek world.[218] In Euripides' *Suppliants* (possibly from the year 423), we find a passage that allows us to explore the reasoning behind the rituals associated with the collection of bodies in war.[219] Speaking to the king of Argos (Adrastus), Theseus says that it is lawful to bury the corpses of the Argive chieftains, in accordance with a universal (panhellenic) *nomos* that must be respected (vv. 522–526 and 560–563):

214 Sternberg (1999: 196–197); Gillespie (2011, 1: 107–108).

215 Sternberg (1999: 199–201).

216 Salazar (2013: 305–307).

217 One might infer from this that, while Greek armies usually included doctors, their number might be insufficient if there were too many victims; cf. Salazar (2013: 306). On this topic, see also Rebuffat (2000: 114).

218 Debidour (2002: 55–58); Gillespie (2011, 1: 111).

219 Tritle (2013: 290).

πόλεμον δὲ τοῦτον οὐκ ἐγὼ καθίσταμαι, ὃς οὐδὲ σὺν τοῖσδ' ἦλθον ἐς Κάδμου χθόνα· νεκροὺς δὲ τοὺς θανόντας, οὐ βλάπτων πόλιν οὐδ' ἀνδροκμῆτας προσφέρων ἀγωνίας, θάψαι δικαιῶ, τὸν Πανελλήνων νόμον.[220]	It is not I who choose this war, seeing that I did not even join these warriors to go unto the land of Cadmus; but still I think it right (*dikaio*) to bury the fallen dead, not injuring any state nor yet introducing murderous strife, but preserving the law of all the Greeks (*ton Panhellenon nomon*).[221]

Theseus employs the same expression that his mother Aethra had used to ask him to take action against the guilty in order that the laws common to Hellas (νόμιμά τε πάσης συγχέοντας Ἑλλάδος, 311) might not be transgressed. Throughout the tragedy, the insistence on this concept, employed in an almost technical sense, is beyond doubt.

The same idea is presented by Sophocles in his *Antigone* (produced in 442), to which I will later refer. In the play, Antigone invokes sacred, unwritten laws as the reason she must bury Polynices, who fought justly (or treasonously, according to Creon) in an effort to drive his brother Eteocles from the throne (vv. 449–459):

οὐ γάρ τί μοι Ζεὺς ἦν ὁ κηρύξας τάδε, οὐδ' ἡ ξύνοικος τῶν κάτω θεῶν Δίκη τοιούσδ' ἐν ἀνθρώποισιν ὥρισεν νόμους. οὐδὲ σθένειν τοσοῦτον ᾠόμην τὰ σὰ κηρύγμαθ', ὥστ' ἄγραπτα κἀσφαλῆ θεῶν νόμιμα δύνασθαι θνητὸν ὄνθ' ὑπερδραμεῖν. οὐ γάρ τι νῦν γε κἀχθές, ἀλλ' ἀεί ποτε ζῇ ταῦτα, κοὐδεὶς οἶδεν ἐξ ὅτου 'φάνη.	Since it was not Zeus that published me that edict, and since not of that kind are the laws (*nomous*) which Justice (*Dike*) who dwells with the gods below established among men. Nor did I think that your decrees were of such force, that a mortal could override the unwritten (*agrapta*) and unfailing (*asphale*) statutes (*nomima*) given us by the gods (*theon*). For their life is not of today or yesterday, but for all time, and no man knows when they were first put forth.[222]

To offer the honors of burial to those fallen in combat is, as Xenophon suggests in describing his agreement with Cheirosophus, in accord with the *nomos* that prevails among good men (ὥσπερ νομίζεται ἀνδράσιν ἀγαθοῖς, *Anabasis*

220 Cf. Murray (1913). Cf. also v. 671.

221 Translation by Coleridge in Oates and O'Neill (1938) with minor corrections.

222 Translation by Jebb (1891).

4.2.23).[223] In Thucydides (4.97.2), the failure of the Athenians and Thebans at Delium to permit the burial of the dead is understood to be a violation of the common laws of the Greeks (οὐ δικαίως δράσειαν παραβαίνοντες τὰ νόμιμα τῶν Ἑλλήνων).[224] Plato affirms that the bodies of dead may not be despoiled or deprived of burial,[225] and Herodotus writes that Pausanias refused to impale the body of Mardonius (a suggestion made by Lampon, who argued that it would repay the treatment of Leonidas's body at Thermopylae) and said that to commit unworthy acts against the dead was condemned by the laws of civilized warfare, to the extent that it would be a cause for reproach even if done by the barbarians (ἐξαείρας γάρ με ὑψοῦ καὶ τὴν πάτρην καὶ τὸ ἔργον, ἐς τὸ μηδὲν κατέβαλες παραινέων νεκρῷ λυμαίνεσθαι, καὶ ἢν ταῦτα ποιέω, φὰς ἄμεινόν με ἀκούσεσθαι· τὰ πρέπει μᾶλλον βαρβάροισι ποιέειν ἤ περ Ἕλλησι, καὶ ἐκείνοισι δὲ ἐπιφθονέομεν, Herodotus 9.79). Such passages seem to suggest the universality of the custom of burying the dead on the field of battle.[226]

3.6 *Protecting Suppliants, Refugees and Asylum-Seekers*

I have examined the religious character of this burial practice and the *nomos* relating to the inviolability of temples: we may also consider the establishment by the Greek *poleis* of a special legal protection for suppliants (ἱκέται, *hiketai*).[227] In their *logos* before the Spartans in 427, the Plataeans redefined the "universal law," claiming that, since they had surrendered, they should be protected. According to this passage, those who extend their hands (χεῖρας προϊσχομένους) may not be attacked, since the "laws of the Greeks" prohibit killing those who surrender (ὁ δὲ νόμος τοῖς Ἕλλησι μὴ κτείνειν τούτους, Thucydides 3.58.3).

A fourth-century decree from Tralleis (in Lydia, Asia Minor), for instance, sets forth explicitly that there should be a right to accept suppliants (*hiketerien*) at the sanctuary of Dionysus, considered to be both sacred (*hieros*) and inviolable (*asylos*). No offence (*me adikein*) could be committed against those asylum-seekers.[228]

---

223 Bernand (1999: 417).

224 De Romilly (1971: 41) imagines that this case of the Athenians at Delium may have inspired the passage in *Suppliants* that we have just discussed. In the account in Thucydides, the Athenian herald was finally authorized to gather up the corpses a few weeks later (Thucydides 4.101.1).

225 Plato, *Republic* 469d. See Gillespie (2011, 1: 111–112).

226 Bederman (2001: 258). *Contra*, see Curchin (1995).

227 Gain (2014: 219). According to Nevin (2017: 132), "[t]he killing of suppliants following battles is used in Greek literatutre as an extreme signifier of a leader's negative characteristics". As I shall explain, there was also a legal side to this moral consideration.

228 *LSAM* 75, 5–12.

In practice, respect for the precept was also appreciated: according to Xenophon, for example, the Spartan king Agesilaus released eighty Theban soldiers who had hidden themselves in a temple, thus demonstrating the nobility of respecting suppliants:[229]

ἱκέτας δὲ θεῶν οὐδὲ ἐχθροὺς ἐβιάζετο, νομίζων ἄλογον εἶναι τοὺς μὲν ἐξ ἱερῶν κλέπτοντας ἱεροσύλους καλεῖν, τοὺς δὲ βωμῶν ἱκέτας ἀποσπῶντας εὐσεβεῖς ἡγεῖσθαι.	To suppliants of the gods, even if his foes, he did no violence, believing it unreasonable to call robbers of temples sacrilegious and yet to consider those who dragged suppliants from altars pious men.[230]

Xenophon also remarks that the king gave orders for the Thebans to be allowed to go wherever they wanted and for them not to be harmed; he even sent an escort to take them to a place of safety (ἐᾶν τε ἀπιέναι ὅποι βούλοιντο ἐκέλευε καὶ ἀδικεῖν οὐκ εἴα, καὶ προπέμψαι ἐπέταξε τοὺς ἀμφ' αὐτὸν ἱππεῖς ἔστε ἐν τῷ ἀσφαλεῖ ἐγένοντο, 2.13).[231]

The list of persons specially protected in times of armed conflict should include refugees. Their protection in international humanitarian law—even if limited to three of the 576 articles in the Geneva Conventions and their Protocols—is, on the one hand, far-reaching (since it covers almost all those who have fled their countries and are in the power of one of the opposing sides[232]) and, at the same time, rather limited.[233]

---

229 Xenophon, *Life of Agesilaus* 11.1; cf. Nevin (2017: 112).

230 Translation by Marchant and Bowersock (1925).

231 On these passages, see Gondicas and Boëldieu-Trevet (1999: 80).

232 In this regard we follow Lavoyer (1995). The protection provided is, however, clearly incomplete and insufficient, insofar as international humanitatian law protects a country's nationals only if, in the event of an international armed conflict (IAC) they have fled to the territory of the enemy State (articles 35–46 of GC-IV). In GC-IV, the State receiving the refugees is required to accomodate them: they should not be treated as foreign enemies simply because of their nationality since on this basis alone they enjoy no protection (article 44). Also protected are all those who were already refugees at the time when the conflict began (article 73 of AP-I, which also applies to stateless persons) and those from occupied territories (article 70.2). Refugee nationals of a neutral State who find themselves in the territory of a belligerent State shall be protected by GC-IV if there are no diplomatic relations between their State and the belligerent State. Article 73 of AP-I maintains this protection, even in cases where there are no diplomatic relations.

233 Furthermore, and despite the fact that GC-IV prohibits (in article 45.4) transferring a protected person to a country where he or she may be persecuted for his or her political or religious views (principle of non-refoulement), the truth is that there are situations that

The silences of international humanitarian law are made up for by the so-called international law of refugees which, at present, complements it.[234] The United Nations Convention Relating to the Status of Refugees of 1951, as well as its 1967 Protocol,[235] now define a refugee (article 1.A.2) to mean any person who:

> … as a result of events occurring before 1 January 1951 and owing to well-founded fear of being persecuted for reasons of race, religion, nationality, membership of a particular social group or political opinion, is outside the country of his nationality and is unable or, owing to such fear, is unwilling to avail himself of the protection of that country; or who, not having a nationality and being outside the country of his former habitual residence as a result of such events, is unable, or, owing to such fear, is unwilling to return to it.

For practical considerations, some regional instruments have advanced a broader notion of who should be considered a refugee, leaving room even for non-international armed conflicts that provide a reason to flee.[236] Thus, the

---

in practice are not covered by international humanitarian law. One such situation, for example, involves refugees who, fleeing a State which is party to an international armed conflict, enter the territory of another State which is not engaged in the conflict (unless, of course, that State is engaged in a separate armed conflict that impacts those who are refugees within that same territory). Despite these legal *lacunae*, however, the provisions of international humanitarian law permit a considerable reduction in the number of persons affected by the devastating consequences of armed violence in their place of origin or habitual residence, even if the needs of these individuals are a long way from being addressed completely; Kälin (2001: 637).

234 On the protection offered to refugees by international humanitarian law and its connections to other provisions in complementary branches of international law, see the comprehensive studies by Jaquemet (2001), Edwards (2008), and Chétail (2014). Jacques's book (2012) is also dedicated to the topic.

235 189 U.N.T.S. 150. The text of the accord was worked out at a conference of ambassadors plenipotentiary held in Geneva in 1951 pursuant to a decision of the United Nations General Assembly (Resolution 429 [V] of December 14; 1950; official documents of the fifth session, Supplement no. 20 [A/1775]); this meeting resulted in the signing of the Convention on July 28 of that year. The treaty entered into force on April 22, 1954. The corresponding Protocol (606 U.N.T.S. 267), in force since October 4, 1967, did not change the scope of the definition.

236 Cf. Arboleda (1991). The recent Syrian crisis has shown the need to improve the current regime, and in December 2016 the United Nations High Commissioner for Refugees

Addis Ababa Convention that regulates specific aspects of the problems of refugees in Africa (1969)[237] and the Cartagena Declaration on Refugees (1984), pertaining to the Americas,[238] both provide expanded protection for those who become refugees as a result of external aggression, violence, or civil unrest.[239]

In spite of its relevance, very little attention has been paid to the subject of refugees in the Greek world.[240] Although the treatment of those claiming territorial asylum is a common and important theme since Homeric times and throughout fifth century tragedy,[241] it is perhaps especially interesting to focus, as a case-study, on the evidence provided by the tragedy *Suppliants* (*Hiketides*), which formed part of a trilogy with the lost *Egyptians* and *Danaids*[242] and

---

(UNHCR) released its Guidelines on International Protection (No. 12) on Claims for Refugee Status Related to Situations of Armed Conflicts and Violence (HCR/GIP/16/12).

237 Article I of this treaty of the Organization for African Unity adds a paragraph that expands the categories defined in the Convention of 1951, establishing that the category of "refugee" should include "… every person who, owing to external aggression, occupation, foreign domination or events seriously disturbing public order in either part or the whole of his country of origin or nationality, is compelled to leave his place of habitual residence in order to seek refuge in another place outside his country of origin or nationality." The extended definition contained in this text thus foresaw, almost fifty years ago, the inclusion of cross-border movements of people because of armed conflicts, and assumed special importance in its applicaion to particular situations such as the mass exoduses resulting from the crises in Mozambique and, later, Rwanda. "La Convention de l'OUA s'inspirait de la Convention de Genève de 1951 et de son Protocole de 1967, mais en l'élargissant considérablement de manière à tenir en compte de réalités spécifiquement africaines comme les exodes massifs" (Wilkinson, 1999: 9). On this expanded definition, see Edwards (2006).

238 The declaration was signed at the Colloquium on the International Protection of Refugees in Central America, Mexico and Panama, which took place in Cartagena de Indias, Colombia, from March 19 to 22, 1984. Among the conclusions of this local instrument, which in principle lacks binding force derived from its legal nature, the third has relevance for our analysis: it proposes that "… the definition or concept of a refugee to be recommended for use in the region is one which (…) includes among refugees persons who have fled their country because their lives, safety or freedom have been threatened by generalized violence, foreign aggression, internal conflicts, massive violation of human rights or other circumstances which have seriously disturbed public order."

239 Arboleda (1991).

240 Exceptions include the books on political refugees by Balogh (1943) and Seibert (1979) and, more recently, Garland (2014).

241 On supplication and hospitality in epic, see Tworek-Hofstetter (2009). Regarding tragedy, one may think of Sophocles' *Oedipus at Colonus* or Euripides' *Children of Heracles* (236–246); cf. Jacquemin (2000: 127–128).

242 On possible reconstructions of this trilogy, see Winnington-Ingram (1961).

which seems to have won Aeschylus a victory in the year 463.[243] Despite doubts concerning this date, it may be significant given the contemporary importance of anti-Spartan diplomatic agreements between Athens and Argos and the increase in democratic confidence—which the work seems to embody—at the time of the reforms of Ephialtes.[244]

The play's story features a chorus of women, the fifty daughters of Danaus (thus known as the Danaids), who arrive with their father in Argos after fleeing Egypt, where they were to be forced into unwanted marriages with their cousins, the sons of Aegyptus (the brother of Danaus).[245] The young women seek asylum and protection in Argos, claiming that they are victims of a war declared by their rejected suitors. Although they demonstrate mythical kinship with the Argives (they descend from Io, priestess at the Temple of Argive Hera who was desired by Zeus), the king of Argos, Pelasgus, initially hesitates to receive them. Nevertheless, taking the view that their plea is directed to his city and not only to himself, he acts as mediator between the women and the Argive people: he submits the issue to a vote of the Assembly in a procedure that would have seemed to the theater audience surprisingly democratic and proper. Ultimately, the city passes a decree granting asylum to the Danaids, accepting them as μέτοικοι (*metoikoi*, "resident foreigners") and assuring them protection.

It is interesting to consider how this mythical material is presented in the context of a specific diplomatic situation in which another party's favor is being sought.[246] The work is centered on the women who make up the chorus.

---

243 This year is the one usually given; it is probable, but not certain. On the historical debates over the date, especially in light of the 1952 discovery of the papyrus fragment *P. Oxy.* 2256, fr. 3, see Lloyd-Jones (1964) and Podlecki (1966: 163–164). Garvie (1969: 1–28) reviews the different points of view and concludes that nothing in the play itself permits the determination of a precise date. The question has been taken up again by Scullion (2002: 87–101).

244 Cuniberti (2001: 140, n. 1).

245 The three plays in the trilogy formed a continuous story. On the basis of Sicherl (1986)—who supposes the existence of an oracle according to which Danaus would be killed by one of his brothers-in-law—and Rösler (1993)—who surmises that the oracle was explained in a play preceding *Suppliants*—Sommerstein (2010) has proposed that this play was the second in the trilogy. According to his point of view, the first play (*Egyptians*) depicted the conflict between Danaus and his brother Aegyptus following the proposal of marriage; in the last play (*Danaids*) the surviving son of Aegyptus, Lynceus, avenged his brothers' murders.

246 The politician Cimon, who had pro-Spartan sentiments, had succeeded in convincing the Athenians to aid the Spartans in their war with the Messenians. The Spartans, however,

Given that the role of women in the Greek world was one of passivity and exclusion,[247] it should not be surprising that the play clearly presents them as victims.[248] In the play, the Danaids do not appear to make their own decisions; instead they are incited to flee and accompanied by their father Danaus, who acts as their representative, advisor, and aide.[249]

Specific elements of the present-day understanding of refugee status appear explicitly in the play, which presents the flight of the girls from their marriage proposals in terms of escape from an armed conflict.[250] Almost two and a half thousand years before the documents produced at Addis Ababa and Cartagena, the women justify their departure from Egypt as the enforced consequence of a state of war: in the third antistrophe of the chorus's song at the beginning of the play, they say that piety for the gods represents for them "an altar that saves from ruin and is the protection of those who flee, oppressed, from war (*ek polemou*)" (ἔστι δὲ κἀκ πολέμου τειρομένοις / βωμὸς ἀρῆς φυγάσιν / ῥῦμα, δαιμόνων σέβας, 83–85).[251] The identification of enforced weddings with armed conflict is reinforced when the Danaids declare that they do not want to be "slaves of Egypt" (δμωὶς Αἰγύπτου γένει, 335), suggesting the possibility that they might

sent the Athenians away; offended, they decided to make an alliance with Sparta's enemy Argos, and Cimon was ostracized in 461. It has been argued that Pelasgus brought about the ruin of the Argives in a similar fashion. Another argument in favor of a date around 460 is based on a possible allusion to Themistocles, who found asylum in Argos after his own ostracism in 470. This nearly caused a war with both Sparta and Athens, which was then pro-Cimon; this situation is similar to Pelasgus' dilemma as he considers the possible consequences of accepting the suppliants into the city.

247 The bibliography on this topic is very extensive; for my purposes, it suffices to mention the summary analysis of the sources recently provided by Pritchard (2014).

248 For an interpretation of the play in terms of genre, see Zeitlin (1988 and 1990).

249 Santiago Álvarez (2013: 61). On the role played by Danaus, cf. Ryzman (1989).

250 Cf. Buis (2016).

251 All Greek quotations from the play come from the edition of West (1990). There have been a number of explanations for the flight of the Danaids: Benveniste (1949) suggested that the reason for their escape would have been provided by the prohibition on incest among cousins; similarly, Mackinnon (1978) has concluded that they were escaping an endogamous marriage—an act contrary to divine justice—forced on them by the sons of Aegyptus, who are described as predators or hunters. Gantz (1978) and Caldwell (1974) have developed interesting psychoanalytic readings concerning a father's love and his replacement by the husband. It is interesting to set against these readings those which understand the marriage in terms of military confrontation (as I have already mentioned).

become spoils of war:[252] this is a claim by people who have had to escape a serious situation involving physical violence.[253]

When the request of the Danaids is presented in this way, it at once becomes clear that the central theme of the work is not marriage but rather the power politics involved in extending protection to vulnerable outsiders.[254] We should note that, since archaic times, hospitality (ξενία, *xenia*) was an important social institution of a private nature. At this point, however, the nature of *xenia*, insofar as it involves a welcoming of foreigners, seems to have shifted from the interpersonal plane to a realm of social action controlled by public authorities.[255] It must be emphasized that *xenia* as a legal-religious institution is relevant, in that the suppliants invoke Zeus Xenios, guardian of outsiders, twice in the course of the play (627, 672),[256] linking him with his daughter Justice (*Themis*), who is also explicitly referred to as "guardian of suppliants" (*hikesia*, 360).

The religious element becomes important in the ritual of supplication, in which the Danaids lay their branches on the altar to obtain divine favor and inviolability.[257] The branch is thus the material symbol of the request for the gods' protection. Supplication (*hiketeia*)—the process in which the interaction of the suppliant and the act of supplicating create a request involving a religious-political ritual—is a legal institution regulated by *nomos*.[258] The legal

---

252 This verse is important in allowing us to understand that the fear experienced by the Danaids is not occasioned by the marriage itself but rather by the possibility of becoming their husbands' prey or subjects. On different views of the chorus-protagonist's motives, cf. Ireland (1974). On foreign female captives as a frequent subject in Greek tragedy, see Rodríguez Cidre (2010).

253 Detienne (2003: 40) has observed that: "The marriage that fills the Danaids with such horror is described in the Argive story as a limitless war (…) It is pure physical violence, perpetrated by physical force …".

254 This is the interpretation of Rohweder (1998). On the political importance of the play's performance in a democratic context characterized by the dilemma of immigration in times of armed conflict, cf. Sommerstein (1997), who argues that the play must have been staged in 461 and that its plot reflects contemporary political reality; see also Bakewell (2013).

255 Santiago Álvarez (2005).

256 Iriarte (2007: 197). Interesting epithets are associated with Zeus in connection with his role as protector of outsiders and suppliants: *Hikesios* (346, 616), *Hiktaios* (385), *Hikter* (479), *Aphiktor* (1); cf. Santiago Álvarez (2005: 63–67, n. 36).

257 On the institutional modalities of supplication in the Greek world, cf. Gould (1973). The usual procedure for seeking asylum in Athens in the classical period is described by Zelnick-Abramovitz (1998).

258 On the relationship between *asylia* and *hiketeia*, between their religious and political

dimension of supplication is present in the play, which describes the Danaids' request for asylum in terms of the requirement to provide proof to the authorities in Argos. The Danaids explain the reasons why they need to ask for the Argives' help and ask for their protection.[259] In presenting their evidence, they employ a procedural vocabulary ("I will now show (*epideixo*) to the men of this country faithful testimonies, and other things will also become clear, even if one would not expect them; everyone will know the full story"; τά τε νῦν ἐπιδείξω / πιστὰ τεκμήρια γαιονόμοις, / τὰ δ' ἄελπτά περ ὄντα φανεῖται. / γνώσεται / δὲ λόγους τις ἐν μάκει; 54–58) and they present themselves as suppliants, promising to respect the rules of the State that takes them in: "Receive (*dexasthe*) this group of women that supplicates (*hiketen*) with a spirit full of respect for your country" (δέξασθ' ἱκέτην / τὸν θηλυγενῆ στόλον αἰδοίῳ / πνεύματι χώρας, 28–30).[260]

Some have argued that the request for asylum and the role of suppliant are subverted in the play, since the girls threaten to commit suicide on the altar and pollute the city if they are not accepted at Argos (465).[261] This threat, however, can be interpreted as part of the aggression that is inherent in the ritual of supplication,[262] which included a series of gestures that accompanied the rhetoric of acceptance. In any event, Aeschylus presents the request for asylum in such as a way as to portray, with precise terminology, the normative issues involved:[263] to reject the suppliants means provoking Zeus's anger but, above all, it means offending against legal justice (*dike ennomos*, 384).

The modern definition of a refugee requires one to have crossed an international border; similarly, in the play, the foreign status of the Danaids and their petition to the authorities of another State are quite clear. The young women—

(divine and human) dimensions, see Naiden (2004), who identifies the four formal stages in the procedure.

259 On feminine supplication in Aeschylus, see Amendola (2006).

260 Respect for the laws of the place of refuge is provided for in article 2 of the Convention of 1951: "Every refugee has duties to the country in which he finds himself, which require in particular that he conform to its laws and regulations as well as to measures taken for the maintenance of public order." In the play, the end shows that the Danaids have left Egypt behind and adopted the *nomoi* of the city that is receiving them: they affirm that they will no longer sing about the Nile but will reserve their songs for Argos (1023–1029).

261 Turner (2001).

262 Brill (2009: 179, n. 23). On the meaning of the threat to commit suicide, see Bednarowski (2010).

263 Daube (1938) has elaborated on legal issues in the work of Aeschylus.

who do not share the local customs despite their distant Hellenic origin—are identified by the citizens of Argos as foreigners (235–238):

ποδαπὸν ὅμιλον τόνδ᾽ ἀνελληνόστολον πέπλοισι βαρβάροισι καὶ πυκνώμασι χλίοντα προσφωνοῦμεν; οὐ γὰρ Ἀργολὶς ἐσθὴς γυναικῶν οὐδ᾽ ἀφ᾽ Ἑλλάδος τόπων.	From where comes this band we address, clothed in foreign attire and luxuriating in closely-woven and barbaric robes? For your apparel is not that of the women of Argos, nor yet of any part of Hellas.[264]

Evidence of persecution directed against the asylum-seekers (an element required in the Convention of 1951) becomes an issue in the play as well. The women of the chorus are upset "by the persecution (διωγμοῖς) to which we have been subjected" (148–149), and they make it clear that they have been harassed as members of a particular group, that of women.[265] At 818–821, moreover, they claim:

γένος γὰρ Αἰγύπτειον ὕβριν δύσφορον ἀρσενογενὲς μετά με δρόμοισι διόμενοι φυγάδα μάταισι πολυθρόοις βίαια δίζηνται λαβεῖν.	For the males of the race of Aegyptus, intolerable in their wantonness, chase after me, a fugitive, with clamorous lewdness and seek to lay hold of me with violence.[266]

264 Translation by Smyth (1926). We should note, in addition, that they present themselves as foreigners by making reference to their barbarian language (*karbana audan*, 118), they claim to have come from far away (*hekathen*, 421), and even when their ancestral ties are recognized, they are understood, in their liminal condition, only as guests in the city (*astoxenoi*, 356).

265 This requirement is also dealt with in article 1.A.2 of the Convention, so that today we would identify the case described in *Suppliants* as one marked by gender violence. There is an increasing tendency to identify forced marriage as a valid reason for claiming refugee status. The issue was raised in the 2002 UNHCR guidebook (UNHCR, "Guidelines on International Protection: Gender-Related Persecution within the Context of Article 1A(2) of the 1951 Convention and/or its 1967 Protocol relating to the Status of Refugees," HCR/GIP/02/01, 2002, in [36], viii) and identified as important six years later in UNHCR, "Guidance Note on Refugee Claims Relating to Sexual Orientation and Gender Identity," (2008, in 13). On the practical difficulty of understanding "forced marriage" as a reason in itself for asylum in some countries like the United Kingdom—in contrast to more successful experiences in Canada and Australia—see the study by Dauvergne and Millbank (2011).

266 Translation by Smyth (1926).

If we turn to the requirement of well-founded fear, it is clear that the daughters of Danaus on several occasions take the opportunity to mention their fear of persecution by the Egyptians. The emotion of fear is connected with their flight in a number of passages: "I gather the flowers of grief, anxious (*daimainousa*) whether there is any friendly kinsman (*kedemon*) here to champion our band which has fled (*tasde phygas*) from the haze-shrouded land" (γοεδνὰ δ' ἀνθεμίζομαι / δειμαίνουσα φίλους, τᾶσδε φυγᾶς / ἀερίας ἀπὸ γᾶς / εἴ τις ἐστὶ κηδεμών, 74–77); "fleeing in terror through loathing (*ekhthei metaptoiousan*) of the marriage-bed" (ἔχθει μεταπτοιοῦσαν εὐναίων γάμων, 333); "your suppliant, a fugitive, running around like a heifer chased by wolves" (ἴδε με τὰν ἱκέτιν φυγάδα περίδρομον, / λυκοδίωκτον, 351–352); "no wonder I am fretful through alarm of mind (*phoboi*)" (οὔτοι τι θαῦμα δυσφορεῖν φόβῳ φρενός, 512); "I am possessed by dreadful fear (*periphobon ... tarbos*) (...) father, I am consumed with fright (*deimati*)" (περίφοβόν μ' ἔχει τάρβος ἐτητύμως [...] παροίχομαι, πάτερ, δείματι, 736–738).[267]

The arguments associated with the suppliants' plea are presented in such detail that the young women even mention that they have not committed crimes of blood that prevent them from being received as refugees; in terms almost like those asserting an absence of grounds for exclusion, as required today,[268] they state (5–11):

Δίαν δὲ λιποῦσαι
χθόνα σύγχορτον Συρίᾳ φεύγομεν,
οὔτιν' ἐφ' αἵματι δημηλασίαν
ψήφῳ πόλεως γνωσθεῖσαν,
ἀλλ' αὐτογενεῖ φυξανορίᾳ
γάμον Αἰγύπτου παίδων ἀσεβῆ
'ξονοταζόμεναι.

For we have fled Zeus' land whose
pastures border Syria, and are fugitives,
not because of some public decree
pronounced against blood crime, but
because of our own act to escape the suit
of man, since we abhor as impious all
marriage with the sons of Aegyptus.[269]

267 All these translations belong to Smyth (1926).

268 Article 1.F of the 1951 Convention declares: "The provisions of this Convention shall not apply to any person with respect to whom there are serious reasons for considering that: (a) he has committed a crime against peace, a war crime, or a crime against humanity, as defined in the international instruments drawn up to make provision in respect of such crimes; (b) he has committed a serious non-political crime outside the country of refuge prior to his admission to that country as a refugee; (c) he has been guilty of acts contrary to the purposes and principles of the United Nations".

269 Translation by Smyth (1926).

Along the same lines, Danaus instructs his daughters on how to justify their claim, and he makes it clear that they must show they are not responsible for any serious crime in their country of origin (193–195):

αἰδοῖα καὶ γοεδνὰ καὶ ζαχρεῖ' ἔπη
ξένους ἀμείβεσθ', ὡς ἐπήλυδας πρέπει,
τορῶς λέγουσαι τάσδ' ἀναιμάκτους φυγάς.

Reply to the strangers, as is fitting for aliens, in piteous and plaintive language of necessity, telling them clearly of your flight, how it was unstained by deed of blood.[270]

After the interested parties have presented their arguments for the granting of asylum, the king expresses his doubts: he fears that granting the girls this status may cause war with Egypt. Instead of rejecting the petition, however,[271] Pelasgus will submit this matter to the Assembly of the *polis* so that the issue can be dealt with there. In the end, the play presents the moment at which asylum is granted and specifies its legal basis in the concept of *asylia*, thereby ensuring respect for the rights of those who were forced to flee a violent fate (606–615):

ἔδοξεν Ἀργείοισιν (…)
ἡμᾶς μετοικεῖν τῆσδε γῆς ἐλευθέρους
κἀρρυσιάστους ξύν τ' ἀσυλίᾳ βροτῶν·
καὶ μήτ' ἐνοίκων μήτ' ἐπηλύδων τινὰ ἄγειν·
ἐὰν δὲ προστιθῇ τὸ καρτερόν,
τὸν μὴ βοηθήσαντα τῶνδε γαμόρων ἄτιμον
εἶναι ξὺν φυγῇ δημηλάτῳ.

The Argives have decided (*edoxen*) (…) that we are settlers (*metoikein*) in this land, and are free, subject to no seizure, and secure from robbery of man; that no one, native or alien, may lead us captive; but, if they turn to violence, any landholder who refuses to rescue us, should both forfeit his rights and suffer public banishment.[272]

270 Translation by Smyth (1926). Coincidentally, Pelasgus, before judging the case, asks the girls to show that in their exile they did not violate the local laws of Egypt (vv. 387–391).

271 Certainly, he could have rejected the petition. Today, it is also possible to impose provisional conditions if there is an issue involving a State's security: "Nothing in this Convention shall prevent a Contracting State, in time of war or other grave and exceptional circumstances, from taking provisionally measures which it considers to be essential to the national security in the case of a particular person, pending a determination by the Contracting State that that person is in fact a refugee and that the continuance of such measures is necessary in his case in the interests of national security" (article 9 of the Convention of 1951).

272 Translation by Smyth (1926) with minor corrections.

The decree, headed by the typical formula for decisions of the Assembly (*edoxe toi demoi*, "it seemed good to the people", "the people decided"), is rich in technical expressions, making the tragedy into a space in which the legal reality of its time is represented theatrically.[273] The play employs many features of the institution of *asylia* as it functioned in the context of wartime and the treatment of foreigners as victims of hostilities; it establishes that the women will receive the specific political status of metics (as reflected in the verb μετοικεῖν, *metoikein*):[274] although they will not become citizens and will not be naturalized, this will allow them to reside in Argos and enjoy certain rights.[275]

The play also refers to the obligations associated with asylum, especially with regard to the granting of housing to the Danaids (957–961):

καὶ δώματ' ἐστὶ πολλὰ μὲν τὰ δήμια, δεδωμάτωμαι δ' οὐδ' ἐγὼ σμικρᾷ χερί. ἔνθ' ὑμίν ἐστιν εὐτύκους ναίειν δόμους πολλῶν μετ' ἄλλων· εἰ δέ τις μείζων χάρις, πάρεστιν οἰκεῖν καὶ μονορρύθμους δόμους.	As for places inside to lodge, there are plenty of the public sort. For on no modest scale do I myself live (*oikein*), where, in company with many others, you may occupy abodes suitably prepared; or, if it is more pleasing to you, it is free for you also to make your home in dwellings of separate sort.[276]

There is also an explicit reference to the duty deriving from the principle of no-return (*non-refoulement*): "But to this purpose a decree has been passed by the unanimous resolve of the people of the State, never, under compulsion (*biai*),

273 The play is rife with language belonging to Athenian democratic thought, centered around concepts such as *psephos* ("vote," 8, 373, 601, 640, 644, 739, 943, 965) and *psephisma* ("decree," 601). By means of legal institutions such as *proxenia* and *prostasia*—referring to foreign representation in Athens—Gauthier (1972: 53–58) has revealed in the play interesting references to the contemporary Athenian political climate. In particular, the decree of *asylia* includes turns of phrase that properly belong to the language of politics; these have been analyzed by Cuniberti (2001: 148, n. 26). Cf. chapter 2, p. 74.

274 Bakewell (1997).

275 This recalls the rights provided for in the 1951 Convention as a consequence of the legal status of refugees (articles 12 to 16).

276 Translation by Smyth (1926). In this connection, article 21 of the Convention of 1951 decrees: "As regards housing, the Contracting States, in so far as the matter is regulated by laws or regulations or is subject to the control of public authorities, shall accord to refugees lawfully staying in their territory treatment as favourable as possible and, in any event, not less favourable than that accorded to aliens generally in the same circumstances."

to surrender (*mepot' ekdounai*) this association of women" (ψῆφος κέκρανται, μήποτ' ἐκδοῦναι βίᾳ /στόλον γυναικῶν· τῶνδ' ἐφήλωται τορῶς / γόμφος διαμπάξ, ὡς μένειν ἀραρότως, 943–945).[277]

Since this is a decision agreed to by the community on the basis of a collective vote, the legal-political character of the grant of asylum in the play is clear. Pelasgus's attitude is surprising in that, even though he is king (399), he voluntarily decides to consult with the Assembly, thus turning Argos into a sort of democratic monarchy.[278] The connection between the on-stage action of *Suppliants* and the Athens of its audience is plain:[279] Aeschylus ultimately gives us a narrative that, through the mythical story of the Danaids, portrays the triumph of liberty over foreign violence. The hallowing on the stage of protection for foreigners allows the spectators to understand the logic of their supplication—and consequently of asylum itself—as an institution that also applies to those who come from a barbarous land like Egypt.

Strictly speaking, however, the antithesis that the play suggests between Greek and barbarian[280] is resolved through diplomatic forbearance when the maidens appeal to Pelasgus by outlining a mythical past that, through their ancestor Io, makes them Argives in some sense. We should point out that the play does not portray the possible opposition between a natural right of sanctuary (*asylia*) and the secular-positivist interest of the State,[281] nor the philanthropy of an Argos willing to take in the marginalized and disadvantaged without much consideration.[282] Rather, it represents a political artifact in which the conceding of rights to the suppliants highlights local benevolence in the service of diplomacy. With Aeschylus's tragedy, Athens thus establishes itself as a

277 The prohibition on expulsion and return is provided for in article 33.1 of the Convention of 1951 as follows: "No Contracting State shall expel or return ("refouler") a refugee in any manner whatsoever to the frontiers of territories where his life or freedom would be threatened on account of his race, religion, nationality, membership of a particular social group or political opinion".

278 Burian (1974).

279 Concerning the good diplomatic relations between Athens and Argos (united in opposition to the Spartans), verses 289–291 and 762–764 of Aeschylus's tragedy *Eumenides*—produced in 458—are rather explicit. In this play, Orestes declares Argos an eternal ally of Athens. We can readily understand how *Suppliants* portrays Athenian benevolence in a propagandistic fashion, by exalting its equity and openness in comparison to "others"; cf. Chou (2012).

280 This interplay is analyzed, in all its subtlety, by Mitchell (2006).

281 This is suggested by Ostwald (1986: 141).

282 Moreover, barbarians are described in the play as disrespectful toward the gods, violent, and impious (750–752, 755–759, 884, 893–894, 903–904, 921, 927).

privileged space, a center of attraction for other Greek communities. In the fiction presented on the stage, the figure of a democratic king who has recourse to the city's popular institutions allows the *polis* of Argos (as Athens' alter ego) to lay the rhetorical groundwork for a legalistic imperialism—founded on generosity—that can only be fully understood in light of interstate relations in the late fifth century.[283]

If this is the case, the tragedy *Suppliants* (to which I have given such emphasis) employs a legalistic narrative concerning *asylia* and supplication (ἱκετεία, *hiketeia*) to establish, through the protection of victims and the weak, humanitarianism as a badge of supremacy, as a form of persuasive rhetoric.[284] But not only this: the voice of Aeschylus, speaking through his characters, also gives us a warning about the risks that the manipulation of the discourse of humanitarianism may involve. Cognizant of the true meanings of social harmony, prudence, and piety, the Greeks teach us that sometimes we cannot distinguish genuine humanitarian manifestos—which were described as the most important starting point for any regulation of armed conflict—[285] from those which, projecting national categories onto "the others," seek thereby to conceal imperialist aims.

The examination of Greek texts on the subject of *ius in bello* reveals how the excesses of war in practice were frequently balanced on the discursive level by the effort to impose legal-political rules of behavior that, once removed from the religious sphere, can serve as useful background for thinking about the traditional basis of modern international humanitarian law. Criticism of abuses in times of armed conflict responded to a logic of compassion for other people's suffering and altruism for the most disadvantaged that does not seem alien to the Greek point of view.[286] On the other hand, if one bears in

283 In an excellent book, Tzanetou (2012) has shown how Greek tragedy served as an ideological vehicle to ensure the consolidation of Athenian supremacy through the institutional practices of supplication. Although Tzanetou does not include *Suppliants* among the texts she studies (because it is not set in Athens itself), her conclusions are fully applicable to our discussion here.

284 This is achieved through the consolidation of moral supremacy at the international level. According to Low (2007: 254), "the appeal to moral criteria frequently relies upon, and more often is used to create or sustain, a position of power in the interstate system".

285 Cf. Pictet (1984: 7).

286 Sternberg (2006). A stronger argument for Greek altruism can be found in Herman (2006: 347–359). According to Low (2007: 173–186), helping the weak was a domestic rule that soon became applicable to international relations.

mind the logic of subordination whose political imposition may be an aim of international law, one cannot ignore the possibility that in many cases these "protections" subserve desires for supremacy. It is well known that fifth-century Athens sought, in the context of the Peloponnesian War, to promulgate and extend—among friends and foes alike—the imperialist models upholding its power; it is therefore reasonable to imagine that references to wartime *nomoi* may often suggest a use of the legal language of humanitarianism connected less closely with the protection of the victims of hostilities than with the hegemonic purposes of a *polis* that wanted to win a war.[287]

4 The Hague in Greece: The *nomos* of the Greeks with Respect to the Restriction of Means and Methods of Warfare

Historical consideration of the nature of the legal provisions that make up the so-called "Law of The Hague" involves an analysis of the restrictions that were progressively imposed on the use of means and methods of combat.[288] Inasmuch as the use of armaments is inherent in the very existence of war, a diachronic examination of the law applicable to armed conflicts must include a historical survey of the rules relating to the limitation of such weaponry as may be disproportionate or may harm those who are not participating in hostilities.[289] In this section, therefore, I shall seek to examine what sources say concerning restrictions on armaments and their uses, thus concluding my inquiry

---

287 "It is doubtful that Athenians differed much from other Greek cities in placing their own interests first in interstate relations, but they do seem to have diverged in the emphasis they placed on the claim that helping other peoples was a national trait. We are left with the paradox that Athenians were strongly drawn to a noble idea of helping others but no more inclined in reality to altruism in interstate relations than was any other Greek state. Whether we view Athenians as Idealists forced to accomodate themselves to a Realist world or as Realists with romantic inclinations, Athenians did not appear to have let helping other states get in the way of pursuing their strategic objectives" (Christ, 2012: 176). The longstanding debate on the popularity of the Athenian imperial foreign policy among the allied cities falls beyond the scope of this study.

288 The "Law of The Hague" refers to the stream of international humanitarian law that is specifically concerned with limiting violence in armed conflicts by limiting the the weapons than can be employed in hostilities (means) as well as the ways in which those arms can be used, tactically or strategically, in the course of military operations (methods). Cf. Verri (1988: 74–77).

289 The work done by Harris and Paxman (2002) is interesting in this respect. Cf. also Wheelis (1999).

into the existence of an inter-*polis* or panhellenic *nomos*.[290] This leg of my journey will be shorter than the last, since weapons and military technology were seen by the Greeks as having limited impact: from the perspective of the warrior mentality, victory was assured not by the instruments of attack but by political and moral superiority.[291]

I should begin by pointing out that the *nomoi* relating to the customary code of honor that regulated behavior in war authorized the use of methods that deceived the opponent by means of military tactics.[292] However, certain religious and ethical guidelines led to a limitation of some means of waging war that were considered excessive by the parties themselves. Thus, we find already in the archaic sources some references to the necessity to limit the use of poisoned weapons due to possible indiscriminate effects of which the gods disapproved. In the *Odyssey*, for example, Odysseus goes to Ephyra to seek a poisonous drug with which to coat his arrows, but Ilus refuses to give it to him, saying that the gods do not condone such things (ᾤχετο γὰρ καὶ κεῖσε θοῆς ἐπὶ νηὸς Ὀδυσσεὺς / φάρμακον ἀνδροφόνον διζήμενος, ὄφρα οἱ εἴη / ἰοὺς χρίεσθαι χαλκήρεας· ἀλλ᾽ ὁ μὲν οὔ οἱ / δῶκεν, ἐπεί ῥα θεοὺς νεμεσίζετο αἰὲν ἐόντας, 1.261–263).[293]

A second example, much later in time, is provided by a passage from Strabo (10.1.12) in which we find one of the few preserved descriptions of a written agreement on wartime *nomoi*.[294] The agreement, reached between the Euboean cities of Chalcis and Eretria and preserved on a stele in the sanctuary of Artemis Amarynthus, limited the weapons that could be used:

τὸ μὲν οὖν πλέον ὡμολόγουν ἀλλήλαις αἱ πόλεις αὗται, περὶ δὲ Ληλάντου διενεχθεῖσαι … οὐδ᾽ οὕτω τελέως ἐπαύσαντο … ὥστ᾽ ἐν τῷ πολέμῳ κατὰ αὐθάδειαν δρᾶν ἕκαστα, ἀλλὰ	Now in general these cities were in accord with one another, and when differences arose concerning the Lelantine Plain they did not so completely break off relations as to wage their wars in all respects according to the will of

290 If, as Prieto Sanjuán (2007: 19) argues, "los métodos y medios de combate son tan antiguos como la misma humanidad," it is also certain that from the earliest use of weapons there was a perceptible desire to limit their pernicious effects.

291 Echeverría Rey (2010: 26). Plutarch, for example, relates that the Spartan king Archidamus, upon seeing a catapult brought from Sicily for the first time, declared that it would mean the end of masculine virtue (*Regum et imperatorum apophthegmata* 191e).

292 On this subject, cf. Krentz (2000: 167–200).

293 Phillipson (1911, ii: 209). On Homeric sources, see Gillespie (2011, 3: 87).

294 Gaurier (2014: 68); Gillespie (2011, 3: 8).

συνέθεντο ἐφ᾽ οἷς συστήσονται τὸν ἀγῶνα. δηλοῖ δὲ καὶ τοῦτο ἐν τῷ Ἀμαρυνθίῳ στήλη τις φράζουσα μὴ χρῆσθαι τηλεβόλοις.

each, but they came to an agreement as to the conditions under which they were to conduct the fight. This fact, among others, is disclosed by a certain pillar in the Amarynthium, which forbids the use of long distance missiles.[295]

The passage shows us a conventional prohibition on the use of missile weapons, agreed to on both sides. Although it seems clear that this is an exceptional measure, inasmuch as "in fact among all the customs (*ethon*) of warfare and of the use of arms there neither is, nor has been, any single custom (*ethos*)" (καὶ γὰρ δὴ καὶ τῶν πολεμικῶν ἐθῶν καὶ τῶν ὁπλισμῶν οὐχ ἓν οὔτ᾽ ἔστιν οὔτ᾽ ἦν ἔθος, 10.1.12), this is nonetheless a case in which a definite agreement was negotiated with the intention of limiting a common means of combat for reasons that were political and perhaps humanitarian.[296] Other texts also address themselves to the uses of certain weapons of the sort that today are prohibited by international multilateral legal instruments.[297]

For example, the first allusion in the Greek world to the use of biological weapons appears in connection with mythology.[298] In the second of the twelve labors that Heracles, son of Zeus and Alcmene, had to perform as a penance imposed by Apollo for killing his children, the hero contronts the fearsome Lernaean Hydra, a merciless aquatic monster in the shape of a multi-headed serpent (its heads numbered from three or five up to 100 or even 10,000 heads, depending on the source) with poisonous breath.[299] According to the legend, Heracles, having arrived at the marsh near Lake Lerna, covered his nose and mouth with a cloth to protect himself from the monster's breath and shot flaming arrows at its refuge (the spring of Amymone) to force it out. With the help of

---

295 Translation by Jones (1924).

296 A detailed analysis of this agreement is provided by Wheeler (1987). On this convention as an example of moderation in war, see Neff (2005: 23). Cf. Polybius (13.3) on the ancient prohibition of hidden weapons.

297 On this topic, it is worth reading Mayor (2003), who examines the various precedents in antiquity for the use of biological, toxin, and chemical weapons. Nevertheless, it should be obvious that in the ancient world there were no "weapons of mass destruction"—the term used today to encompass these three technologies—as Echeverría Rey (2010: 38) makes clear: "The material potential of ancient technology for killing, and the very existence of this 'annihilation principle' as the final goal of ancient warfare should be revised. On the one hand, ancient weapons were not really effective artifacts for mass destruction."

298 I have studied these passages in Buis (2013b).

299 Hyginus, 30. As we shall see, this is an episode that appears repeatedly in Greek literature and in images on ancient pottery; on this, see Venit (1989).

his nephew, Iolaus, who burned the stumps of the Hydra's neck to prevent the severed heads from growing back, Heracles destroyed the creature, took its only immortal head and buried it under a large rock on the sacred road between Lerna and Elis, but not before dipping his arrows in the Hydra's poisonous blood.[300] As mentioned in the story, shortly after his third marriage Heracles and his wife Deianira had to cross a river. A centaur named Nessus carried Deianira across, but then attempted to rape her. Enraged, Heracles shot one of his poisoned arrows[301] from the other bank to kill the centaur in revenge.

Apart from this mythological example, the first documented historical use of biological weapons in western history is probably the contamination of the water of the River Pleistus, a strategy used by the Amphictyonic League to capture and destroy the besieged city of Cirrha (Kirrha) or Crisa at the beginning of the sixth century.[302] This was during the so-called First Sacred War,[303] which took place from 595 to 585 between the Amphictyonic League—a coalition of Greek city-states that included Athens—and the fortified city of Cirrha, which was located in Phocis.[304] The conflict had arisen because of frequent robberies and other abuse committed by the Cirrhaeans against foreigners traveling to Delphi, and because of Cirrhaean encroachment on lands sacred to Apollo.[305] In his speech *Against Ctesiphon*, Aeschines detailed these impious acts (3.107):

300 In his *Description of Greece*, Pausanias (2.37.4) says he believes that the Lernaean Hydra was bigger than other water-snakes and that its venom was so lethal that Heracles used it for his arrows: ἐγὼ δὲ τὸ θηρίον πείθομαι τοῦτο καὶ μεγέθει διενεγκεῖν ὑδρῶν ἄλλων καὶ τὸν ἰὸν οὕτω δή τι ἔχειν ἀνίατον ὡς τὸν Ἡρακλέα ἀπὸ τῆς χολῆς αὐτοῦ τὰς ἀκίδας φαρμακεῦσαι τῶν ὀιστῶν.

301 Significantly, there seems to be an etymological connection in Greek between the words τόξον, *toxon* ("arrow") and τόξις, *toxis* ("poison"). Cf. Chantraine (1990²: 1124–1125, s.v.).

302 The Great Amphictyonic League of Delphi was a confederation of Greek *poleis* united for the protection of the sanctuary of Apollo and for legitimate collective defense; cf. Bonner and Smith (1943).

303 On the First Sacred War, one may consult the works of Sordi (1953) and Forrest (1956). Some historians have called into question the details of this conflict as presented in ancient sources. An overview of their positions can be found in Lehmann (1980: 242–246). See also Robertson (1978), whose arguments are similar.

304 On its geographic location and proximity to Delphi, see Rousset (2002). On its characteristics and peculiarities, cf. Dor, Jannoray, H. van Effenterre and M. van Effenterre (1960). According to more recent studies, the city did not belong to Delphi (even if it functioned as its port) but rather was subject extraterritorially to the administration of the Amphicyonic League. Cf. Mogens and Nielsen (2004: 419–420).

305 Notably, the temple of Apollo at Delphi was a site of crucial importance for the establishment of interhellenic peace, and the influence of the gods' oracles in the conduct of hostilities had great importance in classical times, as Phillipson (1911, ii: 219–221) clearly shows.

ἔστι γάρ, ὦ ἄνδρες Ἀθηναῖοι, τὸ Κιρραῖον ὠνομασμένον πεδίον καὶ λιμὴν ὁ νῦν ἐξάγιστος καὶ ἐπάρατος ὠνομασμένος. ταύτην ποτὲ τὴν χώραν κατῴκησαν Κιρραῖοι καὶ Κραγαλίδαι, γένη παρανομώτατα, οἳ εἰς τὸ ἱερὸν τὸ ἐν Δελφοῖς καὶ περὶ τὰ ἀναθήματα ἠσέβουν, ἐξημάρτανον δὲ καὶ εἰς τοὺς Ἀμφικτύονας. ἀγανακτήσαντες δ' ἐπὶ τοῖς γιγνομένοις μάλιστα μέν, ὡς λέγονται, οἱ πρόγονοι οἱ ὑμέτεροι, ἔπειτα καὶ οἱ ἄλλοι Ἀμφικτύονες, μαντείαν ἐμαντεύσαντο παρὰ τῷ θεῷ, τίνι χρὴ τιμωρίᾳ τοὺς ἀνθρώπους τούτους μετελθεῖν.

There is, fellow citizens, a plain, called the plain of Cirrha, and a harbor, now known as "dedicate and accursed." This district was once inhabited by the Cirrhaeans and the Cragalidae, most lawless tribes, who repeatedly committed sacrilege against the shrine at Delphi and the votive offerings there, and who transgressed against the Amphictyons also. This conduct exasperated all the Amphictyons, and your ancestors most of all, it is said, and they sought at the shrine of the god an oracle to tell them with what penalty they should visit these men.[306]

The same orator indicates that, in response to the inquiry, "[t]he Pythia replied that they must fight against the Cirrhaeans and the Cragalidae day and night, bitterly ravage their country, enslave the inhabitants, and dedicate the land to the Pythian Apollo and Artemis and Leto and Athena Pronaea, that for the future it lie entirely uncultivated; that they must not till this land themselves nor permit another [to do so]" (καὶ αὐτοῖς ἀναιρεῖ ἡ Πυθία πολεμεῖν Κιρραίοις καὶ Κραγαλίδαις πάντ' ἤματα καὶ πάσας νύκτας, καὶ τὴν χώραν αὐτῶν ἐκπορθήσαντας καὶ αὐτοὺς ἀνδραποδισαμένους ἀναθεῖναι τῷ Ἀπόλλωνι τῷ Πυθίῳ καὶ τῇ Ἀρτέμιδι καὶ τῇ Λητοῖ καὶ Ἀθηνᾷ Προναίᾳ ἐπὶ πάσῃ ἀεργίᾳ, καὶ ταύτην τὴν χώραν μήτ' αὐτοὺς ἐργάζεσθαι μήτ' ἄλλον ἐᾶν, 3.108). The religious instructions had immediate practical repercusssions: through a motion proposed by Solon, the words of the god acquired legal force: "Now when they had received this oracle, the Amphictyons voted, on motion of Solon of Athens, a man able as a lawgiver and versed in poetry and philosophy, to march against the accursed men according to the oracle of the god" (λαβόντες δὲ τὸν χρησμὸν τοῦτον οἱ Ἀμφικτύονες ἐψηφίσαντο Σόλωνος εἰπόντος Ἀθηναίου τὴν γνώμην, ἀνδρὸς καὶ νομοθετῆσαι δυνατοῦ καὶ περὶ ποίησιν καὶ φιλοσοφίαν διατετριφότος, ἐπιστρατεύειν ἐπὶ τοὺς ἐναγεῖς κατὰ τὴν μαντείαν τοῦ θεοῦ).[307]

The members of the League thereupon swore to level Cirrha and wreak havoc on the surrounding area. They added a curse in the name of Apollo:

306 Greek text and translation by Adams (1919).

307 Greek texts and translations by Adams (1919).

the Cirrhaeans' land would yield no crops, the offspring of their wives and livestock would be deformed and the whole race that inhabited the city would be eradicated.[308]

According to our ancient sources, the capture of the city of Cirrha required the use of hellebore (*helleborus foetidus*)—a plant capable of seriously affecting the health of the local population—which, by causing widespread illness, allowed the entry into the city of the its enemies. The destruction of this *polis* was attributed to various generals, statesmen, and even doctors.[309] While it seems that the leader of the attack was the tyrant Cleisthenes of Sicyon,[310] who apparently used his powerful fleet to blockade the city's port while the army of his amphictyonic allies besieged Cirrha, ancient historians who describe the episode offer slightly different versions of what occurred.[311]

Although it may be a late source, it is worth reproducing here a passage from Frontinus, a Roman writer of the first century CE, who briefly made reference to Cirrha in his *Stratagemata*, in a chapter that deals with ways of diverting rivers and polluting their waters (*de fluminum derivatione et vitiatione aquarum*) in times of war (3.7.6):

Cleisthenes Sicyonius ductum aquarum in oppidum Crisaeorum ferentem rupit; mox adfectis siti restituit aquam elleboro corruptam, qua usos profluvio ventris deficientes cepit.	Clisthenes of Sicyon cut the water-pipes leading into the town of the Cirrhaeans. Then when the townspeople were suffering from thirst, he turned on the water again, now poisoned with hellebore. When the inhabitants used this, they were weakened by diarrhoea.[312]

Frontinus relates how, by sabotaging the pipe, the allies occasioned great thirst in the city; when they restored it and allowed the water to flow into

308 Of course, one must recognize that this is a quotation from oratory. On the historical value of these literary sources and their closeness to the testimony of historians like Herodotus and Thucydides, see Pearson (1941).

309 The city's destruction was, obviously, the major event of the war, as Jannoray (1937) explains.

310 McGregor (1941); cf. also Parker (1994: 404–424).

311 Mayor (2003: 100–105).

312 Translation by Bennett (1925) with corrections.

Cirrha, the citizens immediately began to drink the water, not knowing that Cleisthenes had poisoned it with hellebore.

Polyaenus, a Macedonian writer of the second century CE, explains how, after the pipe was discovered, the attackers added hellebore to the water at its source, without cutting off the water supply. In his *Stratagemata*, a work in eight books presented to the Roman emperors Lucius Verus and Marcus Aurelius during the Parthian War (163 AD), Polyaenus explains that the strategy used at Cirrha was not devised by Cleisthenes but by the general Eurylochus, who advised his allies to gather a great quantity of hellebore from Anticyra. He writes (6.13):

Ἀμφικτύονες Κίρραν ἐπολιόρκουν καὶ δὴ κρυπτὸν ὑπόνομον εὗρον ἄγοντα ναματιαῖον ὕδωρ πολύ· καὶ τῇ Εὐρυλόχου γνώμῃ συλλέξαντες Ἀντικύραθεν πολὺ πλῆθος ἐλλεβόρου κατέμιξαν τῷ ὕδατι. Κιρραῖοι πιόντες διαφθείρονται τὰς γαστέρας καὶ πάντες ἐκλυθέντες ἔκειντο· Ἀμφικτύονες ἀπονητὶ τὴν πόλιν ἔλαβον κειμένων τῶν πολεμίων.[313]

The Amphictyons, when they were besieging Cirrha, discovered an aqueduct, which supplied the city with water. On the advice of Eurylochus, they poisoned the water with hellebore, which they procured in great quantity from Anticyra. The inhabitants of Cirrha, who made constant use of the water, were seized by a violent sickness, and were unable to continue fighting. Under these circumstances, the Amphictyons easily defeated them, and made themselves masters of the place.[314]

In the second century CE, Pausanias mentions the site of Cirrha in the course of describing his visit to Phocis. Observing the desolation of the countryside and attributing it to a curse resulting from the anger of Delphian Apollo, he introduces a digression relating that it was the great Solon of Athens who decided to divert the course of the river Pleistus so that it did not reach Cirrha. Solon hoped to defeat the Cirrhaeans through thirst, but they were able to obtain water from their wells and from rainwater. According to the passage, Solon added a great quantity of hellebore to the water of the Pleistus and let it flow once more into Cirrha. The poison then allowed the allies to destroy the city (10.37.7–8):

313 The Greek is from the editions of Woelfflin and Melber (1887) and Krentz and Wheeler (1994).

314 Translation by Shepherd (1793).

εὑρέθη δὲ καὶ ἕτερον τῷ Σόλωνι σόφισμα ἐς τοὺς Κιρραίους· τοῦ γὰρ Πλείστου τὸ ὕδωρ ῥέον διὰ ὀχετοῦ σφισιν ἐς τὴν πόλιν ἀπέστρεψεν ἀλλαχόσε ὁ Σόλων. καὶ οἱ μὲν πρὸς τοὺς πολιορκοῦντας ἔτι ἀντεῖχον ἔκ τε φρεάτων καὶ ὕδωρ τὸ ἐκ τοῦ θεοῦ πίνοντες· ὁ δὲ τοῦ ἐλλεβόρου τὰς ῥίζας ἐμβαλὼν ἐς τὸν Πλεῖστον, ἐπειδὴ ἱκανῶς τοῦ φαρμάκου τὸ ὕδωρ ᾔσθετο ἔχον, ἀπέστρεψεν αὖθις ἐς τὸν ὀχετόν. καὶ—ἐνεφορήσαντο γὰρ ἀνέδην οἱ Κιρραῖοι τοῦ ὕδατος—[καὶ] οἱ μὲν ὑπὸ ἀπαύστου τῆς διαρροίας ἐξέλιπον οἱ ἐπὶ τοῦ τείχους τὴν φρουράν, Ἀμφικτύονες δὲ ὡς εἷλον τὴν πόλιν …	Solon invented another trick to outwit the Cirrhaeans. The water of the river Pleistus ran along a channel to the city, and Solon diverted it in another direction. When the Cirrhaeans still held out against the besiegers, drinking well-water and rain-water, Solon threw into the Pleistus roots of hellebore, and when he perceived that the water held enough of the drug he diverted it back again into its channel. The Cirrhaeans drank without stint of the water, and those on the wall, seized with obstinate diarrhoea, deserted their posts, and the Amphictyons captured the city.[315]

Finally, some sources attribute the act to a physician. The writer Thessalus, for example, wrote in the fifth century that the attackers discovered the city's main water pipe after it was damaged by a horse's hoof. According to Thessalus, it was an Asclepiad called Nebrus who recommended to the allies that they poison the water with hellebore; this caused diarrhea in the defenders and left them weak: when they could no longer resist assault, they were destroyed.[316]

Although most scholarship concerning this episode implies a lack of definite consequences following from this form of attack and the later destruction of the city, it is important here to examine a brief passage from Aeschines that mentions a later legal agreement intended to prevent similar actions from happening in the future. In his speech *On the Embassy*, Aeschines explains, as follows, the content of the provisions and regulations agreed to by the amphictyons after the First Sacred War (2.115):

315 Translation by Jones (1918).

316 Mayor (2003) argues that, since Nebrus was supposedly an ancestor of Hippocrates, it would not be too much to suppose that perhaps the use of poison by his forebear led to the creation of the famous "Hippocratic Oath".

ἅμα δ' ἐξ ἀρχῆς διεξῆλθον τὴν κτίσιν τοῦ ἱεροῦ καὶ τὴν πρώτην σύνοδον γενομένην τῶν Ἀμφικτυόνων, καὶ τοὺς ὅρκους αὐτῶν ἀνέγνων, ἐν οἷς ἔνορκον ἦν τοῖς ἀρχαίοις, μηδεμίαν πόλιν τῶν Ἀμφικτυονίδων ἀνάστατον ποιήσειν, μηδ' ὑδάτων ναματιαίων εἴρξειν μήτ' ἐν πολέμῳ μήτ' ἐν εἰρήνῃ, ἐὰν δέ τις ταῦτα παραβῇ, στρατεύσειν ἐπὶ τοῦτον καὶ τὰς πόλεις ἀναστήσειν, καὶ ἐάν τις ἢ συλᾷ τὰ τοῦ θεοῦ, ἢ συνειδῇ τι, ἢ βουλεύσῃ τι κατὰ τῶν ἱερῶν, τιμωρήσειν καὶ χειρὶ καὶ ποδὶ καὶ φωνῇ καὶ πάσῃ δυνάμει· καὶ προσῆν τῷ ὅρκῳ ἀρὰ ἰσχυρά.

At the same time I reviewed from the beginning the story of the founding of the shrine, and of the first synod of the Amphictyons that was ever held; and I read their oaths, in which the men of ancient times swore that they would raze no city of the Amphictyonic states, nor shut them off from flowing water either in war or in peace; that if anyone should violate this oath, they would march against such an one and raze his cities; and if any one should violate the shrine of the god or be accessory to such violation, or make any plot against the holy places, they would punish him with hand and foot and voice, and all their power. To the oath was added a mighty curse.[317]

Total war, then, was prohibited, and was penalized by the league's twelve member cities.[318] Once again, religious and juridical elements come together in support of a means of restricting armed violence.[319] It is reasonable to conclude that, far from there being an indiscriminate use of poison in warfare, there was already, in the wake of its first recorded use, a clear need to establish religious and legal rules which, long before modern international humanitarian law, could avoid the superfluous damage and unnecessary suffering caused by the use of biological or chemical agents for military purposes.[320]

---

317 Translation by Adams (1919). Of course, we cannot say that this oath of the Amphictyons eliminated all violence in armed conflict, but the clause prohibiting the adulteration of waters is significant. According to Lombardo (2002: 49), the fact that such provisions were in place indicates that total destruction was one of war's possible outcomes.

318 Ilari (1980: 57).

319 "With the people of antiquity religion and law were twin-sisters that could not well be sundered; the commission of an offence against the one was usually met by penalties prescribed by the other, in addition to those laid down by itself. So that to offer any violence to a sacred place generally regarded as neutralized, was not only an offence against the presiding gods and rendered the transgressor liable to the unfailing retribution; it was also an infringement of the established 'law of nations'—whether taken universally, or in the more restricted sense of the law of the Hellenic communities—and, as such, was punishable by warlike measures on the part of offended States" (Phillipson, 1911, ii: 302).

320 The current status of the issue is evidenced by the amendment proposed at the Kampala Review Conference of the Rome Statute on the International Criminal Court (2010):

Furthermore, the example also reveals the existence of a discourse that considers inappropriate the manipulation of water or the environment for the purpose of waging war. With respect to the idea of environmental protection, we should remark that for the ancient Greeks nature meant a geographic space bearing the imprint of the divine presence; this did not, however, stand in the way of the exploitation of resources.[321] At a time long before the recognition that natural resources are scarce and the exploitation of the environment must be sustainable[322]—a recognition that does not occur until the second half of the twentieth century—Greek texts express concern for the environmental effects of war in terms of its consequences for agriculture.[323] For example, while it is true that forest fires were not common,[324] a few cases suggest that the destruction of virgin spaces was not done for the purpose of gratuitously harming the enemy but as an effective combat tactic to achieve a military purpose by weakening the adversaries.[325] Thus, during the battle at Pylos

---

seeking to amend Article 8(2)(e) of the agreement, it included as war crimes the use of dum-dum bullets and poison weapons in non-international armed conflict (their use in international armed conflicts being already subject to sanction).

321 See the recent work of Thommen (2012: 19–67).

322 The ancient evidence appears to show that the Greeks were not concerned with the protection of trees, except insofar as they had religious significance (Meiggs, 1982).

323 This is a topic of recent interest among scholars, as is shown by Hughes' addition of a new ninth chapter, "War and the Environment," to the second edition of his well-known book on the environment in antiquity (2014). On the tactic of destroying the enemy's crops—and its drastic consequences—see Hanson (1998: 42–76).

324 Papanastasis, Arianoutsou and Papanastasis (2010: 130), who identify only a few cases where it had a military objective. Herodotus (6.75–81) mentions the Spartan victory at the battle of Sepeia (c. 494), where king Cleomenes tricked the Argives and massacred them by burning the sacred grove of Argos where they were seeking refuge.

325 Hughes (2013: 133), who later argues that "a balance with nature is a condition of peace and is upset by war as a matter of course" (2013: 138). Today, the environment is protected from the effects of hostilities in international armed conflicts: "It is prohibited to employ methods or means of warfare which are intended, or may be expected, to cause widespread, long-term and severe damage to the natural environment." (artícle 35.3 of AP-I). Artícle 55 of the same instrument adds that "care shall be taken in warfare to protect the natural environment against widespread, long-term and severe damage. This protection includes a prohibition of the use of methods or means of warfare which are intended or may be expected to cause such damage to the natural environment and thereby to prejudice the health or survival of the population." It also states that "attacks against the natural environment by way of reprisals are prohibited." These principles are also among the customary rules that have therefore become obligatory (cf. Henckaerts and Doswald-Beck, 2005, rule 45).

a group of Spartan soldiers were on a forested island and a fire, started by chance according to Thucydides (although perhaps it was set deliberately), allowed the Athenians to discover their location and capture them (4.29–30).[326] In 414, the Syracusans cut down olive trees on sacred ground in order to build a defensive work to hold off the Athenians (Thucydides 6.99.3); the Thebans did the same thing in 370 on the occasion of their invasion of the Peloponnese, in order to protect their encampments (Xenophon, *Hellenica* 6.5.30).[327]

To return to Heracles and his poisoned arrows, the question now would be how to reconcile the "humanitarian" version of war that we see in our historical texts with that unrestrained violence that the legends of heroes and angry gods seem to describe. The myths, repeated by the ancient Greeks to the point of exhaustion, should be understood as part of a shared knowledge that inculcated morals and lessons. Heracles' fate is not an exception to this rule; in fact, it demonstrates that, for classical Greek civilization, every disproportionate act, sooner or later and to a greater or lesser extent, carries with it a punishment. The centaur Nessus, dying from Heracles' poisoned arrows after trying to rape his wife, convinced Deianira to collect his blood if she wanted a potion that would guarantee her husband's love. Later, when Deianira suspected that Heracles preferred the company of another woman named Iole, she decided to smear some of his clothes with Nessus's blood. The story tells how, when Heracles' received a cloak from his wife and put it on, the poison in the blood entered his body, causing unbearable pain. Deianira, seeing what she had done, hanged herself. Heracles died willingly, asking for a pyre to be built as a means of ending his agony. The funeral pyre was lit by his friend Philoctetes, who in return for this deed received the bow and poisoned arrows as a legacy; later, the Greeks needed these weapons to win the war at Troy. At the end of his life, however, Philoctetes did not give them

326 We should remember that, nowadays, incendiary weapons may not be used to destroy the environment unless the areas in question are being used by the enemy for a military purpose. Article 2.4 of Protocol III (on incendiary weapons) of the 1980 Convention on Prohibitions or Restrictions on the Use of Certain Conventional Weapons which may be deemed to be Excessively Injurious or to have Indiscriminate Effects (1342 U.N.T.S. 171, adopted on October 10, 1980, in force since December 2, 1983) decrees that "it is prohibited to make forests or other kinds of plant cover the object of attack by incendiary weapons except when such natural elements are used to cover, conceal, or camouflage combatants or other military objectives, or are themselves military objectives."

327 Chandezon (1999: 199). In *Hellenica* 5.2.39, crops are used to protect a retreating army.

away; instead, the texts relate, he dedicated them in the Temple of Apollo, god of healing, so that no one would ever use them again. Perhaps this constitutes a mythical repentance which, along with the historical evidence, demonstrates how even in the bloodiest conflicts of antiquity—and even at the moment when the deadliest means of combat are being employed—humanitarian sentiment can often prevail.

5 Responding to Atrocity after the Conflict: Prosecution of War Crimes?

With respect to responsibility for violations of the "common" law—i.e., of outrages not permitted by the common, inter-*polis* or panhellenic *nomos*—I would call attention to various sources in which we read of courts intervening to judge offences committed in situtations of armed conflict.[328] I should point out that in general the *poleis*, considered as autonomous and self-sufficient entities, were not called to account for their responsibility in such acts.[329] Joining a league or a federation involved some surrender of sovereignty,[330] but although it was usual to have agreements or arbitrating authorities to resolve questions as to the distribution of power, the division of spoils, or disagreements concerning territory, the evidence does not allow us to infer the existence of tribunals established to resolve disputes relating to violations of the "common" law of the Greeks. A notable exception is the Plataean episode in Thucydides, in which the Spartans urged the Plataeans to surrender their city willingly and accept them as judges with the understanding that only the guilty would be prosecuted and that this would be done according to the *nomos* (εἰ βούλονται παραδοῦναι τὴν πόλιν ἑκόντες τοῖς Λακεδαιμονίοις καὶ δικασταῖς ἐκείνοις χρήσασθαι, τούς τε ἀδίκους κολάζειν, παρὰ δίκην δὲ οὐδένα, 3.52.2). The account goes on to say, however, that what followed was far from a conventional trial with the necessary impartiality: when the five Spartan judges arrived, they asked the Plataeans only if they had benefited Sparta and its allies in the war

328 An earlier, less developed version of this section was published as Buis (2013c).

329 It should be recalled here once again that there are sources which show the existence of dependent *poleis*, subject to the control of other city-states; cf. Hansen (1995: 21–44) and my discussion in chapter 2, pp. 77–84. On the absence of permanent tribunals to deal with breaches of international norms, cf. Sheppard (2005: 914). On alternative mechanisms to enforce their respect, such as reprisals, reputational damage, and divine punishment suffered by violators, see Bryant (2016: 35–37).

330 Nielsen (1996: 93).

(εἴ τι Λακεδαιμονίους καὶ τοὺς ξυμμάχους ἐν τῷ πολέμῳ τῷ καθεστῶτι ἀγαθόν [τι] εἰργασμένοι εἰσίν, 3.52.4). After speeches had been given for and against the Plataeans, the judges repeated their question (3.68.1) and finally decided to massacre the Plataean men and enslave the women.[331]

An "international" decision as to the responsibility of a city-state could also be made by leagues or federations. There is evidence that the Delphic Amphictyonic Council, for example, was responsible for judging not only individuals but also the *poleis* who were its members.[332] In our surviving sources, however, there seems to be no recorded case of a league's investigating actions that were carried out as part of a military campaign.[333]

Sources do often mention episodes involving arbitrating authorities. While inter-*polis* arbitrations in the Greek world generally were undertaken to resolve bilateral border disputes,[334] some passages suggest that this mechanism could be employed (and was sometimes required by compromissory clauses) for the discussion of sanctions in cases where wartime commitments were violated.[335] After the Athenians' disastrous Sicilian expedition of 415–413, for example, the Spartans accused their enemies of having broken their agreements (although they had been guilty of prior violations themselves) and we read that, although it had been stipulated that the parties would not resort to arms if the other side chose to have recourse to arbitration (ἐν ταῖς πρότερον ξυνθήκαις ὅπλα μὴ ἐπιφέρειν, ἢν δίκας ἐθέλωσι διδόναι), the Spartans did not accept arbitration when it was proposed by Athens (αὐτοὶ οὐχ ὑπήκουον ἐς δίκας προκαλουμένων τῶν Ἀθηναίων, Thucydides 7.18.2) in response to a violation of *nomos* (παρανόμημα, *paranomema*). Immediately after this, it is pointed out—in similar terms—that, having themselves committed an illicit act (again, a παρανόμημα), the Athenians had refused to accept arbitration despite the Spartans' invitation to do so (ἐς δίκας προκαλουμένων τῶν Λακεδαιμονίων οὐκ ἤθελον ἐπιτρέπειν, 7.18.3).[336]

331 For a rhetorical analysis of the trial of the Plataeans in Thucydides, see Debnar (2001: 125–146).

332 On their role in judging some violations of truces and sacred spaces, cf. Jacquemin (2000: 139–140) and Nevin (2017: 12).

333 Bonner and Smith (1943) report the "international" judgments of the league with respect to the member city-states; all these judgments relate to violations of sacred land or other religious prohibitions.

334 On this topic, see Buis (2006).

335 de Taube (1932: 24–46), Johnston (2008: 196–197), Gaurier (2014: 69). See also Ager (1993: 1–13).

336 Cf. Thucydides 1.140; 1.145.

Classical Greek sources mention some interesting cases of individual responsibility for acts committed in wartime. We should note that the sources contain a number of terms that refer to military stratagems, authorized ways for the combatants to fight:[337] among these permitted tactics, it was commonplace even to organize surprise attacks when the enemy was distracted or was otherwise not prepared to fight.[338]

When an act is identified as a violation, it is precisely because it has exceeded the normal behaviors seen as acceptable in a military context.[339] We should be aware that the domestic *nomos* listed military offenses among the crimes that could be committed against the *polis*.[340] The most serious illicit acts against the city of Athens, for instance, were divided into four substantive categories that were not exclusive of one another: treason (military or civil), subversion of the constitution and government—including the imposition of tyranny (actual, intended, or plotted)—receipt or payment of bribes and—under democracy and even before its establishment—deceiving the people (*apate tou demou*).[341] All these crimes against the administration of the *polis* could be prosecuted through a wide range of public actions available to interested citizens.[342]

---

337 Many of these terms (σοφία, τέχνη, μηχανή, δόλος, ἀπάτη) refer to deception of an adversary; cf. Wheeler (1988: 25–49).

338 For example, we have evidence of attacks by night or at dawn (Montagu, 2006: 57–58), during meals (58–59), and when the enemy was busy setting up or breaking down his encampment (59–60).

339 "Stories of enemy armies behaving badly seem to have been remembered primarily (but not exclusively) by the indignant communities that experienced those wrongs, passing traditions down orally and recording them in sacred histories and other records" (Nevin, 2017: 13).

340 Here I shall begin with a brief examination of military crimes and then proceed to consider some instances of international offenses; in the Greek world, there was a conceptual distinction similar to the one that exists today between illegal acts committed in the armed forces (which are violations of domestic law, whether of the criminal or the military code) and war crimes (which come under the category of international crimes because they involve more serious breaches of *ius in bello*). On this difference, see Solis (2010: 301).

341 Phillips (2013: 464).

342 These public actions—to which I have already referred in chapter 1 of this book—included γραφὴ προδοσίας (a public action—or *eisangelia*—for *prodosia*, "treason"), γραφὴ δώρων or δωροδοκίας (public action for *dorodokia*, "bribery" or "graft"), and γραφὴ κλοπῆς (public action for *klope*, "theft" of public goods). Cf. Hansen (1975), Roberts (1982). Pritchett (1974, ii: 27) has identified fourteen cases of γραφὴ προδοσίας and seven cases of γραφὴ δωροδοκίας in sources from the period. On the use of treason charges during the Peloponnesian War, one may consult Queyrel Bottineau (2010: 180–253).

A piece of evidence from oratory clearly shows that military offenses, including cowardice, desertion, and abandonment of one's post, came under the purview of Athenian justice. Aeschines says in *Against Ctesiphon* (3.175):

πρὸς δὲ ἀνδρείαν βραχύς μοι λείπεται λόγος. εἰ μὲν γὰρ ἠρνεῖτο μὴ δειλὸς εἶναι, ἢ ὑμεῖς μὴ συνήδετε, διατριβὴν ὁ λόγος ἄν μοι παρεῖχεν· ἐπειδὴ δὲ καὶ αὐτὸς ὁμολογεῖ ἐν ταῖς ἐκκλησίαις, καὶ ὑμεῖς σύνιστε, λοιπὸν ὑπομνῆσαι τοὺς περὶ τούτων κειμένους νόμους. ὁ γὰρ Σόλων ὁ παλαιὸς νομοθέτης ἐν τοῖς αὐτοῖς ἐπιτιμίοις ᾤετο δεῖν ἐνέχεσθαι τὸν ἀστράτευτον καὶ τὸν λελοιπότα τὴν τάξιν καὶ τὸν δειλὸν ὁμοίως· εἰσὶ γὰρ καὶ δειλίας γραφαί. καίτοι θαυμάσειεν ἄν τις ὑμῶν, εἰ εἰσὶ φύσεως γραφαί. εἰσίν. τίνος ἕνεκα; ἵν' ἕκαστος ἡμῶν τὰς ἐκ τῶν νόμων ζημίας φοβούμενος μᾶλλον ἢ τοὺς πολεμίους, ἀμείνων ἀγωνιστὴς ὑπὲρ τῆς πατρίδος ὑπάρχῃ.	But as concerns his bravery little remains for me to say. For if he denied that he is a coward, or if you did not know it as well as he does himself, the account of it would have detained me. But since he admits it himself in the assembly, and you are perfectly aware of it, it remains only to remind you of the laws as to this matter. For Solon, the ancient lawgiver, thought it necessary to apply the same penalties to the coward (*deilon*) as to the man who failed to take the field (*astrateuton*) or the man who deserted his post (*leloipota ten taxin*). For there are such things as indictments (*graphai*) for cowardice (*deilias*). Some of you may indeed be surprised to know that there are indictments for inborn defects. There are. To what end? In order that each man of us, fearing the punishment of the laws more than he fears the enemy, may become a better champion of his country.[343]

Athenian sources reveal the existence of specific procedures in response to military offenses: these included actions—all public—for general cowardice (γραφὴ δειλίας, *graphe deilias*), for failure to show up for a military campaign (γραφὴ ἀστρατείας, *graphe astrateias*), and for desertion or breaking ranks (γραφὴ λιποταξίου, *graphe lipotaxiou*).[344] There is debate as to whether the throwing away of one's shield (ῥίψασπις, *rhipsaspis*) could constitute a separate crime, but Theomnestus seems to have been charged with this by Lysitheus (according to Lysias 10, the charge was ultimately dismissed).[345] These judicial

343 Greek text and translation by Adams (1919).

344 Cf. Harrison (1971: 32), Todd (1993: 106). On the difficulty of classifying these actions with precision, owing to the vagueness of our sources, cf. Couvenhes (2005: 443, n. 70).

345 Osborne (1985: 56) has identified four cases in which this charge was employed: in two cases prosecution on the charge seems certain: Lysias 14.15, with reference to the son of Alcibiades, and Demosthenes 59.27, with reference to Stephanos; the other two represent

actions were based on the identification of crimes committed through negligence (ἀμέλεια, *ameleia*)[346] or inaction (βλακεύειν, *blakeuein*),[347] offenses characterized as acts contrary to the *nomoi* (ἀνομία, *anomia*) or the established order (ἀκοσμία, *akosmia*).[348]

An unresolved debate involves the question of what specific authority had jurisdiction over these military crimes. We know that army commanders had significant disciplinary authority and the power to enforce compliance with orders and punish infractions.[349] A passage in Demosthenes suggests that the army was charged with receiving complaints against its members in relation to relevant offenses. In *Against Boeotus* (39.17), the orator states:

ἀπελθόντων δ' ἐξ Εὐβοίας τῶν στρατιωτῶν λιποταξίου προσεκλήθη, κἀγὼ ταξιαρχῶν τῆς φυλῆς ἠναγκαζόμην κατὰ τοὐνόματος τοῦ ἐμαυτοῦ πατρόθεν δέχεσθαι τὴν λῆξιν· καὶ εἰ μισθὸς ἐπορίσθη τοῖς δικαστηρίοις, εἰσῆγον ἂν δῆλον ὅτι. ταῦτα δ' εἰ μὴ σεσημασμένων ἤδη συνέβη τῶν ἐχίνων, κἂν μάρτυρας ὑμῖν παρεσχόμην.	Then, after the soldiers had come back from Euboea, he was summoned on a charge of desertion (*lipotaxiou*), and I, as taxiarch of our tribe, was compelled to receive the summons, since it was against my name, that of my father being added; and if pay had been available for the juries, I should certainly have had to bring the case into court. If this had not occurred after the boxes had already been sealed, I should have brought you witnesses to prove it.[350]

Along with this piece of evidence, another passage, now from Plato, suggests that judicial proceedings should be conducted before military officials, the ἄρχοντες πολεμικοί (*arkhontes polemikoi*). Thus, justice was administered among equals (*Laws* 943a–b):

possible cases: Demosthenes 21.103, with reference to Euctemon, and Lysias 10, with reference to Lysitheus.

346 Xenophon, *Anabasis* 5.8.1. Cf. 5.8.13 on neglect of discipline (ἀταξία, *ataxia*).

347 Xenophon, *Anabasis* 5.8.15.

348 Thucydides 2.87.9; Lysias 3.45; cf. Xenophon, *Anabasis* 3.2.31, 5.7.34; 8.22, where in addition it is mentioned that there are criminal actions for πονηρία (*poneria*) and κακία (*kakia*).

349 See Couvenhes (2005: 440–441), who further points out that the penal powers inherent in their role were delimited by various sorts of military regulations. Although we know of such regulations in hellenistic times, evidence from the classical period is extremely scarce: cf. Fernández Nieto (1997).

350 Translation by Murray (1939).

ἔπαινον μὲν δὴ τοῦτον ἀκούειν τὸν νέον χρῆν δοκεῖν πολεμικοῦ περὶ βίου, νόμους δ᾽ αὖ τούσδε· στρατεύεσθαι τὸν καταλεγέντα ἢ τὸν ἐν μέρει τινὶ τεταγμένον. ἐὰν δέ τις ἐκλείπῃ τινὶ κάκῃ μὴ στρατηγῶν ἀφέντων, γραφὰς ἀστρατείας εἶναι πρὸς τοὺς πολεμικοὺς ἄρχοντας, ὅταν ἔλθωσιν ἀπὸ στρατοπέδου, δικάζειν δὲ τοὺς στρατεύσαντας ἑκάστους χωρίς, ὁπλίτας τε καὶ ἱππέας καὶ τἆλλα ἐμπολέμια ἕκαστα ὡσαύτως, καὶ εἰσάγειν ὁπλίτας μὲν εἰς τοὺς ὁπλίτας, ἱππέας δὲ εἰς τοὺς ἱππέας καὶ τοὺς ἄλλους δὲ κατὰ ταὐτὰ εἰς τοὺς αὑτῶν συννόμους· ἐὰν δέ τις ὄφλῃ, ὑπάρχειν μὲν αὐτῷ μήποτε τῆς ὅλης ἀριστείας ἀγωνιστῇ γενέσθαι μηδὲ ἀστρατείας ἄλλον γράψασθαί ποτε μηδὲ κατηγόρῳ τούτων πέρι γενέσθαι, πρὸς τούτοις δ᾽ ἔτι προστιμᾶν αὐτῷ τὸ δικαστήριον ὅτι χρὴ παθεῖν ἢ ἀποτίνειν.

Such is the laudation of the military life to which, as we hold, the youth ought to hearken, and its laws are these:—He that is enrolled or put on some rota must perform military service. If anyone, through cowardice, fails to present himself without leave from the commanders, he shall be indicted for desertion (*graphas astrateias*) before the military officers (*pros tous polemikous arkhontas*) when they return from camp, and each class of those who have served shall sit by themselves as judge—that is, hoplites, cavalry, and each of the other branches—and they shall summon hoplites before the hoplites, cavalrymen before the cavalry, and all others in like manner before soldiers of their own class; and any man that is convicted shall be debarred from ever competing for any distinction and from ever prosecuting another for shirking service, or acting as accuser in connection with such charges; and, in addition to this, what he ought to suffer or pay shall be determined by the court (*dikasterion*).[351]

The concluding reference to the people's court has raised some doubts concerning the possibility of refering a case to the civilian legal authorities. These uncertainties are reinforced by a passage in Lysias (*Against Alcibiades* 14.5) whose wording seems to confirm the existence of real military courts made up of army officers:

τολμῶσι γάρ τινες λέγειν ὡς οὐδεὶς ἔνοχός ἐστι λιποταξίου οὐδὲ δειλίας· μάχην γὰρ οὐδεμίαν γεγονέναι, τὸν δὲ νόμον κελεύειν, ἐάν τις λίπῃ τὴν τάξιν εἰς τοὐπίσω δειλίας ἕνεκα, μαχομένων τῶν ἄλλων, περὶ τούτου τοὺς στρατιώτας δικάζειν. ὁ δὲ νόμος

For some are bold enough to assert that nobody can be chargeable with desertion (*lipotaxiou*) or cowardice (*deilias*), since no battle has taken place; that the law merely provides for a court-martial (*tous stratiotas dikazein*) on anyone who, from cowardice, has deserted the ranks and retreated while the rest

351 Translation by Bury (1967–1968).

οὐ περὶ τούτων κελεύει μόνον, ἀλλὰ καὶ ὁπόσοι ἂν μὴ παρῶσιν ἐν τῇ πεζῇ στρατιᾷ. ἀνάγνωθί μοι τὸν νόμον.	were fighting. But the provisions of the law apply not only to such a case, but also to that of anyone who fails to appear in the infantry lines. Please read the law.[352]

We need not discuss the various philological interpretations of this passage that have been presented: it is sufficient to note that the phrase τοὺς στρατιώτας δικάζειν (*tous stratiotas dikazein*), which is usually translated as "let the soldiers judge it," could also be translated as "let them judge the soldiers." If the accusative is the object of the infinitive rather than its subject, then this passage in Lysias makes no reference to specialized courts.[353]

In the realm of transitional justice (i.e., the deliberate effort to create an authority to oversee justice and reconciliation following an armed conflict or civil war), Athenian history records a number of effective means of dealing with the aftermath of conflict.[354] In fact, three almost contemporary episodes from the end of the Peloponnesian War allow us to illustrate the multiplicity of available options: what we see is an interesting contrast between the imposition, by the victors, of an *ad hoc* court of allied cities and, in the local Athenian context, the establishment of judicial punishments for treason and the granting of amnesties.

The first episode occurred near the end of the war in the year 405, and its relevance lies in its demonstration of a possible "international" legal aspect of war crimes—specifically, the mistreatment of captured enemy soldiers—in the Greek world. According to Xenophon's *Hellenica*, the Spartan general Lysander sailed from Rhodes to deal with revolted cities on the coast of Asia Minor. Having won a major naval victory in the Dardanelles, and having liberated those captured by the enemy, Lysander transferred his loot and his prisoners—among whom were Philocles, Adeimantus, and other Athenian generals—to Lampsacus. There he summoned his allies to a tribunal in order to judge the atrocities committed by his enemies, especially the Athenians, who had voted that, in the event of victory, they would cut off the hands of the vanquished (2.1.31–32):[355]

352 Translation by Lamb (1930).

353 This is the interpretation elaborated by Bertalozzi (2001).

354 On the different courses available to a State seeking to reestablish a democratic regime in the wake of an outbreak of armed violence, see the several chapters in Teitel (2000) or the synthesis offered by Andrieu (2012). The available options include institutional justice, administrative mechanisms, and historical reparations.

355 On the dangers facing prisoners of war, with special reference to this particular example, cf. Tritle (2013: 289).

Φιλοκλῆς δ' ἦν στρατηγὸς τῶν Ἀθηναίων, ὃς τούτους διέφθειρεν. ἐλέγετο δὲ καὶ ἄλλα πολλά, καὶ ἔδοξεν ἀποκτεῖναι τῶν αἰχμαλώτων ὅσοι ἦσαν Ἀθηναῖοι πλὴν Ἀδειμάντου, ὅτι μόνος ἐπελάβετο ἐν τῇ ἐκκλησίᾳ τοῦ περὶ τῆς ἀποτομῆς τῶν χειρῶν ψηφίσματος· ᾐτιάθη μέντοι ὑπό τινων προδοῦναι τὰς ναῦς. Λύσανδρος δὲ Φιλοκλέα πρῶτον ἐρωτήσας, ὃς τοὺς Ἀνδρίους καὶ Κορινθίους κατεκρήμνισε, τί εἴη ἄξιος παθεῖν ἀρξάμενος εἰς Ἕλληνας παρανομεῖν, ἀπέσφαξεν.[356]

And it was Philocles, one of the Athenian generals, who had thus made away with these men. Many other stories were told, and it was finally resolved to put to death all of the prisoners who were Athenians, with the exception of Adeimantus, because he was the one man who in the Athenian Assembly had opposed the decree in regard to cutting off the hands of captives; he was charged, however, by some people with having betrayed the fleet. As to Philocles, who threw overboard the Andrians and Corinthians, Lysander first asked him what he deserved to suffer for having begun outrageous practices towards Greeks (*eis Hellenas paranomein*), and then had his throat cut.[357]

I need not call attention here to the conceptual similarity, which other authors have explored, between this episode which took place after the battle of Aegospotami and the allied tribunals of the twentieth century's post-world war periods.[358] I am only interested in emphasizing, in light of those similarities, the objectionable nature of the court that was created[359] and the fact that the punishment imposed on the Athenian generals presupposes the application of a law that transcended the geographic boundaries of the city-state. Since Philocles and his colleagues were Athenian, it may be striking that the passage does not indicate a punishment for having violated the laws of Athens or, failing that, the laws of the other city-states whose citizens were affected. I suggest, here again, that the reference to the Greeks collectively (εἰς Ἕλληνας) represents a significant appeal to the existence of legal norms that, insofar as they are

356 Cf. Marchant (1968–1971).

357 Translation by Brownson (1918).

358 Maridakis (1952) has studied the passage and concluded that Lysander's court represented a clear forerunner of the judicial process carried out in the Military Tribunal at Nuremberg: notable similarities include the trial's international character (the involvement of the "allies"), the victors' *ex post facto* decision to create the court, and the death sentence imposed on the accused without the possibility of appeal. See also Kraske (1954). McCormack (1997) also refers to the episode in his exploration of the origins of international criminal law.

359 Bosworth (2012: 19) refers to it as a "kangaroo court."

overarching rules elevated above "national" systems, seem to create rights and obligations at an interstate level: this is a new reference to the "common" law of the Greeks, envisaged as a universal order.

On the basis of this example, I argue that—when it comes to regulations concerning war—the mandatory nature of the legal rules (as discussed in the cases of the narratives regarding the protection of diplomats and envoys, the treatment of prisoners, attacks on suppliants, and the condemnation of those who mistreat captives) was reinforced by a more or less veiled appeal to the divine, which in many instances gives the international provisions their normative force.[360] The ethical, religious, and legal dimension that underlies these models of behavior determines a *ius in bello* that comes into existence between the real and the ideal, between what *actually occurs* in wartime and the way it *should be* on the basis of fundamental principles of respect for humanity.[361]

But, like any convention, even the divine can be manipulated. It should not be forgotten that Lysander's military court is open to criticism because of the bias involved in a form of justice that only punishes transgressions of one's enemies (however unsurprising this may be in a political context involving winners and losers).[362]

This can be seen clearly in my second example, which is connected with events in Athens at the end of the Peloponnesian War that encouraged an extensive role for the courts in determining the responsibility of the *strategoi* for their behavior in the conflict.[363] I am referring to the so-called "trial"

360 This recalls iusnaturalistic philosophical theories, and contrasts with Kelsenian positivism, insofar as the rationale for positive law is not based exclusively on its legal character. On the importance of understanding religious factors if we are to evaluate ancient compliance with legal norms, cf. Goodman and Holladay (1986: 151–171). Nussbaum (1950: 12–14) argues that both the treaties and the customs that supported the interstate norms among the Hellenic *poleis* had clear sacred support. More recently, Bederman (1991) has concluded that religion was not the sole source of obligations among cities in antiquity: he demonstrates that respect for the norms of international law was achieved not only through straightforward fear of the gods' punishments, but also through concern with maintaining the social order and avoiding chaos; political pragmatism contributed as well.

361 It is precisely this twofold nature that explains the frequent contradiction between the formal content of *nomos* and its actual violation in wartime: Payen (2012: 98) points out that the "laws of war" in Greek antiquity are indissociably both descriptive and normative, according to the intentions and needs of those who appeal to them.

362 Nevertheless, this has been characteristic of international criminal justice since its origins, according to the thinking of Zolo (2006).

363 It should be remembered that military officials seldom had much freedom of action, since they were subject to political control; cf. Fröhlich (1999: 121).

of the generals, a procedure that took place before the Assembly—instead of a court—in 406. In that year, despite their great victory in the battle of Arginusae—remembered as the largest naval battle between Greek fleets—[364] the Athenians had lost twenty-five ships and thousands of citizens.[365] By a decision of the Assembly, eight of the generals involved were summoned to Athens to be tried (*Hellenica*, 1.7.1–2).[366] There are doubts as to the grounds on which they were accused, but Xenophon's account indicates that they had failed to rescue men whose ships had been incapacitated or destroyed (1.6.35 and elsewhere)—perhaps also to recover the bodies of the fallen—[367] but that a strong storm had prevented this operation from succeeding (βουλομένους ποιεῖν ἄνεμος καὶ χειμὼν διεκώλυσεν αὐτοὺς μέγας γενόμενος, 1.6.35). It should be noted that the generals did not themselves accompany the detachment that was sent to help the shipwrecked men.

The intricate judicial vicissitudes of the episode left doubts as to the legality of the procedure.[368] These complexities do not permit us a clear understanding of the charges made.[369] Callixenus proposed a joint trial for all the generals and a single vote by tribes to condemn those responsible for a failure to act (*Hellenica* 1.7.9–10):

ἐπειδὴ τῶν τε κατηγορούντων κατὰ τῶν στρατηγῶν καὶ ἐκείνων ἀπολογουμένων ἐν τῇ προτέρᾳ ἐκκλησίᾳ ἀκηκόασι, διαψηφίσασθαι Ἀθηναίους ἅπαντας κατὰ φυλάς· θεῖναι δὲ εἰς τὴν φυλὴν ἑκάστην δύο	Resolved, that since the Athenians have heard in the previous meeting of the Assembly both the accusers who brought charges against the generals and the generals speaking in their own defence, they do now one and all cast their votes by tribes; and that two urns be set

364 In the first century, Diodorus Siculus wrote that this was "the greatest naval battle ever fought by Greeks against Greeks" (13.98.5–102.4; cf. Thucydides 1.1, 21, 23; 6.31; 7.85.5–6).

365 Xenophon, *Hellenica* 1.6.34.

366 Ultimately (according to 1.7.2), only six of them were judged (Pericles, Diomedes, Lysias, Aristocrates, Thrasyllus and Erasinides). The other two generals, Protomachus and Aristogenes, did not return to Athens when they were relieved of command after the battle. Conon, who had remained in Mytilene, and Leon, who had been captured, were not among the eight generals accused.

367 Diodorus Siculus 13.100.1.

368 Gish (2012: 191–195) maintains that this process is an example of the power of the democratic θόρυβος (*thorybos*), "clamor".

369 On the complexities of the case and its political implications, cf. Roberts (1977), Hunt (2001), Kagan (2004: 459–466) and Ostwald (1986: 431–511).

ὑδρίας· ἐφ᾽ ἑκάστῃ δὲ τῇ φυλῇ κήρυκα κηρύττειν, ὅτῳ δοκοῦσιν ἀδικεῖν οἱ στρατηγοὶ οὐκ ἀνελόμενοι τοὺς νικήσαντας ἐν τῇ ναυμαχίᾳ, εἰς τὴν προτέραν ψηφίσασθαι, ὅτῳ δὲ μή, εἰς τὴν ὑστέραν ἂν δὲ δόξωσιν ἀδικεῖν, θανάτῳ ζημιῶσαι καὶ τοῖς ἕνδεκα παραδοῦναι καὶ τὰ χρήματα δημοσιεῦσαι, τὸ δ᾽ ἐπιδέκατον τῆς θεοῦ εἶναι.

at the voting-place of each tribe; and that in each tribe a herald proclaim that whoever adjudges the generals guilty, for not picking up the men who won the victory in the naval battle, shall cast his vote in the first urn, and whoever adjudges them not guilty, shall cast his vote in the second; and if they be adjudged guilty, that they be punished with death and handed over to the Eleven, and that their property be confiscated and the tenth thereof belong to the goddess.[370]

Contrary to this proposal, however, a motion of Euryptolemus sought to ensure a proper defense for the accused[371] and called for individual trials of the generals, according to the established laws (1.7.21–23):[372]

κατὰ τοῦτο τὸ ψήφισμα κελεύω κρίνεσθαι τοὺς στρατηγοὺς καὶ νὴ Δία, ἂν ὑμῖν γε δοκῇ, πρῶτον Περικλέα τὸν ἐμοὶ προσήκοντα· αἰσχρὸν γάρ μοί ἐστιν ἐκεῖνον περὶ πλείονος ποιεῖσθαι ἢ τὴν ὅλην πόλιν. τοῦτο δ᾽ εἰ βούλεσθε, κατὰ τόνδε τὸν νόμον κρίνατε, ὅς ἐστιν ἐπὶ τοῖς ἱεροσύλοις καὶ προδόταις, ἐάν τις ἢ τὴν πόλιν προδιδῷ ἢ τὰ ἱερὰ κλέπτῃ, κριθέντα ἐν δικαστηρίῳ, ἂν καταγνωσθῇ, μὴ ταφῆναι ἐν τῇ Ἀττικῇ, τὰ δὲ χρήματα αὐτοῦ δημόσια εἶναι. τούτων ὁποτέρῳ βούλεσθε, ὦ ἄνδρες Ἀθηναῖοι, τῷ νόμῳ κρινέσθων οἱ ἄνδρες κατὰ ἕνα

Under this decree I urge you to try the generals, and, by Zeus, if it so please you, Pericles, my kinsman, first of them all; for it would be base for me to think more of him than of the general interests of the state. Or if you do not wish to do this, try them under the following law [the decree of Cannonus], which applies to temple-robbers and traitors: namely, if anyone shall be a traitor to the state or shall steal sacred property, he shall be tried before a court, and if he be convicted, he shall not be buried in Attica, and his property shall be confiscated. And whichever of these laws you choose, men of Athens, let the men be tried, each one separately, and let the day be

370 Translation by Brownson (1918).

371 Callixenus's proposal was countered by an action that sought to have it declared illegal, perhaps because it proposed a non-standard type of voting or because it presupposed the culpability of the accused.

372 This was set down in the Decree of Cannonus or in the law established for sacrilege or treason.

ἕκαστον διῃρημένων τῆς ἡμέρας τριῶν μερῶν, ἑνὸς μὲν ἐν ᾧ συλλέγεσθαι ὑμᾶς δεῖ καὶ διαψηφίζεσθαι ἐάν τε ἀδικεῖν δοκῶσιν ἐάν τε μή, ἑτέρου δ' ἐν ᾧ κατηγορῆσαι, ἑτέρου δ' ἐν ᾧ ἀπολογήσασθαι.

divided into three parts, one wherein you shall gather and vote as to whether you judge them guilty or not, another wherein the accusers shall present their case, and another wherein the accused shall make their defence.[373]

Lysias's *Against Eratosthenes*, which mentions the condemnation of the Arginusae generals, allows us to infer that the generals (like Eratosthenes in the speech) were accused of an act of treason, an attempt to subvert the *demokratia* (12.35–36).[374] This clearly shows that, when there was an ideological consensus, it was possible to bring cases involving wartime military conduct before the Assembly for the sake of evaluating the legitimacy of a judicial procedure. The political character of this "treason" trial is thus evident.[375]

The assigning of responsibility for acts contrary to *nomos* is justified by a recognition that fundamental values have been violated. Thus, when the Plataeans try to convince the Spartan judges that the Spartans' reputation—historically an exemplary one among the Greeks—would be compromised if they were to kill the Plataeans, they are appealing to their respect for the values of honor and benevolence (ἀνδραγαθία, *andragathia*, Thucydides 3.57). It might reasonably be argued that the judging of responsibility for acts contrary to the customs of inter-*polis* warfare, although less well documented in our sources than trials resulting from trangressions against the local military authority, reveals to us a true Hellenic conscience which seeks to reinforce positive values and drive out the wrongdoing of those who work against the common good for their own benefit. At the same time, however, it is impossible to deny that the real motive behind proceedings in *polis* courts had less to do with humanitarian altruism—although this was exploited as an argument—than with political battles and partisan interests.

373 Translation by Brownson (1918). On the significance of this speech in the larger debate regarding *graphai paranomon*, cf. Carawan (2007).

374 Some have maintained, however, that the trial's procedure was clearly illegal and politically motivated; cf. Rebuffat (2000: 192).

375 Gilardeau (2015: 23–58) refers to the episode as an example of the manipulation of popular despotism. Even if Hamel (2015: 89–90) arrives at the conclusion that the verdict was reached in accordance with all standing statutes, at the same time the decision seems to be reprehensible: "[t]he Athenians themselves soon came to believe that their condemnation of the generals had been wrong".

The third and final episode that I shall examine is more encouraging and represents, for some, the first authentic example of transitional justice on record.[376] Following the disastrous consequences of the defeat at Aegospotami, an oligarchy was established at Athens in 404; it lasted for four months during which massacres were committed and half of the population was forcibly displaced.[377] This is undoubtedly the best documented instance of *stasis* in the period just after the Peloponnesian War.[378] When the democracy was reestablished, there was a delicate balance between retribution and forgiveness: those who had held the highest offices under the regime of the Thirty Tyrants were prosecuted and found guilty of mass atrocities (they could be condemned to death unless they were in exile at Eleusis) but it was decided to give amnesty to all the rest.[379] *The Constitution of the Athenians*, attributed to Aristotle, records these events, emphasizing that the cancellation of responsibility for past actions was a praiseworthy decision (40.2–3):

δοκοῦσιν κάλλιστα δὴ καὶ πολιτικώτατα ἁπάντων καὶ ἰδίᾳ καὶ κοινῇ χρήσασθαι ταῖς προγεγενημέναις συμφοραῖς· οὐ γὰρ μόνον τὰς περὶ τῶν προτέρων αἰτίας ἐξήλειψαν, ἀλλὰ καὶ τὰ χρήματα Λακεδαιμονίοις, ἃ οἱ τριάκοντα πρὸς τὸν πόλεμον ἔλαβον, ἀπέδοσαν κοινῇ …[380]	But [the Athenians] appear both in private and public to have behaved towards the past disasters in the most completely honorable and statesmanlike manner of any people in history; for they not only blotted out recriminations with regard to the past, but also publicly restored to the Spartans the funds that the Thirty had taken for the war …[381]

The only contemporary evidence that has survived concerning these events comes from indirect references in Andocides' *On the Mysteries*. After having

376 Elster (2004). Cf. *supra*, p. 217.

377 The orator Isocrates relates in his *Areopagiticus* that the Thirty Tyrants killed fifteen hundred people without trial and forced more than five thousand to leave the city and take refuge in the Piraeus (οἱ μὲν γὰρ ψηφίσματι παραλαβόντες τὴν πόλιν πεντακοσίους μὲν καὶ χιλίους τῶν πολιτῶν ἀκρίτους ἀπέκτειναν, εἰς δὲ τὸν Πειραιᾶ φυγεῖν πλείους ἢ πεντακισχιλίους ἠνάγκασαν, 7.67). The Greek text corresponds to Norlin's edition (1980). The *Constitution of the Athenians* (35.4) also notes that no fewer than fifteen hundred individuals were killed.

378 Ober (2002: 128).

379 On this episode and its repercussions in modern cases of transitional justice, cf. Elster (2004: 7–8) and Lanni (2010). On other possible examples of amnesty laws in classical Greece, cf. Smith (1921: 345–346).

380 The Greek text is that of Mathieu and Haussoulier (2002).

381 Translation by Rackham (1952).

been arrested and tried for entering a sacred precinct when forbidden by a decree—because he had participated in the sacrileges of 415—the orator argues that the decree denying him entry to the precinct is null and void as a result of the amnesty following the restoration of democracy in the autumn of 403. It is in this context that Andocides describes the advantages of the new regime in general and the amnesty in particular, in the following terms (1.81):

ἐπειδὴ δ᾽ ἐπανήλθετε ἐκ Πειραιῶς, γενόμενον ἐφ᾽ ὑμῖν τιμωρεῖσθαι ἔγνωτε ἐᾶν τὰ γεγενημένα, καὶ περὶ πλείονος ἐποιήσασθε σῴζειν τὴν πόλιν ἢ τὰς ἰδίας τιμωρίας, καὶ ἔδοξε μὴ μνησικακεῖν ἀλλήλοις τῶν γεγενημένων.[382]	After your return from Peiraeus you resolved to let bygones be bygones, in spite of the opportunity for revenge. You considered the safety of Athens of more importance than the settlement of private scores; so both sides, you decided, were to forget the past (*me mnesikakein*).[383]

The prohibition on bringing up the bad things that had happened (μὴ μνησικακεῖν, *me mnesikakein*)[384] is interpreted as a decision in favor of the salvation of the city and against the survival of a spirit of revenge unsuitable in the public sphere. Later in the speech, Andocides insists upon a strict opposition between an act of public justice (forgetfulness that begets concord) and private retribution (which perpetuates suffering); he stresses the wisdom and prudence of the former (1.140):

382 The Greek text in this and the following quotation corresponds to the edition of Maidment (1968).

383 Translation by Maidment (1968).

384 On the expression and its complex connotations, cf. Carawan (2012), who translates it as "recall-wrong". As Cohen (2001: 339) notes, "the relevant phrase which grounds the amnesty is typically translated as 'to forget' or 'not to remember' what the oligarchs had done. In this context, however, the crucial phrase 'not to *mnesikakein*' actually means not to hold a grudge in the sense in which this is understood in a revenge society: that is, not to seek vengeance". A passage from the *Constitution of the Athenians* repeats the language of Andocides in affirming that "no one was permitted to hold the past against anyone (τῶν δὲ παρεληλυθότων μηδενὶ πρὸς μηδένα μνησικακεῖν ἐξεῖναι) except the Thirty, the Ten, the Eleven, and those who were in charge in the Piraeus; and not even against them if they should render their accounts" (39.6). This evidence is not original, however, since the agreement of 403 did not include exceptions to the obligation of μὴ μνησικακεῖν (according to Carawan, 2006, this passage combines the content of the original agreement with exceptions that were added later).

νυνὶ πᾶσι τοῖς Ἕλλησιν ἄνδρες ἄριστοι καὶ εὐβουλότατοι δοκεῖτε γεγενῆσθαι, οὐκ ἐπὶ τιμωρίαν τραπόμενοι τῶν γεγενημένων, ἀλλ' ἐπὶ σωτηρίαν τῆς πόλεως καὶ ὁμόνοιαν τῶν πολιτῶν. συμφοραὶ μὲν γὰρ ἤδη καὶ ἄλλοις πολλοῖς ἐγένοντο οὐκ ἐλάττους ἢ καὶ ἡμῖν· τὸ δὲ τὰς γενομένας διαφορὰς πρὸς ἀλλήλους θέσθαι καλῶς, τοῦτ' εἰκότως ἤδη δοκεῖ ἀνδρῶν ἀγαθῶν καὶ σωφρόνων ἔργον εἶναι.	The best men among all the Greeks think that you have shown the greatest generosity and wisdom in devoting yourselves, not to revenge, but to the salvation (*soterian*) of your city and the reuniting (*homonoian*) of its citizens. Many before now have suffered no less than we; but it is very rightly recognized that the peaceable settlement of differences requires generosity and self-control (*sophronon*).[385]

This novel means of dealing with *stasis*—eschewing punishment and mandating forgetfulness—is built upon the recognition of a collective and fictitious memory that has assigned responsibility for what happened in the time of the Thirty Tyrants and wishes to set aside the Athenians' widespread complicity in the commission of their crimes.[386] Thus, a sort of contractual negotiation[387] leads to a collective and fictitious narrative concerning the attribution of guilt for ubiquitous violations of the law. The aim of the amnesty was clear: to end the civil war[388] and restore democratic values.[389] In a time of political transition, the sentence and the amnesty permitted the reestablishment of Athenian unity and social peace without the need to return to the past and investigate the underlying truth.[390]

Let us now review these three examples of transitional justice. In the first place, it should be noted that the two responses to large-scale crimes in time of conflict (international or internal) that are illustrated by the aftermath of Aegospotami and the amnesty reflect the permanent tension in Athens at the end of the fifth century, a tension to which I have already repeatedly referred. A political game was taking place that involved, internally, the preservation of

385 Translation by Maidment (1968) with corrections.

386 Judgments concerning the success of the reconciliation between the democrats and the oligarchs (who were known as "the men of the city") have been discussed by Tieman (2002).

387 This is the central thesis of the recent book by Carawan (2013).

388 Joyce (2008: 517–518).

389 The Thirty Tyrants were seen as paradigmatic enemies of the democratic regime. Cohen (2001: 347) clearly states: "In the political discourse of fourth century Athens, the Thirty Tyrants came to stand for the antithesis of the rule of law."

390 Lanni (2010: 593–594).

democratic order and, externally, the effort to achieve supremacy. These two goals were not always compatible, and the difficulty in resolving them explains the existence of various ways in which an autonomous *polis* could react to the mass slaughter of civilians.

The employment of different and even incompatible measures as part of a *ius post bellum* reveals the crucial tension between the effort to create international imbalance, on the one hand, and the consolidation of domestic balance, on the other. The imperialist logic of international law and the quest to sustain an inter-*polis nomos* capable of legitimizing military action allow us to understand Sparta's recourse to these common norms as a way of creating and consolidating an *ad hoc* hegemonic justice that can judge and condemn a conquered enemy. By contrast, the granting of a general amnesty and the encouragement of forgetfulness, alongside the conduct of private proceedings, reflects the desire of post-oligarchic Athens to overcome a division within society and restore the social fabric required by the structure of the new democratic regime.

In summary, the cases studied exemplify the "humanitarian" foundations sustaining different attitudes with respect to international responsibility for the violation of *nomoi*. They serve to illustrate the difficulty of obtaining justice either by uniting the *politai* after a traumatic rupture (equality among citizens) or through the utilitarian desire to secure, by means of a law that legitimizes force, a preeminence over the enemy (inequality among *poleis*). In other words, these episodes reveal the wide range of arguments and ideologies—from democratic self-preservation to the simple desire for power—that provide the historical foundations of an international criminal justice much like that which has been revived in recent times.

Summation: Towards a Framework of Restraint

I hope that my reexamination of the fifth- and fourth-century Greek sources relating to *ius in bello* has called into question traditional assertions—frequently repeated and unfounded—concerning the nonexistence of regulations in armed conflicts in the ancient world. The evidence presented justifies the conclusion that there existed among the Greeks the conception of a genuine "common" (panhellenic or inter-*polis*) law which served to limit the outbreak of armed conflicts and to restrict the excessive use of violence in wartime. The identification of ancient Greek legal regulations relating to the conduct of hostilities, as well as of passages that promote a religious and political expansion of their scope, allows us to contribute some interesting reflections to the discussion concerning the traditional character of the norms that constitute *ius in bello* today.[391] It would not be unjustified to say that ancient wars (projected in their ritual logic onto the last third of the twentieth century) represented a classical conception of limited military action—not unlike a trial, where the conduct of the parties assumes particular forms. The contemporary disappearance of such conflicts and their replacement (since the battle of Solferino) by new types of armed conflict have brought about horrors that positive law has had to control by divesting itself of the performative and auto-regulatory features that characterized premodern and early modern battles.[392]

I should now return to the beginning of this chapter—and to the beginning of Western literature—for some final reflections. In Book 6 of the *Iliad*, in a description of the bloody battles that occurred during the Greek siege of Troy, Glaucus the Lycian and Diomedes the Argive interrupt their combat when they discover that their families are bound by an old tie of guest-friendship, or *xenia* (6.212–231). The fight is called off, and the young men exchange their armor as a gesture of goodwill.[393] Violence is thus limited by an appeal to customary rules based on respect for ancestors. When Sarpedon, the Lycian king, meets death in Book 16 at the hands of Patroclus, it is his cousin Glaucus who will immediately offer prayers to Apollo, asking him to retrieve the

---

391 In discussing the historical foundations of international law, Domingo (2010: 4) contends that the Greek precedent can be useful in understanding our cultural history and, thus, the current importance of law in our legal system: "However, the fact that each age is identified by its law does not mean that in the various legal systems, there are no common points, keys to mutual understanding, recurrent problems, or permanent solutions. This permanence imparts value and meaning to these historical projections and shows that although time may have had great influence in shaping new law, humanity remains the same regardless of the historical moment in which they live. This may be Greece's great contribution to law—adequately resolving the tension between change and permanence by finding a point of equilibrium that makes it possible to go forward without forgetting the past, and building without dismantling what has already been built." Cf. also Purnell (1978: 19–31).

392 This is the interesting thesis of Whitman (2012), who tries to support the hypothesis that the outlawing of war in the last century has removed violence from the field of law, thus permitting the unrestricted intensification of armed conflicts. By contrast, the "classic pitched battle" model was effective in limiting the violence of ancient wars.

393 Respect for ties of hospitality is, incidentally, regarded as a common Greek norm in Euripides' satyr-play *Cyclops* (v. 299).

warrior's body from the field of battle. This request is granted (16.514–683).[394] At the end of the *Iliad* (24.349–620) Priam arrives at Achilles' tent and tearfully supplicates him, begging for the body of his son Hector. Thinking of his own father, the best of the Achaeans will agree to return the corpse of Hector to Priam in order to allow the performance of the required funeral rites.

These three scenes from epic illustrate how restrictions on violence, associated with mutual respect or with the burial of those who die in combat, find meaning in the values that the "common" law—that law which the Greeks shared and which undoubtedly forms the bedrock of our modern international law—must in all cirumstances defend, protect, and guard. This rationale, although it may bear little resemblance to Christian humanism, gave shape, though a moral code and religious fear, to a series of informal *nomoi* that resulted in a customary normative framework of restraint in time of war.[395]

394 On the recovery of bodies from the battlefield, cf. Vaughn (1991) and Garlan (1972: 39–40).

395 One could argue that it is anachronistic to speak of "humanitarian" values in the ancient world. Authors such as Glotz (1923: 96), however, have accepted that "aucun pays ne réunit complètement que la Grèce les conditions politiques et morales qui font éclore le droit de gens", and this results—for Payen (2012: 94)—in evidence of a "signe d'une humanité dans la conduite de la guerre". This idea was expressed similarly by Kiechle (1958) when he spoke of the "humanity" of intra-Hellenic armed conflicts. According to Bryant (2016: 37), "the consensus of scholars is that the common customs of the Hellenes did not express a humanitarian concern for reducing the monstrous suffering of war (…) Nonetheless, it is also notable the ancient Greeks insisted military conflict was subject to constraint". My intention was to prove precisely that these normative limitations of warfare in classical Greece contributed to prepare the ground for the humanitarian basis of modern international legal provisions.

Conclusions: About Apples, Branches, and Humanitarian Strategies

> ἐν μὲν γὰρ εἰρήνῃ καὶ ἀγαθοῖς πράγμασιν αἵ τε πόλεις καὶ οἱ ἰδιῶται ἀμείνους τὰς γνώμας ἔχουσι διὰ τὸ μὴ ἐς ἀκουσίους ἀνάγκας πίπτειν· ὁ δὲ πόλεμος ὑφελὼν τὴν εὐπορίαν τοῦ καθ' ἡμέραν βίαιος διδάσκαλος καὶ πρὸς τὰ παρόντα τὰς ὀργὰς τῶν πολλῶν ὁμοιοῖ.
>
> For in peace and prosperity both states and individuals have gentler feelings, because men are not then forced to face conditions of dire necessity; but war, which robs men of the easy supply of their daily wants, is a rough schoolmaster and creates in most people a temper that matches their condition.
>
> THUCYDIDES 3.82.2 (tr. SMITH)

∴

Taking as a starting point a famous passage by Thucydides (5.89) wherein it is held that, if *dike* is only legally appropriate among equals, in military matters the strong do as they want while the weak do as they can (δυνατὰ δὲ οἱ προύχοντες πράσσουσι καὶ οἱ ἀσθενεῖς ξυγχωροῦσιν), we should not be surprised that the conclusion is that the Greek world established a sort of international *Realpolitik*, where the value of rules derived from the intentionality of the powerful, not so much from a concern to ensure justice. However, as shown throughout this work, such a claim must be contrasted with the specific sources that seem to demonstrate adherence to certain rules and principles that enjoyed inter-*polis* validity.[1] Given that international law is an ideological and political construct, I departed from my interest in observing the origins and background of its rules in order to appraise continuities and fractures, evolutionary lines

1 Blanchet (2013: 80–81) explains this differentiation by arguing that the Athenians followed a double criterion: one for the citizens of the *polis* and another for international relations. In this distinction between domestic democracy and external imperialism, however, a fundamental similarity got lost: at both levels there is one trend towards legal equalization and another towards the imposition of power by the strongest. My aim here has been precisely to show that such coexistence explains the humanitarian rules recorded in surviving sources.

 | DOI: 10.1163/9789004363823_007

and breakpoints, and thus to justify the scope of its current mandatory content. Based on this approach—which is concerned with the diachronic nature of the foundations of any legal system—I proposed throughout this book a particular historical focus. After some methodological considerations to establish a basis for my investigation, I made an attempt to conceptualize the regulation of armed conflict in classical Greece as regards, on the one hand, the lawfulness of the commencement of conflict and, on the other, the way in which the parties must conduct themselves in the course of hostilities.

Based on a survey of available documentary sources, I have shown that at the time of the Peloponnesian War (and even prior to the fifth century) there existed—enshrined in cultural standards connected with ritualism and the performative nature of Greek civilization—a specific thinking regarding a series of legal rules, identified by the Greeks, that mandated specific patterns of conduct during war. Of course, in practice this is not to deny the existence of unlimited armed conflicts in the ancient world or to ignore that too often extremely grave acts were committed during battle. However, the occurrence of atrocities does not negate the existence of a discourse that represents at the same time a true regulatory corpus, itself subject to paradoxical interpretations.[2] This is not unlike what happens nowadays when States resort to the use of force in flagrant violation of international law, even though they cannot deny its existence, enshrined as it is in the Charter of the United Nations.

This study has attempted to answer those who—failing to distinguish between existence and efficacy—argue that regulations aimed at setting limits to war's violence did not exist in the classical world. Ancient sources reveal that warfare was in fact "regulated" to some extent, based on religious and legal criteria and a true code of social conduct.[3] We should not disregard the fact that, inasmuch as this was a system of thought rooted in divine patterns, to a large extent the regulations were inherent to a range of values—honor or fear of the gods—that were translated into ritualized, formally structured

2 "Les 'lois de la guerre' qui se révèlent parfois d'une cruauté et d'une injustice extrême, possèdent alors ce caractère paradoxale: elles prétendent être respectées: elles permettent également de faire main basse sur la propriété d'autrui" (Rebuffat, 2000: 190).

3 Lebow (2010: 196) offered a wise explanation: "The tension between warfare as ritual and a means to political ends was most evident in its conduct. As I noted earlier, the rules of agonal warfare were frequently violated by participants who, throughout the course of Greek history, not infrequently resorted to all kinds of ruses, standoff warfare and sieges to defeat adversaries, and on occasion massacred Greek prisoners and left their bodies unburied. Greeks sometimes regarded the discrepancies between their values and their practice as an aberration and imagined a past in which they had behaved properly".

normativities, undoubtedly subject to the vicissitudes of rhetorical manipulation.[4] The apple of Eris, which triggered the first contest between the goddesses and irrepressible violence in combat between Achaeans and Trojans afterwards, co-exists with the branches of the suppliants, who seek to limit the excesses of war.

Both the need to argue in favor of *belli causae* (which should not surprise us even in times when armed struggle was not prohibited) and the precepts aimed at avoiding the involvement of civilians or the use of weapons capable of causing unnecessary suffering constitute examples of what the Greeks described as "common" rules, as informal standards of conduct that became mandatory in their application. The idea of a *nomos koinos* (common law) or a *nomos ton Hellenon* (law of the Greeks) trascends the legal limits of domestic systems and, takes these rules to a level of universal experiences shared by all city-states. Had the people who fathered philosophy, as a practice and as a discipline, disregarded the excesses of war or failed to prepare an anti-war discourse based on rules of law that translate moral values, it would have probably seemed puzzling.

The philanthropic approach seen in the texts I have analyzed—translated into specific *nomoi*—is ultimately among the most conclusive evidence that the tradition embodied in international humanitarian law (its treaties, its customs and its principles of law) is born from archaic roots.[5] The ambiguity of the rules of war—which are subject to the prevailing political discourse and are strategically manipulated—matches the ambiguous description of a dual Eris, of the irrepressible but sobering Polemos, and of the homicidal Ares who nonetheless was the harmonizer of citizen values.

This study will have achieved its purpose if I have managed to evoke the richness of that ambivalent origin. In the end, the work presented here is aimed at suggesting that Greek sources, as the ultimate basis of Western civilization, express the tension of timeless practices that give rise to the debate as to the customary nature of those rules which now impose limits on interstate violence.[6] I have addressed the strategies of figures, such as Discord or Polemos,

---

4 "On le voit, il y a des usages concernant l'exercice de la guerre, voire une véritable loi morale. Mais les Grecs n'hésitent pas à ruser avec elle, quitte à en subir ultérieurement les conséquences. Ne font-ils pas avec la guerre la même chose qu'avec leurs dieux?" (Corvisier, 2000: 106).

5 Straumann (2015: 6) has already suggested that Hugo Grotius—the so-called father of international law—was heavily influenced by ancient sources.

6 Johnston (2008: 198) concludes that "in at least a rudimentary way, they [i.e., the Greeks] contributed to the state autonomy, order (system-maintenance), cooperation, conflict resolution,

who personify war and its inevitable restrictions. Still today, as in all the sources I have discussed, a two-sided Eris, a protective but cruel Athena, and a brutal but civilizing Ares plead—with words rather than facts—for their inherent ambivalence to be understood.

---

and war prevention-and-management models of world law". As I have shown, the Greek contribution was nevertheless far from rudimentary.

APPENDIX A

Chart of Treaties Signed by Greek *poleis* during the Peloponnesian War (431–404)

The following chart includes a list of agreements registered in the ancient sources, identifying the type of agreement, the year of execution and the contracting parties or *poleis*. The numbers included in the first five columns correspond—respectively—to the numbering of texts in the following editions:

- [B]: Bengston, H. (1962) *Die Verträge der griechische-römischen Welt von 700 bis 338 v. Chr.* (Die Staatsverträge des Altertums, Band II), München: C.H. Beck.
- [C]: Calderini, A. (1949) *Trattati internazionali nell'Antichità greca*, Parte 1, Milano: La Goliardica.
- [PI]: Piccirilli, L. (1973) *Gli arbitrati interstatali greci*, vol. 1 "Dalle origini al 338 a.C.", Pisa: Marlin.
- [FN]: Fernández Nieto. F.J. (1975) *Los acuerdos bélicos en la antigua Grecia*, Santiago de Compostela: Universidad de Santiago de Compostela.
- [PA]: Panessa, G. (1999) (ed.) Philiai. *L'amicizia nelle relazioni interstatali del Greci*, Vol. I "Dalle origine alla fine della Guerra del Peloponneso", Pisa: Scuola Normale Superiore.

[B]	[C]	[PI]	[FN]	[PA]	Type of agreement	Year	Party 1	Party 2	Ancient sources
160			106		Capitulation	435	Epidamnus	Corcyra	Thuc. 1.29.5 [Diodor. 12.31.2]
161					*Epimakhia*	Summer 433	Athens	Corcyra	Thuc. 1.44.1
162	18				Alliance	433/2	Athens	Rhegium	*IG* I 33; *CIC* I 74; *Syll.* I^3 71; *IG* I^2 51 [*IG* I^3 53]
163	19				Alliance	433/2	Athens	Leontinoi	*Syll.* I^3 70; *IG* I^2 52; [*IG* I^3 54]; Thuc. 3.86.3
164					Alliance	Before 431	Lepreon	Eleia	Thuc. 5.31.2

 | DOI: 10.1163/9789004363823_008

(cont.)

[B]	[C]	[PI]	[FN]	[PA]	Type of agreement	Year	Party 1	Party 2	Ancient sources
165				49	Alliance	431	Athens	Sitalkes (King of the Odrysian) and Perdiccas II (King of Macedon)	Thuc. 2.29.4; Thuc. 2.95.2; Ar. *Ach.* 141–150; Diodor. 12.50.3.
166					Treaty	431	Lacedaemon	Confederates	Thuc. 5.31.5.
167				52	Alliance	430–420?	Athens	Unknown	*IG* I^2 53.
168			108		Capitulation	429	Potidaea	Athens	Thuc. 2.70.1 et seq.; Diodor. 12.46.6–7
169			63		Treaty / armistice	Before 427 (428 [FN])	Athens	Mytilene	*IG* I^2 60, 8–9; Thuc. 3.4.2 et seq.
170			110		Capitulation	427	Mytilene	Paques [Athens]	Thuc. 3.28.1 et seq.; [Thuc. 3.35.1 et seq.; Thuc. 3.50.1 et seq.]; Diodor. 12.55.7–10.
171			111		Capitulation	427	Plataea	[Sparta]	Thuc. 3.52.1 [Thuc. 3.68.2–3; Diodor. 12,56.4 et seq.]
172					Defensive alliance	427	Athens	Corcyra	Thuc. 3.75.1
173				56	Alliance	427	Athens	Kamarina	Thuc. 3.86.1; Thuc. 6.75.4; Thuc. 6.52.1; Thuc. 6.78.1 and 6.81.
174				73	Alliance	427/6? (416/5 [PA])	Athens	Egesta	*IG* I^3 11 [*IG* I^2 20; *IG* I^2 19].
175					100-year alliance	Winter 426	Acarnania	Amphilochia and Ambracia	Thuc. 3.114.3; Diodor. 12.60.6
176			64		Armistice	425	Sparta	Athens	Thuc. 4.15.2

[B]	[C]	[PI]	[FN]	[PA]	Type of agreement	Year	Party 1	Party 2	Ancient sources
177			114		Treaty or capitulation[FN]	425	Eurymedon and Sophocles (Athens)	Exiled Corcyraean aristocrats	Thuc. 4.46.1; Polyaenus 6.20
178			115		Capitulation	424	Kythira	Nicias [Athens]	Thuc. 4.54.2–4; Thuc. 4.57.4; [Diodor. 12.65.8]
179			65		Peace congress or armistice [FN]	424	Gela	[Kamarina as per FN]	Thuc. 4.58.1; Thuc. 4.65.1; Timaeus (*FgrHist* n. 566)
180			116		Capitulation	424	Nisaea	Athens	Thuc. 4.69.3–4; Diodor. 12.66.4
181			117		Capitulation	424	Akanthos	Brasidas (Sparta)	Thuc 4.88 [cf. Diodor. 12.67.2]
182			118		Capitulation	424	Amphipolis	Brasidas (Sparta)	Thuc. 4.105.2 [Thuc. 4.106.2]; Diodor. 12.68.3 [Polyaenus 1.38.3]
183				65	Treaty	424/3	Athens	King Darius (Persia)	Andoc. 3.28–29; *IG* II 5, 5c; *IG* II/III^2 8; *Syll.* I^3 118.
184	33			62	Alliance	424/3 (413 [C])	Athens	Halieis	*IG* I^2 87; *SEG* X 80.
185	26	25	66		Armistice	Spring 423	Athens	Sparta	Thuc. 4.117–3.119.1; Diodor. 12.72.5.
186	27			66	Alliance	423/2	Athens	Perdiccas II (Macedon) and Arrhabaeus (Lynkestis)	*IG* I 42; *IG* I 43; *IG* I^2 71; *SEG* X 86; *SEG* XII 16.
187	30			68	Alliance	422	Athens	Bottiaea	*Syll.* I^3 89; *IG* I^2 90; *SEG* X 89.
188	28	27			50-year peace (Peace of Nicias)	Spring 421	Athens	Sparta	Thuc. 5.18–20; Diodor. 12.74.5; Plut. *Nik.* 9.8; Plut. *Alc.* 14.2: Plut. *Nik.* 10.1.

(cont.)

[B]	[C]	[PI]	[FN]	[PA]	Type of agreement	Year	Party 1	Party 2	Ancient sources
189	29				Alliance	Summer 421	Athens	Sparta	Thuc. 5.23.1–25; Diodor. 12.75.2
190					Alliance	421	Mantineia	Elis, Corinth, the Chalcidice and Argos	Thuc. 5.28.1–29.1; Thuc. 5.31.1; Thuc. 5.31.5.
191					Alliance	Spring 420	Sparta	Boeotia	Thuc. 5.39.2–3; Thuc. 5.40.1; Thuc. 5.42.2; Plut. *Nik.* 10.3; Plut. Alc. 14.4.
192		29		70	Treaty negotiation	Spring 420	Argos	Sparta	Thuc. 5.40.1–41.3 and 5.36.1
193	32			71	100-year alliance	420	Athens	Argos, Martineia and Elis	*IG* I^3 86; Thuc. 5.44.1–5.47.12; Plut. *Alc.*15.1; Diodor. 12.77.2.
194	34	31			Alliance	418	Sparta	Argos, Perdiccas II (Macedon) and Chalcidice	Thuc. 5.77.1–7; Thuc. 5.78; Thuc. 5.79.1–4; Thuc. 5.80.2; Thuc. 5.83.4.
195					30-year peace	418/7?	Sparta	Martineia	Thuc. 5.81.1; Diodor. 12.80.2; X., *Hell.* 5.2.2;
196	35				Defensive alliance	Spring 416	Athens	Argos	*IG* I 50; IG I^2 96; *SEG* X 104; Thuc. 5.82.5
197			120		Treaty or Capitulation[FN]	414	Athens	Centoripa	Thuc. 5.94.3; Thuc. 7.32.1 et seq.
198				47	Treaty renewal	413	Athens	Artas (Messapia)	Thuc. 7.33.4
199			121		Capitulation	413	Demosthenes (Athens)	Gyllipus (Sparta) and Syracuse	Thuc. 7.82.2–3; [Diodor. 13.19.2–3]
200 201 202	37 38 39			79	Three treaties	412–411	Sparta	Persia	(A) Thuc. 8.18; (B) Thuc. 8.37; (C) Thuc. 8.58.

[B]	[C]	[PI]	[FN]	[PA]	Type of agreement	Year	Party 1	Party 2	Ancient sources
203		33			Treaty	After 411	Thasos	Neapolis	*IG* XII 5, 109.
204					Treaty	After 411?	Eretria	Histiaea	*IG* XII 9, 188.
205			68		Treaty or armistice [FN] (treaty of Chalcedon)	409	Athens	Pharnabazus (Persia)	X. *Hell.* 1.3.8–12; Plut. *Alc.* 31.1 [Diodor. 13.66.3]
206	41				Treaty	409?	Athens	Selymbria	*IG* I^{2} 116; *Syll.* I^{3} 112; *SEG* X 132.
207				77	Alliance negotiations	406 (414–408/7 [PA])	Athens	Carthage	*IG* I^{2} 47; *SEG* X 136.
208	42				Self-defense treaty	Before 405	Athens	Samos	*IG* II/III^{2} 1.
209					First armistice	405	Dionysus I (Syracuse)	Carthage	Diodor. 13.114.1.
210			125		Peace treaty or Capitulation [FN]	404	Athens	Sparta	Plu. *Lys.* 14 et seq.; X. *Hell.* 2.2.20; Andoc. 3.11–12; Lys. 6.37–38; Isocr. 18.29; [Arist.] *Ath. Pol.* 34.3; Diodor. 13.107.4, Diodor. 14.3.2; Diodor. 14.3.6; Justin 5.8.4
211			126		Capitulation	404	Samos	Lysander (Sparta)	X. *Hell.* 2.3.6.

APPENDIX B

Digital Images of Treaties and Decrees

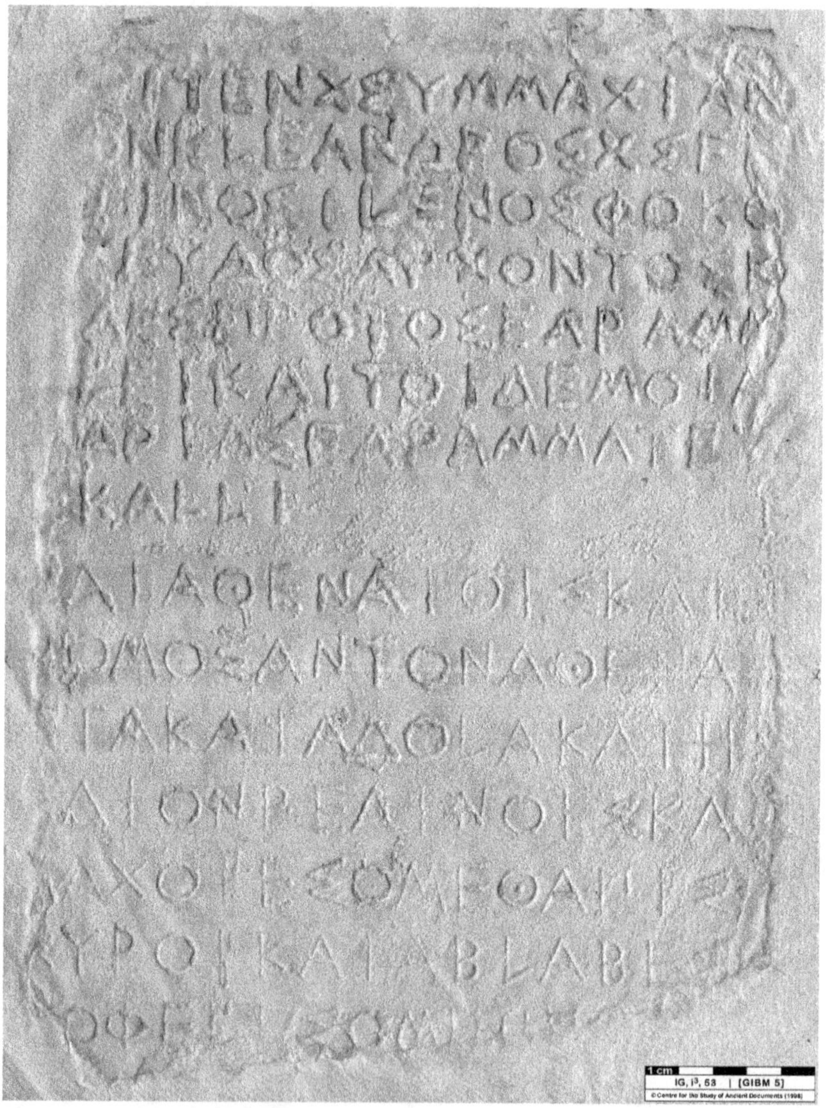

FIGURE 3 *Athenian Alliance with Rhegium* (IG I^3 53)

 | DOI: 10.1163/9789004363823_009

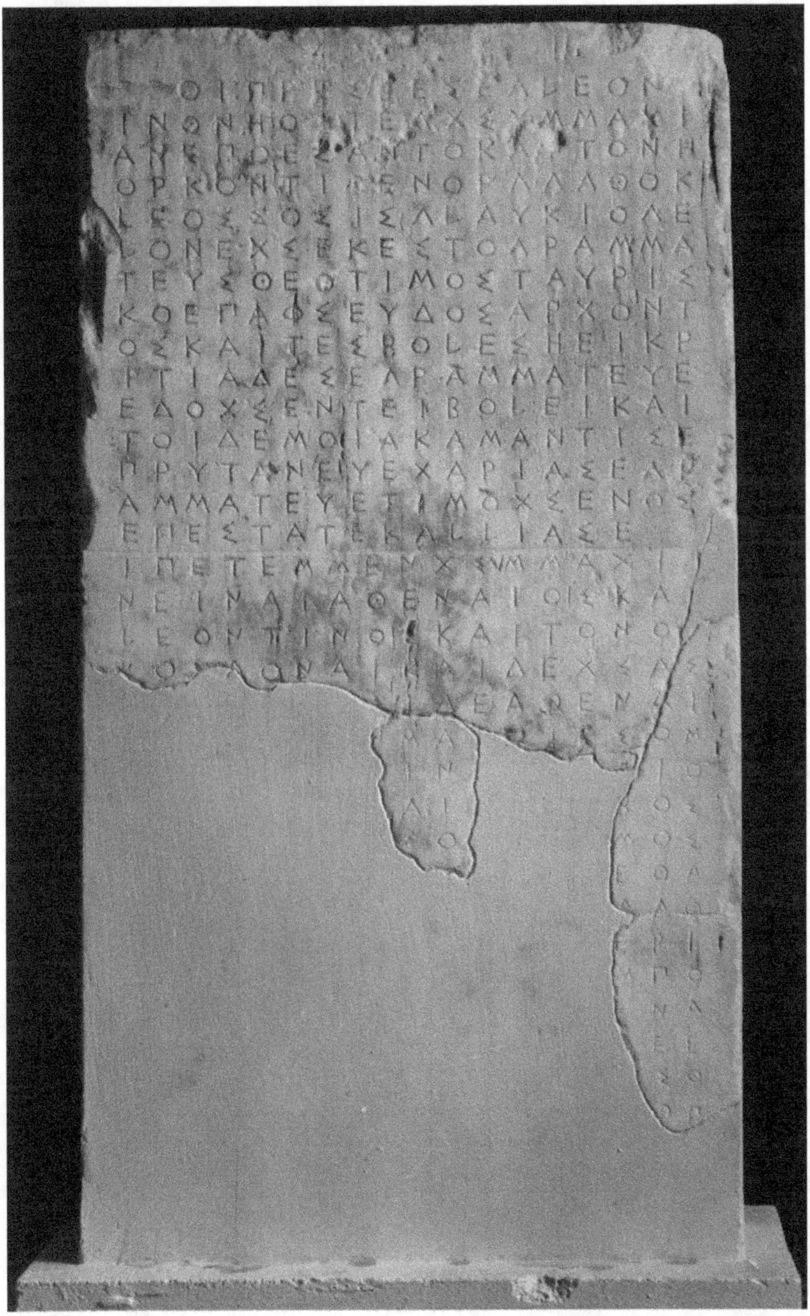

FIGURE 4 *Athenian Alliance with Leontinoi* (IG I^3 54)

FIGURE 5
Quadripartite Treaty between Athens, Argos, Martineia and Elis (IG I^3 83)

Bibliography

1 Editions of Ancient Sources (Texts and Translations)

Adams, Ch.D. (1919) (ed.) *Aeschines*, Cambridge (MA) and London: Harvard University Press and William Heinemann.

Allen, T.W. (1931) (ed.) *Homeri* Ilias, Oxford: University Press.

Bekker, I. (1837) (ed.) *Aristotelis* De Retorica *Libri III*, De Rhetorica ad Alexandrum, De Poetica, Oxonii: e Typographeo Academico.

Bengston, H. (1962) *Die Verträge der griechische-römischen Welt von 700 bis 338 v. Chr*, (Die Staatsverträge des Altertums, Band II), München: C.H. Beck.

Bernardakis, G.N. (1889) (ed.) *Plutarch*. Moralia, Leipzig: Teubner.

Brownson, C.L. (1918) (ed.) *Xenophon*, Vol. 1 (Books 1–4), Cambridge (MA) and London: Harvard University Press and William Heinemann.

Brownson, C.L. (1921) (ed.) *Xenophon*, Vol. 2 (Books 5–7), Cambridge (MA) and London: Harvard University Press and William Heinemann.

Burnet, J. (1924) (ed.) *Plato's* Euthyphro, Apology of Socrates *and* Crito, Oxford: Clarendon Press.

Burnet, J. (1967–1968) (ed.) *Platonis Opera*, Vol. 1–5, Oxford: Clarendon Press.

Butcher, S.H. (1903) (ed.) *Demosthenis Orationes*, Oxonii: e Typographeo Clarendoniano.

Büttner-Wobst, T. (1893) (ed.) *Polybius. Historiae*, Leipzig: Teubner.

Cagnat, R. *et alii* (1927) (eds.) *Inscriptiones Graecae ad res Romanas pertinentes*, IV, Paris: E. Leroux (= *IGR* IV)

Calderini, A. (1949) (ed.) *Trattati internazionali nell' Antichità greca*, Parte 1, Milano: La Goliardica.

Clark, A.C. (1909) (eds.) *M. Tulli Ciceronis Orationes*, Oxonii: e Typographeo Clarendoniano.

Crawley, R. (1910) (ed.) *Thucydides*. The Peloponnesian War, London and New York: J.M. Dent and E.P. Dutton.

Diggle, J. (1994) (ed.) *Euripidis Fabulae*, Vol. 1–3, Oxford: University Press.

Dittenberger, W. (1903–1905) (ed.) *Orientis Graeci Inscriptiones Selectae*, I–II, Leipzig: S. Hirzel (= *OGIS*).

Dittenberger, W. (1915–1924) (ed.) *Sylloge Inscriptionum Graecarum*, 3 ed., Leipzig: S. Hirzel (= *SIG*).

Dunbar, N. (1995) (ed.) *Aristophanes* Birds, Oxford: Clarendon Press.

Emlyn-Jones, Ch. (1999) (ed.) *Plato*. Crito, London: Bristol Classical Press.

Evelyn-White, H.G. (1914) (ed.) *Hesiod, The Homeric Hymns and Homerica*, Cambridge (MA) and London: Harvard University Press and William Heinemann.

Fernández Nieto. F.J. (1975) *Los acuerdos bélicos en la antigua Grecia*, Santiago de Compostela: Universidad de Santiago de Compostela.

Foster, B.O. (1919) (ed.) *Livy. Books I and II*, Cambridge (MA) and London: Harvard University Press and William Heinemann.

Foster, E.S. (1924) (ed.) "The Rhetorica ad Alexandrum", in Ross, W. (ed.) *The Works of Aristotle*, Vol. XI, Oxford: Clarendon Press.

Freese, J.H. (1926) (ed.) *Aristotle in 23 Volumes*, Vol. 22, Cambridge (MA) and London: Harvard University Press and William Heinemann.

Godley, A.D. (1920) (ed.) *Herodotus*, Cambridge (MA): Harvard University Press.

Guarducci, M. (1942) (ed.) *Inscriptiones Creticae*, Vol. 3 "Tituli Cretae orientalis", Roma: Libreria dello Stato (= *IC*).

Hart, H.L.A. (1954) (ed.) *Austin, J. The Province of Jurisprudence Determined*, London: Weidenfeld and Nicolson.

Hercher, R. (1866) (ed.) *Claudii Aeliani de natura animalium libri xvii, varia historia, epistolae, fragmenta*, Vol. 2, Lipsiae: B.G. Teubneri.

Jebb, R. (1891) (ed.) *Sophocles*. The Antigone, Cambridge: University Press.

Jones, H.L. (1924) (ed.) *The* Geography *of Strabo*. Cambridge (MA) and London: Harvard University Press and William Heinemann.

Jones, H.S. and J.E. Powell (1942) (eds.) *Thucydidis* Historiae, Tomus I–II, Oxford: University Press.

Jones, W.H.S. and H.A. Ormerod (1918) (eds.) *Pausanias*. Description of Greece, Cambridge (MA) and London: Harvard University Press and William Heinemann.

Jowett, B. (1881) (ed.) *Thucydides*, Vol. 1, Oxford: Clarendon Press.

Kovacs, D. (1994) (ed.) *Euripides* Cyclops, Alcestis, Medea, Cambridge (MA) and London: Harvard University Press and William Heinemann.

Krentz, P. and E.L. Wheeler (1994) (eds.) *Polyaenus*. Stratagems of War, Chicago: Ares Publishers.

Lafleur, L. (1963) (ed.), *Bentham, J. An Introduction to the Principles of Morals and Legislation* (1789), New York: Hafner.

Lamb, W.R.M. (1930) (ed.) *Lysias*, Cambridge (MA): Harvard University Press.

Leão, D.F. and P.J. Rhodes (2016) (eds.) *The Laws of Solon. A New Edition with Introduction, Translation and Commentary*, London and New York: I.B. Tauris.

Legrand, Ph.-E. (1963–1968) (ed.) *Hérodote*. Histoires, Vol. 1–9, Paris: Les Belles Lettres.

Lewis, D. (1981) (ed.) *Inscriptiones Graecae I: Inscriptiones Atticae Euclidis anno anteriores*, Fasc. 1 *"Decreta et tabulae magistratuum"*, Berlin and New York: Walter de Gruyter (= *IG* I³)

Macan, R.W. (1895) (ed.) *Herodotus*, Books VII–VIII–IX, Vol. I, Part I, London and New York: Routledge.

MacDowell, D. (1982) (ed.) *Gorgias*, Encomium of Helen, Bristol: Bristol Classical Press.

Maidment, K.J. (1968) (ed.) *Minor Attic Orators*, Vol. I "Antiphon-Andocides", Cambridge (MA) and London: Harvard University Press and William Heinemann.

Marchant, E.C. (1968–1971) (ed.) *Xenophontis Opera Omnia*, Vol. 1–4, Oxonii: e Typographeo Clarendoniano.

Marchant, E.C. and G.W. Bowersock (1925) (ed.) *Xenophon. Xenophon in Seven Volumes*, Vol. 7, "Constitution of the Athenians", Cambridge (MA) and London: Harvard University Press and William Heinemann.

Mathieu, G. and B. Haussoulier (2002) (eds.) *Aristote*. Constitution d'Athènes, Paris: Les Belles Lettres.

Meiggs, R. and D. Lewis (1969) (eds.) *A Selection of Greek Historical Inscriptions*, Oxford: Clarendon Press.

Müller, C.F.W. (1889) (ed.) *M. Tullius Cicero. Librorum de Re Publica Sex*, Leipzig: Teubner.

Murray, A.T. (1924) (ed.) *Homer*. The Iliad, Vol. I–II, Cambridge (MA) and London: Harvard University Press and William Heinemann.

Murray, A.T. (1939) (ed.) *Demosthenes*, Cambridge (MA) and London: Harvard University Press and William Heinemann.

Murray, G. (1913) (ed.) *Euripidis Fabulae*, vol. 3, Oxonii: e Typographeo Clarendoniano.

Norlin, G. (1980) (ed.) *Isocrates*, Cambridge (MA) and London: Harvard University Press and William Heinemann.

Oates, W.J. and E. O'Neill Jr. (1938) (ed.) *Euripides. The Complete Greek Drama*, Vol. 1–2, New York: Random House.

Oldfather, C.H. (1989) (ed.) *Diodorus Siculus*, Vol. 4–8, Cambridge (MA) and London: Harvard University Press and William Heinemann.

Panessa, G. (1999) (ed.) Philiai. *L'amicizia nelle relazioni interstatali del Greci*, Vol. I "Dalle origine alla fine della Guerra del Peloponneso", Pisa: Scuola Normale Superiore.

Perrin, B. (1916) *Plutarch*. Lives, Cambridge (MA) and London: Harvard University Press and William Heinemann.

Piccirilli, L. (1973) (ed.) *Gli arbitrati interstatali greci*, Vol. 1 "Dalle origini al 338 a.C.", Pisa: Marlin.

Poste, E. and E.A. Whittuck (1904) (eds.) *Gai Institutiones or Institutes of Roman Law*, with an historical introduction by A.H.J. Greenidge, Oxford: Clarendon Press.

Rackham, H. (1934) (ed.) *Aristotle in 23 Volumes*, Vol. 19, Cambridge (MA) and London: Harvard University Press and William Heinemann.

Rackham, H. (1944) (ed.) *Aristotle in 23 Volumes*, Vol. 21, Cambridge (MA) and London: Harvard University Press and William Heinemann.

Rackham, H. (1952a) (ed.) *Aristotle in 23 Volumes*, Vol. 20, Cambridge (MA) and London: Harvard University Press and William Heinemann.

Rackham, H. (1952b) (ed.) *Aristotle in 23 Volumes*, Vol. 22, Cambridge (MA) and London: Harvard University Press and William Heinemann.

Rauchenstein, R. (1874) (ed.) *Ausgewählte Reden des Isokrates*. Panegyricus *und* Areopagiticus, Berlin: Weidmann.

Rennie, W. (1931) (ed.) *Demosthenis Orationes*, Oxonii: e Typographeo Clarendoniano.

Repgen, K. (1998) (ed.) *Acta Pacis Westphalicae* (Hrsg. von der Nordrhein-Westfälischen Akademie der Wissenschaften in Verbindung mit der Vereinigung zur Erforschung der Neueren Geschichte), Series III [Abteilung B: Verhandlungsakten. Band 1: Die Friedensverträge mit Frankreich und Schweden. 1: Urkunden. Bearb. von Antje Oschmann], Münster: Aschendorff.

Rhodes, P.J. (1994) (ed.) *Thucydides* History, Book III, Warminster: Aris and Phillips.

Rhodes, P.J. and R. Osborne (2003) (eds.) *Greek Historical Inscriptions, 404–323 BC*, Oxford: University Press.

Ross, W.D. (1959) (ed.) *Aristotle*. Ars Rhetorica, Oxford: Clarendon Press.

Ruschenbusch, E. (1966) (ed.) *Solonos Nomoi. Die Fragmente des solonischen Gesetzeswerkes mit einer Text- und Überlieferungsgeschichte*, Wiesbaden: Franz Steiner.

Rutter, N.K. (1996) (ed.) *Thucydides—Books II–IV*, Bristol: Bristol Classical Press.

Sandys, J. (1937) (ed.) *Pindar*. The Odes, Cambridge (MA) and London: Harvard University Press and William Heinemann.

Schweigert, E. (1939) "Greek Inscriptions (1–13)", *Hesperia* 8 (1); 1–47.

Shepherd, R. (1793) (ed.) *Polyœnus's* Stratagems of war, London: G. Nicol.

Shorey, P. (1969) (ed.) *Plato in Twelve Volumes*, Vol. 5–6, Cambridge (MA) and London: Harvard University Press and William Heinemann.

Shuckburgh, E.S. (1889) (ed.) *Polybius*. Histories, London and New York: Macmillan.

Smith, C.F. (1894) (ed.) *Thucydides*, Book 3, Boston and London: Ginn.

Smith, C.F. (1919) (ed.) *Thucydides*. History of the Peloponnesian War, Books I–II, Cambridge (MA) and London: Harvard University Press and William Heinemann.

Smith, C.F. (1920) (ed.) *Thucydides*. History of the Peloponnesian War, Books III–IV, London and New York: William Heinemann and G.P. Putnam's and Sons.

Smith, C.F. (1921) (ed.) *Thucydides*, Vol. III, Books V–VI, Cambridge (MA) and London: Harvard University Press and William Heinemann.

Smyth, H.W. (1926) (ed.) *Aeschylus*. Suppliant Women, Vol. 2, Cambridge (MA): Harvard University Press.

Sommerstein, A.H. (1980) (ed.) *Acharnians* (The Comedies of Aristophanes, Vol. 1), Warminster: Aris & Phillips.

Sommerstein, A.H. (1987) (ed.) *Birds* (The Comedies of Aristophanes, Vol. 6), Warminster: Aris & Phillips.

Susemihl, F. (1884) (ed.) *Aristotle*. Eudemian Ethics, Leipzig: Teubner.

van Effenterre, H. and F. Ruzé (1994) (eds.) *Nomima. Recueil d'inscriptions politiques et juridiques de l'archaïsme grec*, Vol. 1, Rome: École Française de Rome.

Vince, J.H. (1930) (ed.) *Demosthenes*, Cambridge (MA) and London: Harvard University Press and William Heinemann.

Voigt, E.M. (1971) (ed.) *Sappho et Alcaeus*, Amsterdam: Polak and van Gennep.

von der Mühll, P. (1962) (ed.) *Homeri* Odyssea, Basel: Helbing and Lichtenhahn.

Walton, F.R. (1957) (ed.) *Diodorus Siculus*. Library of History, Vol. XI: Fragments of Books 21–32. Cambridge (MA): Harvard University Press.

West, M.L. (1990) (ed.) *Aeschyli Tragoediae*, Stuttgart: Teubner.

West, M.L. (1992) (ed.) *Iambi et elegi Graeci ante Alexandrum cantati*, Vol. II, Oxford: University Press.

Woelfflin, E. and I. Melber (1887) (eds.) *Polyaeni* Strategematon *Libri Octo*, Lipsiae: B.G. Teubneri.

2 Critical Bibliography

Abi-Saab, G. (1987) "La coutume dans tous ses états ou le dilemma du développement du droit international général dans un monde éclaté", in *Le droit international à l'heure de sa codification. Études en l'honneur de Roberto Ago*, Vol. I, Milano: A. Giuffrè; 53–65.

Accame, S. (1935) "L' alleanza di Atene con Leontini e Regio", *Rivista di Filologia* 63; 73–75.

Accame, S. (1952) "Note storiche su epigrafi attiche del V secolo", *Rivista di Filologia* 80, 1952, 111–136.

Adcock, F.E. (1957) *The Greek and Macedonian Art of War*, Berkeley: University of California Press.

Adcock, F.E. and D.J. Mosley (1975) *Diplomacy in Ancient Greece*, London: Thames and Hudson.

Ager, S. (1993) "Why war? Some views on international arbitration in Ancient Greece", *Échos du monde classique / Classical Views* N.S. 12; 1–13.

Ager, S. (2005) "Sacred Settlements: The Role of the Gods in the Resolution of Interstate Disputes", in Bertrand, J.-M. (ed.) *La violence dans les mondes grec et romain*, Paris: Publications de la Sorbonne; 413–429.

Agnati, U. (2009) "*Persona iuris vocabulum*. Per una interpretazione giuridica di 'persona' nelle opere di Gaio", *Rivista di diritto romano* 9; 1–41.

Ago, H.E. (1982) "The First International Communities in the Mediterranean World", *British Yearbook of International Law* 53; 213–232.

Albert, S. (1980) Bellum iustum. *Die Theorie des 'gerechten Krieges' und ihre praktische Bedeutung für die auswärtigen Auseinandersetzung Roms in republikanischer Zeit*, Kallmünz: Lassleben.

Alemany Vilamajó, A. (1997) "Una ambaixada persa a Atenes: Aristoph. Ach. 61–125", in AA.VV. *Homenatge a Miquel Dolç, Actes del XII Simposi de la Secció Catalana i I de la Secció Balear de la SEEC*, Palma, 1 al 43 de febrer de 1996, Palma de Mallorca: Govern Balear; 155–159.

Algarza Roldán, M. (1998) "*Eiréne* y otras palabras griegas sobre la paz", in Muñoz,

F.A. and B. Molina Rueda (eds.) *Cosmovisiones de paz en el Mediterráneo antiguo y medieval*, Granada: Instituto de la Paz y los Conflictos; 123–152.

Allison, J.W. "Thucydides on Delium: War Without Borders", in Rechenauer, G. and V. Pothou (eds.) *Thucydides—A Violent Teacher?*, Göttingen: Vandenhoeck & Ruprecht; 131–144.

Allott, Ph. (1999) "The Concept of International Law", *European Journal of International Law* 10 (1); 31–50.

Allott, Ph. (2004) "International Law and International Revolution. Reconceiving the World", in *The Health of Nations. Society and Law Beyond the State*, Cambridge: University Press; 399–422.

Alonso Troncoso, V. (1987) *Neutralidad y neutralismo en la Guerra del Peloponeso (431–404 a.C.)*, Madrid: Ediciones de la Universidad Autónoma de Madrid.

Alonso Troncoso, V. (1995) "Ultimatum et déclaration de guerre en Grèce classique", in Frézouls, E. and A. Jacquemin (eds.) *Les relations internationales*, Actes du colloque de Strasbourg, 15–17 juin 1993, Paris: De Boccard; 211–295.

Alonso Troncoso, V. (1997) "Tratados y relaciones de alianza en la guerra de Corinto (395–386 a.C.)", *Rivista Storica dell' Antichità* 27; 21–71.

Alonso Troncoso, V. (2001) "Para un corpus de los tratados de alianza de la Grecia Clásica", *Dike* 4; 219–232.

Alonso Troncoso, V. (2002) "La cláusula de la hegemonía en la Liga Délica (Th. 3,10,4; 11,3)", *Ktèma* 27; 57–63.

Alonso Troncoso, V. (2003) "L'institution de l'hégémonie: entre la coutume et le droit écrit", in Thür, G. and F.J. Fernández Nieto (eds.) *Symposion 1999. Vorträge zur griechischen und hellenistischen Rechtsgeschichte* (Pazo de Mariñán, La Coruña, 6.–9. September 1999) (Akten der Gesellschaft für Griechische und Hellenistische Rechtsgeschichte, 14): Köln, Weimar, and Wien: Böhlau; 339–354.

Alonso Troncoso, V. (2007) "War, Peace, and International Law in Ancient Greece", in Raaflaub, K.A. (ed.) *War and Peace in the Ancient World*, Oxford: Blackwell; 206–225.

Amendola, S. (2006) *Donne e Preghiera. Le preghiere dei personaggi femminili nelle tragedie superstiti di Eschilo*, Amsterdam: Adolf. M. Hakkert.

Ames, R.T. (1994) *The Art of Rulership: A Study of Ancient Chinese Political Thought*, New York: State University of New York Press.

Amit, M. (1970), "Hostages in Ancient Greece", *Rivista di Filologia e di Istruzione Classica* 98; 129–147.

Amit, M. (1973) *Great and Small Poleis: A Study in the Relations between the Great Powers and the Small Cities in Ancient Greece* (Collection Latomus, 134), Brussels: Latomus.

Amit, M. (1970) "Hostages in Ancient Greece", *Rivista di Filología e di Istruzione Classica* 98; 129–147.

Anand, R.P. (1986) "Sovereign Equality of States in International Law", *Recueil des Cours de l'Académie de Droit International* 197, Leiden and Boston: Brill and Nijhoff; 9–228.

Anderson, G. (2003) *The Athenian Experiment. Building an Imagined Political Community in Ancient Athens, 508–490 BC*, Ann Arbor: University of Michigan Press.

Anderson, G. (2009) "The Personality of the Greek State", *Journal of Hellenic Studies* 129; 1–22.

Anderson, J.K. (1970) *Military Theory and Practice in the Age of Xenophon*, Berkeley and Los Angeles: University of California Press.

Anderson, J.K. (1991) "Hoplite Weapons and Offensive Arms", in Hanson, V.D. (ed.) *Hoplites: The Classical Greek Battle Experience*, London: Routledge; 15–37.

Andrewes, A. (1959) "Thucydides on the causes of war", *Classical Quarterly* 53 (N.S. 9); 223–239.

Andrieu, K. (2012) *La justice transitionelle. De l'Afrique du Sud au Rwanda*, Paris: Gallimard.

Anghie, A. (2005) *Imperialism, Sovereignty and the Making of International Law*, Cambridge: University Press.

Ansah, T. (2003) "War: Rhetoric and Norm Creation in Response to Terror", *Virginia Journal of International Law* 43; 797–860.

Arboleda, E. (1991) "Refugee Definition in Africa and Latin America: The Lessons of Pragmatism", *International Journal of Refugee Law* 3 (2); 185–207.

Aristodemou, M. (2000) *Law and Literature. Journeys from Here to Eternity*, Oxford: University Press.

Arnaoutoglou, I. (1998) "Between *Koinon* and *Idion*: Legal and Social Dimensions of Religious Associations in Ancient Athens", in Cartledge, P., P. Millett and S. von Reden (eds.) Kosmos. *Essays in Order, Conflict, and Community in Classical Athens*, Cambridge: University Press; 68–83.

Arnaoutoglou, I. (2003) Thusias heneka kai sunousias. *Private religious associations in Hellenistic Athens* (Yearbook of the Research Centre for the History of Greek Law, 37 [4]), Athens: Academy of Athens.

Arnott, P.D. (1967) *An Introduction to the Greek Theatre*, Bloomington: Macmillan.

Arnott, P.D. (1991) *Public and Performance in the Greek Theatre*, London and New York: Routledge.

Ascough, R.S., Ph.A. Harland and J.S. Kloppenborg (2012) *Associations in the Graeco-Roman World. A Sourcebook*, Waco: Baylor University Press.

Aufricht, H. (1943) "Personality in International Law", *The American Political Science Review* 37 (2); 217–243.

Avram, A. (1996) "Der Vertrag zwischen Rom und Kallatis", in Funck, B. (ed.) Hellenismus. *Beiträge zur Erforschung von Akkulturation und politischer Ordnung in den Staaten des hellenistischen Zeitalters*, Tübingen: Mhor.

Avram, A. (1999b) Der *Vertrag zwischen Rom und Kallatis. Ein Beitrag zum römischen Völkerrecht*, Amsterdam: A.M. Hakkert.

Bacon, H.H. (1961) *Barbarians in Greek Tragedy*, New Haven: Yale University Press.

Bacot, G. (1989) *La doctrine de la guerre juste*, Paris: Economica.

Baker, P. (1999) "Les mercenaires", in Prost, F. (ed.) *Armées et sociétés de la Grèce classique. Aspects sociaux et politiques de la guerre aux* V^e *et* IVe *s. av. J.-C.*, Paris: Errance; 240–255.

Bakewell, G.W. (1997) "*Metoikia* in the *Supplices* of Aeschylus", *Classical Antiquity* 16; 209–228.

Bakewell, G.W. (2013) *Aeschylus's* Suppliant Women. *The tragedy of immigration*, Madison: The University of Wisconsin.

Balbín Chamorro, P. (2006) "*Ius hospitii* y *ius civitatis*", *Gerión* 24 (1); 207–235.

Balcer, J. (1978) *The Athenian Regulations for Chalkis. Studies in Athenian Imperial Law* (Historia Einzelschriften, 33), Wiesbaden: Franz Steiner.

Balogh, E. (1943) *Political Refugees in the Ancient Greece from the Period of the Tyrants to Alexander the Great*, Johannesburg: Witwatersrand University Press.

Baltrusch, E. (1994) *Symmachie und Spondai. Untersuchungen zum griechischen Völkerrecht der archaischen und klassischen Zeit (8.–5. Jahrhundert v. Chr.)*, Berlin and New York: De Gruyter.

Bandeira Galindo, G.R. (2005) "Martti Koskenniemi and the Historiographical Turn in International Law", *European Journal of International Law* 16 (3); 539–559.

Banslaugh, R.A. (1991) *The Concept of Neutrality in Classical Greece*, Berkeley: University of California Press.

Barboza, J. (2008) *Derecho Internacional Público*, Buenos Aires: Zavalía.

Barker, E. (1927) "Greek Political Thought and Theory in the Fourth Century", in Bury, J.B., S.A. Cook and F.E. Adcock (eds.) *Cambridge Ancient History*, Vol. 6, Cambridge: University Press; 505–535.

Baslez, M.-F. (1998) "Les associations dans la cité grecque et l'apprentissage du collectif", *Ktèma* 23; 431–440.

Bauslaugh, R.A. (1991) *The Concept of Neutrality in Classical Greece*, Berkeley: University of California Press.

Baviera, G. (1898) *Il diritto internazionale dei Romani*, Modena: Direzione dell'Archivio Giuridico.

Bayliss, A.J. (2013) "Oaths and Interstate Relations", in Sommerstein, A.H. and A.J. Bayliss (eds.) *Oath and State in Ancient Greece* (Beiträge zur Altertumskunde, 306), Berlin and Boston: De Gruyter; 147–325.

Bearzot, C. (2003) "Panellenismo e *asylía* in età classica: il caso dell'Elide", in Dreher, M. (ed.) *Das antike Asyl* (Akten der Gesellschaft für griechische und hellenistische Rechtsgeschichte 15), Köln: Böhlau; 37–58.

Bearzot, C. (2004) *Federalismo e autonomia nelle* Elleniche *di Senofonte*, Milano: Vita e Pensiero.

Beauchet, L. (1897) *Histoire du droit privé de la république athénienne*, Paris: Chevalier Marescq et Cie.

Beaulac, S. (2000) "The Westphalian Legal Orthodoxy—Myth or Reality?", *Journal of the History of International Law* 2 (2); 148–177.

Beaulac, S. (2004) *The Power of Language in the Making of International Law. The Word* Sovereignty *in Bodin and Vattel and the Myth of* Westphalia, Leiden: Martinus Nijhoff.

Beck, H. (1997) Polis *und* Koinon. *Untersuchungen zur Geschichte und Struktur der griechischen Bundesstaaten im 4. Jahrhundert v. Chr.*, Stuttgart: Franz Steiner.

Becker Lorca, A. (2012) "Eurocentrism in the History of International Law", in Fassbender, B. and A. Peters (eds.) *The Oxford Handbook of the History of International Law*, Oxford: University Press; 1034–1057.

Bederman, D.J. (1991) "Religion and the Sources of International Law in Antiquity", in Janis, M.W. (ed.) *The Influence of Religion on the Development of International Law*, The Hague, London and Boston: Martinus Nijhoff; 3–29.

Bederman, D.J. (2001) *International Law in Antiquity*, Cambridge: University Press.

Bednarowski, K.P. (2010) "The Danaids' Threat: Obscurity, Suspense and the Shedding of Tradition in Aeschylus' *Suppliants*", *Classical Journal* 105 (3); 193–212.

Bell, C. (1992) *Ritual Theory, Ritual Practice*, Oxford: University Press.

Bellamy, A.J. (2010) *Guerras justas. De Cicerón a Iraq*, Madrid: Fondo de Cultura Económica (original edition: Cambridge 2006).

Benveniste, É. (1949) "La légende des Danaïdes", *Revue de l'histoire des religions* 136; 134–138.

Benveniste, É. (1969) *Le vocabulaire des institutions indoeuropéennes*, Tome II "Pouvoir, droit, religion", Paris: Les Éditions du Minuit.

Berent, M. (1994) *The Stateless* Polis*: Towards a Re-Evaluation of the Classical Greek Political Community* (PhD, Cambridge University), Cambridge.

Berent, M. (2000a) "Anthropology and the Classics: War, Violence and the Stateless *Polis*", *Classical Quarterly* 50 (1); 257–289.

Berent, M. (2000b) "Sovereignty: Ancient and Modern", *Polis. The Journal of the Society for Greek Political Thought* 17 (1–2); 2–34.

Berent, M. (2004) "In Search of the Greek State: a Rejoinder to M.H. Hansen", *Polis. The Journal of the Society for Greek Political Thought* 21 (1–2); 107–146.

Berent, M. (2006) "The Stateless *Polis*: A Reply to Critics", *Social Evolution and History* 5 (1); 141–163.

Bernabé Pajares, A. (1979) *Fragmentos de épica griega arcaica*, Madrid: Gredos.

Bernand, A. (1999) *Guerre et violence dans la Grèce ancienne*, Paris: Hachette.

Bernard, N. (2000) *À l'épreuve de la guerre. Guerre et société dans le monde grec. Ve et IVe siècles avant notre ère*, Paris: Seli Arslan.

Bertalozzi, M. (2001) "Tribunali militari in Atene?", *Aevum* 75 (1); 57–70.

Bertoli, M. (2009) "La 'guerra giusta' in Tucidide: argomenti giuridici, argomenti religiosi", *Aevum* 83 (1); 7–30.

Best, J.G.P. (1969) *Thracian Peltasts and their Influence on Greek Warfare*, Groningen: Wolters-Noordhoff.

Bettalli, M. (1995) *I mercenari nel mondo greco*, Vol. I "Dalle origine all fine del V sec. a.C.", Pisa: Edizione ETS.

Bettalli, M. (1999) "La guerre du Péloponnèse", in Brulé, P. and J. Oulhen (eds.) *La guerre en Grèce à l'époque classique*, Rennes: Presses Universitaires; 335–354.

Biad, A. (1999) *Droit international humanitaire*, Paris: Ellipses.

Bickerman, E.J. (1950) "Remarques sur le droit des gens dans la Grèce classique", *Revue internationale des droits de l'antiquité* 4; 99–127.

Blanchet, J. (2013) *Gloire et décadence de l'empire athénien*, Nantes: Normant.

Boegehold, A.L. (1963) "Toward a Study of Athenian Voting Procedure", *Hesperia* 32 (4); 366–374.

Boegehold, A.L. (1995) *The Lawcourts at Athens: Sites, Buildings, Equipment, Procedure, and Testimonia* (Athenian Agora, Vol. 28), Princeton: The American School of Classical Studies at Athens.

Boissier, P. (1985) *From Solferino to Tsushima: History of the International Committee of the Red Cross*, Geneva: ICRC and Henry Dunant Institute.

Boll, J. (2008) *War: Interdisciplinary investigations*. Oxford: Inter-disciplinary Press.

Bolmarcich, S. (2007) "Oaths in Greek International Relations", in Sommerstein, A.H. and J. Fletcher (eds.) Horkos. *The Oath in Greek Society*, Exeter: Bristol Phoenix Press; 26–38.

Bolmarcich, S. (2010) "Communal Values in Ancient Diplomacy", in Rosen, R.M. and I. Sluiter (eds.) *Valuing Others in Classical Antiquity*, Leiden and Boston: Brill; 113–135.

Bonk, P. (1974) *Defensiv- und offensivklauseln in griechischen Symmakhieverträgen* (PhD, Rheinischen Friedrich-Wilhelms-Universität), Bonn.

Bonnard, J.-B. (2014) "Le traitement du corps des ennemis vaincus chez Hérodote", in Allély, A. (ed.) *Corps au supplice et violences de guerre dans l'Antiquité*, Bordeaux: De Boccard; 15–25.

Bonner, R.J. and G. Smith (1930–1938) *The Administration of Justice from Homer to Aristotle*, Vol. I–II, Chicago: University Press.

Bonner, R.J. and G. Smith (1943) "Administration of Justice in the Delphic Amphictyony", *Classical Philology* 38 (1); 1–12.

Bonucci, A. (1903) *La legge comune nel pensiero greco*, Perugia: Bartelli.

Borba Casella, P. (2012) *Direito Internacional no mundo antigo*, São Paulo: Atlas.

Börm, H. (2016) "Civil Wars in Greek and Roman Antiquity: Contextualising Disintegration and Reintegration", in Börm, H., M. Mattheis and J. Wienand (eds.) *Civil War in Ancient Greece and Rome. Contexts of Disintegration and Reintegration*, Stuttgart: Franz Steiner; 15–28.

Bosworth, B. (1993) "The Humanitarian Aspect of the Melian Dialogue", *Journal of Hellenic Studies* 113; 30–44.

Bosworth, B. (2012) "Massacre in the Peloponnesian War", in Dwyer, Ph.G. and L. Ryan (eds.) *Theatres of Violence: Massacre, Mass Killing and Atrocity throughout History*, New York: Berghahn Books; 18–26.

Bottici, C. (2004) *Uomini e State: Percorsi di un' analogia*, Pisa: ETS.

Bouchet, Ch. (2014) *Isocrate l'Athénien, ou la belle hégémonie. Études des relations internationales au IVe siècle a.C.*, Bordeaux: De Boccard.

Bouineau, J. (2011) *Droit international et Antiquité: aspects culturels*, Paris: L'Harmattan.

Boutros-Ghali, B. (1960) "Le principe d'égalité des États et les organisations internationales", *Recueil des Cours de l'Académie de Droit International* 100, Leiden and Boston: Brill and Nijhoff; 2–73.

Brandom, R. (1994) *Making it Explicit. Reasoning, Representing and Discursive Commitment*, Cambridge (MA): Harvard University Press.

Brassloff, S. (1928) *Der römische Staat und seine internationalen Beziehungen*, Wien and Leipzig: Perles.

Bravo, B. (1980) "*Sulân*. Représailles et justice privée contre des étrangers dans les cités grecques", *Annali della Scuola Normale Superiore di Pisa* 10; 675–987.

Brelich, A. (2009) *Teatri di guerre, agoni, culti nella Grecia antica* (a cura di E. Dettori), Roma: Riuniti University Press.

Brill, S. (2009) "Violence and Vulnerability in Aeschylus' *Suppliants*", in William, W. (ed.) *Logos and Muthos. Philosophical Essays in Greek Literature*, Albany: State University of New York Press; 161–180.

Broms, B. (1983) "Subjects: Entitlement in the International Legal System", in MacDonald, R.S.J. and D.M. Johnston (eds.) *The Structure and Process of International Law*, Dordrecht, Boston and Lancaster: Martinus Nijhoff; 383–423.

Brown Ferrario, S. (2013) "'Reading' Athens: Foreign Perceptions of the Political Roles of Athenian Leaders in Thucydides", in Tsakmakis, A. and M. Tamiolaki (eds.) *Thucydides Between History and Literature*, Berlin and Boston: De Gruyter; 181–197.

Brutti, M. (2011) *Il diritto privato nell'antica Roma*, Torino: G. Giappichelli.

Bryant, M. (2016) *A World History of War Crimes from Antiquity to the Present*, London: Bloomsbury.

Bryce, T. (1983) *The Lycians*, Vol. 1 "The Lycians in Literary and Epigraphical Sources", Copenhagen: Museum Tusculanum.

Buchanan, A. (2010) "The Legitimacy of International Law", in Besson, S. and J. Tasioulas (eds.) *The Philosophy of International Law*, Oxford: University Press; 79–96.

Buckland, W.W. (1912) *Elementary Principles of the Roman Private Law*, Cambridge: University Press.

Budin, S.L. (2013) *Intimate Lives of the Ancient Greeks*, Santa Barbara: Praeger.

Bugh, G.R. (1988) *The Horsemen of Athens*, Princeton: University Press.

Buis, E.J. (2006) *Propriété privée et frontières dans les cités grecques et les royaumes hellénistiques: conflits territoriaux et les conséquences juridiques de l'occupation fon-*

cière des eschatiai (Mémoire de Master II, UFR d'Histoire de l'Université de Paris I Panthéon-Sorbonne), Paris.

Buis, E.J. (2007) "Entre los compromisos bilaterales y la cláusula de supremacía: contactos jurídicos de Roma con las ciudades helenizadas de Oriente", *I Congreso Internacional Oriente-Occidente "Los campos de la diversidad y el encuentro"* (Facultad de Filosofía y Letras de la Universidad de Buenos Aires, 2 al 4 de mayo de 2007), Buenos Aires.

Buis, E.J. (2008) "Diplomáticos y farsantes (Ar. *Ach.* 61–174): estrategias para una desarticulación cómica de la política exterior ateniense", *Cuadernos de Filología Clásica (Estudios Griegos e Indoeuropeos)* 18; 249–266.

Buis, E.J. (2011) "Sobre gnomos y gigantes: Los tratados grecorromanos y la igualdad soberana de los Estados como ficción histórico-jurídica", *Lecciones y Ensayos* 89; 73–117.

Buis, E.J. (2012) "Las lágrimas de Zeus, la prudencia de Atenea: Normas humanitarias, fuentes históricas y el reconocimiento de un 'derecho internacional' en el mundo griego antiguo", *Revista Jurídica de Buenos Aires* Vol. 2012; 357–383.

Buis, E.J. (2013a) "Échos sophistiques d'une rhétorique du droit dans le langage de Phidippide: Ἀνὴρ ὁ τὸν νόμον θεὶς (*Nuées*, v. 1421)", in Laks, A. and R. Saetta Cottone (dir.) *Comédie et philosophie. Socrate et les "Présocratiques" dans les* Nuées *d'Aristophane*, Paris: Éditions Rue d'Ulm; 151–167.

Buis, E.J. (2013b) "Las flechas de Heracles: Consecuencias jurídicas del empleo de armas tóxicas durante el asedio de Crisa en la Primera Guerra Sagrada (590 a.C.)", in Buis, E.J. and L.M. Giosa (eds.) *Derecho Internacional y Conflictos Armados. Aportes para una comprensión histórica, normativa y práctica*, Azul: Centro de Estudios de Derechos Humanos (CEDH) de la UNICEN; 137–147.

Buis, E.J. (2013c) "El castigo de Ares: los límites de la violencia armada y la responsabilidad por la comisión de crímenes de guerra en la Grecia antigua", in Buis, E.J. and L.M. Giosa (eds.) *Derecho Internacional y Conflictos Armados. Aportes para una comprensión histórica, normativa y práctica*, Azul: Centro de Estudios de Derechos Humanos (CEDH) de la UNICEN; 337–356.

Buis, E.J. (2015) *La súplica de Eris. Derecho internacional, discurso normativo y restricciones de la guerra en la antigua Grecia*, Buenos Aires: Eudeba.

Buis, E.J. (2016) "Huyendo a Argos: La protección jurídica de las mujeres refugiadas y el lenguaje del humanitarismo griego en *Suplicantes* de Esquilo", in Grignon, J. & J. Massé (eds.) *Hommage à (Tribute to, Homenaje a) Jean Pictet par le Concours de droit international humanitaire Jean Pictet*, Montreal: Yvon Blais and Schulthess; 153–174.

Bull, H. (1977) *Anarchical Society. A Study of Order in World Politics*, New York: Macmillan.

Buono-Coro Varas, R. (2012) *El Mediterráneo y la diplomacia en la antigua Grecia* (Serie

Monografías Históricas, 20), Valparaíso: Instituto de Historia, Pontificia Universidad Católica.

Burian, P. (1974) 'Pelasgus and Politics in Aeschylus' Danaid Trilogy', *Wiener Studien* 8; 5–14.

Burkert, W. (1966) "Greek Tragedy and Sacrificial Ritual", *Greek, Roman, and Byzantine Studies* 7; 87–121.

Burkert, W. (1984) *Homo Necans. Anthropology of Ancient Greek Sacrificial Ritual and Myth*, Berkeley and Los Angeles: University of California Press (original edition: Berlin 1972).

Burkert, W. (1985) *Greek Religion: Archaic and Classical*, Oxford: Blackwell (original edition: Stuttgart 1977).

Burkert, W. (1986) "Krieg, Sieg und die Olympischen Götter der Griechen", in Stolz, F. (ed.) *Religion zu Krieg und Frieden*, Zürich: Theologischer Verlag; 67–87.

Calabi, I. (1953) *Ricerche sui rapporti tra le poleis*, Firenze: Nuova Italia.

Calame, C. (1999) "Performative aspects of the choral voice in Greek tragedy: civic identity in performance", in Goldhill, S. and R. Osborne (eds.) *Performance culture and Athenian democracy*, Cambridge: University Press; 125–153.

Calame, C. (2000) "Hélène et les desseins de l'historiographie", in *Poétiques des mythes dans la Grèce antique*, Paris: Hachette; 145–168.

Caldwell, R.S. (1974) 'The Psychology of Aeschylus' *Supplices*', *Arethusa* 7 (1); 45–70.

Calore, A. (2003) *Forme giuridiche del 'bellum iustum'*, Milano: Giuffrè.

Camilleri, J. and J. Falk (1992) *The End of Sovereignty? The Politics of a Shrinking and Fragmenting World*, Aldershot: Edward Elgar.

Cançado Trindade, A.A. (2010) *International Law for Humankind: Towards a New* Jus Gentium, Leiden and Boston: Martinus Nijhoff.

Canfora, L. (1990) "Trattati in Tucidide", in Canfora, L., M. Liverani and C. Zaccagnini (eds.) *I trattati nel mondo antico. Forma, ideología, funzione*, Roma: "L'Erma" di Bretschneider; 193–216.

Carawan, E. (2006) "Amnesty and Accountings for the Thirty", *Classical Quarterly* 56 (1); 57–76.

Carawan, E. (2007) "The Trial of the Arginousai Generals and the Dawn of 'Judicial Review'", *Dike* 10; 19–56.

Carawan, E. (2012) "The meaning of *mê mnêsikakein*", *Classical Quarterly* 62 (2); 567–581.

Carawan, E. (2013) *The Athenian Amnesty and Reconstructing the Law*, Oxford: University Press.

Carey, C. (1998) "The Shape of Athenian Laws", *Classical Quarterly* 48 (1); 93–109.

Carlson, M. (1996) *Performance: A Critical Introduction*, London and New York: Routledge.

Carter, L.B. (1986) *The Quiet Athenian*, Oxford: Clarendon Press.

Cartledge, P. (1977) "Hoplites and Heroes: Sparta's contribution to the technique of ancient Warfare", *Journal of Hellenic Studies* 97; 11–27.

Cartledge, P. (1999) "Laying Down *Polis* Law", *The Classical Review* 49 (2); 465–469.

Cartwright, D. (1997) *A Historical Commentary on Thucydides*, Ann Arbor: University of Michigan Press.

Carty, A. (2017) "International Arbitration in Archaic Greece", in Moloney, E.P. and M.S. Williams (eds.) *Peace and Reconciliation in the Classical World*, London: Routledge; 148–159.

Cassese, A. (2001) "Origins and Foundations of the International Community", in *International Law*, Oxford: University Press; 3–46.

Cataldi, S. (1990) *Prospettive occidentali allo scoppio della Guerra del Peloponneso*, Pisa: ETS Editrice.

Cawkwell, G.L. (1989) "Orthodoxy and Hoplites", *Classical Quarterly* 39; 375–389.

Chaliand, G. (ed.) (1994) *The Art of War in World History: From Antiquity to the Nuclear Age*, Berkeley: University of California Press.

Chalk, F. and K. Jonassohn (2010) *Historia y Sociología del Genocidio. Análisis y estudio de caso*, Buenos Aires: Prometeo (original edition: New Haven 1990).

Chandezon, Ch. (1999) "L'économie rurale et la guerre", in Prost, F. (ed.) *Armées et sociétés de la Grèce classique. Aspects sociaux et politiques de la guerre aux Ve et IVe s. av. J.-C.*, Paris: Errance; 195–208.

Chaniotis, A. (1996) "Conflicting Authorities. *Asylia* between Secular and Divine Law in the Classical and Hellenistic *Poleis*", *Kernos* 9; 65–86.

Chaniotis, A. (2004) "Justifying Territorial Claims in Classical and Hellenistic Greece: the Beginnings of International Law", in Harris, E.M. and L. Rubinstein (eds.) *The Law and the Courts in Ancient Greece*, London: Duckworth; 185–213.

Chantraine, P. (1954) "Grec ΔΙΚΑΝΙΚΟΣ", *Anales de Filología Clásica* 6; 45–56.

Charlesworth, H. and Ch. Chinkin (2000) *The Boundaries of International Law. A Feminist Analysis*, Manchester: University Press.

Charlesworth, H. and J.-M. Coicaud (2010) (eds.), *Fault Lines of International Legitimacy*, Cambridge: University Press.

Cheng, B. (1991) "Introduction to the Subjects of International Law", in Bedjaoui, M. *International Law: Achievements and Prospects*, Dordrecht: Martinus Nijhoff; 23–40.

Chétail, V. (2014) "Armed Conflict and Forced Migration. A Systematic Approach to International Humanitarian Law, Refugee Law, and International Human Rights Law", in Clapham, A. and P. Gaeta (eds.) *The Oxford Handbook of International Law in Armed Conflict*, Oxford: University Press; 700–734.

Chimni, B.S. (2012) "Legitimating the international rule of law", in Crawford, J. and M. Koskenniemi (eds.) *The Cambridge Companion to International Law*, Cambridge: University Press; 290–308.

Chou, M. (2012) "Dramatizing Democracy. Introducing Aeschylus' *Suppliants*", in *Greek Tragedy and Contemporary Democracy*, New York and London: Bloomsbury; 79–91.

Christ, M.R. (1998) *The Litigious Athenian*, Baltimore: Johns Hopkins University Press.

Christ, M.R. (2012) *The Limits of Altruism in Democratic Athens*, Cambridge: University Press.

Christopher, P. (2004) *The Ethics of War and Peace. An Introduction to Legal and Moral Issues*, 3rd edition, Upper Saddle River: Pearson.

Chroust, A.H. (1954) "International treaties in antiquity. The Diplomatic Negotiations between Hannibal and Philip V of Macedonia", *Classica et Mediaevalia* 15; 60–107.

Ciccotti, E. (1971) *La guerra e la pace nel mondo antico*, Roma: "L'Erma" di Bretschneider.

Ciulei, C. (1967) "D. 47.22.4", *Zeitschrift der Savigny-Stifung für Rechtsgeschichte* 97; 371–375.

Clark, M. (1999) "Thucydides at Olympia", in Mellor, R. and L. Tritle (eds.) *Text and Tradition: Studies in Greek History and Historiography in Honor of Mortimer Chambers*, Claremont: Regina Books; 115–134.

Clavadetscher-Thürlemann, S. (1985) Polemos dikaios *und* bellum iustum. *Versuch einer Ideengeschichte*, Zürich: Iuris Druck.

Clerc, M. (1893) *Les méthèques athéniens*, Paris: Thorin and Fils.

Coates, A.J. (1997) *The Ethics of War*. Manchester: University Press.

Cohen, D. (1956) "I.G. I^2 86 and Thucydides V 47 (Treaty of Athens, Argos, Martineia, and Elis, 420/19 B.C.)", *Mnemosyne* 9; 289–295.

Cohen, D. (1995) *Law, Violence, and Community in Classical Athens*, Cambridge: University Press.

Cohen, D. (2001) "The rhetoric of justice: strategies of reconciliation and revenge in the restoration of Athenian democracy in 403 BC", *Archives Européennes de Sociologie* 42 (2); 335–356.

Cohen, J.L. (2004) "Whose Sovereignty? Empire vs. International Law", *Ethics and International Affairs* 18 (3); 1–24.

Combacau, J. and S. Sur (1997) *Droit international public*, Paris: Montchrestien.

Condorelli, L. and A. Cassese (2012) "Is Leviathan Still Holding Sway over International Dealings?", in Cassese, A. (ed.) *Realizing Utopia. The Future of International Law*, Oxford: University Press; 14–25.

Connor, W.R. (1984) *Thucydides*, Princeton: University Press.

Connor, W.R. (1988) "Early Greek Land Warfare as Symbolic Expression", *Past and Present* 119; 3–29.

Contensou, A. (2014) "La guerre dans la mythologie grecque. Quelques elements de réflexion", in Guisard, Ph. and Ch. Laizé (eds.) *La guerre et la paix*, Paris: Ellipses; 233–250.

Corbino, A. (2010) *Diritto privato romano. Contesti, fondamenti, discipline*, Milano: CEDAM.

Corten, O. (2003) *Le retour des guerres preventives: le droit international menacé*. Bruxelles: Labor.

Corvisier, J.-N. (2000) *Guerre et société dans les mondes grecs (490–322 av. J.-C.)*, Paris: Armand Colin.

Corvisier, J.-N. (2012) "Les otages dans le monde grec antique", *Revue internationale d'histoire militaire* 90; 25–50.

Corvisier, J.-N. (2014a) "Guerre et paix dans le monde grec", in Guisard, Ph. and Ch. Laizé (eds.) *La guerre et la paix*, Paris: Ellipses; 55–76.

Corvisier, J.-N. (2014b) "La guerre dans le monde grec antique", in Guisard, Ph. and Ch. Laizé (eds.) *La guerre et la paix*, Paris: Ellipses; 77–94.

Couvenhes, J.-Ch. (2005) "*De disciplina Graecorum*: les relations de violence entre les chefs militaires grecs et leurs soldats", in Bertrand, J.-M. (ed.) *La violence dans les mondes grec et romain*, Paris: Publications de la Sorbonne; 431–454.

Coverdale, J.F. (2004) "An introduction to the just war tradition", *Pace International Law Review* 16; 221–277.

Craig, L.H. (1994) *The War Lover: A Study of Plato's* Republic, Toronto: University Press.

Craven, M. (2007) "Introduction: International Law and Its Histories", in Craven, M., M. Fitzmaurice and M. Vogiatzi (eds.) *Time, History and International Law* (Developments in International Law, Vol. 58), Leiden and Boston: Martinus Nijhoff; 1–25.

Cresci, L.R., F. Gazzano, D.P. Orsi (2002) *La retorica della diplomazia nella Grecia Antica e a Bisanzio*, Roma: "L'Erma" di Bretschneider.

Crowley, J. (2012) *The Psychology of the Athenian Hoplite. The Culture of Combat in Classical Athens*, Cambridge: University Press.

Croxton, D. (1999) "The Peace of Westphalia of 1648 and the Origins of Sovereignty", *International History Review* 21; 569–852.

Csapo, E. and W.J. Slater (1994) *The Context of Ancient Drama*, Ann Arbor: University of Michigan Press.

Cuneo, T. (2007) *The Normative Web. An Argument for Moral Realism*, Oxford: University Press.

Cuniberti, G. (2001) "Le *Supplice* di Eschilo, la fuga del maschio e l'inviolabilità della persona", *Museum Helveticum* 58 (3); 140–156.

Curchin, L.A. (1995) "The Unburied Dead at Termopylae (279 BC)", *Ancient History Bulletin* 9; 68–71.

Cushman, Th. (2005) *A Matter of Principle. Humanitarian Arguments for a War in Iraq*, Berkeley, Los Angeles and London: University of California Press.

Cutler, A.C. (2001) "Critical Reflections on the Westphalian Assumptions of International Law and Organization: A Crisis of Legitimacy", *Review of International Studies* 27; 133–150.

Dabdab Trabulsi, J.A. (2006) *Participation directe et démocratie grecque. Une histoire exemplaire?*, Besançon: Presses Universitaires de Franche-Comté.

Darbo-Peschanski, C. (2010) "Questions sur la normativité dans l'antiquité grecque et romaine", *Mètis* 8; 7–20.

Darmon, J.-P. (1991) "The Powers of War: Ares and Athena in Greek Mythology", in Bonnefoy, Y. (ed.) *Greek and Egyptian Mysteries*, Chicago: University Press; 114–115.

Daube, B. (1938) *Zu den Rechtsprobleme in Aischylos'* Agamemnon, Zürich and Leipzig: Max Niehans.

Dauvergne, C. and J. Millbank (2011) "Forced Marriage and Refugee Status", *Women's Asylum News* 101; 1–4.

Davies, J.K. (1978) *Democracy and Classical Greece*, Sussex: Harvester Press.

Dawson, D. (1996) *The Origins of Western Warfare. Militarism and Morality in the Ancient World*, Boulder: Westview Press.

Dayton, J.C. (2006) *The Athletes of War. An Evaluation of the Agonistic Elements in Greek Warfare*, Toronto: Edgar Kent.

De Babot, J.C. and P.P. de Villalonga (1987) "Las relaciones internacionales entre los griegos", *Actas del Symposium Nacional de Estudios Clásicos 1984*, San Miguel de Tucumán: Asociación Argentina de Estudios Clásicos; 59–69.

De Olloqui, J.J. (2000) "Consideraciones sobre antecedentes del derecho diplomático", *Boletín Mexicano de Derecho Comparado*, N.S. 99, año XXXIII; 1147–1172.

de Robertis, F.M. (1938) *Il diritto associative romano dai collegi della Repubblica alle corporazioni del Basso Impero*, Bari: Laterza.

de Robertis, F.M. (1971) *Storia delle corporazioni e del regime associativo nel mondo romano*, Bari: Laterza.

de Romilly, J. (1947) *Thucydide et l'impérialisme athénien*, Paris: Les Belles Lettres.

de Romilly, J. (1971) *La loi dans la pensée grecque*, Paris: Les Belles Lettres.

de Ste. Croix, G.E.M. (1972) *The Origins of the Peloponnesian War*, London: Duckworth.

de Taube, M. (1932) "Les origines de l'arbitrage international. Antiquité et Moyen Âge", *Recueil des cours de l'Académie de droit international* 42, Leiden and Boston: Brill and Nijhoff.

de Vattel, E. (1758) *Le droit des gens, ou principes de la loi naturelle, appliqués à la conduite et aux affaires des Nations et Souverains*, Tome II, Londres: apud Liberos Tutior.

de Visscher, Ch. (1955) *Théories et réalités en droit international public*, Paris: Pedone.

Deacy, S. (2000) "Athena and Ares: War, Violence, and Warlike Deities", in van Wees, H. (ed.) *War and Violence in Ancient Greece*, London and Swansea: Duckworth and Classical Press of Wales; 285–298.

Debidour, M. (2002) *Les grecs et la guerre. Ve–IVe siècle. De la guerre rituelle à la guerre totale*, Monaco: Rocher.

Debnar, P. (2001) *Speaking the Same Language: Speech and Audience in Thucydides' Spartan Debates*, Ann Arbor: University of Michigan Press.

Debnar, P. (2011) "Rhetoric and Character in the Corcyra Debate", in Rechenauer, G.

and V. Pothou (eds.) *Thucydides—A Violent Teacher?*, Göttingen: Vandenhoek & Ruprecht; 115–129.

Debord, P. (1999) *L'Asie Mineure au IVe siècle (412–323 a.C.): pouvoirs et jeux politiques*, Bordeaux and Paris: Ausonius.

Dedoussi, C. (1995) "Greek Drama and Its Spectators: Conventions and Relationships", in Griffiths, A. (ed.) *Stage Directions. Essays in Ancient Drama in Honour of E.W. Handley* (BICS, Suppl. 66), London: Institute of Classical Studies; 123–132.

Deichgräber, K. (1933) "Πρόφασις. Eine Terminologie Studie", *Festschrift Max Wellmann zum 70. Geburstag*, Berlin: Quellen zur Studien und Geschichte der Naturwissenschaften und der Medizin (Band 3); 209–225.

Demont, P. (1990) *La cité grecque archaïque et classique et l'idéal de tranquillité*, Paris: Les Belles Lettres.

Detienne, M. (1968) "La phalange: problèmes et controverses", in Vernant, J.-P. (ed.) *Problèmes de la guerre en Grèce ancienne*, Paris and La Haye, Mouton; 119–142.

Detienne, M. (2003) "The Danaids Among Themselves: Marriage Founded Upon Violence", in Detienne, M. (ed.) *The Writing of Orpheus. Greek Myth in Cultural Contact*, Baltimore: Johns Hopkins University Press; 37–49.

Detter, I. (1966) "The Problem of Unequal Treaties", *International and Comparative Law Quarterly* 15; 1069–1089.

Dewald, C. (2013) "Justice and Justifications: War Theory among the Ancient Greeks", in Neusner, J., B.D. Chilton and R.E. Tully (eds.) *Just War in Religion and Politics*, Lanham: United Press of America; 27–50.

Deyra, M. (1998) *Droit international humanitaire*, Paris: Gualino.

Diamond, E. (1996) (ed.) *Performance and Cultural Politics*, London and New York: Routledge.

Dickie, M.W. (1978) "*Dike* as a Moral Term in Homer and Hesiod", *Classical Philology* 73 (2); 91–101.

Dickinson, E.D. (1917) "Analogy between natural persons and international persons in the law of nations", *Yale Law Journal* 26; pp. 564–591.

Dickinson, E.D. (1920) *The Equality of States in International Law*, Cambridge (MA): Harvard University Press.

Diels, H. and W. Kranz (1952) (eds.) *Die Fragmente der Vorsokratiker*, vol. 2, Berlin, Weidmann.

Diez de Velasco Vallejo, M. (1973) *Instituciones de Derecho Internacional Público*, Madrid: Tecnos.

Dinstein, Y. (2003) *War, Aggression and Self-Defence*, 3rd Edition. Cambridge: University Press.

Dolan, J. (1933) "Geographies of Learning: Theatre Studies, Performance and 'The Performative'", *Theatre Studies* 45; 417–441.

Domingo, R. (2010) "The *Ius Gentium*, a Roman Concept", in *The New Global Law*, Cambridge, University Press; 1–11.

Dominicé, C. (1991) "La neutralité et l'assistance humanitaire", *Annales de droit international médical* 35; 118–126.

Dor, L., J. Jannoray, H. van Effenterre and M. van Effenterre (1960) *Kirrha. Étude de préhistoire phocidienne*, Paris: De Boccard.

Douzinas, C. (2007) *Human Rights and Empire: the Political Philosophy of Cosmopolitanism*, Abindon and New York: Routledge and Cavendish.

Dover, K.J. (1972) *Aristophanic Comedy*, Berkeley and Los Angeles: University of California Press.

Driver, G.R. and J.C. Miles (1952–1954) *The Babylonian Laws*, Oxford, Clarendon Press.

du Bouchet, J. (2012) "Remarques sur le vocabulaire du conflit en Grèce ancienne", in Ménard, H., P. Sauzeau and J.F. Thomas (eds.) *La pomme d'Eris. Le conflit et sa représentation dans l'Antiquité*, Montpellier: Presses universitaires de la Méditerranée; 61–76.

du Plessis, P.J. (2010) "Corporation Theory", in Bevir, M. (ed.) *Encyclopedia of Political Theory* (A–E), Thousand Oaks: Sage; 305–306.

Dubuisson, M. (2001) "Barbares et barbarie dans le monde gréco-romain: du concept au slogan", *L'Antiquité classique* 70; 1–16.

Ducrey, P. (1986) "The Hoplite Revolution", in *Warfare in Ancient Greece*, New York: Schocken; 45–79.

Ducrey, P. (1968) *Le traitement des prisonniers de guerre dans la Grèce antique*. Ecole Française d'Athènes, fsc. 17. Paris: Editions E. De Boccard.

Ducrey, P. (1985) "Aspects juridiques de la victoire et du traitement des vaincus", in Vernant, J.-P. (ed.) *Problèmes de la guerre en Grèce ancienne*, Paris: Mouton; 231–243.

Ducrot, O. (1982) *Decir y no decir. Principios de semántica lingüística*, Barcelona: Anagrama (original edition: Paris 1972).

Duff, P.W. (1971) *Personality in Roman Private Law*, Cambridge: University Press [1938[1]].

Dunand, J.-Ph. and P. Pichonnaz (2010) *Lexique du droit romain*, Bruxelles: Bruylant.

Dupont, F. (1983) "Le sujet du discours politique en Grèce et à Rome", *Lalies* 5, Actes des sessions de linguistique et de littérature; 265–274.

Dupuy, P.-M. (1974) "Coutume sage et coutume sauvage", in *La communauté internationale. Mélanges offerts à Charles Rousseau*, Paris: Pedone; 75–87.

Durham, H. (2007) "International Humanitarian Law and the Gods of War: the Story of Athena versus Ares", *Melbourne Journal of International Law* 8; 248–258.

Duvignaud, J. (1965) *Sociologie du théatre: essai sur les ombres collectives*, Paris: Presses Universitaires de France.

Easterling, P. (1999) "Actors and voices: reading between the lines in Aeschines and Demosthenes", in Goldhill, S. and R. Osborne (eds.) *Performance culture and Athenian democracy*, Cambridge: University Press; 154–166.

Echeverría Rey, F. (2010) "Weapons, Technological Determinism, and Ancient Warfare", in Fagan, G.G. and M. Trundle (eds.) *New Perspectives on Ancient Warfare*, Leiden and Boston: Brill; 21–56.

Eckstein, A.M. (2006) *Mediterranean Anarchy, Interstate War, and the Rise of Rome*, Berkeley, Los Angeles and London: University of California Press.

Edwards, A. (2006) "Refugee Status Determination in Africa", *African Journal of International and Comparative Law* 14 (2); 204–233.

Edwards, A. (2008) "Crossing Legal Borders: The Interface Between Refugee Law, Human Rights Law, and Humanitarian Law in the 'International Protection' of Refugees", in Arnold, R. and N. Quénivet (eds.) *International Humanitarian Law and Human Rights Law. Towards a New Merger in International Law*, Leiden and Boston: Martinus Nijhoff; 421–446.

Eggers Lan, C. (1997) *Libertad y Compulsión en la Antigua Grecia*, Buenos Aires: Universidad de Buenos Aires.

Ehrenberg, V. (1969) *The Greek State*, London: Methuen.

Elshtain, J.B. (2001) "Just War and Humanitarian Intervention", *Ideas* 8 (2); 1–21.

Elster, J. (2004) *Closing the Books. Transitional Justice in Historical Perspective*, Cambridge: University Press.

English, S. (2012) *Mercenaries in the Classical World to the Death of Alexander*, Barnsley: Pen & Sword Military.

Esfeld, M. (2001) "La normativité sociale du contenu conceptuel", *Cahiers de Philosophie de l'Université de Caen: La normativité* 37; 215–232.

Eslava, L., L. Obregón and R. Urueña (2016) "Imperialismo(s) y derecho(s) internacional(es): ayer y hoy", en Anghie, A., M. Koskenniemi and A. Orford. *Imperialismo y derecho internacional: historia y legado*, Bogotá: Siglo del Hombre Editores, Universidad de Los Andes and Pontificia Universidad Javeriana; 11–94.

Espinel, A.D. (1998) "Fronteras y demarcaciones del territorio egipcio en el Reino Antiguo", *Studia Historica (Historia Antigua)* 16; 9–30.

Evans, N. (2010) *Civic Rites. Democracy and Religion in Ancient Athens*, Berkeley, Los Angeles and London: University of California Press.

Eyffinger, A. (1998) "Europe in the Balance: An Appraisal of the Westphalian System", *Netherlands International Law Review* 45; 161–187.

Fabry, M. (2010) *Recognizing States. International Society and the Establishment of New States since 1776*, Oxford: University Press.

Faraguna, M. (2000), "Individuo, stato e comunità. Studi recenti sulla *polis*", *Dike* 3; 217–229.

Fassbender, B. (2002) "Article 2 (1)", in Simma, B. (ed.) *The Charter of the United Nations. A Commentary*, Volume I, Oxford: University Press; 68–91.

Fernández Nieto, F.J. (1975) *Los acuerdos bélicos en la antigua Grecia (época arcaica y clásica)*, Vol. I, Santiago de Compostela: Universidad de Santiago de Compostela.

Fernández Nieto, F.J. (1995) "Tregua sagrada, diplomacia y política durante la Guerra del Peloponeso", in Frézouls, E. and A. Jacquemin (eds.) *Les relations internationales* (Actes du colloque de Strasbourg, 15–17 juin 1993), Paris: De Boccard; 161–187.

Fernández Nieto, F.J. (1997) "Los reglamentos militares griegos y la justicia castrense en época helenística", in Thür, G. and Vélissaropoulos-Karakostas (eds.) *Symposion 1995. Vorträge zur griechischen und hellenistischen Rechtsgeschichte* (Korfu, 1.–5. September 1995), Köln: Böhlau; 221–244.

Finley, M.I. (1963) *The Ancient Greeks. An Introduction to Their Life and Thought*, London: Penguin Books.

Finley, M.I. (1984) (ed.) *The Legacy of Greece: A New Reappraisal*, Oxford: University Press.

Fisch, J. (2012) "Peoples and Nations", in Fassbender, B. and A. Peters (eds.) *The Oxford Handbook of the History of International Law*, Oxford: University Press; 27–48.

Fisher, N.R.E. (1998) "Violence, Masculinity and the Law in Classical Athens", in Foxhall, L. and J. Salmon (eds.) *When Men Were Men: Masculinity, Power, and Identity in Classical Antiquity*, London: Routledge; 68–97.

Flint, C. and G.W. Falah (2004) "How the United States justified its war on terrorism: prime morality and the construction of a 'just war'", *Third World Quarterly*, 25 (8); 1379–1399.

Flumene, F. (1925) *La 'legge non scritta' nella storia e nella dottrina etico-giuridica della Grecia classica*, Sassari: Stamperia della L.I.S.

Fornara, C. (1977) *Archaic Times to the End of the Peloponnesian War*, Cambridge: University Press.

Forrest, G. (1956) "The First Sacred War", *Bulletin de correspondance hellénique* 80; 33–52.

Forrest, W.G. (1957) "Colonisation and the Rise of Delphi", *Historia* 6; 160–175.

Foucart, P. (1873) *Les associations religieuses chez les Grecs. Thiases, éranes, orgèons*, Paris: Klincksieck.

Foucault, M. (1975) *Surveiller et punir. Naissance de la prison*, Paris: Gallimard.

Fouchard, A. (2003) *Les États grecs*, Paris: Ellipses.

Fowler, R. and Heckster, O. (2005) "Imagining Kings: From Persia to Rome", in Fowler, R. and Heckster, O. (eds.) *Imaginary Kings. Royal Images in the Ancient Near East, Greece and Rome*, Stuttgart: Franz Steiner; 9–38.

Franck, T.M. (2002) *Recourse to force: Threats and Armed Attacks* (Hersch Lauterpacht memorial lectures, Vol. 15), Cambridge: University Press.

Frezza, P. (1938–1939) "Le forme federative e la struttura dei rapporti internazionali nell'antico diritto romano", *Studia e documenta historiae et iuris* 4 and 5; 363–428 and 161–201.

Fröhlich, P. (1999) "Les magistrats de la guerre", in Prost, F. (ed.) *Armées et sociétés de la Grèce classique. Aspects sociaux et politiques de la guerre aux* V[e] *et* IVe *s. av. J.-C.*, Paris: Errance; 108–136.

Gaebel, R.B. (2002) *Cavalry Operations in the Ancient Greek World*, Norman: University of Oklahoma Press.

Gagarin, M. (1973) "*Dike* in the *Works and Days*", *Classical Philology* 68 (2); 81–94.

Gagarin, M. (1986) *Early Greek Law*, Berkeley: University of California Press.

Gagarin, M. (2008) *Writing Athenian Law*, Cambridge: University Press.

Gain, B. (2014) "Les populations civiles et la guerre dans l'antiquité", in Guisard, Ph. and Ch. Laizé (eds.) *La guerre et la paix*, Paris: Ellipses; 214–230.

Galindo Bandeira, G.R. (2005) "Martti Koskenniemi and the Historiographical Turn in International. Law", *European Journal of International Law* 16 (3); 539–559.

Gallego, J. (2011) "La asamblea ateniense y el problema del Estado. Instauración y agotamiento de una subjetividad política", in Campagno, M., J. Gallego, J. and C. García MacGaw (eds.) *El Estado en el Mediterráneo Antiguo. Egipto, Grecia, Roma*, Buenos Aires: Miño y Dávila; 181–222.

Gantz, T. (1978) "Love and death in the *Suppliants* of Aeschylus", *Phoenix* 32; 279–287.

Garapon, A. (1985) *L'âne portant des reliques. Essai sur le rituel judiciaire*, Paris: Le Centurion.

Gardeñez Santiago, M. (2003) "Reflexiones sobre los orígenes históricos del derecho internacional privado", *Anuario Español de Derecho Internacional Privado* 3; 107–135.

Gardner, P. (1920) "A Numismatic Note on the Lelantian War", *The Classical Review* 34; 90–91.

Garlan, Y. (1972) *La guerre dans l'antiquité*, Paris: Nathan.

Garlan, Y. (1989) "Les causes de la guerre chez Platon et Aristote", in *Guerre et économie en Grèce ancienne*, Paris: La Découverte; 20–40.

Garlan, Y. (1999) "L'homme et la guerre", in Brulé, P. and J. Oulhen (eds.) *La guerre en Grèce à l'époque classique*, Rennes: Presses Universitaires; 17–42.

Garland, D.W. (1990) *Punishment and Modern Society: A Study in Social Theory*, Chicago: University Press.

Garland, R. (2014) *Wandering Greeks: The Ancient Greek Diaspora from the Age of Homer to the Death of Alexander the Great*, Princeton: University Press.

Garner, R. (1987) *Law and Society in Classical Athens*, New York: St. Martin's Press.

Garnsey, P.D.A. and C.R. Whittaker (1978) "Introduction", in Garnsey, P.D.A. and C.R. Whittaker (eds.) *Imperialism in the Ancient World*, Cambridge: University Press; 1–6.

Garvie, A.F. (1969) *Aeschylus'* Supplices. *Play and Trilogy*, Cambridge: University Press.

Gastaldi, V. (2007) "Embajadores trágicos: la retórica del *kêryx* en *Heraclidas* de Eurípides", *L'Antiquité classique* 76; 39–50.

Gaurier, D. (2005) *Histoire du droit international. Auteurs, doctrines et développement de l'Antiquité à l'aube de la période contemporaine*, Rennes: Presses Universitaires.

Gaurier, D. (2014) *Histoire du droit international. De l'Antiquité à la création de l'ONU*, Rennes: Presses Universitaires.

Gauthier, P. (1971) "Les *xenoi* dans les textes athéniens de la seconde moitié du v^{o} siècle av. J.-C.", *Revue des études grecques* 84; 44–79.

Gauthier, P. (1972) *Symbola. Les étrangers et la justice dans les cités grecques*, Nancy: Université de Nancy.

Gauthier, P. (1973) "Notes sur l'étranger et l'hospitalité en Grèce et à Rome", *Ancient Society* 4; 1–21.

Gauthier, P. (1987) "Métèques, périèques et *paroikoi*: bilan et points d'interrogation", in Lonis, R. (ed.) *L'étranger dans le monde grec*. Actes du colloque organisé par l'Institut d'Études Anciennes, Nancy: Presses Universitaires; 23–46.

Gauthier, P. (1987–1989) "Grandes et petites cités: hégémonie et autarcie", *Opus* 6–8; 187–202.

Gehrke, H.J. (1985) Stasis. *Untersuchungen zu den inneren Kriegen in der griechischen Staaten des 5. und 4. Jahrhunderts v. Chr*, München: C.H. Beck.

Gera, D. (1997) *Warrior Women: The Anonymous* Tractatus De Mulieribus (Mnemosyne, Suppl. 162), Leiden: Brill.

Gilardeau, E. (2015) *Les grands procès politiques de l'antiquité*, Paris: L'Harmattan.

Gillespie, A. (2011) *A History of the Laws of War*, Vol. 1–3, Oxford and Portland: Hart University Press.

Gillespie, A. (2013) *The Causes of War*, Volume I: 3000 BCE to 1000 CE, Oxford and Portland: Hart Publishing.

Giovannini, A. (1997) "Les relations de parenté entre cités grecques", *Museum Helveticum* 54 (3); 158–162.

Giovannini, A. (2007) *Les relations entre États dans la Grèce antique, du temps d'Homère à l'intervention romaine (ca. 700–200 av. J.-C.)* (Historia Einzelschriften, Heft 193), Stuttgart: Franz Steiner.

Gish, D. (2012) "Defending *Demokratia*: Athenian Justice and the Trial of the Arginusae Generals in Xenophon's *Hellenica*", in Hobden, F. and Ch. Tuplin (eds.) *Xenophon: Ethical Principles and Historical Enquiry*, Leiden: Brill; 161–212.

Glotz, G. (1904) *La solidarité de la famille dans le droit criminel en Grèce*, Paris: Fontemoing.

Glotz, G. (1915) *Le droit des gens dans l'antiquité grecque*, Paris: Imprimerie nationale.

Glotz, G. (1923) "Le droit des gens dans l'antiquité grecque", *Mémoires présentés par divers savants à l'Académie des Inscriptions et Belles Lettres* 13 (1); 91–103.

Goblot-Cahen, C. (2002) "Les hérauts grecs agents et victimes de châtiments", *Hypothèses* 6; 135–144.

Goffman, E. (1959) *The Presentation of Self in Everyday Life*, New York: Anchor Books.

Goldhill, S. (1990) "The Great Dionysia and Civic Ideology", in Winkler, J.J. and F.I. Zeitlin (eds.) *Nothing to Do with Dionysos? Athenian Drama in Its Social Context*, Princeton: University Press; 97–129.

Goldhill, S. (1999) "Programme Notes", in Goldhill, S. and R. Osborne (eds.) *Performance culture and Athenian democracy*, Cambridge: University Press; 1–29.

Goldsmith, J.L. and E.A. Posner (2005) *The Limits of International Law*, Oxford: University Press.

Gómez Castro, D. (2010) "El mercenario en el mundo griego a la luz de los estudios contemporáneos: reflexión teórica y nuevas tesis", *Habis* 41; 95–115.

Gómez Mampaso, M.V. and B. Sáenz de Santa María Gómez Mampaso (2001) *Una aproximación a la historia de las relaciones diplomáticas*, Madrid: Universidad de Comillas.

Gómez Seijo, F. (2017) "Responsabilidad y ambigüedad de Helena en la épica homérica", *Humanitas* 69; 9–45.

Gomme, A.W. (1956a) *A Historical Commentary on Thucydides*, Vol. 2. Books II–III, Oxford: University Press.

Gomme, A.W. (1956b) *A Historical Commentary on Thucydides*, Vol. 3. Books IV–V, Oxford: University Press.

Gomme, A.W., A. Andrewes and K.J. Dover (1970) *A Historical Commentary on Thucydides*, Vol. IV. Books V-VII, Oxford: University Press.

Gomme, A.W., A. Andrewes and K.J. Dover (1981) *A Historical Commentary on Thucydides*, Vol. V. Book VIII, Oxford: University Press.

Gondicas, D. and J. Boëldieu-Trevet (1999) *Guerres et sociétés dans les monds grecs (490–322 avant J.-C.)*, Paris: Bréal.

Goodman, M.D. and A.J. Holladay (1986) "Religious Scruples in Ancient Warfare", *Classical Quarterly* N.S. 36 (1); 151–171.

Gordon Fiala, A. (2008) *The just war myth: moral illusions of war*, Lanham: Rowman and Littlefield.

Gould, J. (1973) "Hiketeia", *Journal of Hellenic Studies* 93; 74–103.

Graf, F. (1996) "Ares", in Hornblower, S. and A. Spawforth (eds.) *The Oxford Classical Dictionary*, 3rd Edition, Oxford: University Press; 152.

Graham, A.J. (1964) *Colony and Mother City in Ancient Greece*, Manchester: University Press.

Grant, J.R. (1965) "A Note on the Tone of Greek Diplomacy", *Classical Quarterly* N.S. 15 (2); 261–266.

Graves, C.E. (1891) *Commentary on Thucydides Book 5*, London: Macmillan.

Gray, Ch. (2000) *International Law and the Use of Force*, Oxford: University Press.

Green, R. and E. Handley (1995) *Images of the Greek Theatre*, London: British Museum Press.

Greenhalgh, P.A.L. (1973) *Early Greek Warfare: Horsemen and Chariots in the Homeric and Archaic Ages*, Cambridge: University Press.

Gregory, J. (1991) *Euripides and the Instruction of the Athenians*, Ann Arbor: University of Michigan Press.

Grelle, F. (1990) "Città e trattati nel sistema romano imperiale", in Canfora, L., M. Liverani and C. Zaccagnini (eds.) *I trattati nel mondo antico. Forma, ideologia, funzione*, Roma: "L'Erma" di Bretschneider; 237–256.

Grewe, W.G. (1984) *Epochen der Völkerrechtsgeschichte*, Baden-Baden: Nomos.

Grinin, L.E. (2004) "Democracy and Early State", *Social Evolution and History* 3 (2); 93–149.

Grinin, L.E. (2008) "Early State in the Classical World: Statehood and Ancient Democracy", in Grinin, L.E., D.D. Beliaev and A.V. Korotayev (eds.) *Hierarchy and Power in the History of Civilizations: Ancient and Medieval Cultures*, Moscow: Uchitel; 31–84.

Grotkamp, N. (2009) *Völkerrecht im Prinzipat. Möglichkeit und Verbreitung* (Studien zur Geschichte des Völkerrechts, 21), Baden-Baden: Nomos.

Guarducci, M. (1935) "Orgeones e tiasoti", *Rivista di Filologia Classica* 13; 332–340.

Guarducci, M. (1969) *Epigrafia greca*, Vol. II, Roma: Istituto Poligrafico dello Stato.

Guizzi, F. (1997) "Conquista, occupazione del suolo e titoli che danno diritto alla proprietà: l'esempio di una controversia interstatale cretese", *Athenaeum* 85 (1); 35–52.

Gutiérrez Posse, H.D.T. (1995) *Moderno derecho internacional y seguridad colectiva*, Buenos Aires: Zavalía.

Gutiérrez Posse, H.D.T. (2014) *Elementos de derecho internacional humanitario*, Buenos Aires: Eudeba.

Gutzwiller, M. (1930) "Le développement historique du droit international privé", *Recueil des Cours, Académie de droit international de La Haye*, 1929-IV, Paris: Hachette; 288–398.

Hall, E. (1995) "Lawcourt Dramas: the Power of Performance in Greek Forensic Oratory", *Bulletin of the Institute of Classical Studies* 40; 39–58.

Hall, J.M. (2007) "International Relations", in Sabin, Ph., H. van Wees and M. Whitby (eds.) *The Cambridge History of Greek and Roman Warfare*, Vol. I, Cambridge: University Press; 85–107.

Hamel, D. (2015) *The Battle of Arginusae. Victory at Sea and its Tragic Aftermath in the Final Years of the Peloponnesian War*, Baltimore: Johns Hopkins University Press.

Hampl, F. (1938) *Die griechischen Staatsverträge des 4. Jahrhunderts v. Christi geb.*, Leipzig: Hirzel.

Hampl, F. (1939) "*Poleis* ohne Territorium", *Klio* 32; 1–60.

Hansen, M.H. (1975) *Eisangelia: The Sovereignty of the People's Court in Athens in the Fourth Century B.C. and the Impeachment of Generals and Politicians*, Odense: University Press.

Hansen, M.H. (1978) "*Nomos* and *psephisma* in Fourth-Century Athens", *Greek, Roman and Byzantine Studies* 19; 315–330.

Hansen, M.H. (1987) *The Athenian Assembly in the Age of Demosthenes*, Oxford: University Press.

Hansen, M.H. (1990) "When Was Selection by Lot of Magistrated Introduced in Athens?", *Classica et Mediaevalia* 41; 55–61.

Hansen, M.H. (1991) *The Athenian Democracy in the Age of Demosthenes*, Oxford: University Press.

Hansen, M.H. (1993) "Introduction. The *Polis* as a Citizen-State", in Hansen, M.H. (ed.) *The Ancient Greek City-State* (Acts of the Copenhagen Polis Centre 1, Det Kongelige Danske Videnskabernes Selskab, Historisk-filosofiske Meddelelser 67), Copenhagen: Munksgaard; 7–29.

Hansen, M.H. (1995) "The 'Autonomous City-State': Ancient Fact or Modern Fiction?", in Hansen, M.H. and K. Raaflaub (eds.) *Studies in the Ancient Greek* Polis (Papers from the Copenhagen Polis Centre 2; Historia Einzelschriften 95), Stuttgart: Franz Steiner; 21–44.

Hansen, M.H. (1996) "City-Ethnics as Evidence for *Polis* Identity", in Hansen, M.H. and K. Raaflaub (eds.) *More Studies in the Ancient Greek Polis* (Papers from the Copenhagen Polis Centre 3; Historia Einzelschriften 108), Stuttgart: Franz Steiner; 169–195.

Hansen, M.H. (1998) *Polis and City-State. An Ancient Concept and its Modern Equivalent* (Acts of the Copenhagen Polis Centre 5, Det Kongelige Danske Videnskabernes Selskab, Historisk-filosofiske Meddelelser 76), Copenhagen: Munksgaard.

Hansen, M.H. (2000) "The Hellenic *Polis*", in Hansen, M.H. (ed.) *A Comparative Study of Thirty City-State Cultures* (Det Kongelige Danske Videnskabernes Selskab, Historisk-filosofiske Skrifter 21), Copenhagen: Munksgaard; 141–187.

Hansen, M.H. (2002) "Was the *Polis* a State or a Stateless Society?", in Nielsen, T.H. (ed.) *Even More Studies in the Ancient Greek Polis* (Papers from the Copenhagen Polis Centre 6; Historia Einzelschriften 162), Stuttgart: Franz Steiner; 17–47.

Hanson, V.D. (1989) *The Western Way of War: Infantry Battle in Classical Greece*, New York: Alfred A. Knopf.

Hanson, V.D. (1991a) "Hoplite Technology in Phalanx Battle", in Hanson, V.D. (ed.) *Hoplites: The Classical Greek Battle Experience*, London and New York: Routledge; 63–84.

Hanson, V.D. (1991b) "Ideology of Hoplite Battle, Ancient and Modern", in Hanson, V.D. (ed.) *Hoplites. The Classical Greek Battle Experience*, New York and London: Routledge; 3–11.

Hanson, V.D. (1998) *Warfare and Agriculture in Classical Greece*, Berkeley, Los Angeles and London: University of California Press.

Hanson, V.D. (1999) *The Other Greeks. The Family Farm and the Agrarian Roots of Western Civilization*, Berkeley: University of California Press.

Hanson, V.D. (2005) *A War Like No Other. How the Athenians and Spartans Fought the Peloponnesian War*, New York: Random House.

Harris, E. (2006) "Antigone the Lawyer or the Ambiguities of *Nomos*", in Harris, E. and L. Rubinstein (eds.) *The Law and the Courts in Ancient Greece*, London: Duckworth; 19–56.

Harris, R. and J. Paxman (2002) *A Higher Form of Killing: The Secret History of Chemical and Biological Warfare*, New York: Random House.

Harrison, A.R.W. (1971) *The Law of Athens*, Vol. II, Oxford: University Press.

Harter-Uibopuu, K. (1998) *Das zwischenstaatliche Schiedsverfahren im achäischen Koinon. Zur friedlichen Streitbeiligung nach den epigraphischen Quellen*, Köln, Weimar and Wien: Böhlau.

Hatzopoulos, C. (1973) *Personae collectivae nach attischem Recht* (PhD. Diss.), Freiburg.

Hayashi, N. (2010) "Requirements of Military Necessity in International Humanitarian Law and International Criminal Law", *Boston University International Law Journal* 28 (1); 39–140.

Hedrik, C.W. (1994) "Writing, Reading, and Democracy", in Osborne, R. and S. Hornblower (eds.) *Ritual, Finance, Politics: Athenian Democratic Accounts Presented to David Lewis*, Oxford: Clarendon Press; 157–174.

Heinimann, F. (1945) Nomos *und* Physis. *Herkunft und Bedeutung einer Antithese im Griechischen Denken des 5. Jahrhunderts*, Basel: Friedrich Reinhardt.

Heitsch, E. (2006) "Der Vertrag des Therimenes: von den Schwierigkeiten einer Thukydides-Interpretation", *Hermes* 134; 26–43.

Henckaerts, J.-M. and L. Doswald-Beck (2005) (eds.) *ICRC Study on Customary Rules of International Humanitarian Law*, Cambridge: University Press.

Henderson, C.W. (2009) *Understanding International Law*, Chichester and Malden: Wiley-Blackwell.

Henry, A.S. (1977) *The Prescripts of Athenian Decrees* (Mnemosyne, Suppl. 49), Leiden: Brill.

Herman, G. (1990) "Treaties and alliances in the world of Thucydides", *Proceedings of the Cambridge Philological Society* 36; 83–102.

Herman, G. (2006) *Morality and Behaviour in Democratic Athens: A Social History*, Cambridge: University Press.

Hesk, J. (1999) "The rhetoric of anti-rhetoric in Athenian oratory", in Goldhill, S. and R. Osborne (eds.) *Performance culture and Athenian democracy*, Cambridge: University Press; 201–230.

Heubeck, A. (1980) "Πρόφασις und keine Ende (zu Thuk. I 23)", *Glotta* 58; 222–236.

Hibbits, B.J. (1992) "Coming to Our Senses: Communication and Legal Expression in Performance Cultures", *Emory Law Journal* 41(4); 874–959

Higgins, R. (1995) *Problems and Process: International Law and How We Use It*, Oxford: University Press.

Hirzel, R. (1907) Themis, Dike *und Verwandtes. Ein Beitrag zur Geschichte der Rechtsidee bei den Griechen*, Leipzig: S. Hirzel.

Hogan, J.C. (1981) "Eris in Homer", *Grazer Beiträge* 10; 21–58.

Holladay, A. (1982) "Hoplites and Heresies", *Journal of Hellenic Studies* 102; 94–103.

Hölscher, T. (2003) "Images of War in Greece and Rome: Between Military Practice, Public Memory, and Cultural Symbolism", *Journal of Roman Studies* 93; 1–17.

Hopper, R.J. (1943) "Interstate juridical agreements in the Athenian empire," *Journal of Hellenic Studies* 63; 35–51.

Hornblower, S. (1991) *A Commentary on Thucydides*, Volume I, Oxford: University Press.

Hornblower, S. (1996) *A Commentary on Thucydides*, Volume II, Oxford: University Press.

Hornblower, S. (2008) *A Commentary on Thucydides*, Volume III, Oxford: University Press.

Hueck, I. (2001) "The Discipline of the History of International Law", *Journal of the History of International Law* 3; 194–217.

Hughes, J.D. (2013) "Warfare and Environment in the Ancient World", in Campbell, B. and L.A. Tritle (eds.) *The Oxford Handbook of Warfare in the Classical World*, Oxford: University Press; 128–139.

Hughes, J.D. (2014) *Environmental Problems of the Greeks and Romans: Ecology in the Ancient Mediterranean*, Baltimore: Johns Hopkins University Press [1994[1]].

Hunt, P. (2001) "The Slaves and the Generals of Arginusae", *American Journal of Philology* 122; 359–380.

Hunt, P. (2010) *War, Peace, and Alliance in Demosthenes' Athens*, Cambridge: University Press.

Hurrell, A. (2009) *On Global Order: Power, Values, and the Constitution of International Society*, Oxford: University Press.

Hurst, A. (1971) "ΕΝ Δ' ΕΡΙΣ?", *Antike Kunst* 14 (2); 123–127.

Husby, T.K. (2009) "Justice and the Justification of War in Ancient Greece: Four Authors" *Classics Honors Papers*. Paper 1, available at http://digitalcommons.conncoll.edu/classicshp/1 [23–02–2015].

Ilari, V. (1980) *Guerra e diritto nel mondo antico*, Parte I, Milano: Giuffrè.

Ilari, V. (1990) "*Ius belli—Toû Polemou Nomos*. Étude sémantique de la terminologie du droit de la guerre", in Sokhna Sow, M. (ed.) *Dépendance et liberté: l'Afrique et le monde méditerranéen dans l'Antiquité*, Toronto: Terebi; 93–108.

Ion, T.P. (1911) "The Sanctity of Treaties", *Yale Law Journal* 20 (4); 268–291.

Ireland, S. (1974) "The Problem of Motivation in the *Supplices* of Aeschylus", *Rheinisches Museum* 117; 14–29.

Iriarte, A. (2007) "La institución de la *xenía*: pactos y acogidas en la antigua Grecia", *Gerion*, Vol. Extra; 197–206.

Iriarte, M. and M. González (2008) *Entre Ares y Afrodita. Violencia del erotismo y erótica de la violencia en la Grecia antigua*, Madrid: Abada.

Isler, C. (1969) *Nike. Der Typus der laufenden Flügelfrau in archaischer Zeit* (Diss., Universität Zürich), Zürich.

Ismard, P. (2007a) "Les associations en Attique de Solon à Clisthène", in Couvenhes,

J.-Ch. and S. Milanezi (eds.) *Individus, groupes et politique à Athènes de Solon à Mithridate* (Actes du colloque de Tours, 7–8 mars 2005), Tours: Presses Universitaires François-Rabelais; 17–34.

Ismard, P. (2007b) "La construction du fait associatif en droit athénien et les limites de la notion de personnalité juridique", *Dike* 10; 57–83.

Ismard, P. (2010) *La cité des réseaux. Athènes et ses associations* (VIe–Ier *siècle av. J.-C.*), Paris: Publications de la Sorbonne.

Jackman, T. (2005) *Political communities in the Greek colonies of archaic and classical Sicily and southern Italy* (PhD, Stanford University), Palo Alto.

Jacquemin, A. (1986) "Droit d'asile et extradition en Grèce antique: le fugitif, le dieu, la cité et le tyran", in Racault, J.-M. (ed.) *Le territoire* (Cahiers CRLH-CIRAOI 3), Saint-Denis de la Réunion and Paris: Université de La Réunion and Didier-Érudition; 7–12.

Jacquemin, A. (2000) *Guerre et religion dans le monde grec (490–322 av. J.-C.)*, Liège: Presses Universitaires de Liège.

Jacquemin, A. (2005) "Images de violence et offrandes de victoire en Grèce ancienne", in Bertrand, J.-M. (ed.) *La violence dans les mondes grec et romain*, Paris: Publications de la Sorbonne; 121–135.

Jacques, M. (2012) *Armed Conflict and Displacement: The Protection of Refugees and Displaced Persons under International Humanitarian Law*, Cambridge: University Press.

Jameson, M.H. (1999) "The spectacular and the obscure in Athenian religion", in Goldhill, S. and R. Osborne (eds.) *Performance culture and Athenian democracy*, Cambridge: University Press; 321–340.

Jannoray, J. (1937) "Krisa-Kirrha et la première guerre sacrée", *Bulletin de correspondance hellénique* 61; 33–43.

Jaquemet, S. (2001) "The Cross-Fertilization of International Humanitarian Law and International Refugee Law", *International Review of the Red Cross* 83, N° 843; 651–674.

Jehne, M. (1994) *Koine Eirene: Untersuchungen zu den Befriedungs- und Stabilisierungsbemühungen in der griechischen Poliswelt des 4. Jahrhunderts v. Chr.*, Stuttgart: Franz Steiner.

Johnson, J.T. (1984) *Can Modern War Be Just*, New Haven: Yale University Press.

Johnson, J.T. (1991) "Historical Roots and Sources of the Just War Tradition in Western Culture", in Kelsay, J. and J.T. Johnson (eds.) *Just War and Jihad—Historical and Theoretical Perspectives on War and Peace in Western and Islamic Traditions*, New York: Greenwood Press; 1–30.

Johnston, D.M. (2008) *The Historical Foundations of World Order. The Tower and the Arena*, Leiden and Boston: Martinus Nijhoff.

Johnstone, S. (1999) *Disputes and Democracy. The Consequences of Litigation in Ancient Athens*, Austin: University of Texas Press.

Jones, C.P. (1999) *Kinship Diplomacy in the Ancient World*, Cambridge (MA) and London: Harvard University Press.

Jones, J.W. (1956) *The Law and Legal Theory of the Greeks*, Oxford: Clarendon Press.

Jones, N. (1999) *The Associations of Classical Athens. The Response to Democracy*, Oxford: University Press.

Jost, M. (1999) "Les divinités de la guerre", in Prost, F. (ed.) *Armées et sociétés de la Grèce classique. Aspects sociaux et politiques de la guerre aux* V*e et* IV*e s. av. J.-C.*, Paris: Errance; 163–178.

Jouan, F. (1966) *Euripide et les légendes des chants cypriens*, Paris: Les Belles Lettres.

Joyce, Ch.J. (2008) "The Athenian Amnesty and Scrutiny of 403", *Classical Quarterly* 58 (2); 507–518.

Kaczorowska, A. (2002) *Public International Law*, London: Old Bailey.

Kagan, D. (2004) *The Peloponnesian War*, New York: Penguin Books.

Kälin, W. (2001) "Flight in Times of War", *International Review of the Red Cross* 83, N° 843; 629–650.

Kallet, L. (2001) *Money and the Corrosion of Power in Thucydides: The Sicilian Expedition and its Aftermath*, Berkeley and Los Angeles: University of California Press.

Kallet-Marx, R.M. (1996) *Hegemony to Empire. The Development of the Roman Imperium in the East from 148 to 62* B.C., Berkeley, Los Angeles and Oxford: University of California Press.

Kalshoven, F. and L. Zegveld (2001) *Constraints on the Waging of War. An Introduction to International Humanitarian Law*, Cambridge: University Press.

Kaplan, P. (2002) "The Social Status of the Mercenary in Archaic Greece", in Robinson, E. and V.B. Gorman (eds.) *Oikistes. Studies in Constitutions, Colonies, and Military Power in the Ancient World, Offered in Honour of A.J. Graham*, Leiden: Brill; 229–244.

Karavites, P. (1982a) *Capitulations and Greek Interstate Relations. The Reflection of Humanistic Ideals in Political Events*, Göttingen: Vandenhoeck & Ruprecht.

Karavites, P. (1982b) "*Eleuthería* and *Autonomía* in Fifth-Century Interstate Relations", *Revue internationale des droits de l'antiquité* 29; 145–162.

Karavites, P. (1992) *Promise-Giving and Treaty-Making. Homer and the Near East*, Leiden: Brill.

Kavoulaki, A. (1999) "Processional performance and the democratic polis", in Goldhill, S. and R. Osborne (eds.) *Performance culture and Athenian democracy*, Cambridge: University Press; 292–320.

Keil, B. (1916) *ΕΙΡΗΝΗ. Eine philologisch-antiquarische Untersuchung*, Leipzig: B.G. Teubner.

Kelsen, H. (1952) *Principles of International Law*, New York: Rinehart and Co.

Kertzer, D.I. (1988) *Ritual, Politics and Power*, London and New Haven: Yale University Press.

Khazanov, A.M. (1978) "Some Theoretical Problems of the Study of the Early State", in Claessen, H.J.M. and P. Skalnik (eds.) *The Early State*, The Hague: Mouton; 77–92.

Kiechle, F. (1958) "Zur Humanität in der Kriegführung der griechischen Staaten", *Historia* 7; 129–156.

Kingsbury, B. and B. Straumann (2010) (eds.) *The Roman Foundations of the Law of Nations. Alberico Gentili and the Justice of Empire*, Oxford: University Press.

Kirchhoff, A. (1877) "Zur Geschichte der Überlieferung des thukydideischen Textes", *Hermes* 12; 366–381.

Kirchhoff, A. (1895) *Thukydides und sein Urkundenmaterial. Ein Beitrag zur Entstehungsgeschichte seines Werkes*, Berlin: W. Hertz.

Kirkwood, G.M. (1952) "Thucydides' words for 'cause'", *American Journal of Philology* 73; 37–51.

Kloppenborg, J.S. (1996) "*Collegia* and *Thiasoi*: Issues in Function, Taxonomy and Membership," in Kloppenborg, J.S. and S.G. Wilson (eds.) *Voluntary Associations in the Graeco-Roman World*, London and New York: Routledge; 16–30.

Kloppenborg, J.S. (2006) "Associations in the Ancient World", in Levine, A.J., D.C. Allison and J.D. Crossan (eds.) *The Historical Jesus In Context*, Princeton: University Press; 323–328.

Kloppenborg, J.S. and R.S. Ascough (2011) (eds.) *Graeco-Roman Associations: Texts, translations, and commentary*. Vol. 1: Attica, Central Greece, Macedonia, Thrace (Beihefte zur Zeitschrift für die neutestamentliche Wissenschaft und die Kunde der älteren Kirche, 181), Berlin: De Gruyter.

Kloppenborg, J.S. and S.G. Wilson (1996) (eds.) *Voluntary Associations in the Graeco-Roman World*, London: Routledge.

Knoepfler, D. (2001) *Décrets érétriens de proxénie et de citoyenneté*, Eretria Fouilles et Recherches XI, Lausanne: Payot.

Koch, C. (1999) "The Athenian Syngrapheis in the Fifth Century B.C.: ad hoc Drafting Committees or Elements of an Integrative Approach?", *Revue internationale des droits de l'antiquité*, 3° série, 46; 13–41.

Kolb, R. (2003) Ius in bello. *Le droit international des conflits armés*, Bâle and Bruxelles: Helbing & Lichtenhahn and Bruylant.

Kolb, R. (2010) *Esquisse d'un droit international public des anciennes cultures extra européennes*, Paris: Pedone.

Konishi, H. (2008) *Power and Structure in Thucydides: An Analytical Commentary*, Vol. II, Amsterdam: Hakkert.

Kooijmans, P.H. (1964) *The Doctrine of the Legal Equality of States: An Inquiry into the Foundations of International Law*, Leiden: Sijthoff.

Korsgaard, Ch. (1996) *The Sources of Normativity*, Cambridge: University Press.

Koskenniemi, M. (1989) *From Apology to Utopia. The Structure of International Legal Argument*, Cambridge: University Press.

Koskenniemi, M. (2001) *The Gentle Civilizer of Nations: The Rise and Fall of International Law 1870–1960*, Cambridge: University Press.

Koskenniemi, M. (2004) "Why History of International Law Today?", *Rechtsgeschichte* 4; 61–66.

Koskenniemi, M. (2012) "International law in the world of ideas", in Crawford, J. and M. Koskenniemi (eds.) *The Cambridge Companion to International Law*, Cambridge: University Press; 47–63.

Kraske, E. (1953–1954) "Klassische Hellas und Nürnberger Prozess", *Archiv des Völkerrechts* 4; 183–189.

Krentz, P. (1985a) "The Nature of Hoplite Battle", *Classical Antiquity* 4; 50–61.

Krentz, P. (1985b) "Casualties in Hoplite Battles", *Greek, Roman and Byzantine Studies* 26; 13–20.

Krentz, P. (2000) "Deception in Archaic and Classical Greek Warfare", in van Wees, H. (ed.) *War and Violence in Classical Greece*, London: Duckworth; 167–200.

Krentz, P. (2002) "Fighting by the Rules: The Invention of the Hoplite Agon", *Hesperia* 71; 23–39.

Krisch, N. (2005) "International Law in Times of Hegemony: Unequal Power and the Shaping of the International Legal Order", *European Journal of International Law* 16; 369–408.

Kunz, J.L. (1948) "Review of *El derecho internacional antes de la Era Cristiana*. By Isodoro Ruiz Moreno", *American Journal of International Law* 42 (1); 237–239.

Kwakwa, E.K. (1992) *The International Law of Armed Conflict: Personal and Material Fields of Application*, Dordrecht, Boston and London: Martinus Nijhoff.

Lafont, B. (2011) "Culture et diplomatie dans le Proche-Orient du IIe millénaire avant notre ère: les prémisses d'un système de relations internationales", in Bouineau, J. (ed.) *Droit international et antiquité. Aspects culturels*, Paris: L'Harmattan; 12–13.

Laghmani, S. (2003) *Histoire du droit des gens: du* jus gentium *impérial au* jus publicum europaeum, Paris: Pedone.

Lambert, S.D. (1993) *The Phratries of Attica*, Ann Arbor: University of Michigan Press.

Lanni, A. (2007) "The Laws of War in Ancient Greece", *Harvard Public Law Working Paper No. 07–24* (= Lanni, A. [2008] "The Laws of War in Ancient Greece", *Law and History Review* 26; 469–489).

Lanni, A. (2010) "Transitional Justice in Ancient Athens: A Case-Study", *University of Pennsylvania Journal of International Law* 32; 551–594.

Larner, D. (1998) "Justice and Drama: Historical Ties and 'Thick' Relationships", *Legal Studies Forum* 22 (1, 2 and 3); 2–17.

Larner, D. (1999a) "Teaching Justice: The Idea of Justice in the Structure of Drama", *Legal Studies Forum* 23 (1 and 2); 201–210.

Larner, D. (1999b) "Justice and Drama: Conflict and Advocacy", *Legal Studies Forum* 23 (4); 417–429.

Laster, K. (2000) *The Drama of the Courtroom*, Annandale: Federation Press.

Laurent, F. (1850) *Histoire du droit des gens et des relations internationales. Études sur l'Histoire de l'humanité*, Gand, Bruxelles and Paris: L. Hebbelynck and Auguste Durand.

Laurot, B. (1981) "Idéaux grecs et barbarie chez Hérodote", *Ktèma* 6; 39–48.

Lauterpacht, H. (1927) *Private Law Sources and Analogies in International Law*, London: Longman, Green & Co.

Lauterpacht, H. (1933) *The Function of Law in the International Community*, Oxford: University Press.

Lavoyer, J.-Ph. (1995) "Réfugiés et personnes déplacées—Droit international humanitaire et rôle du CICR", *Revue internationale de la Croix-Rouge* 77, Nº 812; 183–202.

Le Guen, B. (2001) *Les associations de Technites dionysiaques à l'époque hellénistique*, Nancy: De Boccard.

Lebow, R.N. (2010) *A Cultural Theory of International Relations*, Cambridge: University Press.

Lee, J.W.I. (2010) "Urban Warfare in the Classical Greek World", in Hanson, V.D. (ed.) *Makers of Ancient Strategy. From the Persian Wards to the Fall of Rome*, Princeton: University Press; 138–162.

Lehmann, G.A. (1980) "Der 'Erste Heilige Krieg': eine Fiktion?", *Historia: Zeitschrift für Alte Geschichte* 29 (2); 242–246.

Leiwo, M. (1997) "Religion, or other Reasons? Private Associations in Athens", in Frösén, J. (ed.) *Early Hellenistic Athens. Symptoms of a Change*, Helsinki: Finnish Institute at Athens; 103–117.

Lendon, E.J. (2000) "Homeric Vengeance and the Outbreak of Greek Wars", in van Wees, H. (ed.) *War and Violence in Classical Greece*, London and Swansea: Duckworth and Classical Press of Wales; 1–30.

Lesaffer, R. (1997) "The Westphalian Peace Treaties and the Development of the Tradition of Great European Peace Settlements prior to 1648", *Grotiana* 18; 71–95.

Lesaffer, R. (2004) "Peace Treaties from Lodi to Westphalia", in Lesaffer, R. (ed.) *Peace Treaties and International Law in European History: from the Late Middle Ages to World War One*, Cambridge: University Press; 9–44.

Lesaffer, R. (2005) "Arguments from Roman Law in Current International Law: Occupation and Acquisitive Prescription", *European Journal of International Law* 16 (1); 25–58.

Lesaffer, R. (2007) "International Law and its History: The Story of an Unrequited Love", in Craven, M., M. Fitzmaurice and M. Vogiatzi (eds.) *Time, History and International Law* (Developments in International Law, vol. 58), Leiden and Boston, Brill; 27–41.

Levie, H.S. (2000) "History of the Law of War on Land", *International Review of the Red Cross* 839; 339–340.

Lévy, E. (1983) "Les trois traités entre Sparte et le roi", *Bulletin de Correspondance Hellénique* 107; 221–241.

Lévy, E. (1987) "Métèques et droit de résidence", in Lonis, R. (ed.) *L'étranger dans le monde grec*. Actes du colloque organisé par l'Institut d'Études Anciennes, Nancy; 47–67.

Lewald, H. (1968) "Conflits de lois dans le monde grec et romain", *Revue critique de droit international privé* 57 (1): 419–440 and 615–639.

Lewis, D.M. (1972) "The Treaties with Leontini and Rhegion (Meiggs-Lewis 63–64)", *Zeitschrift für Papyrologie und Epigraphik* 22; 223–225.

Lewis, D.M. (1977) *Sparta and Persia*, Leiden: Brill.

Ley, G. (1991) *A Short Introduction to the Greek Theatre*, Chicago: University Press.

Lipsius, J.H. (1905) *Das attische Recht und Rechtsverfahren mit Benutzung des attischen Prozesses*, Leipzig: O.R. Reisland.

Lissarrague, F. (1990) *L'autre guerrier: archers, peltastes, cavaliers dans l'imagerie attique*, Paris and Rome: La Découverte.

Liu, J. (2008) "Pompeii and collegia: a new appraisal of the evidence", *Ancient History Bulletin* 22 (1–4); 53–69.

Lloyd-Jones, H. (1964) "The *Supplices* of Aeschylus: The New Date and Old Problems", *Antiquité Classique* 33; 356–374.

Lombardo, M. (2002) "La norma e l'eccesso: la guerra tra Sibari e Crotone e alcuni aspetti della '*greek way of war*' in età arcaica", in Sordi, M. (ed.) *Guerra e diritto nel mondo greco e romano* (Contributi dell'Istituto di Storia Antica, 28), Milano: Vita e Pensiero; 43–67.

Longo, O. (1975) "La *polis*, le mura, le navi (Tucidide VII 77,7)", *Quaderni di Storia* 1; 87–113.

Longo, O. (1990) "The Theater of the *Polis*", in Winkler, J.J. and F.I. Zeitlin (eds.) *Nothing to Do With Dionysos? Athenian Drama in Its Social Context*, Princeton: University Press; 12–19.

Lonis, R. (1969) *Les usages de la guerre entre Grecs et Barbares, des guerres mediques au milieu du IVe siècle avant J.-C.*, Besançon and Paris: Les Belles Lettres.

Lonis, R. (1977) "Les otages dans les relations internationales en Grèce classique", in *Mélanges offerts à Léopold Sédar Senghor*, Dakar: Nouvelles Éditions Africaines; 215–234.

Lonis, R. (1979) *Guerre et religion en Grèce à l'époque classique. Recherche sur les rites, les dieux, l'idéologie de la victoire*, Paris: Les Belles Lettres.

Lonis, R. (1988) "Extradition et prise de corps de réfugiés politiques en Grèce", in Lonis, R. (ed.) *L'étranger dans le monde grec* (Actes du colloque de Nancy, mai 1987), Nancy: Presses Universitaires; 69–88.

Lonis, R. (1990) "La condition des réfugiés politiques dans la Grèce antique", in Sokhna Sow, M. (ed.) *Dépendance et liberté: l'Afrique et le monde méditerranéen dans l'Antiquité*, Toronto: Terebi; 131–155.

Lonis, R. (2007) *La cité dans le monde grec*, Paris: Nathan.

Loraux, N. (1981) "Le lit, la guerre", *L'Homme* 21; 37–67.

Loraux, N. (1997) *La cité divisée*, Paris: Payot.

Loraux, N. (2003) *Las experiencias de Tiresias. Lo femenino y el hombre griego*, Buenos Aires: Biblos (original edition: Paris 1989).

Loreto, L. (2001) *Il* bellum iustum *e i suoi equivoci: Cicerone ed una componente della rappresentazione romana del Völkerrecht antico* (Storia politica costituzionale e militare del mondo antico, 1), Napoli: Jovene.

Loreto, L. (2006) *Per la storia militare del mondo antico. Prospettive retrospettive*, Napoli: Jovene.

Lorimer, H.L. (1946) "The Hoplite Phalanx with Special References to the Poems of Archilochus and Tyrtaeus", *Annual of the British School at Athens* 42; 76–138.

Low, P. (2005) "Looking for the Language of Athenian Imperialism", *Journal of Hellenic Studies* 125; 93–111.

Low, P. (2007) *Interstate Relations in Classical Greece. Morality and Power* (Cambridge Classical Studies), Cambridge: University Press.

Low, P. (2008) (ed.) *The Athenian Empire*, Edinburgh: University Press.

Lozano, A. (1996) "Los Seléucidas y sus sistemas de control territorial", *Gerion* 14; 183–194.

Luraghi, N. (2013) "Ruling Alone: Monarchy in Greek Politics and Thought", in Luragui, N. (ed.) *The Splendors and Miseries of Ruling Alone. Encounters with Monarchy from Archaic Greece to the Hellenistic Mediterranean*, München: Franz Steiner; 11–24.

Ma, J. (2003) "Peer Polity Interaction in the Hellenistic Age", *Past and Present* 180; 9–39.

Ma, J. (2013) "Grandes et petites cités au miroir de l'épigraphie classique et hellénistique", *Topoi* 18; 67–86.

MacAloon, J. (1984) (ed.) *Rite, Drama, Festival, Spectacle: Rehearsals toward a Theory of Cultural Performance*, Philadelphia: Institute for the Study of Human Issues.

MacDowell, D. (1963) *Athenian Homicide Law in the Age of the Orators*, Manchester: University Press.

MacDowell, D. (1975) "Law-Making at Athens in the Fourth Century B.C.", *Journal of Hellenic Studies* 95; 62–74.

MacDowell, D. (1986) *The Law in Classical Athens*, Ithaca [1978[1]].

MacDowell, D. (1995) *Aristophanes and Athens. An Introduction to the Plays*, Oxford: University Press.

Mack, W.J.B.G. (2013) "Communal Interests and *Polis* Identity under Negotiation: Documents Depicting Sympolities between Cities Great and Small", *Topoi* 18; 87–116.

MacKechnie, P. (1989) *Outsiders in the Greek Cities in the Fourth Century BC*, London and New York: Routledge.

Mackinnon, J.K. (1978) "The Reason for the Danaids' Flight", *Classical Quarterly* 28; 74–82.

MacMullen, R. (1963) "Foreign Policy for the 'Polis'", *Greece and Rome* 10 (2); 118–122.

Malanczuk, P. (1997) *Akekurst's Modern Introduction to International Law*, New York and London: Routledge.

Mantovani, M. (1990) Bellum iustum. *Die Idee des gerechten Krieges in der römischen Kaiserzeit*, New York: Peter Lang.

Maridakis, G.S. (1952) "Un précédent du Procès de Nuremberg tiré de l'histoire de la Grèce ancienne", *Revue hellénique de droit international* 5; 1–16.

Martin, V. (1940) *La vie internationale dans la Grèce des cités (Vie–Ive s. av. J.-C.)*, Genève and Paris: Recueil Sirey.

Mattaliano, F. (2012) *Atene e Siracusa*. Poleis homoiotropoi, Palermo: Università degli Studi di Palermo.

Mattingly, H.B. (1963) "The Growth of Athenian Imperialism", *Historia* 12; 257–273.

Mattox, J.M. (2006) *Saint Augustine and the Theory of Just War*, London and New York: Continuum.

May, L. (2008) *Aggression and Crimes against Peace*, Cambridge: Cambridge University Press.

Mayor, A. (2003) *Greek Fire, Poison Arrows, and Scorpion Bombs: Biological and Chemical Warfare in the Ancient World*, Woodstock (NY): Overlook Duckworth.

McCormack, T.L.H. (1997) "From Sun Tzu to the Sixth Committee: The Evolution of an International Criminal Law Regime", in McCormack, T.L.H. and G.J. Simpson (eds.) *The Law of War Crimes. National and International Approaches*, The Hague, London and Boston: Kluwer Law International; 31–63.

McGregor, M.F. (1941) "Cleisthenes of Sicyon and the Panhellenic Festivals", *Transactions and Proceedings of the American Philological Association* 72; 266–287.

McGregor, M.F. (1987) *The Athenians and their Empire*, Vancouver: University of British Columbia Press.

Mégret, F. (2012) "International law as law", in Crawford, J. and M. Koskenniemi (eds.) *The Cambridge Companion to International Law*, Cambridge: University Press; 72–81.

Meiggs, R. (1982) *Trees and Timber in the Ancient Mediterranean World*, Oxford: Clarendon Press.

Méndez de Fraboschi, A.M. (1985) "Concepto de Justicia e Injusticia desde Homero hasta el Siglo de Pericles", *Anales de Historia Antigua, Medieval y Moderna*, 1983; 9–40.

Merck Davidson, O. (1979) "Dolon and Rhesus in the *Iliad*", *Quaderni Urbinati di Cultura Classica* N.S. 1; 61–66.

Meritt, B.D. (1940) *Epigraphica Attica* (Martin Classical Lectures, 9), Cambridge (MA): Harvard University Press.

Meritt, B.D. (1946) "The Athenian Alliances with Rhegion and Leontinoi", *Classical Quarterly* 40; 85–91.

Meron, Th. (1998) "Medieval and Renaissance Ordinances of War: Codifying Discipline and Humanity", in *War Crimes Comes of Age. Essays*, Oxford, University Press; 1–10.

Meyer, C. (1955) *Die Urkunden im Geschichtswerk des Thukydides*, München: C.H. Beck.

Meyer, E.A. (2004) *Legitimacy and Law in the Roman World. Tabulae in Roman Belief and Practice*, Cambridge: University Press.

Milchhoefer, A. (1892) *Untersuchungen über die Demenordnung des Kleisthenes*, Berlin: De Gruyter.

Miles, M.M. (2008) *Art as Plunder. The Ancient Origins of Debate about Cultural Property*, Cambridge: University Press.

Miller, M.C. (1997) *Athens and Persia in the Fifth Century B.C. A Study in Cultural Receptivity*, Cambridge: University Press.

Millett, P. (1990) "Sale, credit and exchange in Athenian law and society", in Cartledge, P., P. Millett and S. Todd (eds.), *Nomos. Essays in Athenian law, politics and society*, Cambridge: University Press; 167–194.

Millett, P. (1992) *Lending and Borrowing in Ancient Athens*, Cambridge: University Press.

Millett, P.C. (2013) "Writers on War. Part I. Greece. Winning Ways in Warfare", in Campbell, B. and L.A. Tritle (eds.) *The Oxford Handbook of Warfare in the Classical World*, Oxford: University Press; 46–73.

Missiou-Ladi, A. (1987) "Coercive Diplomacy in Greek Interstate Relations (with special reference to *presbeis autokratores*)", *Classical Quarterly* 37 (ii); 336–345.

Mitchell, L.G. (1997) *Greeks Bearing Gifts: The Public Use of Private Relationships in the Greek World, 435–323 BC*, Cambridge: University Press.

Mitchell, L.G. (2006) "Greeks, Barbarian and Aeschylus' *Suppliants*", *Greece and Rome* 53 (2); 205–223.

Mitchell, S. (1996) "Hoplite warfare in ancient Greece", in Lloyd, A.B. (ed.) *Battle in antiquity*, London and Swansea: Duckworth and Classical Press of Wales; 87–105.

Miyazaki, M. (2007), "Public coercive power of the greek polis—On a recent debate", *Bulletin of the Institute for Mediterranean Studies* 5; 87–100.

Mogens, H.H. and T.H. Nielsen (2004) (eds.) *An Inventory of Archaic and Classical Poleis*, Oxford: University Press.

Momigliano, A. (1966) "Some Observations on Causes of War in Ancient Historiography", in *Studies in Historiography*, London: Weidenfeld and Nicolson; 112–126.

Monaco, M.C. (2015) "Atene e la memoria delle guerre. Appunti per una topografia dei luoghi", in Franchi, E. and G. Proietti (eds.) *Guerra e memoria nel mondo antico*, Trento: Università degli Studi; 153–175.

Moncayo, G., R.E. Vinuesa and H.D.T. Gutiérrez Posse (1997) *Derecho Internacional Público*, Tomo I, Buenos Aires: Zavalía.

Moneti, I. (1991) "La γραφὴ κλοπῆς nel diritto attico", *Civiltà classica e cristiana* 12; 7–10.

Monier, R. (1947) *Manuel élémentaire de droit romain*, Tome I, Paris: Domat Montchrestien.

Montagu, J.D. (2006) *Greek and Roman Warfare. Battles, Tactics, and Trickery*, London: Greenhill.

Moore, M.S. (1967) *The Unwritten Laws of Greece*, Dublin: University College.

Morris, I. (1991) "The Early *Polis* as City and State", in Rich, J. and A. Wallace-Hadrill (eds.) *City and Country in the Ancient World*, London: Routledge; 25–57.

Morrison, J.V. (2006) *Reading Thucydides*, Columbus: The Ohio State University Press.

Mosley, D.J. (1961) "Who 'Signed' Treaties in Ancient Greece?", *Proceedings of the Cambridge Philological Society* N.S. 7; 59–63.

Mosley, D.J. (1965) "The Size of Embassies in Ancient Greek Diplomacy", *Transactions of the American Philological Association* 96; 255–266.

Mosley, D.J. (1971) "Diplomacy and Disunion in Ancient Greece", *Phoenix* 25 (4); 319–330.

Mosley, D.J. (1972) "Diplomacy in Classical Greece", *Ancient Society* 3; 1–16.

Mosley, D.J. (1973) *Envoys and Diplomacy in Ancient Greece* (Historia-Einzelschrift, 22), Wiesbaden: Franz Steiner.

Mugerwa, N. (1968) "Subjects of International Law", in Sørensen, M. (ed.) *Manual of Public International Law*, London: Macmillan; 247–310.

Muller, Y. (2014) "La mutilation de l'ennemi en Grèce classique: pratique barbare ou préjugé grec?", in Allély, A. (ed.) *Corps au supplice et violences de guerre dans l'Antiquité*, Bordeaux: De Boccard; 41–72.

Müllerson, R. (2000) *Ordering Anarchy: International Law in International Society*, Leiden: Martinus Nijhoff.

Murray, O. (1997) "Rationality and the Greek *polis*: the evidence from Kamarina", in Hansen, M.H. (ed.) *The Polis as an Urban Centre and as a Political Community* (Acts of the Copenhagen Polis Centre 4. Det Kongelige Danske Videnskabernes Selskab, Historisk-filosofiske Meddelelser 75), Copenhagen: Munksgaard; 493–504.

Murray, O. (2000) "What is Greek about the Polis?", in Flensted-Jensen, P., T. Heine Nielsen and L. Rubinstein (eds.) *Polis and Politics. Studies in Ancient Greek History Presented to Mogen Herman Hansen on his Sixtieth Birthday*, Copenhagen: Museum Tusculanum; 231–248.

Murray, O. (2009) "The Culture of the Symposion", in Raaflaub, K.A. and H. van Wees (eds.) *A Companion to Archaic Greece*, Chichester and Malden: Wiley-Blackwell; 508–523.

Nagler, M.N. (1988) "Toward a Semantics of Ancient Conflict: *Eris* in the *Iliad*", *The Classical World* 82 (2); 81–90.

Naiden, F.S. (2004) "Supplication and the Law", in Harris, E. and L. Rubinstein (eds.) *The Law and the Courts in Ancient Greece*, London: Duckworth; 71–91.

Nail, C. (2014) "La guerre et la paix dans l'antiquité", in Guisard, Ph. and Ch. Laizé (eds.) *La guerre et la paix*, Paris: Ellipses; 3–36.

Neff, S.C. (2005) *War and the Law of Nations. A General History*, Cambridge: University Press.

Nevin, S. (2017) *Military Leaders and Sacred Space in Classical Greek Warfare. Temples, Sanctuaries, and Conflict in Antiquity*, London: I.B. Tauris.

Newiger, H.-J. (1980) "War and Peace in the Comedies of Aristophanes", *Yale Classical Studies* 26; 219–237.

Nicholas, B. (1962) *An Introduction to Roman Law*, Oxford: Clarendon Press.

Nicolson, H. (1955) *La diplomacia*, México: Fondo de Cultura Económica.

Nielsen, T.H. (1996) "A Survey of Dependent *Poleis* in Classical Arkadia", in Hansen, M.H. and K. Raaflaub (eds.) *More Studies in the Ancient Greek Polis* (Papers from the Copenhagen Polis Centre 3; Historia Einzelschriften 108), Stuttgart: Franz Steiner; 63–105.

Nijman, J.E. (2004) *The Concept of International Legal Personality: An Inquiry into the History and Theory of International Law*, The Hague: T.M.C. Asser Press.

Nikitas, A. (1976) *Zur Bedeutung von* Prophasis *in der altengriechischen Literatur*, Wiesbaden: Franz Steiner.

Nörr, D. (1991) *Die Fides im römischen Völkerrecht*, Heidelberg: Müller.

Nussbaum, A. (1947) *A Concise History of the Law of Nations*, New York: Macmillan.

O'Connell, D.P. (1963) "La personnalité en droit international", *Revue générale de droit international public* 67; 4–43.

Oakeshott, M. (1991) *On Human Conduct*, Oxford: University Press.

Ober, J. (1985) *Fortress Attica. Defensa of the Athenian Land Frontier, 404–322 BC* (Mnemosyne, Suppl. 84), Leiden: Brill.

Ober, J. (1989) *Mass and Elite in Democratic Athens: Rhetoric, Ideology and the Power of the People*, Princeton: University Press.

Ober, J. (1994) "Classical Greek Times", in Howard, M., G.J. Andreopoulos and M.R. Shulman (eds.) *The Laws of War. Constraints on Warfare in the Western World*, New Haven and London: Yale University Press; 12–26.

Ober, J. (1996a) "The Rules of War in Ancient Greece", in *The Athenian Revolution. Essays on Ancient Greek Democracy and Political Theory*, Princeton: Princeton University Press: 53–71.

Ober, J. (1996b) "The Nature of Athenian Democracy", in *The Athenian Revolution. Essays on Ancient Greek Democracy and Political Theory*, Princeton; 107–122.

Ober, J. (2002) "Social Science History, Cultural History, and the Amnesty of 403", *Transactions of the American Philological Association* 132 (1/2); 127–137.

Ober, J. and B. Strauss (1990) "Drama, Political Rhetoric and the Discourse of Athenian Democracy", in Winkler, J.J. and F.I. Zeitlin (eds.) *Nothing to Do with Dionysos? Athenian Drama in its Social Context*, Princeton: University Press; 237–270.

Onuma, Y. (2010) *A Transcivilizational Perspective on International Law*, Leiden and Boston: Martinus Nijhoff.

Oppenheim, L. (1908) "The Science of International Law", *American Journal of International Law* 2 (2); 313–356.

Orestano, R. (1968) *Il problema delle persone giuridiche in diritto romano*, Tomo I, Torino: Casa Editrice Torinese.

Orford, A. (2011) *International Authority and the Responsibility to Protect*, Cambridge: University Press.

Ormerod, H.A. (1914) *Piracy in the Ancient World*. Liverpool: University Press.

Osborne, R. (1985) "Law in action in Classical Athens", *Journal of Hellenic Studies* 105; 40–58.

Osborne, R. (1993) "Competitive Festivals and the Polis: A Context for Dramatic Festivals in Athens", in Sommerstein, A.H., S. Halliwell, J. Henderson and B. Zimmermann (eds.) *Tragedy, Comedy, and the Polis: Papers from the Greek Drama Conference* (Nottingham, 18–20 July 1990), Bari: Levante; 21–38.

Osborne, R. (2014) "Intoxication and Sociality: The Symposium in the Ancient Greek World", *Past and Present* (Suppl.) 9; 34–60.

Osiander, A. (2001) "Sovereignty, International Relations, and the Westphalian Myth", *International Organization* 55 (2); 251–287.

Ostwald, M. (1965) "Pindar, *Nomos*, and Heracles", *Harvard Studies in Classical Philology* 69; 109–138.

Ostwald, M. (1969) *Nomos and the Beginnings of Athenian Democracy*, Oxford: Clarendon Press.

Ostwald, M. (1982) *Autonomia: Its Genesis and Early History*, Chico (CA): Scholars Press.

Ostwald, M. (1986) *From Popular Sovereignty to the Sovereignty of Law. Law, Society, and Politics in Fifth-Century Athens*, Berkeley, Los Angeles and London: University of California Press.

Ostwald, M. (1988) *Ἀνάγκη in Thucydides*, Atlanta: Scholars Press.

Paiaro, D. (2011) "Las ambigüedades del Estado en la democracia ateniense: entre la libertad y la coacción", in Campagno, M., J. Gallego, J. and C. García MacGaw (eds.) *El Estado en el Mediterráneo Antiguo. Egipto, Grecia, Roma*, Buenos Aires: Miño y Dávila; 223–242.

Paiaro, D. (2012) "*Ándres gàr pólis*. Algunas reflexiones acerca de los debates recientes en torno a la estatalidad de la ciudad griega antigua a la luz del caso ateniense", in Dell'Elicine, E., H. Francisco, P. Miceli and A. Morin (coords.) *El Estado en las sociedades precapitalistas. Pertinencia, límites y condiciones del concepto de Estado*, Buenos Aires: Universidad Nacional de General Sarmiento; 51–77.

Panessa, G. (1999) Philiai. *L'amicizia nelle relazioni interstatali del Greci*, Pisa: Scuola Normale Superiore.

Paoli, U.E. (1976) "Diritto attico e diritto greco", in *Altri studi di diritto greco e romano*, Milano: Cisalpino-La Goliardica; 1–18.

Papadopoulos, I. (1998) *Pratiques juridiques interprétatives et herméneutique littéraire. Variations autour d'un thème de Ronald Dworkin*, Québec: Éditions Yvon Blais.

Papanastasis, V.P., M. Arianoutsou and K. Papanastasis (2010) "Environmental conservation in classical Greece", *Journal of Biological Research (Thessaloniki)* 14; 123–135.

Paradisi, B. (1957) "Due aspetti fondamentali nella formazione del diritto internazionale antico", *Annali di Storia del Diritto* 1; 169–259.

Pardo, M.L. (1996) *Derecho y lingüística: cómo se juzga con palabras*, Buenos Aires: Nueva Visión [1992[1]].

Parke, H.W. (1933) *Greek Mercenary Soldiers*, Oxford: The Clarendon Press.

Parke, H.W. (1977) *Festivals of the Athenians*, London: Thames and Hudson.

Parker, V. (1994) "Some Aspects of the Foreign and Domestic Policy of Cleisthenes of Sicyon", *Hermes* 122 (4); 404–424.

Parker, V. (2016) "War and Religion in Ancient Greece", in Ulanowski, K. (ed.) *The Religious Aspects of War in the Ancient Near East, Greece, and Rome*, Leiden and Boston: Brill; 123–132.

Parlett, K. (2011) *The Individual in the International Legal System. Continuity and Change in International Law*, Cambridge: University Press.

Parra, J.D. (2010) "Political Psychology in Plato's *Alcibiades* I", *Praxis filosófica* 31; 25–44.

Patterson, C. (2000) "The Hospitality of Athenian Justice: The Metic in Court", in Hunter, V. and J. Edmondson (eds.) *Law and Social Status in Classical Athens*, Oxford: University Press; 93–111.

Payen, P. (2012) *Les revers de la guerre en Grèce ancienne*, Paris: Belin.

Pearson, L. (1941) "Historical Allusions in the Attic Orators", *Classical Philology* 36 (3); 209–229.

Pearson, L. (1952) "*Prophasis* and *Aitia*", *Transactions of the American Philological Association* 83; 205–223.

Pearson, L. (1972) "*Prophasis*: A Clarification", *Transactions of the American Philological Association* 103; 381–394.

Pecírka, J. (1966) *The Formula for the Grant of Enktesis in Attic Inscriptions*, Acta Universitatis Carolinae Philosophicae et Historica Monographica XV, Praha: Univerzita Karlova.

Pepe, L. (2012) Phonos. *L'omicidio da Draconte all'età degli oratori*, Milano: Giuffrè.

Pérez Bernárdez, C. (2009) "Personalidad jurídica internacional", in Sánchez, V.M. (dir.) *Derecho internacional público*, Barcelona: Huygens; 133–138.

Pérez Martín, E. (2001) *Los extranjeros y el derecho en la antigua Grecia*, Madrid: Universidad Rey Juan Carlos and Dykinson.

Perlman, S. (1976) "On Bribing Athenian Ambassadors", *Greek, Roman and Byzantine Studies* 17; 223–233.

Perreau-Saussine, A. (2010) "Immanuel Kant on International Law", in Besson, S. and J. Tasioulas (eds.) *The Philosophy of International Law*, Oxford: University Press; 53–75.

Perrin-Saminadayar, É. (1999) "*Si vis pacem, gere bellum*. L'aspiration à la paix dans la société athénienne, de la Guerre du Péloponnèse à la Guerre Lamiaque", in Prost, F. (ed.) *Armées et sociétés de la Grèce classique. Aspects sociaux et politiques de la guerre aux Vᵉ et IVᵉ s. av. J.-C.*, Paris: Errance; 147–162.

Phillipson, C. (1911) *The International Law and Custom of Ancient Greece and Rome*, Vol. i–ii, London: Macmillan.

Picard, O. (1980) *Les Grecs devant la menace perse*, Regards sur l'histoire—Histoire ancienne, Paris: Société d'édition d'enseignement supérieur.

Piccirilli, L. (2001) "La diplomazia nella Grecia antica: temi del linguaggio e caratteristiche degli ambasciatori", *Museum Helveticum* 58; 1–31.

Piccirilli, L. (2002) *L'invenzione della diplomazia nella Grecia antica*. Roma: "L'Erma" di Bretschneider.

Pickard-Cambridge, A.W. (1927) *Dithyramb, Tragedy and Comedy*, Oxford: Clarendon Press.

Pickard-Cambridge, A.W. (1946) *The Theatre of Dionysus in Athens*, Oxford: Clarendon Press.

Pickard-Cambridge, A.W. (1968) *The Dramatic Festivals of Athens* (Revised by Gould, S. and D. Lewis), Oxford: Clarendon Press.

Pictet, J. (1983) *Développement et principes du droit international humanitaire*, Genève and Paris: Institut Henry-Dunant and Pedone.

Pictet, J. (1984) *The Fundamental Principles of the Red Cross and Peace*, Geneva: Henry-Dunant Institute.

Pinto, M. (2004) *El derecho internacional. Vigencias y desafíos en un escenario globalizado*, Buenos Aires: Fondo de Cultura Económica.

Pistorius, T. (1985) *Hegemoniestreben und Autonomiesicherung in der griechischen Vertragspolitik klassischer und hellenistischer Zeit*, Frankfurt am Main, Bern and New York: Peter Lang.

Plattner, D. (1996) "ICRC Neutrality and Neutrality in Humanitarian Assistance", *International Review of the Red Cross* 311; 161–179.

Podlecki, A.J. (1966) *The Political Background of Aeschylean Tragedy*, Ann Arbor: University of Michigan Press.

Portmann, R. (2010) *Legal Personality in International Law*, Cambridge: University Press.

Pouncey, P.R. (1980) *The Necessities of War. A Study on Thucydides' Pessimism*, New York: Columbia University Press.

Powell, A. (2005) "Les femmes de Sparte (et d'autres cités) en temps de guerre", in Bertrand, J.-M. (ed.) *La violence dans les mondes grec et romain*, Paris: Publications de la Sorbonne; 321–335.

Pownell, F. (2004) *Lessons from the Past: The Moral Use of History in Fourth-Century Prose*, Ann Arbor: University of Michigan Press.

Preiser, W. (1976) *Frühe völkerrechtliche Ordnungen der aussereuropäischen Welt. Ein Beitrag zur Geschichte des Völkerrechts*, Wiesbaden: Franz Steiner.

Price, J.J. (2001) *Thucydides and Internal War*, Cambridge: University Press.

Prieto Sanjuán, R.A. (2007) "De la vigencia y necesidad del derecho relativo a los medios y métodos de combate", in Prieto Sanjuán, R.A. (ed.) *Conducción de hostilidades y derecho internacional humanitario. A propósito del Centenario de las Convenciones de La Haya de 1907*, Bogotá: Pontificia Universidad Javeriana and Biblioteca Jurídica Diké; 19–55.

Pritchard, D.M. (2014) "The Position of Attic Women in Democratic Athens", *Greece and Rome* 61; 174–193.

Pritchett, W.K. (1971) *Ancient Greek Military Practices* 1, Berkeley, Los Angeles and London: University of California Press.

Pritchett, W.K. (1974) *The Greek State at War*, Berkeley, Los Angeles and London: University of California Press.

Prost, F. (1999) "Les combattants de Marathon: Idéologie et société hoplitiques à Athènes au Ve siècle", in Prost, F. (ed.) *Armées et sociétés de la Grèce classique. Aspects sociaux et politiques de la guerre aux Ve et IVe s. av. J.-C.*, Paris: Errance; 69–88.

Purnell, R. (1978) "Theoretical approaches to International Relations: the contribution of the Graeco-Roman World", in Taylor, T. (ed) *Approaches and Theory in International Relations*, London and New York: Longman; 19–31.

Quass, F. (1971) Nomos *und* Psephisma. *Untersuchung zum griechischen Staatsrecht* (Zetemata, Heft 55), München: C.H. Beck.

Queyrel Bottineau, A. (2010) Prodosia. *La notion et l'acte de trahison dans l'Athènes du Ve siècle*, Paris: Ausonius.

Raaflaub, K.A. (1991) "City-State, Territory, and Empire in Classical Antiquity", in Molho, A., K. Raaflaub and J. Emlen (eds.) *City States in Classical Antiquity and Medieval Italy*, Stuttgart: Franz Steiner; 565–588.

Raaflaub, K.A. (1999) "Archaic and Classical Greece", in Raaflaub, K.A. and N. Rosenstein (eds.) *War and Society in the Ancient and Medieval World*, Washington DC: Center for Hellenic Studies; 129–161.

Raaflaub, K.A. (2001) "Father of All, Destroyer of All: War in Late Fifth-Century Athenian Discourse and Ideology", in McCann, D.R. and B.S. Strauss (eds.) *War and Democracy: A Comparative Study of the Korean War and the Peloponnesian War*, Armonk (NY) and London: M.E. Sharpe; 307–356.

Raaflaub, K.A. (2006) "Introduction: Searching for Peace in the Ancient World", in Raaflaub, K.A. (ed.) *War and Peace in the Ancient World*, London: Blackwell; 1–33.

Raaflaub, K.A. (2007) "Warfare and Athenian Society", in Samons II, L.J. (ed.) *The Cambridge Companion to the Age of Pericles*, Cambridge: University Press; 96–124.

Radin, M. (1910) *The Legislation of Greeks and Romans on Corporations* (PhD, University of Columbia), New York.

Raeder, A. (1912) *L'arbitrage international chez les Hellènes*, Kristiania: H. Aschehong & Co.

Rajagopal, B. (2003) *International Law from Below*, Cambridge: University Press.

Rappaport, R.A. (1979) *Ecology, Meaning, and Religion*, Richmond (CA): North Atlantic Books.

Rawlings, H. (1975) *A Semantic Study of Πρόφασις to 400 B.C.* (Hermes Einzelschrift 33), Wiesbaden: Franz Steiner.

Rawlings, L. (2007) *The Ancient Greeks at War*, Manchester: University Press.

Rawlings, L. (2013) "War and Warfare in Ancient Greece", in Campbell, B. and L.A. Tritle (eds.) *The Oxford Handbook of Warfare in the Classical World*, Oxford: University Press; 3–28.

Rawls, J. (1999) *The Law of Peoples*, Cambridge (MA): Harvard University Press.

Rebuffat, F. (2000) *Guerre et société dans le monde grec (490–322 av. J.-C.)*, Paris and Liège: Sedes.

Redslob, R. (1923) *Histoire des grands principes du droit des gens depuis l'antiquité jusqu'à la veille de la grande guerre*, Paris: Librairie A. Rousseau.

Reeves, J.D. (1966) "The Cause of the Trojan War: A Forgotten Myth Revived", *The Classical Journal* 61 (5); 211–214.

Remec, P.P. (1960) *The position of the individual in international law according to Grotius and Vattel*, Leiden and Boston: Martinus Nijhoff.

Renaut, M.-H. (2007) *Histoire du droit international public*, Paris: Ellipses.

Rhodes, P.J. (1972) *The Athenian Boule*, Oxford: University Press.

Rhodes, P.J. (1984) "*Nomothesia* in Fourth Century Athens", *Classical Quarterly* 35 (1); 55–61.

Rhodes, P.J. (1987) "Thucydides on the causes of the Peloponnesian War", *Hermes* 115; 154–165.

Rhodes, P.J. (2007) *The Greek City States. A Source Book*, 2nd Edition, Cambridge: University Press.

Rhodes, P.J. and D.M. Lewis, D.M. (1997) *The Decrees of the Greek States*, Oxford: University Press.

Ribeiro Ferreira, J. (2004) "Próxeno e proxenia", in Leão, D.F., L. Rossetti and M.d.C.G.Z. Fialho (eds.) *Nomos. Direito e sociedade na Antiguidade Clássica / Derecho y sociedad en la Antigüedad Clásica*, Coimbra and Madrid: Imprensa da Universidade de Coimbra and Ediciones Clásicas; 227–239.

Richardson, J.S. (1990) "Thucydides I.23.6 and the Debate Around the Peloponnesian War", in Craik, E.M. (ed.) *Owls to Athens: Essays on Classical Subjects Presented to Sir Kenneth Dover*, Oxford: Clarendon Press; 151–161.

Richmond, J.A. (1998) "Spies in Ancient Greece", *Greece & Rome* 45 (1); 1–18.

Ridley, R.T. (1972) "The Hoplite as Citizen: Athenian Military Institutions in their Social Context", *L'Antiquité classique* 48; 508–548.

Rigsby, K.J. (1996) Asylia*: Territorial Inviolability in the Hellenistic World*, Berkeley, Los Angeles and London: University of California Press.

Robert, J. (1976) *"Prophasis"*, *Revue des études grecques* 89; 334–335.

Roberts, J.T. (1977) "Arginusae Once Again", *Classical World* 71 (2); 107–111.

Roberts, J.T. (1982) *Accountability in Athenian Government*, Madison: University of Wisconsin Press.

Robertson, N. (1978) "The Myth of the First Sacred War", *Classical Quarterly* N.S. 28 (1); 38–73.

Robinson, P. (2003) *Just War in Comparative Perspective*. Aldershot and Burlington: Ashgate.

Robinson, P. (2006) *Military Honour and the Conduct of War. From Ancient Greece to Iraq*, London and New York: Routledge.

Rodin, D. (2002) *War and Self-Defense*, Oxford: University Press.

Rodin, D. and Shue, H. (2008) *Just and Unjust Warriors. The Moral and Legal Status of Soldiers*, Oxford: University Press.

Rodin, D. and Sorabji, R. (2006) *The ethics of war: shared problems in different traditions*. Aldershot and Burlington: Ashgate.

Rodríguez Cidre, E. (2010) *Cautivas troyanas. El mundo femenino fragmentado en las tragedias de Eurípides*, Córdoba: Ediciones del Copista.

Rohweder, Ch. (1998) *Macht und Gedeihen. Eine politische Interpretation der* Hiketiden *des Aischylos*, Frankfurt am Main: Peter Lang.

Roisman, H.M. (2006) "Helen in the *Iliad*: *Causa Belli* and Victim of War: From Silent Weaver to Public Speaker", *American Journal of Philology* 127; 1–36.

Rood, T. (1998) *Thucydides. Narrative and Explanation*, Oxford: University Press.

Rösler, W. (1993) "Der Schluss der "Hiketiden" und die Danaiden-Trilogie des Aischylos", *Rheinisches Museum* 136; 1–22.

Roth, M. (1995) *Law Collections from Mesopotamia and Asia Minor*, Atlanta: Scholars Press.

Roussel, D. (1976) *Tribu et cité. Études sur les groupes sociaux dans les cités grecques aux époques archaïque et classique*, Paris and Besançon: Les Belles Lettres.

Rousset, D. (2002) *Le territoire de Delphes et la terre d'Apollon*, Paris: De Boccard.

Rubinstein, L. (2000) *Litigation and Cooperation: Supporting Speakers in the Courts of Classical Athens*, Stuttgart: Franz Steiner.

Ruiz Moreno, I. (1946) *El derecho internacional antes de la Era Cristiana*, Buenos Aires: Facultad de Derecho y Ciencias Sociales de la UBA.

Ruschenbusch, E. (1975) "Die Verträge Athens mit Leontinoi und Rhegion vom Jahre 433/2 v. Chr.", *Zeitschrift für Papyrologie und Epigraphik* 19; 225–232.

Russell, F. (2013) "Finding the Enemy. Military Intelligence", in Campbell, B. and L.A. Tritle (eds.) *The Oxford Handbook of Warfare in the Classical World*, Oxford: University Press; 474–492.

Ruzié, D. (2008) *Droit international public*, 19e édition, Paris: Dalloz.

Rybacki, K.C. and D.J. Rybacki (2000) *Advocacy and Opposition: An Introduction to Argumentation*, 4th edition, Boston: Allyn and Bacon.

Ryder, T.T.B. (1965) Koine Eirene: *General Peace and Local Independence in Ancient Greece*. Oxford: University Press.

Ryzman, M. (1989) "The Psychological Role of Danaus in Aeschylus' *Suppliants*", *Eranos* 87; 1–6.

Sage, M.M. (1996) *Warfare in Ancient Greece: A Sourcebook*, London and New York: Routledge.

Saito, N.T. (2010) *Meeting the Enemy. American Exceptionalism and International Law*, New York: University Press.

Salazar, Ch.F. (2013) "Treating the Sick and the Wounded", in Campbell, B. and L.A. Tritle (eds.) *The Oxford Handbook of Warfare in the Classical World*, Oxford: University Press; 294–311.

Salmon, J. (1977) "Political Hoplites?", *Journal of Hellenic Studies* 97; 84–101.

Salmon, J. (2002) *Dictionnaire du droit international*, Bruxelles: Bruylant.

Santi Amantini, L. (1985) "Semantica storica dei termini greci relativi alla pace nelle epigrafi anteriori al 387/6 a.C.", in Sordi, M. (ed.) *La pace nel mondo antico*, Milano: Vita e Pensiero; 45–68.

San Nicolò, M. (1913–1915) *Ägyptisches Vereinswesen zur Zeit der Ptolemäer und Römer*, München: C.H. Beck.

Santiago Álvarez, R.A. (1998) "Griegos y bárbaros: arqueología de una alteridad", *Faventia* 20 (2); 33–44.

Santiago Álvarez, R.A. (2005) "Acogida y protección de mujeres extranjeras: el testimonio de *Suplicantes* de Esquilo", in Nieto Ibañez, J.M. (ed.) *Estudios sobre la mujer en la cultura griega y latina* (XVIII Jornadas de Filología Clásica de Castilla y León, León, 2–5 noviembre de 2004), León: Universidad de León; 143–178.

Santiago Álvarez, R.A. (2005) "La condición de extranjero en el mundo griego antiguo: algunas observaciones", in Alvar Esquerra, A. and J.F. González Castro (eds.) *Actas del XI Congreso de la Sociedad Española de Estudios Clásicos* (Santiago de Compostela, 15–20 de septiembre de 2003), vol. I, Madrid: Sociedad Española de Estudios Clásicos; 587–596.

Santiago Álvarez, R.A. (2013) "Esquilo, *Las Suplicantes*: una "hospitalidad" plasmada en leyes", in Oller Guzmán, M. (ed.) *Contacto de poblaciones y extranjería en el mundo griego antiguo. Estudio de fuentes* (Faventia, Suppl. 2), Barcelona: Universitat Autònoma; 57–74.

Santiago Álvarez, R.A. and S. Gardeñes Santiago (2002) "Interacción de poblaciones en la antigua Grecia: algunos ejemplos de especial interés para el derecho internacional privado", *Faventia* 24 (1); 7–36.

Sartori, F. (1958) "Il diritto di associazione nell'età soloniana ed una notizia de Gaio (D. 47.22.4)", *Iura* 9; 100–104.

Sassòli, M. (1976) "Means of Warfare: The Traditional and the New Law", in Sassòli, M. (ed.) *The New Humanitarian Law of Armed Conflict*, Napoli: Editoriale Scientifica; 161–198.

Sassòli, M. (2003) *Legitimate Targets of Attacks under International Humanitarian Law*. Background Paper prepared for the Informal High-Level Expert Meeting on the Reaffirmation and Development of International Humanitarian Law (Cambridge, January 27–29, 2003), Harvard University.

Sassòli, M. and A. Bouvier (1999) *How Does Law Protect in War? Cases, Documents and Teaching Materials on Contemporary Practice in International Humanitarian Law*, Geneva: International Committee of the Red Cross.

Savalli-Lestrade, I. (2013) "Remarques sur les 'grandes' et les 'petites' cités aux époques classique et hellénistique d'après les sources littéraires et épigraphiques", *Topoi* 18; 117–129.

Schachermeyr, F. (1953) "La formation de la Cité grecque", *Diogène* 4; 22–39.

Schäublin, C. (1971) "Wider einmal πρόφασις", *Museum Helveticum* 28; 133–144.

Schechner, R. (1977) *Performance Theory*, London and New York: Routledge.

Scheibelreiter, Ph. (2013) *Untersuchungen zur Vertragsrechtlichen Struktur des delisch-attischen Seebundes* (Akten der Gesellschaft für griechische und hellenistische Rechtsgeschichte, 22), Wien: Verlag der Österreichischen Akademie der Wissenschaften.

Scheid-Tissinier, É. (2011) "Les dèmes, lieux de citoyenneté, lieux de conflits", in Azoulay, V. and P. Ismard (dir.) *Clisthène et Lycurgue d'Athènes. Autour du politique dans la cité classique*, Paris: Publications de la Sorbonne; 275–291.

Scheidel, W. (2013) "Studying the State", in Bang, P.F. and W. Scheidel (eds.) *The Oxford Handbook of the State in the Ancient Near East and Mediterranean*, Oxford: University Press; 5–57.

Schiavone, A. (2003) (ed.) *Diritto privato romano. Un profilo storico*, Torino: Einaudi.

Schmidlin, B. (2008) *Droit privé romain*, Vol. I, Genève and Bruxelles: Bruylant.

Schmitt-Pantel, P. (1990) "Collective Activities and the Political in the Greek City", in Murray, O. and S. Price (eds.) *The Greek City from Homer to Alexander*, Oxford: Clarendon Press; 119–213.

Schmitt, M.N. (2010) "Military Necessity and Humanity in International Humanitarian Law: Preserving the Delicate Balance", *Virginia Journal of International Law* 50 (4); 795–839.

Schreuer, Ch. (1993) "The Waning of the Sovereign State: Towards a New Paradigm for International Law?", *European Journal of International Law* 4; 447–471.

Schuller, S. (1956) "About Thucydides' use of αἰτία and πρόφασις", *Revue belge de philologie* 34; 971–984.

Schweigert, E. (1939) "Greek Inscriptions 1–13", *Hesperia* 8; 8.

Scullion, S. (2002) "Tragic dates", *Classical Quarterly* 52; 81–101.

Seager, R. (1969) "The Congress Decree: Some Doubts and a Hypothesis", *Historia* 18; 129–141.

Seager, R. (1976) "After the Peace of Nicias: Diplomacy and Policy, 421–416", *Classical Quarterly* 26; 249–269.

Sealey, R. (1957) "Thucydides, Herodotos, and the Causes of War", *Classical Quarterly* 7 (1/2); 1–12.

Sealey, R. (1975) "The causes of the Peloponnesian War", *Classical Philology* 70; 89–109.

Sebillotte Cuchet, V. (2006) *Libérez la patrie! Patriotisme et politique en Grèce ancienne*, Paris: Belin.

Seibert, J. (1979) *Die politischen Flüchtlinge und Verbannten in der griechischen Geschichte*, Darmstadt: Wissenschaftliche Buchgesellschaft.

Selb, W. (1993) "Griechisches Recht", in *Antike Rechte im Mittelmeerraum*, Wien, Köln and Weimar: Böhlau; 80–96.

Sepúlveda, C. (1995) *El derecho de gentes y la organización internacional en los umbrales del siglo XXI*, México: UNAM.

Severyns, A. (1950–1951) "Pomme de discorde et Jugement des déesses", *Phoibos* 5; 147–172.

Shanske, D. (2007) *Thucydides and the Philosophical Origins of History*, Cambridge: University Press.

Shanske, D. (2011) "Thucydides and Lawfulness", in Rechenauer, G. and V. Pothou (eds.) *Thucydides—A Violent Teacher?*, Göttingen: Vandenhoeck & Ruprecht; 199–212.

Shaw, M.N. (2008) *International Law*, Cambridge: University Press.

Sheets, G.A. (1994) "Conceptualizing International Law in Thucydides", *American Journal of Philology* 115 (1); 51–73.

Sheppard, S. (2005) "The Laws of War in the Pre-Dawn Light: Institutions and Obligations in Thucydides' Peloponnesian War", *Columbia Journal of Transnational Law* 43; 905–925.

Sherwin-White, A.N. (1984) *Roman Foreign Policy in the East, 168 B.C. to A.D. 1*, London: Duckworth.

Shipley, G. (1993) "The Limits of War", in Rich, J. and G. Shipley (eds.) *War and Society in the Greek World*, London: Routledge; 1–24.

Sicherl, M. (1986) "Die Tragik der Danaiden", *Museum Helveticum* 43; 81–110.

Sidebottom, H. (2004) *Ancient Warfare. A Very Short Introduction*, Oxford: University Press.

Siewert, P. (1982) *Die Trittyen Attikas und die Heeresreform des Kleisthenes*, München: C.H. Beck.

Simpson, G. (2004) *Great Powers and Outlaw States: Unequal Sovereigns in the International Legal Order*, Cambridge: University Press.

Sinagra, A. and P. Bargiacchi (2009) *Lezioni di diritto internazionale pubblico*, Milano: Giuffrè.

Sinclair, R.K. (1988) *Democracy and Participation in Athens*, Cambridge: University Press.

Sini, F. (2003) "*Ut iustum conciperetur bellum*: guerra "giusta" e sistema giuridico-religioso romano", in Calore, A. (ed.) *"Guerra giusta"? La metamorfosi di un concetto unico*, Milano: Giuffrè; 31–76.

Smart, J.D. (1972) "Athens and Egesta", *Journal of Hellenic Studies* 92; 128–146.

Smith, G. (1921) "The Prytaneum in the Athenian Amnesty Law", *Classical Philology*, 16 (4); 345–353.

Snodgrass, A.M. (1965) "The Hoplite Reform and History", *Journal of Hellenic Studies* 85; 110–122.

Solis, G.D. (2010) *The Law of Armed Conflict. International Humanitarian Law in War*, Cambridge: University Press.

Sommerstein, A.H. (1997) "The Theatre Audience, the *Demos*, and the *Suppliants* of Aeschylus", in Pelling, Ch.B. (ed.) *Greek Tragedy and the Historian*, Oxford: Clarendon Press; 63–79.

Sommerstein, A.H. (2010) "The beginning and the end of Aeschylus' Danaid Trilogy", in *The Tangled Ways of Zeus*, Oxford: University Press; 89–117.

Sordi, M. (1953) "La prima guerra sacra", *Rivista di filologia e di istruzione classica* 81; 320–346.

Spence, I.G. (1993) *The Cavalry of Classical Greece: A Social and Military History*, Oxford: Clarendon Press.

Stachenfeld, A.J. and C.M. Nicholson (1996) "Blurred Boundaries: An Analysis of the Close Relationship Between Popular Culture and the Practice of Law", *University of San Francisco Law Review*, 30 (4); 903–916.

Starr, C.G. (1974) *Political Intelligence in Classical Greece* (Mnemosyne, Suppl. 31), Leiden: Brill.

Steinhoff, U. (2008) *On the Ethics of War and Terrorism*, Oxford: University Press.

Stern, J. (1987) "Le traité d'alliance entre Rome et Maronée", *Bulletin de correspondance hellénique* 111; 501–509.

Sternberg, R.H. (1999) "The Transport of Sick and Wounded Soldiers in Classical Greece", *Phoenix* 53 (3/4); 191–205.

Sternberg, R.H. (2006) *Tragedy Offstage. Suffering and Sympathy in Ancient Athens*, Austin: University of Texas Press.

Steup, M. (2001) (ed.) *Knowledge, Truth, and Duty*, Oxford: University Press.

Stocker, M. (1990) *Plural and Conflicting Values*, Oxford: University Press.

Stouder, G. (2006) "Πόλεμος ἀκήρυκτος: la guerre sans héraut", in Caire, E. and S. Pittia (eds.) *Guerre et diplomatie romaine. IVe–IIIe siècles av. J.-C. Pour un réexamen des sources*, Aix-en-Provence: Université de Provence; 209–222.

Straumann, B. (2008) "The Peace of Westphalia as a Secular Constitution", *Constellations* 15 (2); 173–188.

Straumann, B. (2015) *Roman Law in the State of Nature. The Classical Foundations of Hugo Grotius' Natural Law*, Cambridge: University Press.

Sturm, F. (1979) "Comment l'Antiquité réglait-elle ses conflits de lois?", *Journal du droit international* 106 (2); 259–273.

Swinarski, C. (1984) "La notion d'un organisme neutre et le droit international", in Swinarski, C. (ed.) *Studies and essays on international humanitarian law and Red Cross principles in honour of Jean Pictet*, Geneva: International Committee of the Red Cross; 819–835.

Talamanca, M. (1981) "Il diritto in Grecia", in Bretone, M. and M. Talamanca. *Il diritto in Grecia e a Roma*, Roma and Bari: Laterza; 3–89.

Tasioulas, J. (2002) "From Utopia to Kazanistan: John Rawls and the Law of Peoples", *Oxford Journal of Legal Studies* 22 (2); 367–396.

Tasioulas, J. (2010) "The Legitimacy of International Law", in Besson, S. and J. Tasioulas (eds.) *The Philosophy of International Law*, Oxford: University Press; 97–116.

Tausend, K. (1992) *Amphiktionie und Symmachie. Formen zwischenstaatlicher Beziehungen im archaischen Griechenland* (Historia Einzelschriften, 73), Stuttgart: Franz Steiner.

Taylor, M.C. (2010) *Thucydides, Pericles, and the Idea of Athens in the Peloponnesian War*, Cambridge: University Press.

Teitel, R.G. (2000) *Transitional Justice*, Oxford: University Press.

Ténèkides, G.C. (1954) *La notion juridique d'indépendence et la tradition hellénique. Autonomie et fédéralisme aux* V^e *et* IVe *s. av. J.C.* Athènes: Presses de l'Institut Français d'Athènes.

Ténèkides, G.C. (1956) "Droit international et communautés fédérales dans la Grèce des cités (Ve–IIIe s. av. J.C.)", *Recueil des cours de l'Academie de droit international de La Haye*, 90 II, Leiden and Boston: Martinus Nijhoff; 475–652.

Ténèkides, G.C. (1970) "Esquisse d'une théorie des droits internationaux de l'homme dans la Grèce des cités", *Revue des droits de l'homme* 213; 195–244.

Ténèkides, G.C. (1993) *Les relations internationales dans la Grèce antique*, Athènes: Fondation A.G. Leventis.

Teschke, B. (2002) "Theorizing the Westphalian System of States: International Relations from Absolutism to Capitalism", *European Journal of International Relations* 8 (1); 5–48.

Thalmann, W.G. (2004) "'The Most Divinely Approved and Political Discord': Thinking about Conflict in the Developing Polis", *Classical Antiquity* 23 (2); 359–399.

Thirlway, H. (2014) *The Sources of International Law*, Oxford: University Press.

Thomas, R. (1996) "Written in Stone? Liberty, Equality, Orality and the Codification of Law", in Foxhall, L. and A.D.E. Lewis (eds.) *Greek Law in its Political Setting. Justifications not Justice*, Oxford: Clarendon Press; 9–31.

Thommen, L. (2012) *An Environmental History of Ancient Greece and Rome*, Cambridge: University Press.

Thomsen, Ch.A. (2015) "The *Eranistai* of Classical Athens", *Greek, Roman, and Byzantine Studies* 55; 154–175.

Tieman, W. (2002) "'Cause' in History and the Amnesty at Athens: An Introduction", *Transactions of the American Philological Association* 132 (1/2); 63–69.

Tod, M.N. (1913), *International Arbitration amongst the Greeks*, Oxford: Clarendon Press.

Todd, S.C. (1990) "*Lady Chatterley's Lover* and the Attic Orators: The Social Composition of the Athenian Jury", *Journal of Hellenic Studies* 110; 146–173.

Todd, S.C. (1993) *The Shape of Athenian Law*, Oxford: Clarendon Press.

Todd, S.C. (1996) "Lysias against Nikomachos: The Fate of the Expert in Athenian Law", in Foxhall, L. and A.D.E. Lewis (eds.) *Greek Law in its Political Setting. Justifications not Justice*, Oxford: Clarendon Press; 101–131.

Todd, S.C. and P. Millett (1990) "Law, Society and Athens", in Cartledge, P., P. Millett and S. Todd (eds.), *Nomos. Essays in Athenian law, politics and society*, Cambridge: University Press; 1–18.

Tompkins, D.P. (2013) "Greek Rituals of War", in Campbell, B. and L.A. Tritle (eds.) *The Oxford Handbook of Warfare in the Classical World*, Oxford: University Press; 527–541.

Triantaphyllopoulos, J. (1985) *Das Rechtsdenken der Griechen* (Münchener Beiträge zur Papyrusforschung und antiken Rechtsgeschichte, 78 Heft), München: C.H. Beck.

Tritle, L.A. (2013) "Men at Work", in Campbell, B. and L.A. Tritle (eds.) *The Oxford Handbook of Warfare in the Classical World*, Oxford: University Press; 279–293.

Trundle, M. (2004) *Greek Mercenaries. From the Late Archaic Period to Alexander*, New York and London: Routledge.

Trundle, M. (2013) "The Business of War: Mercenaries", in Campbell, B. and L.A. Tritle (eds.) *The Oxford Handbook of Warfare in the Classical World*, Oxford: University Press; 330–350.

Truyol y Serra, A. (1998) *Historia del derecho internacional público*, Madrid: Tecnos.

Turner, Ch. (2001) "Perverted Supplication and Other Inversions in Aeschylus' Danaid Trilogy", *Classical Journal* 97; 27–50.

Tworek-Hofstetter, M. (2009) *Suppliant, Guest, and the Power of Zeus in Homeric Epic* (MA Report, University of Texas), Austin.

Tzanetou, A. (2012) *City of Suppliants. Tragedy and the Athenian Empire*, Austin: University of Texas Press.

Valdés Guía, M. (2003) "El espacio ciudadano: integración/exclusión en el imaginario y la realidad ateniense del s. VI a.C.", *Studia Historica—Historia Antigua* 21; 29–45.

van der Vliet, E. (2005) "*Polis*. The problem of Statehood", *Social Evolution and History* 4 (2); 120–150.

van der Vliet, E. (2008) "The Early State, the *Polis* and State Formation in Early Greece", *Social Evolution and History* 7 (1); 197–221.

van Wees, H. (1994) "The Homeric Way of War: The *Iliad* and the Hoplite Phalanx", *Greece and Rome* 41; 1–18 and 131–155.

van Wees, H. (1995) "Politics and the Battlefield: Ideology in Greek Warfare", in Powell, A. (ed.) *The Greek World*, London and New York: Routledge; 153–178.

van Wees, H. (2000) "The Development of the Hoplite Phalanx: Iconography and Reality in the Seventh Century", in van Wees, H. (ed.) *War and Violence in Classical Greece*, London: Duckworth and The Classical Press of Wales; 125–166.

van Wees, H. (2004) *Greek Warfare. Myths and Realities*, Swansea: The Classical Press of Wales.

Varela, C.A. (1984) "Los orígenes del pensamiento jurídico en la Antigua Grecia", *Prudentia Iuris* 12; 67–82.

Vaughn, P. (1991) "The Identification and Retrieval of the Hoplite Battle-dead", in Hanson, V.D. (ed.) *Hoplites: The Classical Greek Battle Experience*, London and New York: Routledge; 63–84.

Venit, M.S. (1989) "Herakles and the Hydra in Athens in the First Half of the Sixth Century B.C.", *Hesperia: The Journal of the American School of Classical Studies at Athens* 58 (1); 99–113.

Verma, S.K. (2004) *An Introduction to Public International Law*, New Delhi: Phi Learning Pvt.

Vernant, J.P. (1968) (ed.) *Problèmes de la guerre en Grèce ancienne* (Ecole pratique des hautes études, Sorbonne, Civilisations et sociétés, 11), La Haye: Mouton and Co.

Verri, P. (1988) *Dictionnaire du droit international des conflits armés*, Genève: Comité International de la Croix-Rouge.

Verzijl, J.H.W. (1968) *International Law in Historical Perspective*, Vol. I, Leiden: Martinus Nijhoff.

Verzijl, J.H.W. (1978) *International Law in Historical Perspective*, Part IX-A, Alphen aan den Rijn: Sijthoff & Noordhoff.

Vetta, M. (1999) "The Culture of the Symposium", in Flandrin, J.-L. and M. Montanari (eds.) *Food: A Culinary History from Antiquity to the Present*, New York: Columbia University Press; 96–105.

Vial, C. (1999) "Le jugement des auteurs athéniens sur la guerre du Péloponnèse", in Prost, F. (ed.) *Armées et sociétés de la Grèce classique. Aspects sociaux et politiques de la guerre aux Ve et IVe s. av. J.-C.*, Paris: Errance; 137–146.

Vian, F. (1968) "La fonction guerrière dans la mythologie grecque", in Vernant, J.-P. (ed.) *Problèmes de la guerre en Grèce ancienne*, Paris and La Haye: Mouton; 53–68.

Vidal-Naquet, P. (1991) *Le chasseur noir: formes de pensée et formes de société dans le monde grec*, Paris: La Découverte.

Virgilio, B. (1969) "Rassegna di studi sulle prossenie greche", *Rivista di Filologia e di Istruzione Classica* 97; 494–501.

von Glahn, G. (1965) *Law Among Nations. An Introduction to Public International Law*, New York: Macmillan.

Vondeling, J. (1961) *Eranos*, Groningen: J.B. Wolters.

Walbank, M.B. (1978) *Athenian Proxenies of the Fifth Century B.C.*, Toronto and Sarasota: Samuel Stevens.

Wallace, R.W. (1997) "Poet, Public, and 'Theatrocracy': Audience Performance in Classical Athens", in Edmunds, L. and R.W. Wallace (eds.) *Poet, Public, and Performance in Ancient Greece*, Baltimore: Johns Hopkins University Press; 97–111.

Waltzing, J.P. (1895) *Étude historique sur les corporations professionnelles chez les Romains*, Louvain: C. Peeters.

Walzer, M. (1992) *Just and Unjust Wars: A Moral Argument with Historical Illustrations*. New York: Basic Books [1977[1]].

Walzer, M. (2004) "The Triumph of Just War Theory", in *Arguing About War*. New Haven: Yale University Press; 3–23.

Welwei, K. (1996) "Zur 'Herrschaftsterminologie' in der Quadrupleallianz von 420 v. Chr.", *Zeitschrift für Papyrologie und Epigraphik* 111; 88–92.

Wéry, M. (1967) "Le fonctionnement de la diplomatie à l'époque homérique", *Revue internationale des droits de l'antiquité* 14; 169–215.

Westermann, W.L. (1907) "Interstate Arbitration in Antiquity", *The Classical Journal* 2 (5); 197–211.

Westermann, W.L. (1910) "Notes Upon the Ephodia of Greek Ambassadors", *Classical Philology* 5 (2); 203–216.

Wheeler, E.L. (1987) "Ephorus and the Prohibition of Missiles", *Transactions of the American Philological Association* 117; 157–182.

Wheeler, E.L. (1988) *Stratagem and the Vocabulary of Military Trickery* (Mnemosyne, Suppl. 108), Leiden: Brill.

Wheelis, M. (1999) "Biological Warfare Before 1914", in Geissler, E. and J.E. van Courtland Moon (eds.) *Biological and Toxin Weapons: Research, Development and Use from the Middle Ages to 1945*, Oxford: University Press; 8–34.

Whibley, L. (1889) *Political parties in Athens during the Peloponnesian War*, Cambridge: University Press.

Whitehead, D. (1986) *The Demes of Attica, 508/7 ca.–250 B.C. A Political and Social Study*, Princeton: University Press.

Whitehead, D. (1996) "*Polis*-toponyms as personal entities (in Thucydides and elsewhere)", *Museum Helveticum* 53 (1); 1–11.

Whitman, J.Q. (2012) *The Verdict of Battle. The Law of Victory and the Making of Modern War*, Cambridge (MA) and London: Harvard University Press.

Wick, T.E. (1976) "Athens' Alliances with Rhegion and Leontinoi", *Historia* 25; 288–304.

Wiles, D. (2000) *Greek Theater Performance: An Introduction*, Cambridge: University Press.

Wilkinson, R. (1999) "Trente ans plus tard …", *Réfugiés* 2, nº 115; 4–13.

Wilson, J.R. (1979) "Eris in Euripides", *Greece and Rome* 26 (1); 7–20.

Wilson, P. (2000) *The Athenian Institution of the* Khoregia. *The Chorus, the City and the Stage*, Cambridge: University Press.

Windrow, M. (1985) *The Greek Hoplite*, New York: Franklin Watts.

Winkel, L. (2004) "The Peace Treaties of Westphalia as an Instance of the Reception of Roman Law", in Lesaffer, R. (ed.) *Peace Treaties and International Law in European History. From the Late Middle Ages to World War One*, Cambridge: University Press; 222–237.

Winnington-Ingram, R.P. (1961) "The Danaid Trilogy of Aeschylus", *Journal of Hellenic Studies* 81; 141–152.

Wise, J. (1998) *Dionysus Writes: The Invention of Theatre in Ancient Greece*, Ithaca: Cornell University Press.

Wogasli, D. (1895) *Die Normen des altgriechischen Völkerrechtes* (Nomoi Koinoi tôn Hellénon) (Inaug.-Diss.), Freiburg.

Wohl, V. (2010) *Law's Cosmos: Juridical Discourse in Athenian Forensic Oratory*, Cambridge: University Press.

Wolfke, K. (1961) *Great and Small Powers in International Law from 1814 to 1920*, Wroclaw: Zakad Narodowy im. Ossoliânskich.

Wolpert, A. (2002) *Remembering Defeat: Civil War and Civic Memory in Ancient Athens*, Baltimore and London: Johns Hopkins University Press.

Woodhead, A.G. (1997) "Inscriptions. The Decrees", *The Athenian Agora* 16, American School of Classical Studies, Princeton: University Press.

Zack, A. (2001) *Studien zum* Römischen Völkerrecht. *Kriegserklärung, Kriegsbeschluss, Beeidung und Ratifikation zwischenstaatlicher Verträge, internationale Freundschaft und Feindschaft während der römischen Republik bis zum Beginn des Prinzipats*, Göttingen: Duehrkohp & Radicke.

Zarilli, P. (1986) "Towards a Definition of Performance Studies", *Theatre Journal* 38; 372–376 (I) and 493–496 (II).

Zeitlin, F.I. (1988) "La politique d'Éros: féminin et masculin dans les *Suppliantes* d'Eschyle", *Mètis* 3; 231–259.

Zeitlin, F.I. (1990) "Patterns of gender in Aeschylean drama: *Seven against Thebes* and the Danaid trilogy", in Griffith, M. and D.J. Mastronarde (eds.) *Cabinet of the Muses: Essays on Classical and Comparative Literature in Honor of T.G. Rosenmeyer*, Atlanta: Scholars Press; 103–115.

Zelnick-Abramovitz, R. (1998) "Supplication and Request: Application by Foreigners to the Athenian Polis", *Mnemosyne* 51 (5); 554–573.

Zelnick-Abramovitz, R. (2004) "The Proxenoi of Western Greece", *Zeitschrift für Papyrologie und Epigraphik* 147; 93–106.

Ziebarth, E.G.L. (1896) *Das griechisches Vereinswesen*, Stuttgart: S. Hirzel.

Ziegler, K.-H. (1972) "Das Völkerrecht der römischen Republik", *Aufstieg und Niedergang der romischen Welt* I (2); 68–114.

Ziegler, K.-H. (2007) *Völkerrechtsgeschichte: Ein Studienbuch*, München: C.H. Beck.

Zolo, D. (2006) *La giustizia dei vincitori. Da Norimberga a Baghdad*, Roma and Bari: Laterza.

Zumbrunnen, J. (2008) *Silence and Democracy. Athenian Politics in Thucydides'* History, Pennsylvania: Penn State University Press.

3 *Instrumenta studiorum*

Bailly, A. (2000), *Dictionnaire Grec Français*, rédigé avec le concours de E. Egger, Édition revue par L. Séchan et P. Chantraine, Paris: Hachette [1894[1]].

Brandenstein, W. (1964) *Lingüística griega*, Madrid: Gredos.

Buck, C.D. (1968) *The Greek Dialects*, Chicago: University Press.

Chantraine, P. (1967[2]) *Morphologie historique du grec*, Paris: Klincksieck.

Chantraine, P. (1990[2]) *Dictionnaire étymologique de la langue grecque. Histoire des mots*, Vol. I–II, Paris: Klincksieck.

Daremberg, C. and M.E. Saglio (1918) *Dictionnaire des Antiquités Grecques et Romaines*, Paris: Hachette.

Denniston, J.D. (1954[2]) *The Greek Particles*, Oxford: Clarendon Press.

Goodwin, W. (1890) *Syntax of the moods and tenses of the greek verb*, Philadelphia: William H. Allen Bookseller.

Grimal, P. (1986) *Diccionario de Mitología Griega y Romana*, Barcelona: Paidós.

Hofmann, J.B. (1949) *Etymologisches Wörterbuch des griechischen*, München: R. Oldenbourg.

Hornblower, S. and A. Spawforth (1999[3]) (eds.) *The Oxford Classical Dictionary*, Oxford: University Press.

Humbert, J. (1982[3]) *Syntaxe Grecque*, Paris: Klincksieck.

Kirchner, J. (1901–1903) *Prosopographia Attica*, Berlin: Ares.

Kühner. R. (1966) *Ausführliche Grammatik der griechischen Sprache*, Vol. I–IV, Hannover: Hahnsche.

Liddell, H.G. and R. Scott (1996) *A Greek-English Lexicon*. Revised and augmented throughout by Sir Henry Stuart Jones, with the assistance of Roderick McKenzie, with a revised supplement edited by P.G.W. Glare, Oxford: Clarendon Press [1843[1]].

Mossé, C. (1998) *Dictionnaire de la civilisation grecque*, Bruxelles: Complexe.

Osborne, M.J. and S.G. Byrne (1994) "Attica", in Fraser, P.M. and E. Matthews (eds.) *A Lexicon of Greek Personal Names* (Vol. II), Oxford: University Press.

Rodríguez Adrados, F. (1992) *Nueva sintaxis del griego antiguo*, Madrid: Gredos.

Rodríguez Adrados, F. (1999) *Historia de la lengua griega*, Madrid: Gredos.

Rodríguez Adrados, F. et al. (1980–) *Diccionario Griego-Español*, Vol. I–VI, Madrid: CSIC.

Schwyzer, E. (1939–1953) *Griechische Grammatik*, Vol. I–III, München: C.H. Beck.

Smyth, H.W. (1984) *Greek Grammar*, revised by Gordon M. Messing, Cambridge (MA): Harvard University Press [1920[1]].

Index of Greek Terms

Index of Ancient Sources

Literary Texts

Inscriptions

Index of Subjects and Names

www.ingramcontent.com/pod-product-compliance
Lightning Source LLC
LaVergne TN
LVHW010640300926
849161LV00005B/1001